D1452805

BEHIND THE GLASS

BEHIND THE GLASS

The Villa Tugendhat and Its Family

Michael Lambek

UNIVERSITY OF TORONTO PRESS
Toronto Buffalo London

© University of Toronto Press 2022
Toronto Buffalo London
utorontopress.com
Printed in Canada

ISBN 978-1-4875-4219-1 (cloth)   ISBN 978-1-4875-4222-1 (EPUB)
                                   ISBN 978-1-4875-4221-4 (PDF)

_____

Library and Archives Canada Cataloguing in Publication

Title: Behind the glass : the Villa Tugendhat and its family / Michael Lambek.
Names: Lambek, Michael, author.
Description: Includes bibliographical references and index.
Identifiers: Canadiana (print) 20220245533 | Canadiana (ebook) 20220245614 |
   ISBN 9781487542191 (cloth) | ISBN 9781487542221 (EPUB) |
   ISBN 9781487542214 (PDF)
Subjects: LCSH: Tugendhat family – History – 20th century. | LCSH: Tugendhat
   family – Homes and haunts – Czech Republic – Brno – History – 20th century. |
   LCSH: Tugendhat House (Brno, Czech Republic) – History – 20th century. |
   LCSH: Jewish families – Czech Republic – Brno – History – 20th century. |
   LCSH: Jews – Czech Republic – Brno – History – 20th century. |
   LCSH: Brno (Czech Republic) – Genealogy.
Classification: LCC CS539 .T84 2022 | DDC 929.2094371 – dc23

_____

Every effort has been made to contact copyright holders; in the event of an error or
omission, please notify the publisher.

We wish to acknowledge the land on which the University of Toronto Press
operates. This land is the traditional territory of the Wendat, the Anishnaabeg, the
Haudenosaunee, the Métis, and the Mississaugas of the Credit First Nation.

This book has been published with the help of a grant from the Federation for the
Humanities and Social Sciences, through the Awards to Scholarly Publications
Program, using funds provided by the Social Sciences and Humanities Research
Council of Canada.

University of Toronto Press acknowledges the financial support of the Government of
Canada, the Canada Council for the Arts, and the Ontario Arts Council, an agency of
the Government of Ontario, for its publishing activities.

Canada Council
for the Arts
Conseil des Arts
du Canada

ONTARIO ARTS COUNCIL
CONSEIL DES ARTS DE L'ONTARIO
an Ontario government agency
un organisme du gouvernement de l'Ontario

Funded by the   Financé par le
Government   gouvernement
of Canada   du Canada

Canadä

MIX
Paper from
responsible sources
FSC® C016245

Contents

Part III: Grete and Her World

Part IV: The Family Regrouped and Represented

Illustrations

Figures

Kinship Diagrams

Preface

This book brings together two dimensions of my life and experience: the first as a member of a particular family, a diasporic and self-important one; and the second as an anthropologist, someone who has made a profession of seeking out and trying to understand other lives and families. If being a member of my family has led me to anthropology and to the kind of anthropologist I am, so too anthropology has come to shape how I approach my family. This book is a product of that recognition. Perhaps one can call it a marriage, but if so, like any marriage, it is one in which the partners do not absorb or dissolve into each other or reach a final resolution of their differences.

The past, in the famous phrase of L.P. Hartley, is a foreign country.[1] This statement is literally true for all migrants and members of diasporic families, and it is also an imagined truth. It is true for each of us in the course of our lives; childhood is past, and it becomes foreign to adults. At the same time, though, the past follows us and helps compose who we are; its knowledge, silences, fantasies, and unresolved conflicts remain ours. There have been moments in writing this book where the perceptions I had as a child were confirmed, but more frequently I have had to acknowledge that how I understood things then was partial or mistaken. And there have been moments when I have felt myself again that child, prying at the parents' bedroom door. Opening that door can be frightening, and it can be inappropriate. Sometimes it could be necessary.

The present too is a foreign country, at least for me. It may be true for any historian, biographer, or memoirist, as it is for anthropologists. Anthropologists live, in part, vicariously. We enter other peoples' worlds as privileged interlopers, sometimes also as pariahs or parvenus (to twist Hannah Arendt's terms), and, shaped by those experiences, we return to live as partial outsiders back home. In living our lives we attempt to transcend our immediate condition, if only by gaining insight into its affordances and deficits. We could call this striving for some kind of maturity.

If that illuminates the inner workings of this book, it is not what the book is explicitly about. My subject is both a family and a concept of family. I write also about individual members of the family. Some of their achievements are found in encounters with famous people of the age, notably with Mies van der Rohe and Martin Heidegger. Readers primarily interested in Mies and the house he designed will want to turn to chapters 1, 10, 15, and 16. Readers concerned with Heidegger or with the philosopher Ernst Tugendhat will be most interested in chapters 13 and 14, and on Ernst's childhood, chapters 10 and 11. But the book treats other subjects as well: the emancipation of Moravian Jews and their role in capitalist textile production in Austria-Hungary; upper bourgeois life and marriage towards the end of the long nineteenth century; encounters with modernity and then with Nazism and communism; the place of Jews in the reimagination of history in the Czech Republic (in particular, in Brno); and the fundamental nature of representation in the constitution of family and what is both continuous and discontinuous in it.

PART I

House and Family

Nothing is so difficult as not deceiving oneself.

                                        – Ludwig Wittgenstein, *Culture and Value*

Chapter One

People Who Live in Glass Houses

Remember the impression one gets from good architecture, that it expresses a thought. It makes one want to respond with a gesture.

– Ludwig Wittgenstein, *Culture and Value*

In 2009 British novelist Simon Mawer published to some acclaim a work of historical fiction called *The Glass Room*. Mawer is a good writer – the book was shortlisted for the Man Booker Prize – albeit not of the calibre of Pat Barker, Julian Barnes, or Ian McEwan. I had enjoyed an earlier book of Mawer's, *The Fall*, about rock climbers. By contrast, *The Glass Room* was disappointing, with characters who appeared, shall I say, smaller than life.

The Glass Room is a work of fiction, but it is anchored around one character who is incontrovertibly real. This character is not a human being but a house. The architectural drawings of the house placed in the book establish authenticity. They demonstrate beyond any doubt that the house is the one that my maternal grandparents commissioned in 1928, moved into in 1930, and abandoned in 1938 before it was summarily appropriated by the German Reich. My mother, born in 1924, spent her childhood in the house.

Mawer begins with an author's note that states: "Although *The Glass Room* is a work of fiction, the house and its setting are not fictional. I have disguised both with name changes, but that will not fool anyone who knows the building … However, penetrating those thin disguises will not lead to any further revelations: [the characters] are creatures of my own imagination and their story has no basis in fact."[1] And yet, the fiction is *historical*, and the human characters in the novel *are*, in a way, my grandparents as Mawer imagined them. Two other central characters are women who would have been my grandmother's best friend and my mother's nanny. The main characters are actually very little like the real people, but there are uncanny resemblances – including the central presence of the friend and the nanny.

Did Mawer have some secret knowledge? Letting my imagination run wild, I wondered, might he be an illegitimate son of said nanny? She had relocated to London just before the war and after an unnerving experience serving in the house of a British aristocrat who, seeing she was German, proudly showed her his Nazi paraphernalia, found alternative work with Anna Freud to care for displaced refugee children. But Mawer had few of these delicious facts at his disposal and is certainly not her son.

In fact, Mawer learned what he knew of the family from other books, notably one co-edited and written by my mother's youngest sister, Daniela, from which I too draw extensively.[2] This book is not a piece of fiction but a serious architectural and historical study of the house. My aunt Dani, who is only four years my senior, is an art historian, and her husband Ivo is an architectural restorer; although their professional work has been on gender in Dutch and Flemish painting on Dani's side, and conserving historic monuments on Ivo's, much of their later adult lives have been concerned with seeing that the house – which is no longer in our family, but still very much *of* it – receives proper treatment and exact restoration. They were furious with Mawer and his book.

You may wonder why the house is so interesting. Houses, as I learned in an episode of *Last Week Tonight with John Oliver* on civil asset forfeiture, can be treated, at least in the United States, as legal persons and can be found guilty of crimes. And houses, as anthropologists know, are central to what Claude Lévi-Strauss called house societies.[3] In such societies, the house provides a stable unit or core in a way that individuals who are born into it, who move into it or out, and who die are not. We do not live in such a society,[4] and the house in question has not been directly in our family's hands since 1939; and yet it has served as a kind of family anchor – at once a real, material place and building *and* a piece of powerful symbolic capital and site of fantasy. Houses, we also know from the anthropological literature, can serve as materialized metaphors – of body, mind, the cosmos, or in this case, of an idea or an ideal.

Our house has been the subject of both devotion and conflict. Family members still identify and are identified with it. If the material house was appropriated and is no longer our legal property, it remains an object over whose preservation and representations we still feel some responsibility and moral rights.

The house is not simply of personal or sentimental value but was from the start, and has remained, a kind of public figure. A lauded and debated icon of architectural modernism, the house stands in the Moravian city of Brno – Brünn, as my German-speaking grandparents called it. It has stood witness to late Weimar intellectual life, the short-lived independence of interwar multi-ethnic Czechoslovakia, the German conquest, the flight and extermination of the Jews, and the communist epoch in central Europe. The house was successively confiscated by the Gestapo, inhabited by Soviet cavalry, turned into a dance studio, and then became a rehabilitation centre for children with spinal defects.

In November 1967 my grandmother was invited back to Brno by a Czech architect and revisited the home she had left almost thirty years earlier. On another visit, with great poise and no bitterness, in a public speech delivered in Czech on 17 January 1969, she gave the house to the city; that is, she relinquished her rights to it. She did so on two conditions: that it be properly restored and maintained, and that it be accessible to the public. In planning this event Grete presciently wrote: "What I am also afraid of is that if the house as it stands were to become a museum, one's first thoughts on seeing it would not be the beauty of the space, but: so this is how capitalists live. Of course it is true that only capitalists could afford to have such a house built, but that was neither our fault nor [the architect's], and I find that one should take the

Figure 1. Villa Tugendhat from the garden post-restoration, showing the "glass room" with curved dining area, chrome-plated steel support columns, and the onyx wall. Image from David Židlický via www.tugendhat.eu/en

opportunity to show how especially this house is perfectly capable of serving another purpose."[5]

The pact between capitalist owner and socialist government stalled with the repercussions of the Russian re-invasion. But the house did become a government hospitality building. The decision and then the signing of the divorce between the Czech and Slovak Republics took place in the house in 1992. I have been told that Prince Charles once slept in it. The city occasionally leased it for filming commercials and even pornography. There ensued several decades of very complex struggle among too many interested parties at local, national, and global scales, including a short period when the family sued to take it back. In 2001 the house became a UNESCO World Heritage site. The deteriorating house was finally properly restored between 2010 and 2012 under the partial supervision of my uncle Ivo and is now managed by the City of Brno as a museum and the site of prestigious events.[6] Some years ago, my friend Maurice Bloch sent me a gleeful email saying guess where he had been for an academic workshop. In 2018 *The Glass Room* was filmed there, and the house continues to be a subject of representation. *The Spectator* had an article in which the journalist took the liberty to "sense" (wrongly) that the children's toys would have all been "sharp-edged, geometric," and he ended wittily by extending the architect's famous remark "less is more" to "sometimes less is much more expensive."[7]

Here is the *Guardian*'s summary of *The Glass Room*:

> The novel hangs around a building. In 1929, newlyweds Viktor and Liesel Landauer commission the visionary architect Rainer von Abt to build them a house overlooking their hometown in Czechoslovakia. The result is a modernist masterpiece: a sculptured confection of glass, concrete and steel, holding light and air and the dream of a transparent future free from the freight of the past. But the light that pours through the glass walls isn't bright enough to illuminate the murkier corners of family life. Nor is it capable of dispersing the rising shadow of National Socialism: barely a decade later, Czechoslovakia's nascent democracy is subsumed and the Landauers are forced to flee. Through the story of the house and its occupants, Mawer shines a light on central Europe through the 20th century as it drowned under successive waves of invaders and was forced to abandon dreams to concentrate on survival.[8]

It is those "murkier corners of family life" that are the trouble and the fact that the characters are one-dimensional compared to the real persons, people who were very smart and very intense, living lives that were interesting enough without the addition of imagined sexual escapades.[9]

Historical fiction is fraught with ambiguity about the kind of pact it makes with events and readers. I once participated in a workshop organized by the late Gina Feldberg concerning Pat Barker's wonderful *Regeneration Trilogy* and the role of the great psychiatrist and anthropologist W.H.R. Rivers in diagnosing shellshock during the First World War. As a historian of medicine, Gina was disturbed by Barker's freedom with the facts and especially the depiction of character, whereas I was more appreciative. In retrospect, Gina's attitude was likely influenced by the fact that one of Barker's characters, the poet Siegfried Sassoon, was also *her* relative. In any case, with respect to matters of authorial pact and fact, Mawer himself was quoted in the *Guardian* to say unambiguously: "I'm a novelist. I don't want to tell the truth. I want to manipulate things as I choose. I want to lie."[10]

In other words, the novelist, or at least Mawer, makes no pact with his subjects or his readers. But surely it is not correct to conflate fiction with lying? I thought perhaps I should follow up on my fantasy and write a novel in which Mawer *is* the illegitimate son of the nanny and a British lord who dressed up in Nazi uniforms. My brother Bernie retorted that in criticizing Mawer I was mistaking his genre. *The Glass Room* is not *historical* fiction, he suggested, but fiction, pure and simple. Like any realist fiction, it must specify a time and place.

For another view, there is the documentary film *Haus Tugendhat*.[11] It includes interviews with several of my relatives and has their blessing. The film is stiflingly pretentious at the beginning and has its genuinely surreal moments, notably when the daughter of the German industrialist who inhabited the house from 1943 to 1945 reminisces how they had to add internal partitions and "a little farmhouse parlour" to make it *heimlich* (cozy). Incidentally, she punctures a long-held family myth that the resident had been Willy Messerschmitt, the airplane manufacturer. In fact, as she explains, they were Messerschmidt spelled differently, albeit also manufacturing for the war effort.[12] In another striking moment my iconoclastic cousin Michael Guggenheim, who teaches sociology at Goldsmiths, suggests blowing up the house. Particularly moving for me are images of my mother as a girl that I had not seen before, as well as some of her visiting the house in 1990 shortly before her death.

My aunts were seriously unamused by the ostensible portrayal of their parents in Mawer's book. And yet, as authors and as interviewees for articles and for *Haus Tugendhat*, my relatives have also engaged in representing. Indeed, my grandmother herself had a good deal to say in public and had planned to write a book together with the Czech architect.[13] And here I come: writing about being subject to representation, I too am doing a good deal of representing.

The genre of this book is, for want of a better answer, what Clifford Geertz called "blurred."[14] It is the biography of a family, with the aspirations to objectivity that biography requires, yet it includes subjective elements that could be described as memoir. The ambiguity of the stance towards the real made by the historical novelist has parallels with the ostensible pact of the memoirist. Anthropologist Bianca Dahl cites Philippe Lejeune's depiction of the "autobiographical pact" as "the often subtle means by which writers of memoirs convince their readers of the authenticity and authority of their self-depictions – essentially, balancing between fulfilling the necessity to establish that they are writing the truth, and the reader's expectation of an autobiographer's introspection and aesthetics."[15] This pact is complicated or undermined by the vagaries of memory and the conscious and unconscious motivations of the memoirist. The urge to speak objective truth is surely distorted by the wish to settle accounts and other unsavoury motives. Adding a few doses of ambivalence, screen memories, repression, and suppression on my part, as well as on the part of family members whose words I draw upon, suggests a certain infelicity, but one that is far from outright fabrication.

My interest in the family, and my ambivalence, derive in part from a mix of envy and wonder. I grew up in a modest suburban bungalow and wore hand-me-down clothes. Every three years during my childhood my grandmother invited us to Europe, where we encountered another world. We travelled by ocean liner from Montreal or New York, truly among the most exhilarating experiences of my life. My brothers and I roamed the ship and escaped the confines of the economy decks to taste surreptitiously the lifestyle of the first-class passengers. In Europe we tasted a different lifestyle as well. We spent some weeks at the seaside or in the Alps and some in my grandparents' house in Switzerland, a house commissioned and built in the 1950s. This house, with its own large glass room, expansiveness, and order, made a big impression on me. At its heart was an enclosed unroofed internal courtyard where we ate our lunch and mid-afternoon *torte*, seated formally and drawing our linen napkins from their silver napkin rings.

The stark differences in class and culture were exacerbated by an intellectual one. My formidable grandmother was a deep reader of Heidegger; my father, a mathematician and logician who had no scruples in telling his mother-in-law what he thought was nonsense. These were two of the most intelligent but also most certain people I have ever met, and I came early to the conclusion that I would never be capable of understanding either continental philosophy or mathematics.

A point not often recognized in the anthropological study of kinship is that families reproduce certain complexes from generation to generation. In my mother's extended family, it was a matter of idealizing one or two members every generation and a consequent feeling of inadequacy among the rest. Those idealized included my grandmother, Grete, and her son, my uncle Ernst, who read Heidegger with her in early adolescence, went to Stanford at fifteen, and then studied with Heidegger himself after the war. Ernst became one of Germany's leading philosophers of the later twentieth century, albeit executing a sharp turn away from the thought of his teacher. People like me have a sense of being not quite real intellectuals and possibly imposing that feeling on others, while those family members who did spectacularly well in business never felt themselves Grete's equal.

Grete came from a family of textile manufacturers, the Löw-Beers. Their antecedents lived in Boskovice, a small town in Moravia that contained a large Jewish ghetto. Family graves are still standing; in the late twentieth century the town reinvented itself with a Wild West theme park alongside the tourist attraction of the ghetto. Early members of the family, so a story incorrectly went, made money outfitting Napoleon's soldiers on their way to the Russian front, and one of them went to Manchester to learn textile engineering. The original siblings established two independent textile firms. The ancestor of my branch of the family set up his first factory in a village with a stream and watermill for power. Two generations later the family built an adjacent garden compound with villas for themselves, and they provided housing and a nursery for the workers. There was a careful division of labour, with some of the men in the family specializing in the business side and others in the technical side. In my grandparents' generation, the women and some of the men seized the opportunity to explore intellectual, artistic, and political interests.

The firm expanded, and the family rapidly became very wealthy, their prosperity consolidated by astute marriages. Notably, my great-grandfather was one of three brothers who married three Viennese sisters. Thus my grandmother, Grete, was one of a set of eight double cousins, and they all lived a kind of hothouse life. In 1922 Grete married young to Hans Weiss, from a family that ran another large textile factory. The Weiss family, originally from Boskovice as well, lived over the border in what was then German (now Polish) Silesia, and so both Hans and eventually my mother had German passports, while her maternal family were Czech citizens after the First World War when Czechoslovakia became an independent country.[16]

My grandfather Hans managed the business while his siblings explored intellectual pursuits. One of his sisters, Helene (Lene) Weiss, went off in 1919 to study with Husserl and Heidegger, and communicated those interests to Grete. Lene eventually taught philosophy in the United Kingdom but died young, and her legacy is now food for intellectual historians.[17] Among her fellow students, with whom she transcribed Heidegger's lectures, were Hans Loewald, subsequently one of the most interesting psychoanalytic thinkers in the United States, and Herbert Marcuse. My grandfather's youngest brother, Paul, became a distinguished mathematician. A sister, Anni, was a psychiatrist who helped identify Asperger's syndrome. Another sister, Gerti, married Kurt Lewin, a founder of social psychology. In fact, my mother first became a subject of representation as a toddler in one of the earliest observational films in child psychology, made by Lewin. During the war Lewin taught at the University of Iowa, where my mother wanted to study with him. In one of the many twists of fate in her very fateful life, the day before she was to pick up her visa from the American consulate in Caracas was Pearl Harbor. All visas were cancelled, and she went many months later to Montreal instead, only to be disappointed that the psychologists at McGill were studying rats not people, but with the consolation of meeting my father.

Grete was a decisive woman. She divorced Hans Weiss, and on her second marriage, in 1928 to Fritz Tugendhat, a man from another interconnected textile manufacturing firm in Brno, but very much a love match, she requested the gift of a house from her father. This house was, in effect, her inheritance, a piece of immobile property. Grete was deeply interested in both philosophy and art, and wanted to break from the ornate houses and heavy furniture that continued to characterize the life of rich people in the wake of the Austro-Hungarian Empire. Whereas her parents looked back, towards Vienna, for art and culture, Grete turned forward, towards Berlin. There, she attended the open house of Eduard Fuchs, a communist and art historian, later the subject of an essay by Walter Benjamin.[18] (Benjamin himself took up with the wife of one of Grete's first cousins.) And so, at the age of twenty-five and having already given birth four times and seen three infants die, Grete encountered the early work of a charismatic architect whom she then hired.[19] At the same time as he constructed her house, the architect was designing what I consider one of the most stunning buildings ever made, namely the German Pavilion for the 1929 Barcelona International Exhibition. It is a building (dismantled in 1930 and reconstructed in 1983–86) in which inside and outside fold into each other in pure harmonious form.

The Barcelona Pavilion is not fully enclosed; it is not an actual house. But Mies van der Rohe did create such a house for Grete. It was startling at the time for its open concept on the public floor; huge windows in place of walls; steel, chrome, travertine, and glass materials; unified heating and air conditioning system; and its absolute precision. Not only were these windows the first floor-to-ceiling windows in a family home, but unlike virtually any since, they retracted into the floor at the press of a button. Grete wrote: "Everyone in Brno assured us during the construction that because of the large windows we would freeze to death. In fact, on sunny winter days the sunlight falling through the 10mm plate-glass windows heated up the lower room so much that even when it was very cold outside we did not have to heat it; we would even lower the large window-panes electrically, sitting as if in the open."[20] The room contained a partition made from slabs of translucent onyx from the Atlas Mountains and a dining alcove encircled by panels of Macassar ebony. These panels later lined a Gestapo bar and subsequently a student canteen before they were recovered. Each piece of furniture was designed and had its precise place.[21] Although the materials were luxurious, the house exemplified the famous remark attributed to Mies that "less is more."

Here is how Grete remembered that period in her speech of 1969:

I had always wanted a spacious modern house of clear and simple forms, and my husband had been almost horrified by the interiors of his youth, stuffed with trinkets and lace. After we decided to have a house built, we made an appointment with Mies van der Rohe. And from the very first moment we met him, it was clear to us that he should be the one to build our house, so impressed were we by his personality ... Above all, the way he talked about architecture gave us the feeling that we were dealing with a true artist ... He added that a house should not be built starting from the façade, but from the inside, and that the windows in a modern building should no longer be holes in a wall but fill the space between floor and ceiling, thereby becoming elements of the structure.[22]

Early afternoon on New Year's Eve we expectantly entered [Mies's] studio [to see the designs]. We were due for a New Year's Eve celebration with friends, but instead the meeting with Mies went on until one o'clock in the morning. First we saw the plan of an enormous room with a curved and a rectangular free-standing wall. [We immediately realized that the room was something unheard of; something never seen before; handwritten note by G.T.] ... [For the semicircular dining alcove] Mies designed a round table, whose steel leg, of exactly the same shape as the steel supports of the house, was lowered into the floor. The table-top was made of black pear wood, and on its underside were metal bars with inserted slats on which circular segments were put, so that the table could be enlarged twice while retaining its circular form ... When fully extended, the table could accommodate 24 people, and looked extremely festive.[23]

[We moved in] at the beginning of December 1930. We loved the house from the very first moment.[24]

In her contributions to the book in which this speech has been published, Grete's daughter Daniela humanizes the house, deliberately including pictures taken by her father, a gifted photographer, of the family life within it (see chapter 10). The photographs are a significant part of how the house and family have been represented. As Dani points out, "photographs, which show buildings without their inhabitants, present a merely formal and aesthetic view of architecture. Architectural photography is invariably more than simply 'objective' images of architecture; it is also an interpretation of it."[25] The house was built on a hillside that sloped down to the large Art Nouveau (Viennese Secessionist style) house of Grete's parents below. Dani writes: "Not only did the house open out towards the green space outside, nature was also brought, as it were, inside; on the eastern façade a lushly green conservatory mediated between interior and natural exterior space. The large onyx wall – another natural element – was part of the interior structure. Landscape, plants, and flowers played a central role."[26]

Dani also provides some social context. She writes: "As far as I know most of the Jews in Brno, at least those acquainted with my parents, had long become assimilated, but still used to socialize only among themselves. The German minority was thus divided into a Jewish and a non-Jewish community ... My parents did not observe Jewish holidays but they did observe Christmas."[27] However, the name Tugendhat, which translates – literally – as "has virtue," I am told, is instantly recognized by German speakers as "Jewish" – like Goldberg or Shapiro in North America. Unlike Mayer, the great-grandfather of Ludwig Wittgenstein, and unlike Stanley Cavell (né Goldstein) or Robert Merton (Meyer Schkolnick),[28] Fritz and Grete did not change their name.

Figure 2. Villa Tugendhat living room with the onyx wall, torso by Wilhelm Lehmbruck (1914), and the conservatory in the background. Photo by Fritz Tugendhat, c. 1932; Archive Daniela Hammer-Tugendhat

Despite the presence of several servants – nanny, chauffeur, cook, and housemaid – the Tugendhats were not idle. Dani writes: "During the day my father was at the textile mill. After 1933, my mother went almost every morning to the bureau of the Human Rights League, which organized help for the refugees from Germany."[29]

My mother's happy childhood in the house was abruptly shattered in March 1938. As her German passport put her in more immediate danger, her father, Hans Weiss, swooped in from England, where he had already relocated, and within twenty-four hours left again with my mother and deposited her in a rigid (and frigid) British boarding school. Grete and her two sons left for Switzerland immediately thereafter, and Fritz followed later. The last to leave was Grete's father, Alfred. Alfred disappeared en route. His corpse was later identified at the border by British secret agent Sir Paul Dukes, hired by Hans Weiss on behalf of his former mother-in-law. Dukes then published a memoir, *An Epic of the Gestapo*, using pseudonyms for the family.[30]

In 1940 while my mother was visiting Grete during summer holidays, the Germans invaded France, and she was unable to return from Switzerland to England. Hanna recalled being the only person pleased by the circumstances. In 1941 she accompanied her maternal family by train to Lisbon and thence by ship to Venezuela, where Fritz managed a woollens factory. In 1950 Fritz and Grete returned to Switzerland, with two young daughters born in Venezuela, and in 1957 they completed their new house, like the former one in many ways but without the excessively luxurious materials. This beautiful building was described bizarrely in the local Swiss newspaper as "a mixture between a pigsty and an Indian mosque," exhibiting a far more provincial attitude than the one prevalent a quarter century earlier in what had been the self-consciously modern City of Brno.[31] Fritz died the following year, and Grete stayed there until her death in 1970.

From the start, the Brno house was subject to public debate. In 1931 it was discussed in the Werkbund review *Die Form*. Walter Riezler saw the house as "indicative of a new spirit and even of a new humanity," to which Justus Bier replied: "Surely one has to agree … [with] the impression of 'an extremely high and refined spirituality' [quoting Riezler]. But will the dwellers, one is bound to ask, be able to support such relentlessly elevating splendor for long without inner resentment? The style of the Tugendhat House is wonderfully pure, but is it not, in its severity and monumentality, unbearable to live in, is it not *representative* [my emphasis] in the true and proper sense of the word, befitting reception halls such as the Barcelona Pavilion … but not to a private residence, whose inhabitants would be forced to live in a show room dwarfing their individual lives?"[32] For his part, Roger Ginsburger wrote of "immoral luxury," comparing it to a church or palace whose aim is "to give the impression of affluence, of particularity, of something never experienced before" instead of comfort and coziness. In this assessment, the Marxist critic agreed with the subsequent National Socialist inhabitants. He continued: "Are you allowed to simply walk through it or do you have to stalk and strut?"[33]

Leaving aside the peculiar German fixation with spirit, itself a very inadequate translation of *Geist*, this debate had partly to do with the place of aesthetics in the move to architectural functionalism and partly the sense in that period that architecture could be a key force for change. The deeper discomfort was a social one, namely with the radical openness of the design – both the interior spaces to one another and to the outside – in the face of the idea that people needed small and fully enclosed spaces to feel at home.[34] Moreover, the critics imply that the inhabitants would be self-conscious, forced, as it were, into a permanent state of representation.

The critics grossly underestimated my grandparents. Each of them published replies emphasizing their affinity with Mies and his architecture.[35] Grete wrote: "Mies is trying to ... restore the primary spiritual sense of life to its proper place, beyond the mere necessities." Noting that "the central point of Mr Bier's criticism is that the pathos of the interior space compels the inhabitants to representational living," Grete responded in 1931 that "I never experienced the rooms as possessing pathos. I find them large and austerely simple – however not in a dwarfing but in a liberating sense." Later she wrote: "The large room – precisely because of its rhythm – has a very particular tranquility, which a closed room could never have."[36] Grete concluded: "We love living in this house, so much so that we find it difficult to go away and are relieved to leave cramped rooms behind us and return to our large, soothing spaces."

In his reply, Fritz asserted that "technically [the house] possesses everything a modern person might wish for." He complements this resort to function by adding: "Whenever I let these rooms and all they contain take their effect, I am overcome by the feeling that this is beauty, this is truth. Truth – there are many ways of looking at it, but anyone seeing these rooms will sooner or later come to the conclusion that here is true art."[37]

In 1934 Grete published an essay on the trust between architect and client, who "should share the same basic feeling of being." She wrote: "I also believe that beauty – in architecture and elsewhere – can never be calculated, but always has to be created anew."[38]

Dani makes an astute comparison between the sources of Mies's ideas in Aquinas and the theologian Romano Guardini and those of her parents in Heidegger, finding the correspondence between Mies and Heidegger "stunning." She points out that Guardini felt "the forces of technological progress had to be bridled to leave enough room for 'life.' Guardini strove for a new 'unified consciousness,' a totality which could overcome modern age subjectivism, but could neither be grasped by rational thought nor by intuition alone ... According to Mies the crucial task of the architect is not of a practical, technical, or formal nature, but essentially philosophical. Mies is concerned with the nature of building, with its spiritual side, with truth. It never becomes clear, however, what he precisely means by words like 'the spiritual' or 'truth.'"[39]

Both Heidegger and Mies, citing Augustine, refer to beauty as the "shining of truth." Moreover, "for Mies, to represent the Zeitgeist in architecture was a moral question."[40] As Fiona MacCarthy in a *Guardian* article of 2012 writes: "Mies was a formidable philosopher architect, imbued with a belief in architecture as a moral question of truthfulness. Robert Hughes, the late art critic, saw Mies's great importance in his period as bringing his individual buildings 'closer to the status of a pure Idea than any 20th-century architect had yet done.'"[41]

It is worth remarking that in the late 1920s Ludwig Wittgenstein helped design his sister's house in Vienna, a house that, in the words of Hans Sluga, "shuns all decoration and all reminders of the architectural styles of the past. Aesthetic values are, instead, to be realized in pure architectonic forms. In pursuit of this ideal, Wittgenstein dedicated himself to the design of the smallest details: the exact height of the ceilings, the metal and glass doors, the glass-enclosed elevator showing the inner mechanics, the door handles, the vents of the under-floor heating system, the radiators, even the feet on which those radiators stood. Austerely minimalistic (there were bare light bulbs hanging from the ceilings instead of the traditional chandeliers), the house is indubitably a specimen of cultural modernism. It is also, however, a direct expression of the *Tractatus*. One of Ludwig's younger sisters called it appositely, 'logic turned into a house, not a human habitation.'"[42] The last remark is of course reminiscent of responses to the Tugendhat House.

Unlike Wittgenstein of the *Tractatus*, Heidegger's concept of truth is not logical but poietic. "In the presence of the temple truth is happening. With this is not meant that something is being correctly presented and represented but that being as a whole is being brought into unhiddenness and held in it."[43]

Dani writes that from her perspective "the Tugendhat House is an ideal architectural expression of my parents, at least how I saw and experienced them, also in their ambivalence: on the one hand, there was the admirable striving towards 'spirituality' and 'truth' which, on the other hand, implied an attitude of excessive strictness and demands."[44]

MacCarthy concludes her piece with the following words:

> In Brno itself the novel is not lauded. Tugendhat descendants forbid it to be mentioned in public discussions of the restoration. There is no reference to Mawer in the guidebook to the villa. On my recent visit to Brno a city official, while admitting he had not even read it, referred to *The Glass Room* as "probably pornography."

She continues:

> Such hostility is puzzling. The Landauers are quite evidently not the Tugendhats. The fictional nanny, who has a long intense affair with Mr Landauer, bears little resemblance to the Tugendhat's governess, Irene Kalkofen, who left Brno to live blamelessly in London from 1938 until her death in 2004. Fiction is not fact, but it can amplify reality. Viewing Villa Tugendhat having read Mawer's novel is a doubly unforgettable experience.[45]

Perhaps the hostility is not so puzzling. My aunts fought long and hard to have the house restored. Ivo writes: "Not only has the house itself been expropriated, but this was also an attempt to expropriate the history of the Tugendhat family."[46] Dani sees the book – and the film made from it – as the final acts of provocation and appropriation. Not all family members share her view; my cousin Michael says reasonably that one cannot expect to control representations of what has become a public object.

It is evident that both Mies and my grandparents were captivated by a search for truth and specifically by the connection between truth and beauty in the work of art that the house exemplified for them. When juxtaposed against the concerns of his subjects, this ideal makes Mawer's remark about the novelist's freedom to lie all the more unfortunate.

My grandparents' ideal also raises enormous challenges for me, challenges at once empirical, aesthetic, and ethical, as I tell my story of the family who commissioned and inhabited the house. I place the story within two intersecting frames: a historical one that situates my grandparents within the deeper and broader context of successive generations of a modernizing family, moving from a Jewish ghetto, through wealth and social prominence, to flight, dispersal, and ambiguous return; and an anthropological one concerning the concept and workings of family. As forms of representation – memoir, family biography, history, auto-ethnography, in whatever mix – each raise tough questions concerning voice and silence, truth and tact.

Perhaps the act of representing is precisely to be no longer in the presence of truth.

Chapter Two

Writing the Family

Much has been written on the Tugendhat House, less about its original inhabitants. The family appears to be represented in *The Glass Room*; Mawer's admonition to the contrary, many people read it that way. I want to correct that. But correcting falsehood does not imply that I reach truth. My account is accurate as far as it goes, but also necessarily subjective and partial, and without the purity and exactitude, the spiritual "something more" of the house itself.

Deciding to tell the family story left me with many questions. I wanted to understand Grete, and I wanted to recount the experience of my mother, Hanna. But I also wanted to place them in context, to understand how Grete had the capacity, the wealth, and the imagination to commission such a house, to understand where she came from and how she lived.

This book is a kind of biography, not of a person, a single life, but of a family. It is a family, not in the sense of a small self-enclosed group of parents and children but in a more extensive sense – both historically deeper, encompassing multiple generations, and socially broader, including siblings, cousins, spouses, and in-laws.[1] It is about how they lived but also how they saw themselves *as* a family.

Families in this sense are the subject of fictional sagas but rarely of non-fiction books. In biography family forms a background to the central figure. In this work the "figure" *is* the family. The family is larger, more salient, and more continuous than any of its members, even as each member transcends it in the course of their life. At the same time the family is not an objective phenomenon but a product contingent on the acts of its members.

If one person is central, it is my mother's mother, Grete Tugendhat. This book is about the world Grete inherited, the world she inhabited, and the world she bequeathed. But the family is not primarily the Tugendhats. Tugendhat is the name of Grete's second husband, my mother's stepfather. The more comprehensive name is Löw-Beer, which was Grete's maiden name, the patronym (family name) of my maternal great-grandfather and his siblings. It is they and their spouses and descendants who comprise the core of the family described here. Some chapters include their antecedents and the families into which they married, all, in some contexts, considered part of the same family.

Many years ago, when I was conducting research in Madagascar, I suggested to my Malagasy friend Emmanuel Tehindrazanarivelo that we make an exchange: I would write about his remarkable family, and he would write the story of mine.[2] Had Emmanuel accepted, he would have produced a fascinating account, with many unspoken assumptions brought to the fore. I am an anthropologist, but I am also here a native, an insider, and this position constrains me in at least two ways. In the first place, it leaves much taken for granted, unremarked. In the second, my subjectivity and deep motivations play a greater role than they do when I study people at arm's length, as I have in Madagascar – though subjectivity is never ruled out in ethnography.

As members of any family exercise practical judgment concerning who counts with respect to love, care, attention, and resources, and how to think about themselves as and in a family, so I, as a self-declared member of this family, inevitably exercise judgment as to who "counts," who is in focus and who out of focus, where the family begins, and where my coverage stops.

In preparing this book I found myself tracking the lives of one person after another. There quickly turned out to be far too many family members, and I had to make hard choices. I am most comprehensive in my great-grandparents' and grandparents' generations. I do not do justice to all their children and grandchildren.

I do not even note the existence of most members of the younger generations, and even if I did, the list would quickly be out of date. Inevitably, I end up reinforcing certain biases, spending more time on family members who were admired during their lifetime, or who lived longer and left more traces. And inevitably, I give precedence to people more directly related to me than not. But I do not privilege those closest to me – my mother receives less space than I imagined at the outset. Hanna's immediate family were very important to her, but she was not a central member of the broader one. Key figures include my great-grandfather's older brother, Rudolf Löw-Beer, whom I call the patriarch; my great-grandmother, Marianne Löw-Beer, known as Mutzi; my grandmother, Grete Tugendhat; Grete's first cousin, Paul Löw-Beer; and my grandfather's sister, Lene Weiss, and my mother's brother, Ernst Tugendhat, who were each students of Martin Heidegger, respectively before and after the war. One of the puzzles the book raises, but does not solve, is the attraction of Heidegger for several family members.

The book represents a triumph over my ambivalence in writing it. It has had many false starts. The idea first gelled in 1987, two weeks after my son Simon was born. My mother came to visit in Toronto, and by chance the weekend edition of the *Globe and Mail* carried a review of a show on Mies van der Rohe to be broadcast on TVOntario. Among the contents mentioned was footage of the Tugendhat House.

Hanna would miss the broadcast as she was returning to Montreal, but she expressed little regret. She lived intensely in the present, albeit with regular visits to her sisters in Europe. She did not dwell on the past, and she did not reminisce about life in the house. She never used the connection to show off. Hanna died less than four years later, having suffered from multiple myeloma for a decade. I was forty years old, and she was sixty-six.

Hanna took her background for granted, something I never could. I had been taken to Europe regularly since the age of two, and I knew some of her relatives. But I felt an outsider, desiring the unselfconsciousness and confidence I thought I saw there. Though I could not then have understood it in this way, it was as though people were living their lives in truth and beauty, exactly as my grandparents had once put it. There was an assurance born of money, of cultural capital, and of character, as epitomized in Grete. The strength of Grete's voice is evident from the quotations in the previous chapter. She had decided tastes in art and philosophy, and she could be scornful of those who appeared incapable of sharing them. A Renoir hung in her bedroom and a Picasso by the dining table. She took us to comfortable but unostentatious resorts where we swam and hiked. She presided over a wonderful house, which I did not realize was modelled on her earlier one (a house that during my childhood I knew nothing about), and she served delicious meals at an orderly table at punctual mealtimes. She was decisive concerning comportment and evidently disapproved of mine. She appraised people on their intelligence and character. There were standards and ideals that were at once unquestionably worthy and not quite mine to aspire to.

How enticing to write about this, yet how impossible.

Over the years I endeavoured in small spurts to learn more about the family, to draw closer or gain mastery over it. I also repeatedly withdrew from the task and displaced it, living in faraway places and writing about other families. I became an anthropologist, a discipline that is more a calling than a profession, which has become as fully a part of my life as my family origins. The kind of anthropologist I became is undoubtedly shaped by my experience in the family, and this account of my family is shaped by my anthropology. But this book is not written as a work of anthropology, and it underplays reference to concepts and scholarly work in the discipline.

In 1988 I went to Brno, then still within the communist bloc, spoke to neighbours, local historians and ethnologists, and talked my way into the empty house. I came away thinking that a project on the industrial revolution and textile manufacturers in Moravia would be worthwhile, but also that the linguistic challenges were too much for me and that I did not have the patience to work in archives. I pursued some relatively informal interviews with family members in Vienna, Zurich, London, and Montreal but didn't fully commit to the project. I have notes from relatives telling me to hurry up and speak to older ones while they were still alive. Mostly I did not do so, partly because of distance, partly out of shyness and a sense I could not live up to the expectations the project might generate. What gave me the final push was a coincidence of events. There was Mawer's book that invited a response. There was opportunity and support during a fellowship in Berlin, with an invitation to consider the project legitimate. And then, there was the surprise announcement of a family reunion courtesy of the City of Brno. It was clearly now or never.

Many questions remained. First and most stubbornly, what kind of book was I writing: memoir, family history, auto-ethnography? A memoir retraces experiences in the life of its author. This book is at once considerably more and considerably less than that. It draws on my memory and on my selection of other people's memories. It offers portraits of people and relationships that are filtered through my subjectivity, both conscious and unconscious. But it is not fully a memoir, if only because I have had to acknowledge how poor my memory is and perhaps how poor and removed were my interactions as a child, and even as a young man, with these relatives, who seemingly revolved like distant planets in their own orbits, some visible, some never glimpsed in the flesh, none fully accessible to my understanding. I thought of them mostly in the third person rather than engaging with them in the second, never such that I could appreciate who they were in and for themselves. Writing has entailed acquiring an adult's view of what the family was and is – and of my position in it. So this book is less a memoir than an anti-memoir – catching up on things in my own family that I did *not* see or understand as I grew up.

And so I have pulled away from the more subjective approach of the memoirist towards the more objective stance of the biographer, historian, or anthropologist. This perspective results in a less unified narrative but one that is fairer to the people who enter it. And yet, as I am a part of the story, and as the book is motivated by my subjectivity, I am present as well.

The book is ethnographic insofar as it explores a mode of life in the round. Ethnography is constituted through a method that is no method, but rather a sustained, if temporary, being with others and a particular focus of attention. Like the memoir, it takes its shape and authority from the author's presence, but like a work of history, it draws its contents and authority from the world it tries to grasp, at once in the terms of that world and as accurately and objectively as possible.[3] The book is *auto*-ethnographic insofar as the way of life to which it turns its attention is in some respect mine.[4] But it is not auto-ethnographic insofar as I recognize my family's past as "another country" – and indeed, my grandparents did live quite literally in another country as well as in another time.

Most cogently, the book is a kind of social history of a family, hence simultaneously a broader history as told through a specific family. Yet it is not exhaustive with respect to sources, as the discipline of history demands. And where a historian might focus on a topic like class, the collapse of Austria-Hungary, or the transformation of Jewish life, these serve as backdrops here, which is in some respect true to the experience of the family. As I will show, the primary attachment of its members, through my age cohort, has been less to nation, religion, or ethnicity than to the family itself. Identification with the family was reinforced by circumstances: from collective ownership of a firm through the invitation to visit Brno in 2017. I follow several generations across the nineteenth and twentieth centuries and use historical experience to think about family along a dimension not often taken in anthropology: a study of successive generations can say something about family that the more common focus on one period of time cannot. In this historical span, it is like a family saga, but it differs from that genre of fiction insofar as it attends to real people and actual events, and is not overdetermined by plot.

It is best not to discriminate among these genres too precisely. The most original books are often ones whose genre cannot be pinned down. I have been inspired by writers like Janet Malcolm, whose works of journalism consistently transcend that genre. I think of Jamaica Kincaid, whose passionate writing about her former home and family is at once tract, memoir, and fiction. I think of W.G. Sebald, who displaces his melancholy onto figures whose fictional journeys he follows with exquisite attention to empirical detail, interspersing subjective ruminations with photographs that document realities of landscape, time, and person. I think of John Berger and Carolyn Steedman, and of the elegant historical accounts of Edmund de Waal and Philippe Sands.[5]

A related question arose: Whom is this book about? When I began, I thought naïvely it would be the story of "my family" but with little thought of what that comprised. I was encouraged by some of my relatives and received with scepticism by others. But I quickly realized that my view of the family – where its centre was and where its outer limits might be – was different from that of my cousins. There was no steady subject for whom my book could serve as portrait. To write about the family was also to question the very content and even the concept of "family."

I also realized how odd it was to think of the subject as "my" family when it does not treat my wife and children, and says very little about my brothers or my father and "his" family. The subject is my mother's family or, as members of that family refer to it, "*the* family" – as if it *were* some kind of steady object. As if there were no other.

While at one level nothing could be more evident than family or "a" family, reflection shows that things are not so simple. Family presents both a practical and conceptual problem: a group of interconnected people whose centre and boundaries and whose commitments to one another are never fixed. We talk as if families were closed wholes, but they are not. And we don't agree; no one can say definitively who is in or out, whose family it is or was, who has the right to speak on its behalf.

Indeed, Wittgenstein used the concept of "family" precisely to define amorphous groupings – units in which each member shares at least one thing in common with at least one other member but in which some members will have nothing in common with each other.[6] Wittgenstein's metaphor can be turned back to inform the very subject he drew upon. My mother's and my father's cousins each have something in common with me but nothing with each other. The question is not whether we are all one family in some objective sense, but in what respects or contexts, to what ends and with what signification, some of us act as one.

I gradually came to realize that if the book were to be about my family, it would need to be about how that family constitutes itself *as* a family. The family is a family in the manner in which the members understand and imagine themselves as family. The family – any family – is constituted through the way it enacts itself, and the way representations on the part of insiders and outsiders mutually work on each other. In a way, then, the subject of the book is coterminous with the problems of writing it: problems of conceptualizing, delimiting, representing, and simply being a family.

If the family is both subject and object of representation, a related question concerns my position within it, and hence within the story, and the challenges my acts of representation raise.

I write about a family that I can imagine, in the first instance, only from my place within it. I am the first born of my biological generation, as was my mother of hers; in age I am close to cousins a generation older than me and only four years younger than Dani, my mother's youngest sister. Being out of synch in terms of generation has shaped how I see things and have been seen. I am at one further remove from material inheritance and social engagement than my age peers of the older generation. I was born and raised in Canada, of refugee parents, whereas most of the people who figure in this book were raised in Europe. I grew up in a household in which an absence of money was offset by my parents' implicit disparagement of those whose lives seemed oriented primarily towards money rather than intellectual or socially progressive activity. We were poor members of a wealthy family, awkward relations.

To write about family members raises difficult ethical questions. To begin with, it means that you cannot please everyone and that you will betray expectations if not presumed confidences.[7] After I circulated the first draft of the previous chapter, my brother Bernie, who had a friendly exchange with Simon Mawer, responded that I was being unfair. In confronting the different responses of family members to Mawer, do I take sides?

Evidently, you cannot write about your own family without being indiscrete, since one of the things that characterizes or defines "family" is what it keeps to itself, a disposition children learn very early. This dilemma is a matter of the ethics of representation. Are the dead entitled, as Dani asked me, to their privacy? Is holding back a matter of tact (positive) or concealment (negative)? How should I balance between discretion and disclosure, or conversely put, between a betrayal of truth or attention and a betrayal of intimacy? Unlike ethnography, I cannot resort to pseudonyms. Family members will not all share my judgment concerning what should have been made public or should have remained untold.

Whatever one's response to Mawer's right to lie in fiction, the question of truth is pressing here. It was central to Grete and Fritz, and to their philosopher son, Ernst. They asked: What is truth? Is truth what is unconcealed? Does unconcealment manifest as beauty, and conversely, is beauty a sign of truth? More practically, and at a different scale, does candour take precedence over the feelings of the person one is addressing? If "less is more," does that include silence – or a preference for blunt speech over tactful circumlocution? Finally and most saliently, is truth the primary value, and is its pursuit the key to living life ethically, seriously, and well?

The house with its wide windows and open interior was criticized, incorrectly, for exposing its inhabitants. The inhabitants *were* exposed to criticism from architectural reviewers, and subsequently to Nazi violence and then to the renewed anti-semitism and indifference of the communist regime. Recently, they were exposed, as some see it, to gratuitous portrayal in *The Glass Room*. People are not transparent like glass windows, but they are vulnerable both to exposure and to misinterpretation. Insofar as this book is another exposure, I would like to think of it less with respect to the *glass* room than to the *dark* room. I think of the delicate way Fritz Tugendhat exposed his photographic negatives of the family to reveal something at once true and beautiful.

My indiscretion concerns not only other members of the family. I worry too about what I reveal about myself. I have asked myself whether I am writing to settle scores or redress insecurities. In drawing from my own past I return to a period in which I was small and relatively ignorant, a time when my parents seemed fully adult and my grandparents very old, even if they were then considerably younger than I am today. This perceived family is perhaps less an actual family than a fantasy family, the family of childhood imagination that never was quite mine and yet is a part of me. It is thus a matter not only of trying to recapture the past – like the smell of a garden in Europe after it rains, so different from Canada – but also of dissolving its hold and growing up.[8]

The larger point is that in writing about a family, especially your own, you cannot present fairly and equally each person's point of view, you cannot write without a complex mix of motivations, and you cannot write without exposing or misinterpreting people or revealing lingering resentments and conflict. You could well spark new conflict.

There is also the question, one central to anthropology, of whether to accept the images the family has of itself or subject them to analysis, appraisal, and recontextualization. Family members speak of the progressive outlook of the factory owners and their enlightened treatment of the workers. Undoubtedly, there is some relative truth here, both in the fact and in the thought. But the stories say little about the material conditions of the workers, the hours of work, or the size of the wages, and they are silent on the fact that the wealth of the family must have been predicated on exploitation of the workers (and maybe also of the consumers). The bitter strikes evident in newspaper accounts are not part of the family narrative.

Relatives who have anticipated this book on "the family" will inevitably discover it is not quite what they wanted and that my perspective differs from theirs. Inevitably, our experience of the family is personal and our view of it structural. By personal, I refer to how our individual early experience has enabled the engagement and expansion, or else the contraction, of our capacities for work, wonder, happiness, and love. By structural, I refer to the fact that each of us has a distinct place within the family – son of one person, sister to another, and so on – and moreover, a different conception of who counts as family. This relativity of position is intrinsic to what we mean by kinship or family.

While some family stories are held in common, each person has their own experience and memories. I draw on the knowledge and perspectives of as many family members as I can. Mostly they complemented each other. Sometimes someone assured me of facts that proved objectively false, for example, which of a set of siblings was the first to marry. These small inaccuracies illustrate how family knowledge can be based on assumptions made in childhood that later take on the ring of truth. Naïvely for an anthropologist, I was surprised when people whom I took to be authorities on the family knew about only one branch. Something as central to my world as my uncle Ernst's connection to Heidegger was unknown to some of his second cousins.

My interest in the past is not a matter of my personality alone; it is common among my generation and age cohort in the diaspora. Silences between parents and children are often reopened by grandchildren, which is evident in the many accounts of the Holocaust written by grandchildren of victims and survivors. However, although my family is of Jewish background and was affected by Nazi brutality, this book is not primarily a story of the Holocaust, the abjection of victims, or the dignity of survivors. Only in places does it pull those emotional strings. Most of my mother's closest relatives were wealthy enough to leave, though some of them left by the skin of their teeth. Of those who didn't make it, no one spoke.

For family members the interest in the past lies less in the bad things that happened than in the positive world that was lost, not least the sense of being at home in the world that we imagine, possibly mistakenly, the older generations had. There is also a feeling that life then was lived to a higher standard, with greater intensity and conviction. Things truly counted back then and over there.

This feeling – is it nostalgia? – emanates in part from the ideals that my grandmother herself lived by. These did not need to be explicitly stated; one could say that she had achieved her ideal insofar as it was manifest in her manner of being and mode of life. If the house in Brno was a materialization of these ideals, so she and Fritz built in Switzerland, after the war, a second house that shared some features with the original (though not in slavish imitation and with some lovely additions). She lived there in what seemed absolute presence and authority. People visited as though on pilgrimage. And family members were frequently in awe of the seriousness and rigour she exemplified and expected in others.

At least, so it seemed to me.

꒰꒱

As noted, any representation of a family on the part of one of its members is inevitably partial. It is partial in both meanings of the term: part and not whole, and taking one perspective rather than another. Who is included also changes according to the context: widening or narrowing according to the issue or occasion.

Anthropologists have experience in addressing these matters. But for the most part they write about other people's families, not their own. And for the most part they conceive of their subject not as "family" but under the rubric of "kinship." Kinship is not a group of real people but an abstract concept, an ideal, and a set of ideas about relationships. In some hands it is highly formal, represented by diagrams on the page. This approach has great conceptual advantages, but it is also bloodless, dry, and impersonal, unlike family as we experience it day to day – messy, unbound, direct, comforting, irritating, boring, dramatic, confrontational, and loving. The idea of *kinship* is idealized as "diffuse, enduring solidarity" or "mutuality of being."[9] The image of *family*, as exemplified and perhaps exaggerated in the core narratives of our culture, from Abraham and Isaac to Hansel and Gretel, Sophocles to Shakespeare, Freud to soap operas, is bloody, replete with desire, jealousy, competition, neglect, ambivalence, substitution, betrayal, and violence.

On anthropological kinship diagrams, there is a focal person. It could be an ancestor, followed by their descendants. Or it could be someone of the current generation, figured as an abstract "ego" in a diagram that lays out all the terms and relations possible in relation to that ego within a given kinship system.

"Ego" is neutral on these diagrams and could be anyone. But of course, that is not the case when the kin terms are replaced by real people. Ego then is someone in particular; it is each of us with respect to our own family. The layout and extent of kin in a diagram in which I am ego will look different from one in which my cousin is ego. So, when I decide to write a history of what my mother's relatives call "the family," what is first at stake is the identity of the ego around whom the family is defined. When my mother's first cousin Susan encourages me to write about "the family," we share an idea of the subject, but in practice her imagination and her reality of the family overlaps with, but is not identical, to mine. Intrinsic to a family is that each person's position within it is unique. Family is something that binds its members together and that they share, and yet family is also different for each of its members, not fully shared and pulling them apart.

If the person selected as ego is arbitrary on an anthropologist's abstract kinship diagram, in the depiction of an actual family it matters a good deal. The identity of ego is evident in genres of biography or memoir, but not in a family history. As author, orchestrator, and narrator, the position of ego is mine, but I can also assign it elsewhere. In some respects, the ego in this book, the person around whom the family is defined, is my mother's mother, Grete. She is also a key personality and a central figure in the story; it is largely thanks to Grete that the piece of symbolic capital, the Mies house, came into being, remained part of our heritage, and continued to tie us together as "one" family; thanks to her that "we" have a story to tell, and one that some strangers take an interest in or tell a story about us. But the book is about her family – including her parents, their siblings and antecedents, her two husbands and their kin, her siblings and cousins, and all of their children.

If the centre of any family remains arbitrary, so do its borders. This concept became clear at the reunion where an entire branch we had not expected appeared. Included within this large other branch, connected to me through a common ancestor six generations back (we have my great-grandfather's great-grandfather in common) was a sub-branch whose existence none of us had even suspected, a line that had survived the Holocaust hidden in Czechoslovakia and who relocated to Germany when post-war life under the communist regime became too difficult.

This incident illustrates as well that if we trace back in time, hoping to find a source, an anchor for defining who we are, the further back we go, the more people come into view and the larger and more amorphous a family becomes. As sociologist Rogers Brubaker aptly puts it, "paradoxically, the more we know about our ancestry, the less unambiguously [the more ambiguously] that ancestry determines our identity."[10]

The more generations back you are able to trace, potentially the wider the number of their descendants in the present. The exercise illustrates that in practice genealogical knowledge is limited; only some names and people are remembered from the infinite number who could be included. The depth, scope, and layout of the known genealogy depend on many factors. To begin with, there is only so far back that people remember. Moreover, the names and social identities of members of intervening generations between the present speaker and a named ancestor are often forgotten. If we are all descended from Adam (see chapter 3), or from Lucy, that is a lot of people.

A notable feature of genealogies is that they are segmentary, branching at each generation, such that the descendants of one sibling are differentiated from the descendants of each other sibling. At each new generation the branches split further apart, and those who are closer to one another genealogically are more likely to interact and have more interests in common. However, it is also a principle of segmentation that on specific occasions or for particular events, a wider group of living people come together and identify with one another on their basis of acknowledgment of descent from a common ancestor further generations back. That is what happened at our family reunion.

Genealogy depends also on how a particular society understands *how* people pass on connections to one another and hence who count as kin. In a given society, relations through nurture could be more important than relations through biological connection ("blood" or "genes"). Marriage could be understood as intrinsic to relations among kin, or the choice of spouses could be seen as external, individual, and contingent.

Many societies emphasize connection through men, while others prioritize connections through women or recognize connections equally through men and women. It was evident at our family reunion that relations through men – as indicated by a shared last name – weighed more heavily than those through women. People with the patronym Löw-Beer connected through eight generations, whereas genealogically much closer ties through women with different last names were forgotten. We do not know who or where they are; hence, they are not part of the family in any socially meaningful sense. Some perished in the Holocaust.

The application of such principles depends on practical considerations concerning residence, property, authority, citizenship, and the like. Lines break off; mutual ancestors are forgotten; boundaries are redrawn. There are also contingent factors of demography – fertility, mortality, and morbidity. It remains a mystery why each of my mother's three full siblings died a few days after birth, or why she survived. Following the vast numbers of male soldiers killed in the First World War, many women went unmarried (though not in my family) and sometimes, as in the Freud family, lived in the household of a married sister.[11] Inspected closely enough, no genealogy works out strictly according to an ideal; there will be adoptions, untimely deaths, and contested conceptions, marriages, inheritances, and successions.

Families are often identified with respect to property, whether the estate is a house or business, land or title, stocks or privileges. Sometimes family units are defined as corporate, the members sharing certain rights and obligations, and functioning to outsiders as an undifferentiated legal unit. In this case, membership is regulated by rules that are narrower and more specific than those of birth and that are overseen or legitimated by the state.

Grete's father, Alfred Löw-Beer, was a member of such a corporate family. They were industrial capitalists. Established by Alfred's grandfather, Moses, the family firm grew from modest means in the mid-nineteenth century until by the early twentieth century it owned and managed several factories. The family was shaped by its estate. Membership in the firm passed exclusively from fathers to sons, and so Grete and her children were not members. When I describe the family, my perspective is from someone who has been outside the firm for three generations. The family in this sense includes those who were within the firm, or who remained connected to it after it was disbanded, through inheritance or a common last name. That name is Löw-Beer. In German, the first syllable is pronounced like the French word for egg and the second like the animal: *l'oeuf*-bear. That name (sometimes without the umlaut or the hyphen – Low Beer, Lowbeer, Lowber) remains the salient patronym, the name that above all enables this family to consider itself a single family. Its potency is evident in those Löw-Beer daughters who have chosen since the war to keep the name or hyphenate it with that of their husbands. Some of their sons have kept it as well.

From this perspective, the focal member is not Grete but a male ancestor, the founder of the firm, Moses Löw-Beer. The other branch to appear at the reunion, descended from two of his brothers, who founded their own firm, share the last name; that, along with mutual class interests, is what has maintained the connection.

Despite my anthropological training, it took me some time to fully recognize with respect to my own family the difference between the family constituted through birth, marriage, and sentiment, and largely through women, and the family constituted through property, passed on exclusively to and through men; hence, the distinction between the family as an amorphous network of people related by "mutuality of being" and the family as a bounded corporation related through ownership and inheritance of common (now formerly common) property (means of production).[12] At the same time, these principles partially coincided because of marriages between sets of brothers and sisters. Alfred was one of three brothers who married three sisters. Their offspring were double cousins to one another, tied simultaneously through men and women. This situation also illustrates that marriage practices can be as critical to the constitution of family as are principles of descent.

Over the next few chapters I reconstruct the world of kinship for successive generations of the family. Each chapter starts from a different period, cohort, or individual.

From the perspective of the firm, writing the family is less a matter of going back in time, from living members to their parents and grandparents, than starting with a founding ancestor, Moses Löw-Beer. The Löw-Beer family, moving from past to present, is constituted effectively as a line of men, whereas from my perspective, going from present to past, the connection is through women – to my mother's mother's mother, Marianne, who died when I was twenty-five. Grete and Marianne were at the centre of the postwar diasporic network of family. Both women long outlived their husbands, and both were strong, albeit very different, personalities. So, if the firm was constituted through men, an effect of the demise of the firm was that the prominence of women became more evident.

Grete was the last Löw-Beer in my line of ascendance. She was a member by birth, and she received the house from her father as a dowry or pre-mortem inheritance. But with that gift, she was also set outside the Löw-Beers. Her children, including my mother, and therefore me, were not owners; their economic interests did not include ours. In part II, I write about the family as a firm from its origins through Alfred and his two brothers and their children,

Kinship Diagram 1. Moses to Michael (partial)

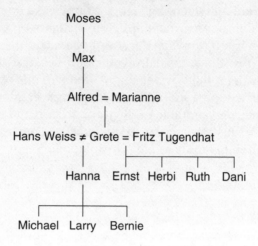

but I also consider the sisters and wives, as well as the husbands of Löw-Beer women. In part III, I focus on Grete and her son Ernst, before turning in part IV to the recent family reunion.

Alongside this core are many other figures. My mother was the only live product of the union between Grete and her first husband, Hans Weiss, and she is the only one of Grete's five children not a Tugendhat.[13] The Weiss family are not part of the story of the house, which my grandmother commissioned for herself and her second husband, Fritz Tugendhat. But consider that the Löw-Beers, Weiss, and Tugendhats were all German-speaking Jews of Moravia, each with antecedents in the small town of Boskovice and each the owners and managers of textile factories, in which the Löw-Beers had shares. The families were closely connected socially and financially, connections that continued after Hans and Grete's divorce in 1928. Their factories were among the largest and technically most advanced in central Europe. Of the three patronymically distinguished families, the Löw-Beers were at once the richest and the most self-conscious. Each of these families produced successful businessmen and intellectuals, some of whom became eminent in their fields.

Of course, neither artistic and scholarly nor worldly achievement, nor sheer intelligence, is a criterion of being a good person or a necessary or sufficient condition for happiness. The family values did not come without cost.

In recent decades anthropologists have reconfigured the study of kinship as one of relations rather than descent groups. The influential work of Marilyn Strathern emphasizes what she calls "dividuals" and the ways people are constituted as sharing parts of one another.[14] In this perspective, "dividuality" is the background condition and individuality a kind of unusual and marked form of personhood. Strathern and her followers examine cultural models of shared bodily substances; more sociologically inclined writers like Pierre Bourdieu add the significance of shared class-based habits, skills, interests, and taste.[15]

The turn to relationality by anthropologists is complemented by developments in psychoanalysis. A family is composed of people who identify with and unconsciously internalize one other and, conversely, defend themselves from projections and over-identification. Notably, children identify with but also separate from and ultimately displace their parents. In lived experience, relations among kin are characterized by ambivalence. There is plenty of love, but also disappointment, resentment, jealousy, and even hate. Our recognition of these matters obviously owes much to Sigmund Freud, himself from a family of assimilated Moravian Jews. There was even a modest connection. Leah Bernays (1829–1924), married to a nephew of Moses Löw-Beer, provided some assistance to her niece Martha Freud when the family was in financial difficulty.[16]

Not only might the family have shared some of Freud's tacit assumptions or manifest the kinds of relations that provided the empirical basis for his theorizing, but some of them read Freud or were influenced by his ideas. Some members described others as "neurotic." However, it was only well after the Second World War that several women in the family became practising psychoanalysts.[17]

In contemporary psychoanalysis the focus is less on the bounded autonomous ego than on the ways in which the self is constituted in and through relations with significant others and the internalization of particular modes of relating to others. While each person's unconscious and conscious fantasy life is their own, they are produced in relation and response to the fantasy lives and modes of relationship of adults whom they encounter at a young age. Yet, if psychoanalysis theorizes such intersubjective or "dividual" relations, in practice it focuses on individual patients. The biography of families can reveal how particular character traits, dispositions, neuroses, or modes of relating are reproduced or transformed from generation to generation.

A particular characteristic of my family is a proclivity to idealization. Those idealized were the dominant personalities and highest achievers of their generation, and they get a prominent place in the narrative. This pattern extended beyond individuals to an idealization of the family as a whole, something in which I am obviously complicit. However, I hope to set idealization alongside recognition of what these people and this family were actually like. This intent is not to disparage them or pivot from idealization to denigration.

I am not only representing a certain family but writing about – representing – the way that family is and has been represented, both how family members represent it to themselves and how representations of the family have been used in other projects, by people outside the family, not least how various interested parties have represented the Tugendhat House and its inhabitants since it was built.

I've suggested that a family, any family, exists as such in and through its enactments and representations of itself. Representations materialize in and as everyday interactions, daily meals, holiday gatherings, photo albums, letters and Facebook posts, wills and contracts, property, care, love, and conflict. Here is an excerpt from my notes:

> *Thanksgiving 2017.* My brothers Larry and Bernie and Bernie's wife Linda celebrate with us in Toronto. Bernie and Linda combine the occasion with a memorial event for one of Linda's aunts – a part of Bernie's family but not mine. Bernie brings me a copy of Georgia Hunter's *We Were the Lucky Ones* and says there is a surprise inside. Bernie was told about the book by Ellen Pollak, a Löw-Beer cousin we had only recently discovered [see chapter 5]. The cover asserts that it is a novel, but in fact it is equally Hunter's family history.[18] The contradiction is manifest in the surprise. Among the characters are a pair of distant Löw-Beers, whose exploits in the book match their actions in real life as put forward by our fifth cousin Daniel Low-Beer in his family history, unpublished at the time Hunter's book appeared.[19]
>
> Bernie has asked Mawer to blurb his own book, a work of pure fiction but one that does contain certain names recognizable to close family members.[20]

What else is a family than the representations it makes of itself and its responses to those that are made of it? Necessarily then, the project is recursive.

PART II

Family and Firm

How strange it is, to be standing leaning against the current of time.
– W.G. Sebald, *Vertigo*

Before Löw-Beers

The Löw-Beers sometimes talked as if the emergence of their enterprise was purely a matter of individual genius. While the first Löw-Beers were particularly enterprising, the industrial revolution took place earlier and more strongly in Moravia than in other parts of central Europe. Conditions in the nineteenth century were conducive to industry and relatively hospitable to Jews. Contrary to the family story, the Löw-Beers were hardly the first to establish textile factories.

The period saw not only rapid industrialization and accumulation of wealth but also secularization. The older way of Jewish life was holistic, one in which it was impossible to separate religious from political and social activities. But as Jews moved into the cities, these features became disaggregated. Jews were no longer under control of their rabbis or community elders. Social horizons broadened. People began to ease up on ritual practices and prohibitions. Some converted to Christianity, while others, like the Löw-Beers, retained an identity as Jews but abandoned religious practice.

The Löw-Beer story moves between three locations. First is the small Moravian town of Boskovice (Boskowitz in German). At the beginning of the story the Löw-Beers live entirely in Boskovice, but by the First World War virtually no family member (among those remembered today) is still there. Second is Brno, capital of Moravia, an industrial hub known in the nineteenth century as "the Manchester of the Habsburg Monarchy."[1] Brno is 42 kilometres south of Boskovice. And third is Vienna, capital of the Habsburg Empire, where policies were set and where many of the wealthiest and most modernized Jews settled when they could. Vienna is 134 kilometres south of Brno.

The Czech Republic (Czechia) today is comprised of Bohemia and Moravia. Bohemia, the larger region, is centred on the beautiful city of Prague. Moravia lies adjacent to its east. Today the two Czech-speaking regions are highly integrated, but that was less the case in the past. For this story, Moravia's relations with Silesia to the north, Austria to the south, and Slovakia and Hungary to the east and southeast have equal if not greater importance. Of course, connections between these various places have changed over time. From the Middle Ages, there were shifting layers of feudal overlords, subordinated eventually to a single empire governed from Vienna. During the nineteenth century in both Bohemia and Moravia, the majority of people, especially in the countryside, spoke Czech, but German speakers formed a large proportion of city dwellers. In 1900, 77 per cent of Jews in Moravia declared German their mother tongue.[2] Moravia was then oriented more towards Vienna than towards Prague. Not only did Austria provide the seat of government but also the main market for its products. Brno is considerably closer (by 70 kilometres) to Vienna than to Prague. For German speakers, as the Löw-Beers became, Vienna was also a cultural hub, with music, art, theatre, university, and superior medical facilities.

The shifting geopolitical boundaries and names can be confusing. Moravia is part of what are sometimes called the historical Czech lands; during the feudal period Moravia was under the Bohemian crown, and its ruler, known as a margrave, was often the younger brother or son of the monarch in Prague. In 1526 Moravia became subject to Habsburg rule, in what was known until 1867 as the Austrian Empire and thereafter as the Austro-Hungarian Empire or Austria-Hungary.[3] When the empire was dismantled at the end of the First World War and divided into nation-states, Moravia became the central region of the nation-state of Czechoslovakia, bordered by Bohemia to the west and Slovakia to the east. Twenty years later it was occupied by the Germans, and then from 1948 to 1989 it was part of the Soviet bloc. In 1992 Czechs and Slovaks divided the country into two separate states. The decision was made peacefully in Grete's house in Brno.

Jews are mentioned in Brno from the eleventh century. In medieval times they were generally treated quite well; a thirteenth-century charter forbade forced conversion, protected their lives and property, and freed restrictions on dress and occupation.[4] By the fourteenth century they were self-governing; in 1345 Brno was explicitly granted the right to admit Jews, and there were probably around 1,000 Jewish inhabitants at the time. But in 1454 the tide abruptly turned; Jews were expelled from six so-called royal cities, among them Brno, not to be officially readmitted until 1848. They settled in smaller towns under the protection of local lords, some of whom believed in religious tolerance. Many of the Jews expelled from Brno moved to Boskovice.[5]

Jews in Moravia still had it better than those in most other parts of central and eastern Europe. They inhabited towns rather than villages and were "permitted to consolidate tight self-ruled settlements ... where they lived in relative comfort."[6] Jews were free, not serfs, but they had to pay an annual tax and lived in bounded neighbourhoods, that is, in ghettos. However, they were quite mobile, and most of them appear to have engaged in trade. Jews were able to enter Brno during the day to attend the markets and could sleep in the suburbs. Moreover, they were permitted to engage in petty manufacturing as long as they produced for Jewish consumption and did not compete directly with the town-based Christian guilds.

While life in the eighteenth century was undoubtedly harsh at times, Jews had certain advantages. They were, for the most part, self-governing, subject to a chief rabbi for Moravia who arbitrated judicial matters and to a regional council and local "deputations" of wealthy Jewish citizens who supervised collection of the annual tax. The tax promoted some interest in their well-being and protection from the nobles on whose land their settlements were. Unlike the peasants, Jews could move between districts in the face of war or famine.[7] When in 1726 Emperor Karl (Charles) VI declared 20,000 to 25,000 the upper limit for the population of Jews in Moravia and allowed only one son per family to marry, some people of marriageable age resituated to Hungary, which, after war with Turkey and before the influx of Galician Jews, had a very low Jewish population. Since Hungary then included Slovakia, they did not have to go very far. Once the population restriction was removed, the Jewish population of Moravia rose from around 30,000 in 1830 to 45,000 in 1890 and then began a gradual decline through the Second World War, when some emigrated and most were deported and murdered.

When Maria Theresia became empress in 1740, she raised the tax on Jews steeply, but other policies came indirectly to favour them insofar as she tried to undermine the feudal system in the western territories. Royal officials offered support for commercial and financial activities.[8] The wealthiest Jewish money lenders became influential at court, and many took on Christian modes of dress and comportment, as well as the German language. Jews in places like Boskovice began to emulate the wealthier and most assimilated Jews. Schooling in German was supported by the empress.

Maria Theresia's successor, Joseph II, who reigned from 1780 to 1790, abolished serfdom, terminated the body tax on Jews, and gave Jews the right to attend schools, enter the professions, and found factories.[9] He even ordered half the tax to be placed in a fund to pay the chief rabbi and officials; from 1831 the fund was used to support needy communities.[10] Joseph II also undermined the separatism in the Jewish way of life, forbidding the use of Hebrew in public documents, encouraging modern modes of dress, and abolishing Jewish civic law. With the spread of coeducational schooling in German, Yiddish was supplanted by German.[11] As a consequence, German became "the lingua franca of Central Europe's Jews, who tended to view it as a supranational language of culture, enlightenment, and commerce, not as a 'national' idiom."[12] Although he kept residence restrictions, the emperor's initiatives, in historian William McCagg's view, "unmistakably constituted the first great generalized attack in modern European history by a Christian ruler against the medieval restrictions that burdened Jewish life."[13]

The assessment of "burdensome restrictions" is of course a modernist one, and not all Jews saw it that way. Throughout the empire, in different ways and at somewhat different times, there developed a polarization between what came to be called orthodox and reformist Judaism. While the orthodox strove to maintain their separateness with respect to school, dress, family, law, and ritual observance, secularization brought the idea that Jews were not an internally self-governing people with a distinct way of life but citizens of a diverse empire who happened to practise a specific religion. One effect of increased mobility was that Jews were no longer subject to conservative rabbis and could practise as they pleased. To the degree that they were not hampered by anti-semitism, they could assimilate into the wider society as individual citizens. In fact, it was likely easier for Jews to imagine being part of the plural society of the empire prior to the First World War than to fit into the nation-states propagating internal ethnic homogeneity that emerged after.

By the time residence restrictions were officially removed in 1848–49, they had already been ignored for some time by the wealthy. In 1820 there were 130 legally tolerated Jewish families in Vienna; in 1826 they opened a "modern temple." By 1848 Vienna had between 4,500 and 10,000 Jews.[14] McCagg goes so far as to say that "the Jewish emancipation of 1848 was achieved at Vienna because leading figures of the Jewish community were indigenized."[15] In 1867 Jews were given full rights under the constitution.

From 1848 poorer Jews began pouring into the cities. By 1869 they formed slightly over 10 per cent of Vienna's population of 400,000. Of these, some 20.6 per cent were from Moravia and Silesia. As McCagg puts it, "in no other part of Habsburg Jewry was there such a pronounced flow from the old small-town ghettos into modern cities in the decades after 1848."[16] This period was an exciting time in Vienna with the construction of the opulent Ringstrasse, along which the mansions of the wealthiest Jews went up adjacent to those of the aristocracy. In Brno, a Jewish cemetery was opened in 1852, and a synagogue in 1855, the first building in the city to be supplied with electric lighting. By 1900 there were over 8,000 Jewish residents.[17]

McCagg adds that in the second half of the nineteenth century, one could observe the embourgeoisement of even the smaller communities.[18] At the same time, however, these places grew impoverished as Jewish taxpayers who had once supported synagogues, schools, ritual baths, hospitals, burial houses, and cemeteries moved away. Moreover, in cities like Brno, they didn't necessarily pay the Jewish communal taxes, thereby asserting their separation from tradition and their autonomy as citizens.

By 1880 there were over 72,000 Jews in Vienna. The wealthy, some 6 per cent of the total, "displayed their luxury and cosmopolitan culture, and put a premium on modern education. They were German speakers who looked down on Yiddish. They were relaxed in their ritual observance of Judaism, and open to modern ideas."[19] McCagg describes the ethos as one of "accepting pseudo-aristocratic social values, aesthetic escapism, and economic speculation as a way of life."[20] The wealthy played the stock market and encouraged the middle class to do so as well. When in 1873 the market bubble burst and many people lost their savings, anti-semitism rose up again. From 1897 to 1910 Vienna elected an anti-semitic mayor, Karl Lueger. His election did not halt Jewish immigration or enterprise. In 1900 there were nearly 147,000 Jews in Vienna, and within the decade the Jewish population rose to 182,700. By the First World War, many were middle class and "indulged in cheerful sublimation into culture ... as was habitual among the Viennese."[21]

While I once assumed that Moses or a close family member had gone to Manchester to learn textile production, that appears to have been unnecessary and not the case. In fact, there was a long tradition of wool production in Moravia, and conditions favoured the development of the textile industry, eventually including Jews. Several Jewish families from Boskovice developed textile factories, and there were more in Brno.

Habsburg policies from the mid-eighteenth century encouraged industrialization and weakened the power of the Christian guilds that controlled production and excluded Jews. In his admirable study of the origins of industrial production in Moravia and, more specifically, of the Brno Fine-Cloth Factory established in 1764, economic historian Herman Freudenberger shows that it took place under the direct and massive support of the Habsburg monarchy. Mercantilist policies attempted to use agricultural products more effectively, create a pool of workers who could be taxed, and reduce the import of fine woollens. The aim was also to replace Silesia, which had been the main producer of textiles for the empire until Austria lost possession in 1740.[22]

Freudenberger clarifies the process by which craft was transformed into industrial production. The legal definition of "factory" (*Fabrik*) was established in order to overcome the limitations of the guilds. Factories were "larger productive enterprises especially chartered by the government and protected against the interference of municipalities and guilds. These factories were not subject to any limitations concerning their output, their employment of workers or their methods of manufacturing." Freudenberger adds that "despite government protection, they did not, however, enjoy a good reputation among the population. During the entire century people looked upon them as akin to penitentiaries and workhouses."[23]

Brno was, for social and geographic reasons, well placed to benefit from this intervention. The proto-factory "proved to be the main stem from which the textile industry grew" and served as a training institution for the diffusion of the new technology.[24] In 1788 there were over 100 looms in the city, and by 1802 there were 600 looms in woollen cloth factories, with some 10,000 workers.[25] Brno attracted immigrant Germans entrepreneurs as well as a British manufacturer who set up a machine shop. By the first decades of the nineteenth century, spinning and shearing machines were manufactured locally.[26] Once the hand wheel was replaced by a mechanical wheel in 1793, a steady supply of yarn was secured. Brno also benefitted from direct rail connection with Vienna from 1839, thanks to a steam railroad financed by a joint stock company whose major investor was Salomon Rothschild. This "northern line" led from Breslau and the Silesian mining and iron works to Vienna via Brno. By 1841 Brno was "the largest producer in the Austria Empire of woolen textiles by value."[27]

The guilds were finally abolished in 1859. One consequence was that the artisan class became poorer, and many of their members started producing piece work for the factories. The mass of the labour force moved downwards, and the poor were ripe for exploitation in the factories. Working conditions were very bad, provoking in 1843 a large strike in Brno.[28] McCagg adds that because Protestant nobility had been chased out of the Czech lands in the 1620s, there was a much lower ratio of gentry to commoners than elsewhere in the realm and serfdom had been more limited. Hence, there was more available labour.[29] A further consequence of the demise of the guilds was that Jews were able to step in and intensify production.

The transformation from the 1860s of Brno into a planned modern nineteenth-century city with its own Ringstrasse was supported by the Jewish population and their capital. The city attracted planners, architects, and artists. The first "villa colony" in Brno was developed on the slopes above the Augarten (Lužánky Park), the neighbourhood where the Löw-Beers eventually settled.

Until the mid-nineteenth century, most of the ancestors of my family inhabited Boskovice, a small town surrounded by rolling hills in a lush countryside. Founded in the eleventh century, Boskovice retains material evidence of its history, including a ruined thirteenth-century castle, a town hall tower with a Gothic portal from the late fifteenth century, a château from the 1820s, and a large Jewish quarter and cemetery. Boscovice is considered one of the oldest Jewish communities in Moravia, with a tombstone in Hebrew dated 1069 and a court document of 1243 attesting to the presence of Jews.[30]

The website of Brno's tourist office explains that the Boskovice ghetto extended over 12 acres and comprised 13 streets and 138 houses. Today the quarter is a tourist destination in which "since 1999, the 27 most attractive sights have been presented as part of an educational trail winding through the Jewish quarter." An annual arts festival is held to raise funds to preserve and restore the quarter.[31] In sum, the ghetto is a source of tourist revenue, the synagogue has become a museum, and the commemoration of the death, disappearance, and dispersal of its former Jews now enlivens the town.

The houses in the Jewish "quarter" (a friendlier word than "ghetto") are described as baroque or classicist in style and are more than humble dwellings. According to the same website, "the baroque synagogue ... was built in 1639 by an Italian builder Sylvester Fiota of Chiavenna. In 1698 the synagogue was extended with a side aisle ... [T]he vaults and interior walls ... were covered with decorative fresco paintings including ornamental and plant motifs and Hebraic liturgical texts ... Another two synagogues, the Synagogue Minor from the 18th century and the Löw-Beer Synagogue from 1884, were pulled down after WWII." The interior of the remaining synagogue is indeed very beautiful. The Jewish cemetery, one of the largest in the Czech Republic, contains 2,400 tombstones.

There were 1,531 Jews in Boskovice in 1727, the year that the Jews were confined to a single quarter and limited to 326 families. The population revived, peaking at 2,018 in 1857 and comprising approximately one-third of the town's population. In 1848 the Jewish community was singled out as one of the first two places in the Czech lands to be established as its own municipality, with a mayor, police, and fire department.[32] The mayor was officially a representative of Count Mensdorff-Pouilly, whose family, originally from Lorraine, retained feudal overlordship, but in 1850 it was the count himself who was elected mayor.[33]

During the seventeenth and eighteenth centuries, most Jews were engaged in petty trade and crafts. The first Jewish textile

enterprise was founded in Boskovice at the beginning of the nineteenth century but ran into conflict with the Christian spinners'
guild and was closed in 1812. Later in the century, a number of
Jewish families began textile and ready-made clothing production.[34] As Jews began to move elsewhere, the population declined
to 850 in 1900 and 395 in 1930. In 1939 Jews were forced to re-enter
the ghetto, and in 1942 they were transported to Theresienstadt
and then to Auschwitz. Some 473 Jews from Boskovice and its
immediate neighbourhood perished in the Holocaust.[35]

Although you wouldn't know it from subsequent Löw-Beers,
Boskovice was an "important center of Jewish learning in the eighteenth and nineteenth centuries."[36] Religious life was intense and
turbulent. The town was party to revival movements that swept
through Judaism during this period. In 1782 Nathan Adler, a well-
known kabbalist from Frankfurt, was elected rabbi of the community, but his "excessive and mystical piety" made enemies so that
he returned to Frankfurt three years later.[37] The challenge came no
doubt from Samuel ha-Levi Kolin (1720 or 1724–1806), who led a
yeshiva in Boskovice.[38] Samuel will reappear shortly. A later rabbi,
Abraham Placzek, served also as chief rabbi of Moravia (1851–84),
provisionally moving the seat of the chief rabbinate to Boskovice.
His son Baruch married Karolina Löw-Beer and became rabbi of
Brno and of Moravia as well, so there was a Löw-Beer, of the same
generation as my great-grandfather, albeit an older female second
cousin, firmly ensconced in Judaism. Baruch is described as a kind
of Renaissance man who was interested in natural science, a friend
of Mendel, and a correspondent with Darwin. Their son began in
one of the Löw-Beer factories and became a wealthy textile industrialist himself.[39]

Finding the "First" Löw-Beer

The two Löw-Beer firms that emerged from Boskovice were
respectively the Aron-Jakob and the Moses firms. All three of these
men were brothers. But who were their antecedents? The historians in Brno concerned with documenting the family history offer

one answer and I another. The historians note that in neither the Boskovice tract list of 1677 nor the "Protocollum" of 1727, a kind of census, are Löw-Beers mentioned.[40] Hence, they suppose that the ancestor of the brothers arrived in Boskovice after 1727. However, given the non-existence of last names at the time, the absence is not surprising.

It was only from 1 January 1788 by edict of the emperor that every Jewish resident was obliged to select a surname, which had to be German. Judas Löw-Beer appears in a tax record of 1788 and then in the 1799 register of Boskovice families and "free Jews" (the *Sub-Repartition bei der Boskowitzer Juden Gemeinde fur das Jahr 1799*); Salomon, Samson, and Nathan Löw-Beer are also named. The Brno historians surmise that Judas was the first Löw-Beer. Historian Jaroslav Bránský locates the name in the Book of Seats of the main synagogue. Seat number 38 was inherited by Judas Löw-Beer from his father. The historians guess the father was called Salomon Löbl since Salomon was also the name that Judas apparently gave his first-born son. But that would only have been the case were Judas's father already deceased. They also suggest that Judas Löw-Beer had been called Jehuda Löw, or Löb, before 1788 and that he lived from 1724 to 1800. They mention only two children of Judas / Jehuda: Salomon, who lived from 1746 to 1832, and Samson or Shimon, 1753 to 1824. Salomon was the father of Nathan, mentioned in the register, and later of Aron, Jakob, and Moses, founders of the Löw-Beer firms. Samson appears to have moved elsewhere, following the limitation on the number of Jewish families.

Before offering my alternative "origin" story, I need to make an aside to discuss Jewish naming practices. Until Judas's time, most Jewish men were called by a single name and took their father's name to qualify it. Were someone to ask *which* Shlomo you were referring to, you could add the name of his father, say, Shlomo Nathan. Because children were given the names of deceased grandparents, names often recurred. It is easy to find in the genealogies a Shlomo Nathan, followed by a Nathan Shlomo, and then again a Shlomo Nathan. It is also easy to get confused and to delete past generations by mistake. Women were referred to through their fathers, thus Miriam *bat* (daughter of) Nathan. Daughters were added to the genealogies when a man had no sons; then it is a woman who forms the connecting link between two generations of men.

Primary names had additional identifiers. People were often distinguished according to the place where they lived or from where they or an ancestor had come, like Samuel ha-Levi Kolin, so called because he came from Kolín, a town in eastern Bohemia. Samuel's son Wolf, who led yeshivas in Moravia and Hungary and returned to Boskovice from Budapest to deliver the oration at his father's funeral, became known as Wolf Boskowitz, identified through his place of origin. In rabbinical genealogies, places of origin were often passed on for many generations, thereby maintaining a geographical as well as genealogical memory and functioning rather like a last name. Eventually, when last names were introduced, many of these appellations were drawn upon. Thus there are families named Boskowitz, most commonly in Hungary. A better-known example is people with a distant origin in the town of Speyer in the Rhineland, called Spira by the Romans and subsequently by the French, who became known as Spira or Spiro and later as Shapira or Schapiro, and so on. Pronunciation changed over time, as did spelling when people moved from a Hebrew alphabet without vowels to a Latin one.

Further elaborations and affectionate epithets were added as extra terms. Among Jews, "Löw" was originally not a family name but a substitute or nickname (Hebrew *kinnui*) for Judah, Judas, or Jehuda.[41] It was, in effect, the secular version in the local language of the biblical Hebrew name. Jehuda refers back to one of Jacob's sons in the Torah, the founder of the tribe of Judah. Biblical Judah was associated with a lion, for which the word in German is *Löwe*. In the Torah (Genesis 49:9) Jacob calls his son Judah a "*Gur Aryeh*, a Young Lion" when he blesses him. (In modern Hebrew, *Aryeh* – Lion – is a common personal name.) The Geni website entry adds: "In Jewish naming tradition the Hebrew name and the substitute name are often combined as a pair." Judas (Judah, Jehuda) Löw is a common pair. *It is not a first and last name, but an amplification of the same name in two languages.*

In other words, Judas or Jehuda Löw gives no direct indication of parentage. During Jehuda's lifetime there were many people with Löw appended to their personal name in Boskovice and in the region more broadly. In the first instance it would appear that Löw indicates a descendant of the original Judah rather than an immediate kinship connection between two people who had the name. But nowhere would it be more appropriately used than for someone with the first name Judah/Jehuda. Here the two words replicate and mirror each other as a kind of poetic confirmation and bilingual coupling. Nevertheless, not all men named Jehuda hailed from the tribe of Judah, nor were they all also called Löw. Conversely, not everyone called Löw was also named Jehuda or associated with the tribe of Judah. Moreover, women too could be called Löw but not Jehuda.

Judas or Jehuda Löw who became a Löw-Beer did not necessarily share the term *Löw* with his father or brothers. He did, however, happen to share this coupling with the famous rabbi of Prague who died in that city in 1609. From 1553 to 1588 *that* Jehuda Löw was the *Landesrabbiner*, the chief rabbi, for all Moravia and lived in Nikolsburg (Mikulov), south of Brno, before he returned to Prague and then went briefly to Pozen as chief rabbi of Poland. His more complete name was Judah Löw *ben* (son of) Bezalel.[42] Rabbi Löw is famous for his scholarship. Indeed, his well-known work is called in Hebrew the "*Gur Aryeh al HaTorah*," "Young Lion [commentary on] the Torah." This title reinforces the point that Judah and Löw were identified with lion. Moreover, Rabbi Löw was said to be descended patrilineally from King David, hence of the line of Judah.

It is worth saying a few more words about Rabbi Judah Löw of Prague. He was widely known and respected during his life as a philosopher, Talmudic scholar, and mystic, once even invited to speak with the emperor about Kabbalah. His work inspired Polish Hasidism. As chief rabbi of Moravia he was active in directing community affairs. Rabbi Löw had six daughters but only one son, who became a rabbi in Kolín.

What Rabbi Löw is best known for has little to do with any of this biographic detail. In the nineteenth century he became subject of a legend that he had raised the golem, an animate being fashioned of clay. This monster, prototype of Frankenstein's monster, was a product of the rabbi's mystical powers and based on secret knowledge of how God created and gave life to Adam. Rabbi Löw created the golem to defend the Jews of Prague from anti-semitic attacks. But when the golem went out of control, he had to render it lifeless again. According to one tradition, the golem was animated by writing the Hebrew letters *aleph, mem, tav* on its forehead. This spells *emet*, which means "truth." To de-animate the golem, Rabbi Löw simply wiped off the first letter, leaving the word *met*, which means "death."[43]

Rabbi Löw is said to be the ancestor of a number of famous individuals, including Menachim Schneerson, the Lubavitcher rebbe, and Yehudi Menuhin, the violinist. Whether he was an ancestor of the Löw-Beer family is debatable. There was such a story in the family; my mother once raised it in order to discount it. I assumed she was correct, but I now think otherwise.

Let me return to the question of the first man to take the name Löw-Beer. When I began to investigate life in Boskovice, I came across the name of a well-known rabbi who lived there in the eighteenth century and had a son called Jehuda Löw, born in Boskovice in 1751 and dying in 1800, listed without reference to a wife or children. I began to think this man could be our Judas Löw-Beer. However, the dates suggested he was more likely a brother of Salomon than his father. I proposed that the father of both Salomon and Judas was the rabbi in question and that we are descended from Salomon but not from Jehuda/Judas.

In my reconstruction, Salomon Löw-Beer's father was a man mentioned earlier, called Rabbi Shmuel Halevi Kelin Kolin (Löw), otherwise known as Samuel *ben* Nathan Ha-Levi Löw.[44] Samuel's birthdate is listed as 1720 or 1724, the very date the Brno historians assigned to Jehuda. He died in Budapest, presumably on a visit to his son Wolf Boskowitz, but he was buried in Boskovice in 1806. Kelin or Kolín is his place of birth, a town some 55 kilometres east of Prague on the River Elbe that contained a significant Jewish community. Two of his brothers, Jakob and Nathan, were each born in Boskovice, suggesting he arrived as a child with his parents. Each brother had the appellation Löw. Samuel Kolin or Kelin – the spelling is flexible – was a Talmudist and authority on Jewish law.[45] He never held an official rabbinical position, but he presided over a yeshiva and was an influential teacher and writer in Boskovice for some sixty years. He is described in the *Jewish Encyclopedia* of 1906 as "the most eminent person of Boskowitz" and someone whose teaching enabled the citizens to be "too practical to follow the religious extravagances" of other rabbis and to "embarrass [them] by their acumen."[46] He also approved of secular education, as long as it assisted understanding of the Torah. Nevertheless, "he regularly recited mystical midnight prayers (*Tikkun Chatzot*) and wore sackcloth to mourn the destruction of the Temple."[47]

Samuel was supported by the wool business of his wife, Elka Esther Loeb or Löw (both spellings are used). Her paternal grandfather, Jehuda Arye Loeb-Isserl ("lion" appears three times here), and her great-grandfather were noted rabbis. Samuel and Elka had several children, including a son listed as Judah Löw.

What about Samuel's parents? Can we go further back in the paternal line? While Samuel's immediate antecedents are somewhat confused, it seems that his mother was Bela Löw, who was in fact descended from the famous rabbi of Prague. This lineage could explain why her sons had Löw applied to their names. Samuel's father, Nosson Notah (Halevi) Kellin, also known as Nate or Nathan, was a wealthy merchant descended in turn from a long line of rabbis bearing the Spira name and tracing back to Samuel Zalman Shapira or Spira (c. 1345–1414), recognized as the first Shapira, from Speyer in the Rhineland. They trace further back in the Klonimus line to seventh-century Lucca and Rome, and via Julia Minna Vergentlin (c. 1350–1427), through French and Rhineland rabbis back to Rashi (1040–1105), the great medieval commentator on the Talmud and the Torah. From the Geni website, it is easy to trace the lines of Ashkenazi Jewry through their leading rabbis over the centuries across Europe, from the south and west to the northeast, but very mobile in both directions in any given lifetime, producing a vast network of kinship and learning. Most of the links are father to son, but in some generations, like that of Rashi himself, the line passes through daughters. From Rashi, one can trace back to the Sanhedrin Court in Jerusalem at the beginning of the Christian era, and from there, to King David and the original Judah himself. From Judah, it is easy to go back via Abraham and

Noah to Adam and Eve. Following these lines and accepting the number of generations listed in the Jewish records, Samuel Kolin is approximately the 135th generation down from Adam and my children the 143rd.

If I can trace back to Adam, surely my genealogical work is done! Of course, my point is the pointlessness of trying to find ultimate origins. This descent is a fantasy – manifest today in genetic testing – but a powerful one that speaks to the way kinship is supposed to anchor identity in some original source. But the source is arbitrary: first, because it is always possible to go back one generation more, and second, because of the cultural bias to picture founding ancestors as men and to trace back to them through men. Few people ask or know about the ascendants of the mothers, grandmothers, or wives of the Löw-Beer men. I myself have weeded many of them from what would otherwise be a manuscript choked with ancestors.

The interesting social questions are which connections out of the multitude are broken or forgotten and why, and which remembered. Salomon's father was largely forgotten insofar as there was no last name to connect father and son, and insofar as interests changed. From Rashi to Samuel Kolin, the people remembered at each generation were Talmudic scholars and rabbis, while from Salomon onwards, not a single descendant became a rabbi, and adherence to religious practice and scholarship declined, until by my grandparents' generation it was completely gone.[48] A very sharp break indeed.

The story depends on Salomon Löw-Beer being the son of Samuel rather than of Judas. The Brno historians had traced the Löw-Beer line back to a Judas/Jehuda Löw with no known antecedents. I found a different Jehuda Löw who was a recorded son of Samuel. I hypothesized that the two Jehudas were one and the same, but I could not make the dates work. There were not enough years between them for Salomon to be a grandchild of Samuel through this Jehuda. Salomon's birth date of 1746 did, however, fit neatly as Samuel's son. If both Jehuda and Salomon took the name Löw-Beer, as we know from the records, then it is more likely they were brothers than father and son. Admittedly, there was no genealogical record to support my hypothesis. While the dates fit perfectly, no Salomon is listed as a son of Samuel, although some versions of his genealogy do indicate additional unnamed children. It was exciting to think I had solved the paternal ancestry of the Löw-Beers and not only confirmed we had a rabbi in the family but one who linked us to the senior Ashkenazi rabbinical lineages across Europe. But in the end, with no genealogical record of a Salomon among Samuel's sons, it seemed implausible and could not be defended.

However, my reconstruction was unexpectedly confirmed about a year later when I came across Traudl Schmidt's account of the life of my grandmother's cousin Paul Löw-Beer. Paul was Rudolf's son, and Rudolf was the person most likely to have known the family patriline. In her description of Paul's roots, Schmidt indicates that our line stems from Rabbi Samuel Ha-Levi Kolin, exactly as I had hypothesized. She says specifically that Moses's father, Salomon Löbl (1746–1832) *was* "said to have been" Samuel's son.[49] As Rabbi Samuel was born c. 1724 (or 1720) and Salomon in 1746, the dates fit. Moreover, insofar as the birthdate of Samuel corresponds with that of Judah in the Brno historians' account, there is a slim possibility that Judah could simply have been another appellation for Samuel rather than a distinct person. In sum, the putative Jehuda Löw is none other than either Samuel himself, or more likely, Salomon's brother.[50]

At the time there were many other residents of Boskovice to whom the name Löw was applied. Once last names were taken on, Beer was likely added precisely to distinguish the family from all the others named Löw. Why the name Beer was selected remains unknown. The Brno historians suggest that Judas's wife was called Buny Beer (Bär or Berisch). They do not mention other people named Beer, and there is no evidence the name was associated with either Samuel or Salomon's wife. Paul Löw-Beer did tell me that the name would not originally have been hyphenated, a hyphen being the sign of nobility. Paul said his mother, Elise, introduced the hyphen to avoid confusion, but that his father, Rudolf, didn't use it.

꙰

Salomon married Paulina Perl Kolin (b. 1753). It is possible that she was Samuel's daughter and Salomon his son-in-law. Indeed, I have seen a genealogy in which Salamon Löbl, son of Judas, is indicated as married to a daughter of Samuel. Moreover, on that genealogy Judas is the son of a Rabbi Beer from Prosnitz where Beer is short for Bernard, a plausible source of the name. However, Samuel's daughter is listed as Sara not Perl, and other records show Sara married someone else. Remember too that Kolin was not a last name but rather the town Perl/Paulina or her antecedents came from.

Whatever the case, we can start the Löw-Beer line firmly with Salomon and Paulina. They had five sons of whom the oldest was Nathan (1779–1817), mentioned in the 1799 register and presumably named for Samuel's father, followed by Aron (1782/3–1849), Abraham (b. 1789), Moses (1793–1851), and Jakob (1795–1864). If there were daughters, I have not seen mention of them. Salomon is listed in the land register as owning the house at what is now Plačkova 10 in the ghetto.[51]

Salomon was active in the Boskovice Jewish community. In 1810 he served as *Judenrichter*, the annually elected head of the board of elders. Salomon's second son, Aron, and Aron's son, another Nathan, were also active. The Brno historians record that in 1849 Aron donated 400 golden coins to found a charitable foundation (*Stiftung*) in his name. Nathan purchased two adjacent houses that he interconnected and in which he placed a prayer room and a classroom. In 1883–84 he established the institution known as "The Orphan and Old-Age Nathan Löw-Beer Foundation," which housed three old men and three orphans under the age of fourteen. Nathan presented this establishment to the community in honour of his parents and built a vaulted room at the back that became

Kinship Diagram 2. Samuel to Elliott (partial)

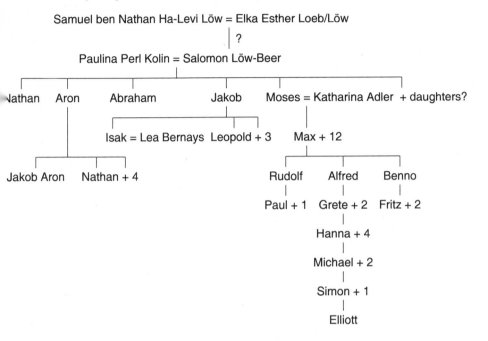

Boskovice's third synagogue. The historians say it was "used even by the orthodox Jews," suggesting that the Löw-Beers were not orthodox.

In 1855–56 the community founded a children's school and an industrial school for low-income families. In 1857 these institutions included 128 girls. Women from richer families worked as teachers; here, otherwise missing sisters, wives, and daughters make their appearance, including Hani, Pepi, and Antonie Löw-Beer. Antonie, Nathan's wife, was also a donor to the school in 1856. In 1859 Nathan also founded a *Spar und Vorschussverein* (savings and loan association) into which some of the wealthier inhabitants of Boskovice deposited money. The association made loans to craftsmen and entrepreneurs, and operated until it was closed by the Nazis in 1939.

Chapter Four

Founding the Firm

With Salomon we shift from origin stories to an actual beginning of the Löw-Beer line and family firms. This shift also marks a break from the long religious tradition, a transition from the pre-modern to the modern.

Salomon was a wool merchant like his mother, and he also traded in leather and owned a distillery. According to Hans Löw-Beer, a great-grandson of Salomon's son Moses, the family started as rag collectors. As he explained to me in 1987, you make woollens from rags by tearing them apart and reconstructing threads; in other words, a form of recycling. Hans's cousin Paul Löw-Beer suggested that many of the rags were old uniforms collected from the Napoleonic and subsequent armies. This story seems more likely than the converse suggestion that the family supplied the armies with clothing. In an interview in 1988 Paul said that the Brno method of textile production using rags had been developed in Yorkshire and was also found near Florence. It required a good deal of ingenuity. When the rags are broken down you get short threads. For spinning, some longer threads should be added. They used cotton or artificial silk, buying up waste material from the artificial silk industry. The skill, Paul explained, lay in knowing what waste material you could purchase and adjusting production accordingly.

Three of Salomon's five sons began to industrialize wool production. They created two distinct firms and therefore two branches of the family. Aron and Jakob jointly founded the *Aron und Jakob*

Löw-Beer, Wollhandel und Wollgespinsterzeugung in Boskovice around 1820, producing and selling woollen thread. On Aron's death in 1849, his widow, Rebekka, applied for and received a concession to trade wool in Brno. On the basis of a legal agreement that came into effect 1 May 1853, her sons Jakob Aron and Nathan (the philanthropist noted in the previous chapter) as well Aron's brother Jakob and Jakob's sons Isak and Leopold were listed as partners.[1] They built a spinning factory and textile business in Brněnec (Brünnlitz) and also purchased a woollen yarn manufacture on Václavská Street in Brno, later extending the business with a weaving and finishing mill. By the 1880s the company employed some 1,200 people and introduced health and pension insurance.

Salomon's youngest son, Moses (Mois, 1793–1851), is the ancestor of my branch, the grandfather of my great-grandfather. For reasons I do not know, he created his own firm apart from his older brothers.[2] Moses began collecting rags (often discarded military uniforms) and leasing the schnapps distillery in Boskovice from 1814. As he prospered, he began to invest his earnings by starting a woollen mill in the village of Svitávka. Here, he had access to waterpower and a water turbine, and was closer to markets. Svitávka is only 5.5 kilometres from Boskovice and 39 kilometres from Brno. Moses's older brothers sold some of the wool and linen yarns he produced in their shop in Boskowitz.

In a long letter dated 1971, Fritz Löw-Beer, another great-grandson of Moses, wrote: "Moses left the ghetto in Boskovice, probably around 1825, and started a wool washing business in what used to be a mill (*Mühle*) in Svitávka." After some years he began to manufacture cloth woven on handlooms and founded the firm of Mos. L.-B. He purchased work woven to his specifications by piece workers who owned their own looms and processed them into fabrics he could sell at a profit. He then decided to control each step of the production – spinning, weaving, dyeing, and finishing – and built a factory that drew on hydropower to do so. Fritz wrote: "We think that this happened in 1839 but [the] factory people celebrated the 130 years' jubilee only some weeks ago [basing] this on some documents they found." This statement would place the founding of the cloth manufacture in 1841, the same date at which Paul places Moses's authorization to operate the wool weaving business.[3] According to Paul, by 1847, 130 workers sat at seventy mechanical looms in a two-story factory. Vladimír Velešik offers a substantial history of the enterprise, noting the complex demand for permits, conflicts over water rights, and pollution of the river. Things stabilized only in 1850, when Moses moved his family from Boskovice to Svitávka. Moses died the following year.[4]

In a letter to Joan Inoue dated 21 July 1974, Fritz adds that he learned more in 1937 or 1938 when lightning hit the "old factory" (already replaced with newer buildings) and "the firemen threw a lot of old books, etc. out of the attic. Among them were dozens of little *Notizbucheln* (notebooks), many of them filled with notes in Hebrew letters (Yiddish, I suppose) which I could not read. In one of them I found the date 1829." In Fritz's lifetime "the old factory consisted mainly of a two-storied building in front with a low wing along the '*Mühlgraben*' (millrace) extending to the rear, a courtyard and some lower buildings, containing stables, harness rooms and '*Wagenremisen*' (coach houses) in the back ... Grandmother Pauline lived in part of the main building in the summer. The other parts were inhabited by a janitor, by Blažek, my father's chauffeur (both on the ground floor), and by the gardener, and one factory employee on the second floor. Until 1902 grandmother's apartment provided the only living quarters for the whole family in Svitávka."

Fritz writes Joan that he regrets he knows nothing about "great-grandfather Moses and his emergence from the Boskowice ghetto. He must have been very much 'a Jew' and might, perhaps, have felt somewhat uneasy at first living among 'goyim.' Some seventy years later the Low-Beers had become almost feudal patrons of Svitávka, and I wish I knew something about the course of this development. I have heard that grandfather Moses was very 'anti-religious' and this might have contributed to a change in 'status.' But, of course, by the end of the 19th century, 'we' had become the biggest employer of labour within a radius of 10 km, and there was no real feudal patron, i.e., no old aristocratic family, in Svitávka itself as there were in several of the surrounding towns and villages."

Moses lived only until 1851. By the time Rebekka was consolidating her firm, "ours" was in the hands of Moses's son Maximilian,

Figure 3. The factory in Svitávka, date unknown. Image from Villa Tugendhat, https://www.tugendhat.eu/en/svitavka.html

known as Max (1829–87). Like his cousin Leopold, he was given a German rather than a Hebrew name, although a second name, Marcus, was appended to the Max. The Löw-Beers were not always very original in their names; there is another Max (1838–99), a son of Jakob Aron. Each Max married a woman named Pauline, and each couple had a son named Alfred.

The Aron-Jakob family firm consolidated through marriages between first cousins over two generations. Leadership passed from Isak and Leopold to Jonas, a son of Jakob Aron, and Arnold, a son of Leopold. As neither Isak nor Jonas had live offspring, ownership and management then passed to Arnold's three sons, Felix, August, and Walter (no more biblical names!).[5] In the decades before the Second World War, they lived in Brno and had cordial relations with members of my branch. Hans said there was no strenuous competition between the firms, but they were completely distinct. The brothers, together with their wives and children, successfully relocated to Britain and Brazil, where they prospered. They will appear from time to time in the narrative, their descendants turning up at the family reunion. A sister, Mitzi, and her son did not escape. During the war, the Brněnec factory was appropriated by Oskar Schindler, a Catholic and ethnic German from nearby Svitavy. · Schindler used captured Jewish workers to make arms, possibly intending to protect them from the gas chambers. Daniel Low Beer, a great-grandson of Arnold, has made the connection between the abandoned factory and the story and film of Schindler's supposed heroism central to his portrait of the family.[6]

Max joined his father's company at fourteen and took over the firm after Moses's death in 1851 at the young age of twenty-two. The story I heard was simply that Max inherited from his father and subsequently passed the firm on to his three sons. But what about Max's siblings? Fritz writes that "Max's brothers were in the firm originally, and I do not know why and how they left." Hans mentioned that Max had sisters but said he had not heard of any brothers. In fact, three brothers, Max, Josef, and Šalamoun (Salomon), along with their mother Katharina, became the partners on Moses's death. In both 1853 and 1854 their requests for a provincial licence to produce woollen goods were rejected on the grounds that they had insufficient machinery, only a dozen looms. Authorization came in 1858 and, in addition to weaving, they introduced machines with copper cylinder blocks for colour printing on the fabric.[7] The firm grew very prosperous. Katharina stepped out of the company in 1860, and, for reasons that are unclear, so did Josef in 1867 and Salomon in 1879, leaving Max the sole proprietor of the Moses Löw-Beer company. Presumably he bought out his brothers.[8]

A little more digging brings out the remarkable fact that within a twenty-year period, between 1820 and 1841, Moses and his wife Gittel Güttl, in German, Katharina Adler (1801–83), about whose background I know nothing, produced thirteen children. They were, in order of birth, Charlotte, Josephine, Joseph, Krösl, Sara, Max, Anna, Salomon, Leopold, Therese, Zipperl, Blümele, and

Kinship Diagram 3. Aron-Jacob Line (partial)

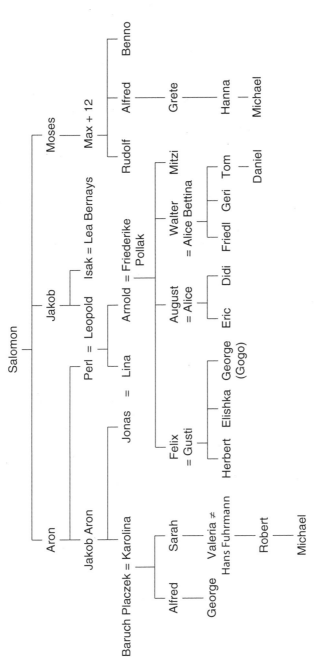

Figure 4. Graves of Moses and Katharina, Jewish Cemetery, Boskovice, 2017. Photo courtesy of Jacqueline Solway

Nathan.[9] It is worth pausing a moment to think about these siblings. Of Krösl, Sara, Anna, and Blümele, I know nothing; perhaps they died young, as suggested by the diminutive Yiddish names. Of Charlotte, Josephine, and Zipperl, I know only the names of their spouses. Joseph had five daughters and no sons. Several of his descendants were murdered.

About the other siblings I risk cluttering the manuscript with more names in order to illustrate social mobility and to honour the disappeared. Salomon, born c. 1833 and named for his recently deceased grandfather, was twice married, having two daughters and a son with his first wife and a daughter with his second. The son, Viktor, died in 1916. Salomon's eldest daughter, Helene, married Karl Popper, a lawyer in Brno and the consul of Mexico. His second daughter, Emma Mandler, was murdered 21 September 1942 in Treblinka. Emma's eldest daughter, Auguste, born in

Figure 5. Death notice for Leopold Löw Beer, Max's brother. Image copied from Geni

Vienna in 1897, together with her husband Otto, committed suicide in Prague in January 1942 to avoid deportation. Emma's son Karl, born in 1901, escaped. Salomon's last daughter, Marie Kuffler, died in 1938 in Vienna. Her son John, described on Geni as a merchant of wholesale textiles, died in New York in 1965. His younger brother Robert, born in 1902, was shot by the SS on 20 April 1945.

After Salomon came Leopold (1834–1906), who married Bertha Löw from Zlinsky. Bertha was the sister of Max's wife Pauline. Thus, two brothers married two sisters, a pattern that was to be repeated. Leopold and Bertha had two daughters. What happened to them after marriage or whether Leopold participated in the firm, I don't know. Leopold is listed on his death announcement (Figure 5) as president of the Moravian-Jewish Orphans Auxiliary Association. The only surviving siblings listed were Therese and Nathan, as well as the widows of Max, Joseph, and Salomon, and the widower of the eldest sister.

Therese, born in 1836 in Boskovice like her siblings, is linked to the business. She married Heinrich Feldhändler from Brno; the two children of their son Sigmund (b. 1866) were born in Svitávka, suggesting that Sigmund worked in the Löw-Beer factories. Sigmund was also a partner with Benno Tugendhat in the Feldhendler textile company, later run by Fritz Tugendhat. The company was confiscated in 1945. Sigmund's son Heinrich became a bank clerk in Brno and died 12 June 1942, murdered near Lublin. Nathan had a son and three daughters. Some of his descendants were murdered, and some survived.

One thing evident in this account of Gittel's descendants is a demographic transition. None of her children had as many children as she did, nor in as quick succession. We can also see the disappearance of Yiddish or Hebrew names in favour of German ones. The siblings and their descendants move out from Boskovice to Brno and Vienna, and tend to marry people from those places. Several of their children are murdered by the Nazis. Critical to the picture is that none of Max's brothers left any recorded descendants through men. Whatever legacies were left his other children, Moses's firm appears to have passed entirely to Max's offspring. Remarkably, none of the descendants of Max's siblings have been remembered by our line. I have never heard mention of a single one. The priority of firm over family and the salience of descent through men are evident in that the family does include male descendants of Moses's brothers, from a generation earlier.

⚜

Max was born 17 September 1829. Fritz Löw-Beer, who never saw his grandfather in the flesh, writes that "Max was short, fat, bald and bearded." I expect Fritz drew his description from a photo, as far as I know undated but, surprisingly, apparently taken in Berlin (Figure 6). But Max also looks forceful, self-satisfied, almost belligerent – the picture of a successful entrepreneur. Indeed, Paul describes him as "full of the spirit of the industrial world revolution, which developed in Austria-Hungary later than in England or Germany. He was a gifted financier and speculator with carefree optimism. He took out bank loans, with which he erected multi-storey factory buildings, very firmly built to support heavy machinery."

The beautiful woman encumbered by the heavy dress is his wife, Pauline. Born in 1838, Pauline was some nine years younger than Max and lived much longer. Pauline's father was Samuel Löw (1810–91) and her mother Fränziska Fanny Kohn (1813–92). According to Fritz, Samuel was a wool merchant from Olomouc, another town in Moravia. However, Samuel's brother Benjamin

Figure 6. Max and Pauline. Photo
courtesy of Roger Pollak

was born in Boskovice. Tracing Benjamin and his second wife Betty
Spitzer's descendants provided two surprises. One of their daughters, Marie (1843–1912), became the grandmother of Grete's husband Fritz Tugendhat. Thus, although I never heard it mentioned
in the family, Grete and Fritz were kin, the great-grandchildren of
siblings; put another way, their grandmothers were first cousins.

The second surprise came via Benjamin's granddaughter Ida
who, with her shoe merchant husband Friedrich Kohn, emigrated
to the United States before 1901. One of Ida's grandchildren is John
Kerry, former secretary of state and US presidential candidate.
Kerry's appearance in the narrative illustrates what happens when
one traces up to multiple ancestors and then looks for each of their
descendants. My mother and John Kerry are fourth cousins, but
they surely did not know this, and Kerry is mentioned here only
because he is famous; I have ignored all the other people in his line.[10]

Kinship Diagram 4. Grete, Fritz, and John Kerry (partial)

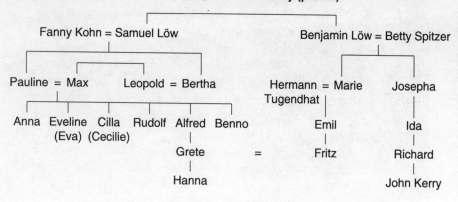

Returning to closer family, Fritz Löw-Beer remembered Max's wife "'Grossmama Pauline' [as] a very kind, dignified old lady with beautiful silvery hair," an image borne out in another photograph (Figure 7). Fritz's cousin Hans said she was the daughter of a rabbi and that she was very religious and maintained a small synagogue in Svitávka. He added that she had a strong personality, reminiscent of that of his own sister, Grete (Pauline's granddaughter), whom everyone admired. On another occasion he told me she was very beautiful. When he knew her, she lived in Brno, opposite the theatre, but returned to her apartment in Svitávka in the summers. A third grandson, Paul, described Pauline as a very educated woman and the only intellectual on his paternal side, the rest being "robust businesspeople." During the summer they visited her once a week. The visits were quite formal, and Paul felt he had no adult contact with her.

Unlike many wealthy families, the Löw-Beers did not convert. Yet Pauline, who died in 1919 at the age of 81 or 82, appears to have been the last observant Jew. Religious practice had precipitously declined; hence Hans's recollection of Pauline as "very" religious must be taken as relative to other members of the family.

Figure 7. Pauline Löw-Beer. Photo
courtesy of Roger Pollak

By 1876 the Löw-Beer textile firms were well established. A manual entitled *Handbook of European Commerce: What to Buy and Where to Buy It* says of Brünn: "Population 55,000 … The number and extent of its woollen, silk, and cotton manufacturies have obtained for it the name of 'a second Bradford.' Its woollens are particularly prized." Among the "most prominent manufacturing firms" are listed Max Löw Beer, A. & J. Löw Beer Söhne, and Max Kohn. "The commercial intercourse between Brünn and the United States has been important, the declared values of exports to the United States having reached nearly half-a-million florins."[11]

Max considerably expanded the firm. He enlarged and modernized the factory in Svitávka. In 1862 he added a textile factory in Brno itself, on Čechyňská Street, connected to a freight train track by 1890. In 1870 he founded a beet distillery in Záhorská Ves, on the riverine plain at the Slovakian/Austrian frontier at Angern, which became the largest producer of sugar in central Europe. He cleverly built near a rail line and connected the factory to it in 1892. In 1912 the factory also began producing alcohol as an additive

Figure 8. Maximilian (Max) Markus
Löw-Beer. Photo courtesy of Roger
Pollak

to automotive gasoline.[12] Max expanded into Austria with the purchase of a textile factory in Fischamend near Vienna from the English Jupp brothers. He established a branch of the Moses Löw-Beer firm in Sagan in what was then Prussian Silesia (now Zagan, Poland) in 1876. The Sagan textile factory is one about which I will have more to say in the following chapters because its subsequent co-owner and manager, Hans Weiss, became my grandfather. In 1882 Max began major expansion of the factory buildings in Svitávka. Max was a member of the chamber of commerce and a "censor" of the Moravská eskontní banka in Brno, as well as a member of the board of directors of the Jewish religious community. He died 31 May 1887 of a stroke in the spa town of Mariánské Lázně, and is buried in what is apparently the largest tomb in the Jewish cemetery in Brno.

Fritz suggests that Max overextended, as "the firm's finances were quite shaky in his time." Hans said explicitly that he went into debt. This trouble will be the starting point, another sort of "founding myth," for the next phase of the family's story under the leadership of Max's son Rudolf.

Chapter Five

The Patriarch and His Siblings

Once upon a time there were three brothers who married three sisters. The brothers were rich and the sisters were cultured and beautiful, themselves well-off cousins to one of the wealthiest families in the empire. The brothers were young when their father died, and they found the business they inherited at risk. Under the brilliant management of the eldest brother and the devoted attention of the younger two, the business rebounded and the family grew very wealthy. Even the workers received some benefit. The three sets of paired brothers and sisters had among them eight children, who played together in a beautiful estate and grew up to be talented, complicated people. The family successfully survived the First World War and the dissolution of the empire in which they had grown up, and they carried on brilliantly until, very suddenly, as it seemed, and at the last minute, they fled for their lives.

Such is the gist of the tale I tell over the next few chapters. This chapter and the next focus on the generation of my great-grandparents, through the First World War and up to the Second. The story of their children – the generation of my grandparents – comes later. My method here is to follow generational cohorts as they move across time, like overlapping waves.[1]

Moses founded the factory; his son Max expanded the business; and then Max's son Rudolf took over and made the family very rich. Rudolf's generation came of age after the emancipation of the Jews in central Europe and before the collapse of the Austro-Hungarian Empire. A cohort of wealthy bourgeois, they were more or less Viennese in culture and taste, comportment and prejudices. My great-grandmother, Marianne, remembered dancing at the emperor's ball.

My great-grandfather, Alfred Löw-Beer, was one of six siblings, and my great-grandmother, Marianne Wiedmann, was one of five siblings, all sisters, who lived to adulthood. It happened that after Alfred and Marianne's wedding, Alfred's two brothers married two of Marianne's sisters, creating a dense node of kin. Somewhat to one side were what anthropologists call collateral kin: Alfred's three sisters and their husbands, and Marianne's additional two sisters and theirs. One effect of marrying women who were sisters was that the wives were more fully incorporated into "the family" – and family took on, for this and the following generation, more of a bilateral than a distinctively patrilineal look. Conversely, however, the Löw-Beer sisters were somewhat marginalized.

This chapter is about the Löw-Beer siblings and the ways in which they composed both a family and a firm. It is also a story of patriarchy. Rudolf, the eldest of the brothers (but younger than his three sisters), was the unquestioned head of the family from his father's death in 1887 to his own death in 1953, thus for sixty-six years: admired, respected, feared, and obeyed by everyone. Marianne (his brother's wife and equally his wife's sister) played a strong role as well; after Rudolf's death she became the node and informal leader of the Löw-Beer family, until her own death at the age of ninety-three in 1975. Rudolf had the advantages of birth order, gender, and personality and was an extremely shrewd and successful businessman; Marianne's character and longevity granted her much respect as well. After her death, the family had no apical figure.

I begin with the three Löw-Beer brothers and then move to their sisters. In the following chapter I discuss the Wiedmann sisters, three of whom were Löw-Beer wives. The broad aim is to understand the life of this wealthy bourgeois family and the generation composed of people who experienced as adults the transition from empire to nation-states. Only one fought (briefly) in the First World War – on the side of their homeland, Austria-Hungary. The great catastrophe for them was not the First World War but the Second.

Kinship Diagram 5. Löw-Beer and Wiedmann Siblings

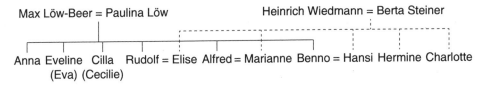

Max Löw-Beer = Paulina Löw   Heinrich Wiedmann = Berta Steiner

Anna Eveline Cilla   Rudolf = Elise Alfred = Marianne Benno = Hansi Hermine Charlotte
      (Eva)   (Cecilie)

Of the original eleven members of the two sibling sets, one died in a concentration camp, one committed suicide in exile, and my great-grandfather, Alfred, was killed at the Czech border in 1939. Rudolf and Marianne, and her sisters Charlotte and Elise, survived the war.

I draw on various sources, including lengthy conversations with Marianne's son Hans and Rudolf's son Paul in the late 1980s, as well as the master's thesis written about Paul's life.[2] I also spoke in 2018 to several grandchildren of the siblings. Eva was especially helpful because she had asked many of the same questions of Paul when he was alive as I was asking now. Another source is the long letter about the family, already cited, written in New York by a son of Alfred's younger brother Benno. Fritz Löw-Beer began the letter on 19 December 1971, when he was sixty-five. By the time he finished, on 23 December, it had grown to some 5,000 words. Fritz's son John circulated the letter to family members on 15 May 2016, explaining that the original addressee, a daughter of Fritz's Czech friend Ferenc, gave it to John when they met in Boskovice in 2014. Fritz provides additional observations in a letter to his cousin Helene's daughter Joan, dated 21 July 1974. Fritz himself lived from 1906 to 1976. He, Hans, and Paul were contemporaries and double first cousins, each the son of one of the three pairs of wedded siblings.

The letters are candid and full of information, some of which I had known but much of which was new to me. The writer is very insightful, but also quite opinionated. I draw extensively on the letters but do not repeat all his remarks. I was surprised that Fritz said little about his wife and children or his siblings, or even his own adult life, until I realized I was doing exactly the same.

Members of the diaspora turn towards the past. But each generation sees the past differently. Fritz remembers a time that ends with his coming of age, but also his exile. I only *imagine* a past, one that in its historical and generational distance carries a kind of grandeur.

※

One of Herman Freudenberger's conclusions in his book on the Moravian textile industry is that "success seems to have been determined by the direct interest of forceful personalities."[3] This finding was certainly true of the Löw-Beer firm, both as an objective fact and in the stories the Löw-Beers tell.

The forceful personality is Rudolf, born 5 October 1865 in Brno, the fourth child and first son of Max and Pauline. His granddaughter Eva thinks he was raised in Svitávka, where his parents lived in the *Alte Fabrik*, the old factory. Rudolf was an unruly child with too much energy. Around the age of twelve, he was sent to a Prussian school in Silesia, where he lived in the home of a rabbi. Eva thinks this decision was less for bar mitzvah preparation, though he had that, than because his parents didn't know what to do with him. Rudolf thrived on the discipline, rose to the top of the class, and played chess with the rabbi. He also developed into an authoritarian personality.

When Max died young, in 1887, power of attorney and management of the firm passed to Rudolf, who was no more than twenty-two, the same age Max had been when he succeeded Moses. Rudolf's son Paul thought that Rudolf had not even graduated Gymnasium. "Barely an adult, he had to take over the company and the factory." Rudolf rose to the challenge. His mother Paulina relinquished her position as public shareholder in 1896 and was replaced by her other two sons.[4]

The firm was in a precarious position, and Rudolf had to make some quick decisions. Max "must have been quite enterprising," Fritz wrote. "However, he may not have been such a good businessman as the firm's finances were quite shaky in his time." Max had overextended with the purchases described in the previous chapter, and there were massive bank loans, which Rudolf repaid within ten years. The sugar factory was losing money. Rudolph concluded that the problem lay with the large estate, presumably on which the beets were grown, and so he sold the land. Rudolf soon had the textile factories working profitably again. His philosophy, as Paul explained, was to buy raw materials cheaply and keep production costs down: the Löw-Beers produced cheap material. They imported wool in bulk from England and Australia. The two key resources in addition to wool were waterpower and labour power. The manpower at the beginning was virtually entirely German-speaking, and the firm was run in German, even though Svitávka was a Czech-speaking village. However, Czech farmers were glad for factory work in order to avoid having to split their land into too small parcels, and they soon became the main work force.

Paul explained the production strategy as follows. The basic idea was to attend to coming fashions and buy raw materials accordingly. Fabrics were produced from a mix of waste wool, purchased mainly from Yorkshire, plus a combination of torn rags and some good wool. This material was carefully sorted by colour and content, whether wool, cotton, or artificial silk. The latter was a nuisance because it was not dyeable in the same way as wool or cotton. Every stage of production was carefully planned and skillfully enacted. "You had to know the entire production process, the selection of the respective waste materials for the corresponding fashion, sorting, mixing of fibres, spinning, weaving, and then finishing. You had to master everything, so that something sound came out, something very nice and very soft." This form of production was unique to Brno with the exception of Prato in Italy. Paul said: "The whole thing was an artistic synthesis and at the same time a mass production. The result was unbeatable: low production costs and correspondingly low selling prices. 'The goods have to sell themselves,' he [Rudolf] said – and they did, throughout the whole monarchy."[5]

Rudolf used the considerable profits to found new factories, while remaining, as Paul put it, "the full-time conductor of the increasingly complex orchestra." There were four textile factories in addition to Svitávka. Svitávka itself was expanded to include two large five-storey factory buildings by 1905 and a housing estate for workers by 1910. Rudolf was a creative technician, said Paul. "The sugar factory was terribly old-fashioned and ugly, because he put no value on exteriors, but thermally it was the best factory in the world," with the lowest consumption of coal per kilo of sugar of any in the industry. Rudolf insisted on diversification. He invested in a screw factory in Bielitz, run by his sister Eveline's husband. He founded a wood pulp (cellulose) factory in Austria, outside Leoben. Production continued through the Second World War, managed during that time by Swiss partners who returned it to the family afterwards. Rudolf also gradually acquired the majority share of a cement factory in Maloměřice, on the outskirts of Brno. "The cement factory ... got along without any external power, as it drew on steam produced by the cement kilns." Fritz writes that the cement business, known as "Leo Czech & Co.[,] was a *Kommanditgesellschaft* [limited partnership][6] shared between Ing. Max Kohn, Dr. Cornel Hože and Mos. L.-B." By Mos. L.-B. he refers to the family business run by Rudolf and his brothers. Cornel Hože, a doctor of law, was the husband of their sister Cilla. Fritz writes that "Onkel Cornel had been taken in as the partner in charges of sales." It is unclear whether the partnership was Cilla's dowry or whether Hože had his own money. As Eva put it, "the ownership of Maloměřice was one-third Löw-Beer and one-third Hože – and that meant two-thirds Löw-Beer!"[7]

The third partner, Max Kohn, refers to another company, comprising a textile factory owned by Fritz Tugendhat's father and uncles. In other words, the cement factory was an enterprise that incorporated additional kin and one that drew on and perhaps anticipated marriages between members of the partner families. The Tugendhat textile factory was unusual for Brno in that it produced luxury fabrics.

Fritz Löw-Beer wrote that the cement factory was the only Löw-Beer industry to be greatly expanded during the interwar period. Hans described it as the largest Portland cement factory in interwar Czechoslovakia. Cornel and Cilla's son Max Hože appears to have eventually managed the factory.

Business prospered under Rudolf's management. Of the many textile factories that sprang up in Brno, the Löw-Beers likely had the largest. Expansion slowed after the First World War, but the Villa Tugendhat website affirms that the Löw-Beers "contributed significantly to the industrialization of Czechoslovakia during the between-the-wars period. They owned and operated a range of textile factories, sugar refineries [*sic*] and cement works within the territory of the former Austria-Hungary Monarchy."[8] However, as Jews, they had no political influence.

During the First World War, Rudolf oversaw the rags used in textile production across Germany and Austria-Hungary, fixing production costs and setting margins. He made many people angry because he set prices very low. This "self-administration of industry," said Paul, impressed Lenin and served in his model of a planned economy. Rudolf's activity enabled him to avoid active duty. Alfred enlisted but served only a short time as he was deemed indispensable for the factories. The company was also able to supply the army. After the war, the imposition of customs duties between the new states forced many factories to close, but the diversification among the Löw-Beer enterprises enabled them to survive.

Fritz writes of this period: "The war, my father's death [of pernicious anemia in 1916] and the collapse of the Habsburg Empire had a considerable influence on the family. Rudolf had to take over father's work, and he resented the new Czechoslovakia which expropriated the big landowners, conducted a predominantly agrarian policy which harmed industrial interests and whose government officials were frequently corrupt. I think that he had lost interest in any further expansion and that running especially the woolen plants on which he spent most of his time became merely a kind of 'sport' for him." The next day he added to the letter: "The Russian revolution probably influenced him as well."

Fritz appears to share the view he attributes to Rudolf. He continues: "The various nations which had constituted the Habsburg Empire were unfortunately too chauvinistic and their leaders were too ignorant about economics to realize the unwisdom of splitting a relatively large economic area into several small units.

Comparatively small Czechoslovakia was left with the major part of Austria-Hungary's industry, but ... it conducted an agrarian policy because the Agrarians dominated parliament. This policy meant reducing agrarian imports to a minimum with the result that the other successor states put up customs barriers against Czechoslovak industrial products and made an effort to build industries themselves. They also found that Germany was ready to buy their agricultural surpluses in exchange for machinery, and since the Germans were not at all anxious to deliver on schedule, these small eastern countries were piling up credit balances in Berlin and thus became dependent on it politically as well as economically. Masaryk had been a well-meaning idealistic intellectual and a fool as far as his politics were concerned because it just was not realistic to believe that half a dozen little states would be able to maintain their independence for long."

Despite these difficulties, the firm flourished and was exporting goods throughout Europe as well as to Palestine, Syria, South Africa, and South America. After Benno's death, his underage sons joined the company in 1919, and Max, Hans, and Paul joined in 1922.[9]

Here is how Hans described his uncle's style of work. Rudolf focused on both the financial and technical affairs. He requested regular reports from each factory representative and frequently inspected the factories in person. On one occasion he asked Hans for a report on the lubrication of the machines in a factory. When Hans submitted the report, Rudolf knew the contents already, and Hans realized that Rudolf had been testing him. "He always had an immediate solution to any problem," continued Hans. Rudolf was active in both the sugar and the pulp factories. He put Hans in charge of the former towards the end. Hans recalled it was very old-fashioned, with oxen transporting the coal to run it.

Rudolf worked extremely hard and didn't make much personal use of his wealth. He appears to have had the ascetic disposition that Max Weber famously attributed to early capitalists, albeit in Rudolf's case without thoughts of a gracious god. Rudolf's passion lay in efficient and innovative production, of which financial success was a by-product. Paul remembers his father travelling continually. He spent the week managing Svitávka, going once every month or two to Sagan (in Silesia) and once a week to consult with Alfred in Brno.[10] Rudolf was able to sleep on the train and to wake up exactly when he reached his stop. He arrived in Vienna Friday evenings and spent Saturday inspecting the Austrian factory.[11] On Sunday morning he would see buyers in the flat, and "Sunday afternoon we all went for a walk in the Vienna woods, which we hated." Rudolf took two two-week holidays a year.

Hans said that Rudolf's staff were afraid of him. He was fantastically organized and had an incredible knowledge and memory: he could ask to see letters that had been written twenty years earlier. He had a reputation in the industry as a genius.

Hans remembered a man named Leopold Weiss (not Jewish and no relation to Hans Weiss) who was a trusted financial assistant and special sidekick of Rudolf's, as Leopold's father had been of Max. Leopold was a short man with a beard and was invited along to family events. His son Otto gambled, and Leopold stole to pay off the debts. Rudolf discovered this theft in 1921 and fired him but decided not to prosecute in order to avoid a scandal in the newspapers that could have hurt the firm's reputation.

What can I say about the lives of the workers? Family recollections are somewhat self-congratulatory. Fritz wrote: "The 3 L.-B. brothers were hard-working men, and they also were fairly progressive socially. Thus the firm provided its own *Krankenkasse* (medical insurance) for its workers and employed a doctor for it. This was however given up after 1918 when the government *Krankenkassen* were established. I do not think that this change was for the better in this particular case." The firm also provided a canteen and social rooms for workers, support for widows and orphans from 1906, a free daycare and kindergarten with food, staffed by German nuns, which covered working hours that lasted from 7:00 am to 5:00 pm.[12] There was a small school, taught in German, which angered the Czech ethnonationalists.

Figure 9. Rudolf Löw-Beer, taken by
Edith Tudor-Hart in England, 1940s.
Photo courtesy of Roger Pollak

In his late life recollections to Traudl Schmidt, Paul said: "I do not think my father exploited his workers. To give him justice, at least he was a strict and fair boss. The company was successful, and the workers had great security. If you talk to them about Löw-Beers today, they say that was the best time they ever had in their lives. I suppose – after all that has happened in the meantime – that's true too. Much depended on performance, but wages were not bad. There were also houses for the workers, still standing today. The first ones did not have interior bathrooms or lavatories, but these were installed later. There really was good workers' housing in Svitávka and social amenities, such as a kindergarten." The workers called the Löw-Beers, Pan Rudolf, Pan Max, and so forth. Paul pointed out how well received they were on the visit to Svitávka on his ninetieth birthday in July 2000. Rudolf's granddaughter Joan said that Rudolf knew each worker by name; he may have been distant with his daughter, but he was good with the workers.

In 1988 Paul described the textile factory as exemplifying a philosophy of liberalism. But Fritz called Svitávka "feudal." Certainly, it represents a form of what one might call paternalism. Some family members enjoyed the sense of being patrons, while others, like Paul himself, were embarrassed and tried to escape it.

An independent source exposes quite another view, albeit for a period before Paul was born. Traudl Schmidt cites extensively from an article by Karl Kraus in his famous magazine *Die Fackel* (*The Torch*). Kraus writes in May 1899:

> The 12,000 weavers and spinners of Brno have been on strike a full month. Their socialist desires are not for an increase in wages. It is true that the business situation in the textile industry has become strong again, but the workers are not demanding a share in the increased profits of the entrepreneurs. They want to continue to enjoy the 2 to 7 guilders that are paid to them on a weekly basis, and they challenge neither the capitalist order at large, nor the rate of profits of Messers Strakosch, Löw-Beer, and Schoeller. Their fight is solely for the attainment of a ten-hour instead of the existing eleven-hour workday. However, since they are willing to give up the break for breakfast, the entrepreneurs would lose no more than 3¾ hours a week of actual work time. The workers also claim that this shortening of hours would not affect production, that the increased intensity and meticulousness of the work, and the savings on heat and light, would more than make up for it, and that the experiences of the three Brno companies that have already introduced the ten-hour workday confirm this view. On top of this, the workers originally did not even demand the definitive introduction of the ten-hour workday, but only requested it be granted on a trial basis for one year, during which the advantages of the innovation would also become apparent to the entrepreneurs.
>
> ...
>
> In fact, only the special circumstances of the Brno industrial area make understandable the emphasis which the workers put on this demand. Because so far our emaciated industrial slaves are unlike the proud English proletarians who could fight principled struggles to win respect from the entrepreneurs for the claims and rules their unions teach. What is going on in Brünn right now is a naked, desperate struggle for basic human existence ... We learn (from a leaflet of the strikers) that the majority of Brünn workers do not live in the city. They travel daily for six hours to and from villages that are three hours on foot each

way. Six hours of daily march alongside eleven-hour work, that's what the forces of our blossoming industry have brought ... Most of them are women, and many of them only see their children in daylight on Sundays ... Others, who live in more distant places, spend the whole week in Brünn, in dank, dirty quarters. Men, women, and children are mixed together, five to ten people crammed in a room, without exception two in a bed, if not lying on a pallet of straw on the ground, and sometimes with a strange adaptation to the shift system so that in the morning the night worker gets into the still warm bed which the day worker has just left. The health statistics with their awful numbers, the appalling percentage of deaths from tuberculosis, highlight the state of misery ... The manufacturers call this goal (the ten-hour workday) the "subjugation of entrepreneurship" ... currently an economic impossibility ... and they have opposed it to any sociopolitical progress.[13]

This account of the strike in Svitávka is complemented by Nela Ledvinová, who cites the Chronicle of the Svitávka Township from 1899: "The repeal of the language regulations by which Czech in the Czech lands was equated with German resulted in a major political storm. Hatred turned against the liberal Germans and especially the supporters of unassailable Germanism – the Jews ... At the same time local factory workers contested the owners of the Löw-Beer factory over wages and other social benefits ... This led to a strike that was put down by the police and, unfortunately, not without bloodshed. The workers did make some gains."[14]

To be sure, conditions had improved by the time Fritz and Paul came of age, but these were the conditions (perhaps exaggerated) under which Rudolf presided earlier. The 1899 strike was preceded by one in 1869 and followed in 1905 by labour unrest in the factory in Svitávka when Benno refused to allow the workers time off to join demonstrations for universal suffrage. They attacked the factory buildings and went on to smash windows of the mayor and the doctor, and loot pubs. When the military were called in and a few strikers arrested, the protesters attacked the prison and Jewish shops in Boskovice, ending with a proclamation of martial law.[15]

Despite fears of an "anti-Jewish pogrom," some workers were Jewish as well. In Hans's time Jews worked at all levels of the firm and not just in the management jobs. Hans observed that there were sufficient observant employees to have a minyan at the synagogue in Svitávka, but Jewish workers were not in the majority. The sugar factory in Slovakia also had Jewish employees, especially at the top. There, most of the Jewish employees spoke Hungarian, which was the language of the ruling class. Hans said that not many women worked in textiles; in the sugar industry there were many more.

Rudolf, said his son Paul, was afraid of communism. "The growth of socialist and communist movements and of workers' councils in his factories in the twenties filled my father with great concern." During the 1920s Rudolf continued to invest in rebuilding the factories but by 1932 he was very pessimistic about the future of European industry and no longer put his heart into the firm; instead of further expansion, he began removing capital, sending it to Switzerland before laws constraining foreign exchange came into effect. This money created a material basis for the emigration of the family and what they lived on afterwards.[16] Rudolf did so less out of fear of National Socialism than of communism. Indeed, said Paul, he would have agreed with fascism if it hadn't been anti-semitic!

Paul's wife Ala explained that Rudolf's fear of communism was also the reason he refused to return to Austria after the war; he said he wouldn't set foot in Austria again while one Russian soldier remained there.

Rudolf's first move on succeeding his father, Fritz suggested, was to expand woollens production to incorporate a large factory, located in Sagan, north of Boskovice, in what was then Prussia. This factory has an interesting history, one in which family dynamics played a significant role. Max had originally established a factory there in 1876. By Rudolf's time there was an additional factory, owned by the Weiss brothers. Rudolf formed a partnership with them, creating the largest woollens plant in Germany.

In fact, the Weiss and Löw-Beer families already had a long relationship. The Weiss brothers Hermann (1852–1921) and Ignaz (1860–1922), sons of Simon Weiss, came from Boskovice like the Löw-Beers. Hermann and Ignaz's mother, Therese (1822–1902), daughter of Jakob Hanak, was also born there. Hermann's older sister, Charlotte, married another Jakob Hanak from Boskovice, and their sons ran a "Weiss and Hanak" woollen textile business. I am guessing that Herman and Ignaz were involved. In any case, Hermann and Ignaz seem also to have been hired by Max Löw-Beer to work in Svitávka, and when he expanded, they were deployed as managers of his woollens factory in Sagan.

What happened next is intriguing. When Max's daughter Anna (c. 1856–1939), eldest sister to Rudolf and Alfred, wanted to marry Hermann Weiss, Max forbade it. At this refusal, Hermann and Ignaz left the firm. The Weiss brothers obtained capital in Hamburg and built another factory directly across the Bober River that runs through Sagan, which provided the waterpower for both factories. After Max's death, as Fritz explains in his letter, "Rudolf made up the quarrel with Hermann Weiss, bought out the Hamburg group, and took over the new factory. The brothers Weiss became partners, they received 50% of the profits of Sagan but they owned only about 10% of it."[17] They also ran the expanded factory.

I am guessing that the Hamburg capital came from their new in-laws. Hermann and Ignaz married two sisters from Hamburg, respectively, Babette, called Mumma (1872–1943), and Harriet (1874–1942), daughters of banker Wilhelm Rosenbacher (1838–1915) and Anna Maultner. The pair of brothers and their sister wives set up adjacent houses in Sagan, and the families interacted a good deal. Babette eventually died a refugee in London; Harriet was murdered in Auschwitz.

The Rosenbachers, north German Jews with roots also in Prague, had been assimilated longer than the Löw-Beer or Weiss families and were evidently quite well-to-do.[18] Wilhelm's great-grandfather had been a printer in Salzbach, Bavaria. There is a photograph of Wilhelm on Geni, in which he looks quite distinguished with one of his granddaughters on his lap.

Kinship Diagram 6. Rosenbacher and Weiss Marriages (partial)

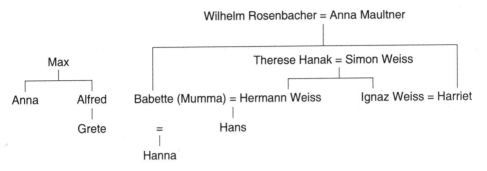

I will have much more to say about the Weiss family because Hermann's eldest son, Hans Weiss, became my grandfather. If Max had forbidden the marriage between Hermann and Anna, by the next generation the parents were glad to see the marriage of Hermann's son Hans to Alfred's daughter (Max's granddaughter, Anna's niece) Grete. But I am getting ahead of the story here.

Family members all attributed the success of the business to Rudolf. As Paul said, "he learned everything from scratch and handled the organization masterfully." But Rudolf not only led the business; as Fritz suggests, he also became the head of the family. The family was constituted around the firm, and the firm was passed on through men. Moreover, although we will meet many strong women, at that time authority within the family was vested in men. And while Rudolf's sisters moved into the spheres of their respective husbands, he seems to have helped two of his brothers-in-law in business.

Rudolf was seven years older than his next brother, Alfred (b. 1872), and nine years older than Benno (b. 1874). It took these men some years to come of age after their father died, and they must have done so under Rudolf's tutelage. Paul described Rudolf as the senior partner and the only one of the brothers who was especially gifted. The brothers seem to have got along well; the younger two were incorporated as partners and eventually given significant responsibilities, but for his lifetime Rudolf remained the unquestioned head of firm and family. Alfred was described as weaker and softer, and Benno died in 1916. Rudolf considerably outlived them both, dying in Lugano on 19 May 1953 at the age of eighty-eight.

As head of the business, Rudolf decided whom to include and in what capacity they would work. He assigned roles to younger men in the family, and told them what to study in order to contribute expertise to the firm. Some resented their assignments, but they all respected him. Rudolf was strict, but as one of his granddaughters said, they put their trust in him. She added that he thought of women as a secondary class. They were consumers, not producers, and he had contempt for consumers. He did not give his daughter Helene the same recognition he gave his son Paul.

In the accounts of various family members Rudolf was "highly esteemed," "a genius at business," and "a financial wizard." Hans told me he wrote poems in Latin and other languages, yet he never went to university and was entirely self-taught. He was described as "impressively clear" and an "enormous presence," in sum, the idealized figure of his generation. Fritz concluded: "Rudolf ... gave most of us an inferiority complex because of his superior intelligence and his extraordinary memory."

Fritz depicted Rudolf as "the genius and in a way also the bane of the family." Fritz writes in his forthright way: "Rudolf was undoubtedly an extraordinarily intelligent man, but I think he remained psychologically immature. He was almost totally egocentric and apparently quite unable to understand that any views or opinions could be right if they differed from his own. He was hard, or at least insensitive to the feelings of other people, although he could be generous and charitable if he felt like it. He dominated the family and most of its members were afraid of him, I certainly was."

"Rudolf," Fritz continued, "was totally devoid of any interest in small children, even his own. In those days children were of course left largely in the care of nurses and governesses, but my father, at any rate, was not as detached as Rudolf."

Paul had a different view of his father. He said once that if Rudolf was conservative politically, in terms of personal relations he was "liberal." He thought Rudolf did have some personal distance from the firm, despite working so hard for it, and could have seen himself doing something else; it wasn't his total identity. He tried to live this other life through his son. Paul was a bit contradictory here, saying Rudolf encouraged him to study and would have accepted whatever profession he chose, but adding that in fact chemistry was chosen for him as his father foresaw a need for it.

Rudolf's reputation continued to the generation of his grandchildren and grand-nieces and grand-nephews. One told me Rudolf had power over the family and made all the decisions, especially about money. Another said Rudolf may have thought himself omnipotent, and a third said Rudolf must have been very impressive but also very nasty. His granddaughter Kitty said: "Rudolf had a way of interacting with people. He was very certain in his thinking and what he said. Wherever he was, he was the boss. He knew exactly what he wanted and what he thought. There were no arguments; he was simply louder in voicing his opinions and you wouldn't contradict him." Another time she remarked: "He was so smart." Unlike Fritz, she felt appreciated by him as a child. She referred several times to what he wrote in her journal: "You are not the centre of the world." Yet somehow that is how he acted or appeared to others.

When Kitty spoke, I was struck with the similarity of how I remembered Grete.

Rudolf figures large for his granddaughter Eva. She attributes to him the securing of the family's fortunes twice over, first when he succeeded his father and second when he had the foresight to move capital before the Second World War. Rudolf, she said, was the only one sufficiently aware of the direction things were heading and willing to risk removing a significant amount of money. Others thought their lifestyle wouldn't be disturbed. Rudolf had a large and difficult family to deal with, and he tried to look after them. It was "a tough job, but he probably loved it. He was made for doing that."

Nevertheless, Eva thought Rudolf did not invest wisely after the war. He believed only in commodities, and he put money into

Cuban sugar. Rudolf disapproved of collecting art, didn't understand it, and found it a waste of money. That was a shame, she concluded: "If there had been art we could have found and claimed it." She reported her mother saying that Rudolf "knew a little about a lot. He read newspapers and kept himself informed about multiple subjects," but he lacked an appreciation of "culture" that the women had.

Here is a final illustration of how people were under Rudolf's spell. Hans's sunny Canadian wife Edith said: "Hans once didn't speak to me for three days because I said his uncle Rudolf was an unpleasant person."

The Patriarch's Brothers

Alfred was more outgoing and well-rounded than his older brother. He was a horseman and liked to hunt. Hans described his father as honourable and honest, not too shrewd, practical, or cunning. Fritz was unflattering: "Alfred ... was probably the least significant of the brothers. He ran the factory in Brno and was in charge of selling; he also was the 'official' representative of the firm and in that capacity vice president of the Chamber of Commerce (the president had to be an ethnic Czech after 1918), president of the *Verein der Wollindustriellen* [association of woollens producers] in Brünn, etc. He was good-natured, egocentric, naïve, always trying to assert himself and actually quite under Rudolf's and to some extent also under his [own] wife's thumb. Unlike Rudolf, who was *Bescheidenheitsprotz* [ostentatiously modest in his tastes and requirements], Alfred enjoyed some luxury but without being generous. He was not well organized at work and shouted at people often without justification. If one shouted back he would shut up right away and become quite meek and reasonable. Rudolf shouted rarely, and it was frightening when he did."

Alfred was the public face of the firm in Brno; indeed, he was the only one of the three brothers to set up house in the city. He served on various boards, as Fritz noted, and he and Marianne actively socialized. They engaged with the German-speaking elite, sat on the board of the German theatre, and Alfred was a member of the riders club, together with non-Jewish industrialists.[19] The city belatedly recognized Alfred in 2016, placing his name on one of the large new city buses bestowed with the names of prominent citizens.[20]

In a conversation in Montreal in 1987, Alfred's son Hans suggested that relations between the two brothers were very good. Rudolf was the unquestioned leader of the family. He ran the firm, and everyone knew it. He dealt with the financial and technological sides, while Alfred was "minister of foreign affairs" and also worked on the finishing end of the textile production. Alfred made sales and production decisions, but all financial decisions were made by Rudolf. The complementarity of talents and absence of competition between the brothers was something that Eva noted as well. As she put it, Alfred was the social one and would spend money.

Fritz was most complimentary of his own father, Benno, who died when Fritz was ten. "The picture I have of my father is of course largely based on what I was told about him by all kinds of people. He seems to have been the most human as well as the most humane of the brothers." He once threw his nephew Paul up in the air, and Paul regretted no one ever did that again. Rudolf and his wife Elise appear to have shown little physical affection to their children. Benno spent a year as a volunteer in the imperial army (*Einjahrigfreiwilliger*). While the usual term of service for draftees, Fritz thought, was three years, recruits who were better educated (*Mittelschulmaturanten*) could volunteer for one year's service, which included officer's school, and then leave with the position of lieutenant in the reserve.

Benno became resident manager in Svitávka, and he raised his family there. Fritz continues: "Papa was liked by the workers and employees in Svitávka despite his frequent shouting. They used to say: 'He shouted at you and then he turned around and gave you 5 crowns.'" Benno "loved horses and he knew a great deal about them. Since my mother disliked horseback riding, father had given it up too and confined himself to driving a pair of sometimes too spirited American trotters." There is even a photo of Benno driving a carriage with his wife at his side and the coachman sitting in back. In Fritz's youth, the family maintained "five or six carriages and ... a sleigh. The coachman wore dark blue livery, the buttons of which, as well as the horses' harness, bore father's monogram in relief." Fritz could recall the names of his father's coachman, Franz Růžička, and that of "Grandmother Pauline," Karl Blanar.

Fritz grants Benno Rudolf's approval. "He seems to have been close to Rudolf as the only sign of emotion, apart from anger, I ever saw in Rudolf's face was during father's funeral when he almost cried. Papa was apparently generous, and he was the only one who spent money relatively freely."

In his letter to Joan, Fritz says, with underlining in the original: "The egocentricity of most Löw-Beers was and is most remarkable. (I know that this is true of myself.) Neither Rudolf nor Alfred had even a slight trace of self-criticism, and neither even conceived that any but their own views on life in general or on any specific matter could be 'right.' This meant, of course, that they were quite intolerant. They could maintain such an attitude because they had no contacts with the 'outside' world, i.e., with people who were not in business or connected with it."

The Löw-Beer Sisters

Growing up, I knew of the three brothers marrying three sisters but little of relatives beyond them. The fact that Rudolf, Alfred, and Benno themselves had three sisters was not mentioned. Indeed, many of the Löw-Beers appear to have forgotten about them. My mother remembered some older female relatives being very strict. One of them always checked her hands for cleanliness. But they were not described as individuals, and we never spoke about their descendants. I knew vaguely that there were relatives named Pollak in New York, but not how they were connected to the family.

I learned about the sisters only in 2016 when I and a large number of other relatives received an email from an Israeli lawyer, Erez Bernstein. Bernstein appeared to make his living in the somewhat unsavoury business of digging around for unclaimed assets left by victims of the Holocaust and then digging further to discover the nearest kin to whom he offered his services at accessing the money. Bernstein had discovered the estate of a certain Max Hože who, along with his mother and wife, was murdered by the Nazis. He found papers concerning the estate drawn up in 1939 and a statement from the *Reichsprotektor* from 21 April 1943. Bernstein proposed requesting the money on behalf of the rightful heirs, but to do that he needed to track down each and every one of us, that is, every descendant of Max Hože's maternal grandfather, Max Löw-Beer.

What most surprised family members was that we had relatives who had been murdered in the death camps. As someone said, "we were always told that everyone in the family got out. No one had ever mentioned them. It was shocking to learn." However, not only did we discover a sister of Rudolf and Alfred's whose family were killed by the Nazis, but Bernstein's request also brought to our consciousness the existence of two additional sisters and the live descendants of one of them. My aunt replied that she did not know these sisters had even existed. Evidently, Grete and Marianne had not spoken of relatives who died before the war. The lawyer's message also brought into email contact a vast number of Löw-Beers who knew (more or less vaguely, depending on their generation) of each other's existence but many of whom had never met each other. It was to this list that John Low-Beer circulated his father Fritz's letter.

Here is what I learned about the three daughters of Max Löw-Beer. Born into the family but not into the firm, they were assured marriages within the Jewish upper bourgeoisie and must have been given either a dowry or an inheritance (although as Max died with the firm financially overextended, the arrangements are unclear). When their husbands needed assistance, Rudolf set them up in business. It is significant that the sisters were considerably older than the brothers.

Max Hože (1888–1942) was the only child of my great-grandfather Alfred's sister Cilla (Cecilie or Zilla; 1864–1942). Cilla married Cornelius (Cornel) Hože (1854–1936), a lawyer in Brno. As noted, Cornel had a partnership in the cement factory and managed the sales. Hans said he proved incapable. Cornel then invested in an

Figure 10. Rudolf and his siblings Cilla, Anna, Alfred, and Eva as children.
Photo courtesy of Roger Pollak

apartment building and lost so much money that apparently his family did not have the means to leave. This information makes the fact of our inheriting from them painfully ironic. In May 1942 they were transported to Thereseinstadt; Cilla died there in September; in June, Max and his wife Fritzi Kessler were gassed in Majdanek.

Cilla owned a house known as the Arnold Villa, around the corner from Alfred and Marianne, which she expanded and renovated in Art Deco style between 1909 and 1915. Fritz wrote: "Cilla I knew somewhat better than the other two aunts as she lived in Brno, and she and her husband used to come to Svitávka fairly often when I was a child." He added: "Tante Cilla called Cornel 'Manni' and ordered him around a good deal ... I quite liked Onkel Cornel as a child and also his son Max who must have been about 15 years older than I [actually 18] and who used to squeeze my hand very hard and to praise me for not crying ... Cilla was generally feared in Brno because she was very outspoken and told people all kinds of more or less disagreeable things. This is a family failing in general, but Cilla was worse than any of the others."

Fritz illustrates the point with an anecdote from the wedding of my grandparents. "Around 1922 Hermann Weiss's older son, Hans, married my double cousin Grete, Alfred's daughter, which was quite a family occasion ... Hans had a younger brother Rudi, who was not exactly handsome, and Cilla met him at the wedding. Afterwards, she told Rudi's mother, Mumma Weiss: 'You know, I met your son Rudi. I think he is not really as ugly as people told me he was.'"

Fritz himself wrote that Rudi "looked rather Jewish and not at all like his quite handsome brother." Nevertheless, Rudi had a way with the ladies and an interest in older ones, as we will see.

In 1988 Grete's daughter Dani told me that the only sister of Alfred she knew about was Cilla, who, her mother told her, always had rude things to say. So the description is one that gets reproduced, and now by me. At the time, neither Dani nor I spoke of the Holocaust; Cilla's death was something of which we had never been told. Nor had we asked.

I think of the Hožes as though they were giant shadow figures destined to repeat themselves for eternity, Cilla caught forever in the unpleasantness of her remarks; Cilla and Cornel haughty in their photo (Figure 11); Max and Fritzi young and vulnerable in theirs, so clumsy and innocent, with the overlarge cap and handbag (Figure 12). Or perhaps they are released from ignominy by their fate: our appreciation of the photo overdetermined by what we know befell them after it was taken, a fate foreshadowed by the man in uniform (but likely a chauffeur) standing behind them.

Older than Cilla was Eveline, called Eva (1859–1925). She married Theodor Pollak (1853–1912) who, Fritz writes in his critical way, "seems to have been inefficient. Rudolf started 2 or 3 businesses for him, the last was a screw factory in Bielitz which prospered reasonably well, especially after Theodor's death when it was taken over by one of his two sons, Bruno." Bruno's granddaughter Ellen had a somewhat different account. "Theodor emigrated to Bielsko-Biala from Prague and began working in the textile trade, first with an outfit named Leopold Popper & Co. and

Figure 11. Cornel and Cilla Löw-Beer Hože. Photo courtesy of Roger Pollak

then setting up his own factory devoted to the production of Turkish cloth and the manufacture of Fez hats. Eventually, though, he moved into metal goods and opened a screw factory in 1909. That factory is now owned by the Swedish company Bulten."[21] Ellen added that Theodor declared he was dividing the business into two parts equally between his sons so long as Bruno ran it and Max stayed away. Apparently Max had tried to organize the workers into a union. Fritz continues: "Max Pollak was much more

Figure 12. Max Hože and Fritzi Kessler Hože. Photo courtesy of Roger Pollak

intelligent than Bruno but not interested in business; he became a *Privatgelehrter* [private scholar] and was, indeed, a kind of walking encyclopedia."[22] Hans, always more generous than Fritz, described Max as a genius. Although they lived in Bielitz, Fritz says that "Tante Eva and Onkel Theodor visited in Svitávka fairly often but both died quite early."

Shortly after the lawyer put us all in touch, we received emails from Roger and Ellen Pollak, grandchildren of Bruno. Ellen wrote: "I am thrilled to have made these family connections. About a year ago, I was looking through a friend's copy of Libor Teplý's beautiful book about Villa Tugendhat and stumbled on the name of Alfred Low-Beer. I was pretty sure he was a relative of mine, but I couldn't make all the connections … When the emails began to come from Mr. Bernstein, a number of stray pieces of information finally fell into place. Amazing."[23] The next day she wrote my brother Bernie: "I go to a Hadassah book club at my synagogue, where we happened to read the novel *The Glass Room* by Simon Mawer. Do you know it? It's a heavily fictionalized account of the

Figure 13. Eveline (Eva) Löw-Beer
Pollak. Photo courtesy of Roger Pollak

history of the Tugendhat Villa. One of the members of the club ...
brought Teplý's book to show us. As it went around the table, I
noticed Alfred L-B's name."

So here, the house and even Simon Mawer have helped provide a connection for a line of kin who had drawn apart. Ellen
wrote later that afternoon: "I didn't mention *The Glass Room* in my
first message, partly because I wasn't sure how the characters in it
might have been received by the family. I had very mixed feelings
about the book myself, and that was before I knew it mattered!"

Ellen continued: "I knew we had a Low-Beer connection ... My
late father, John Pollak, was a great family historian ... But the presence of actual flesh and blood Low-Beers always seemed remote ...
I also did not have a clear sense of the Low-Beer family tree, so
although the name Alfred Low-Beer felt familiar, I had no idea that
he was a brother of my great-grandmother Eveline, or even that
there were 6 siblings in that generation. I also didn't know at that
time what his connection was to the Tugendhat house. Perhaps he
was just someone who worked for the architectural firm?"

Figure 14. Eveline (Eva) and Theodor Pollak, Pauline Löw-Beer, and Frl. Wahlmann, Marienbad, 1908. Photo courtesy of Roger Pollak

Ellen added another piece of family lore that I have heard more than once. "Eveline L-B's son Max (my great-uncle) lost his first wife (Dora Kellner) to the philosopher and cultural critic Walter Benjamin, with whom he and Dora spent a great deal of time in Berlin, where they were involved together in the Free Student Movement before WWI." She continued: "Max spent time as a political prisoner in Dachau during the early 30s. Somehow, the family got him out and he found asylum in Haiti, where he lived for many years before reuniting with the rest of the family in NYC. As it turns out, my father also got out of Europe via Haiti, before eventually getting to the U.S. More long stories."

Ellen included a photo of the very large (c. twelve-foot high) tombstone of Eveline (Eva) and Theodor in the Jewish Cemetery of Bielsko-Biala. It is marked there that Eveline died in 1925 at the age of sixty-six. She died in Merano, Italy, where she must have been on vacation. Four grandsons are listed: Bruno's sons Theodore/ Teddy, Robert, and Hans/John; and Max's son Peter. Peter was born in 1918, in Davos, of all places. Curiously, Dora's son Stefan Benjamin was also born in 1918 in Switzerland (in Bern). Dora and

Kinship Diagram 7. Max and the Pollaks (partial)

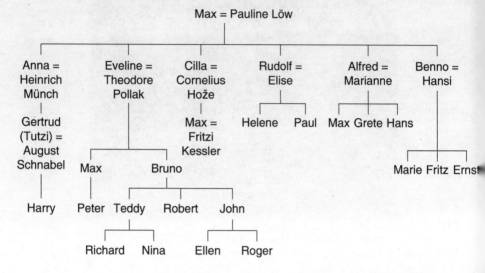

Max were married from 1912 to 1916; she and Walter Benjamin are said to have lived in part from the "considerable fortune" she brought from the marriage.[24]

I turn last to the oldest Löw-Beer of Alfred's generation, Anna, born around 1856. I have already mentioned her frustrated attempt to marry Hermann Weiss. According to Fritz, "Anna was forced to marry Dr. Münch with whom she was unhappy." With Heinrich Münch (1844–1932), a lawyer, she had two daughters, Gertrud born in 1880 and Käthe who died at the age of two. They lived in Vienna. Gertrud, known as Tutzi, married August Schnabel and had only one child, Erwin Harry, in 1902. Hans described Anna as "very vivacious and a good bridge player." Paul, who seems to have confused Eveline with Anna, recalled that "she had a phenomenal personal memory and knew the entire Viennese society with all the ramifications and connections."

Fritz wrote: "I last saw Anna in London in 1939 when she told me that the flight from Vienna to London had been one of the most

Figure 15. Anna Münch, 1938. Photo
courtesy of Roger Pollak

beautiful experiences of her life. I thought this quite remarkable as
coming from an old lady who had never flown before." She went
on, with Tutzi and Harry, to Haiti, where she committed suicide a
year later.[25]

Harry moved to New York and died in 1989. Fritz said he
wouldn't recognize him, but Ernst Löw-Beer's daughter Joan
remembers "Harry as my father's bridge partner. I used to go to
his house to watch the games. I think it was somewhere in Queens
… I remember a wife vaguely but not children. I really just sat and
watched Dad, Harry and two other men play bridge. It was interesting because my father rarely socialized." This socializing likely
took place during the 1950s. Harry was nine years older than Ernst
but a generation younger; Joan did not realize they were related.
Harry seems to have been childless; the lawyer could track down
no living descendants of Anna.

Chapter Six

The Wiedmann Sisters

The relationship among the three Löw-Beer brothers, and hence the integration of the firm, was further solidified through marriage to three Wiedmann sisters. Marrying the Löw-Beer brothers would have been attractive to the sisters for the economic security, especially because they had no brothers of their own. On the other hand, they were well-to-do and well connected and certainly did not arrive penniless. This was the generation in which women had the least opportunity to participate directly in the firm or indeed to have professional lives. They were supported by nannies and servants. Nevertheless, they could invest their own money and engage in charitable activity. Their presence was critical in enlivening family life and enriching the cultural milieu.

Alfred and Marianne were the first to marry. Marianne was born in Payerbach, southwest of Vienna, on 2 September 1882, just before the family were to return to Vienna at the end of their vacation. She was taught first grade by her sister Elise and then went to school at the Lyceum, where her older sisters had excelled. In her unpublished memoir, from which I draw extensively, she wrote of "dancing classes in school, but only for girls. We learned Lancier, Quadrille, Polka, and naturally the Waltz. Then we started having parties at home and of course boys were invited too. When I was 17 Mama gave a ball for me. The only music I wanted was waltzes ... [I]t went on till 5 am. Mama never went to bed, and started clearing up as soon as it was over."

Alfred was first attracted to Marianne's older married sisters. Alfred met Elise in Bielitz, where he went weekly to work in a family textile factory (presumably run by his sister Eveline's husband Theodor Pollak). He was also taken with Charlotte, an active presence on the Brno social scene. Alfred joined Elise and Charlotte and their husbands on a vacation in Abbazia, a fashionable seaside resort (now Opatija, in Croatia). Marianne wrote: "There was speculation after this holiday if there wasn't another sister somewhere? And so Alfred begged Charlotte to be allowed to visit her parents' home. At my next *Kränzchen* (small party), he sent me flowers, but then I didn't hear from him for a very long time. He had promised Charlotte not to be in touch for at least half a year as I was still a child."

"That summer [1900] in Reichenau-Payerbach," Marianne continued, "Elise and Charlotte were with us. Alfred was in Wiener-Neustadt at the Emperor's manoeuvres with three horses, having joined the army as an ordinance officer. He told himself, as he was only one hour away from Reichenau, it would be polite to call on my two sisters ... However, the next Sunday, August 18th the Emperor's birthday, he called again, and on that day my sisters were no longer there. On September 2 [her birthday], I received flowers – and my oldest sister, Hermine, spoke the memorable words: 'Marianne, I too received red roses on my 18th birthday, and within a few months I was engaged!'" Shortly after, the Wiedmanns took Marianne and her younger sister Hansi on a trip to Paris. "On our return we heard that Alfred had lost two front teeth in a rencontre with his horse. I was curious how he would look, but it wasn't that bad. From then on, he spent nearly every weekend with us. And, in November, we became engaged."

"A little later," Marianne added, "I went to stay with my sister Charlotte in Brünn, to meet Alfred's family. Rudolf and Benno from the start made things easy for me. The sisters were a little more reserved. At a big family dinner, there was already then discussion of the merits of being fat or thin. I said '*ich bin gerade recht*' I am just right – this caused great hilarity. The wedding was set for May, and until then Alfred made the two and a half hours journey by train every weekend – when we would dutifully pay calls on all the relatives, rejoicing when we found them not at home."

"The dowry preparations began in earnest," wrote Marianne. "We were to take over my parents-in-law's apartment, and furnishings were part of my dowry. I received new double beds, two single beds, which were especially beautiful, 4 dozen sheets, 5 dozen underpants, dozens of shirts, stockings – all things which no one would wear now. Alfred was also completely re-equipped. Then we received silver cutlery for 24." Her mother-in-law, Pauline, gave Marianne a gold chain and a small watch, and for the wedding a diamond bow with emerald drop. Rudolf presented her a silver mirror and silver objects for her dressing table, and Benno gave the couple a grand piano, "which had to match the woodwork in the Salon – later it had to be painted black when we moved to the Parkstrasse."

They wed on 27 May 1901 in Vienna. Alfred was twenty-nine and Marianne eighteen. The evening before, the immediate family dined at the Hotel Sacher. "The service was in the Seitenstetern Temple – Rabbi Midermann married us. Then we drove in a Fiaker with grey directly to the Prater – where there was a meal for 50 – the usual toasts and speeches, a band, singing, and finally dancing. We disappeared unnoticed." They took a four-week honeymoon through "Salzburg, Munich, Baden-Baden with the marvellous forest, Heidelberg, Basel, then Interlaken, Lauterbrunnen and up to Murren, Luzern, Lake Como and Bellagio, and finally Venice. All this by train with huge steamer trunks. How silly and impractical!"

The first summer they spent in the home of Pauline in Svitávka, in the old factory building. Marianne recalled the village fire brigade played a serenade for her nineteenth birthday. She wrote: "I loved being in Svitávka. The first few years, I was spoiled by the two single brothers-in-law. When Alfred stayed for several days in Brünn, one or other of them would play tennis with me, or Benno would drive me out with his 'Lady' … She was Benno's first horse and great love."

Marianne had a lot of zest; she liked tennis and music, eating and entertaining. Hans said of his mother that if she were not the best looking of the sisters, she was the most cheerful and well balanced. She was a charming woman in a charmed existence, but also a strong person capable of surviving the vicissitudes life later threw at her, and serving, as her grandson Frank said, as a kind of guardian angel to many of her younger relatives.

On the birth of Max (1902), her first child, Benno brought her red roses the next morning. Rudolf gave her a ring with a black and a white pearl, and Alfred added a fourth row to her pearl collar. She was looked after first by her mother and then by Charlotte. She had to stay in bed for three weeks, and a lot of fuss was made over her. Her white silk negligee "was so elegant that I wore it to Hansi's wedding when I was pregnant with my second child." The second summer they went first to her parents' summer villa and then to Pauline's in Svitávka. By the third summer the Grosse Villa in Svitávka had been completed, and Rudolf lent them his suite while he stayed with his mother. "After two summers using Rudolf's apartment, he declared we must build! 'I need this for myself and my bride-to-be, Elise.' And in this way, we learned of the engagement." Alfred planned the Kleine Villa, which they built on the same property.

On a trip to London with Rudolf and Alfred, Marianne became pregnant with Grete (b. 1903). "The doctor forbade me to go to Vienna for Hansi's wedding but I, frivolous as always, ignored the advice, and even waltzed away the night with the wonderful dancer, Ernst Kronbach. Hansi was a beautiful bride." Marianne went into labour at the theatre a few weeks later. At the birth of her third child, Hans (1911), the older children had whooping cough and were sent to Alfred's sister Cilla before the birth. "They were allowed to visit me after four weeks, and the baby not until six weeks when the cough had completely gone."

The position of women was tricky. At one point Hans dismissed his mother, saying, after Rudolf, that Marianne was "only a consumer." It is true she enjoyed the finer things of life. But Hans added that she was the enterprising one among her sisters and the only one to take an active interest in the company. Apparently, she started a nursery or elementary school for the children of the factory workers, hiring Catholic staff. She was also active in community affairs, by which I suppose Hans meant social activities among people of her class.

Fritz admits that Marianne "had a lot of vitality," even at the age of eighty-nine. But he described her as "only moderately intelligent. She enjoyed running the household and being hostess to the cream of the mostly Jewish society of the Brno industrialists. She also liked to meddle in other people's affairs, especially ours after my father's death, so that Ernst (my brother) called her the 'head mistress.' We did not enjoy this, since she completely accepted Rudolf's and Alfred's opinion of ourselves." Marianne was probably quite right to become involved, as their mother, her sister Hansi, was herself needy.

Marianne told one of her granddaughters that she didn't know what to do on her wedding night; no one had ever informed her. But she was hardly repressed. Irene Kalkofen (see chapter 10) described her as flirtatious and "quite a number." The marriage with Alfred was by all accounts a very good one. As Marianne wrote, "I had wonderful years with Alfred. We were still together to celebrate our silver [twenty-fifth] wedding anniversary. I didn't want the children to make a fuss. They gave us a Cézanne – it was very beautiful – it remained with all other valuables in Brünn plundered by the Germans."

Benno, the youngest of the three brothers, was the next to marry. He did so in 1903, and he chose as his wife Marianne's younger sister, Johanna, known as Hansi (1883–1948). Benno and Hansi had three children, Marie (b. 1904), Fritz (b. 1906), and Ernst (b. 1911). Hansi was described as passive. As a child she wanted to be pulled in her sled. As an adult she was "long suffering" and considered a hypochondriac. But it was Benno who died first, in 1916 at the age of forty-two of pernicious anemia. After that, Hansi became needier, keeping Marie tied to her. Her condition "got steadily worse so that her health had become her overriding interest by the time I [her son Fritz] was 20." Hansi returned to Vienna, where she maintained her own household. She never remarried and was presumably supported by Rudolf, that is, by the firm.

Rudolf finally made his move and married two years after Benno, in 1905, at the age of forty-one. His granddaughter Eva thinks the reason Rudolf didn't marry younger was simply that he was focused on the business. She suggests he married in order to produce an heir and notes insightfully that his brothers each had children by then, and in Alfred's case his first-born was a son.

Rudolf's interest in having heirs was affirmed a generation later. When Ala, the wife of Rudolf's son gave birth to Martin, her second child and first son, Rudolf gave her his ring.

Rudolf selected as his bride an older sister of Marianne and Hansi. Elise (1874–1957) was the middle of the five Wiedmann sisters, and had been married previously at the age of seventeen in Bielitz to Ahron Alfred Fränkel. It had been an arranged marriage; Elise's father came from Bielitz.[1] Paul described his mother then as a sporty, enterprising, and popular young woman who, as a new bride, enjoyed cycling excursions with her husband, often as much as 100 kilometres in a day. "The catastrophe was that Mr. Fränkel infected her with syphilis. That ended the marriage, of course." Elise returned to Vienna where, said Paul, she began treatment with Salvarsan, which was extremely unpleasant. As Salvarsan was only synthesized in 1907 and marketed in 1910, and Rudolf and Elise married in 1905, something is not right in Paul's account. Nevertheless, Elise was cured.

Paul reflected that Elise married Rudolf in a period of resignation and probably without any idea of what a hard and dominant personality he was, albeit not vicious. As Eva phrased it, Rudolf didn't waste a lot of time and energy courting. Elise was a "damaged woman." She was also the right wife for him. Like Rudolf, she was very frugal. He might have been attracted to more outgoing women, but he didn't want to marry one. Elise, she said, was ideal for him.

Before marrying, Rudolf confirmed that there would be no danger to any offspring. But other versions have percolated in the family. Someone said Rudolf had not known about the syphilis when he married, while another suggested, surely incorrectly, that it was Rudolf himself who infected her. They assumed he had lots of relations with women before marrying, and possibly after as well. One younger relative imagined him a virile lover. In any case, Elise gave birth to Helene in Vienna in 1908 and, under some trepidation with an unknown doctor, to Paul in Svitávka in 1910. It was midsummer and presumably she was expected to be there.

Whether there was love on either side I cannot say. Paul described the marriage as solid but said it put an end to Elise's independence.

Marriages between sets of siblings were not uncommon. I have already noted Pauline and her sister marrying Max and his brother in the previous generation and the Weiss brothers marrying the Rosenbacher sisters. One reason for this kind of marriage among entrepreneurs is that the wives supply additional capital, as the Rosenbachers did.[2] No one I spoke to knew whether that was the case with the Wiedmann sisters, and most thought it unlikely, but it is at least plausible. In any case, such marriages served to consolidate the firm, creating a pool of closely related owners with common interests and mutual trust. The Weiss families lived next door to each other. The Löw-Beer/Wiedmann couples lived separately during the winter months but came together in the summers.

Relations were intense. Indeed, sometime after Benno died, "there was an affair with Rudolf," as Fritz neutrally put it, "for which Mama [Hansi] was blamed." I wonder about the response of those who held Rudolf in such esteem. It certainly was further evidence of his patriarchal rule. An affair with his brother's widow was simultaneously one with his wife's sister, and on Hansi's part, she was having an affair with her sister Elise's husband. Attraction aside, for Rudolf perhaps this affair was a way of keeping Hansi from remarrying outside the family, exercising a kind of leviratic responsibility, or simply exerting his control. From Hansi's perspective it may have been about ensuring the good will of the man who controlled her children's future. Elise told her daughter Helene that she knew about the affair.

People remember that Elise walked with a bit of a hunch and always a few steps behind Rudolf, carrying his jacket for him. Fritz writes that Rudolf "seems to have suppressed Elise's personality entirely ... She had been very gay and lively as a girl, but as Rudolf's wife she was scarcely more than a household slave." Hans called Elise a toady to Rudolf.

Although Rudolf and Elise were the senior couple, they were not outgoing. Elise lived for most of the year in Vienna, from where Rudolf commuted to the factories in Moravia and elsewhere. They inhabited what Paul called "a large impractical apartment" in the city hall district (*Rathausviertel*). This living arrangement was one instance where Elise exerted control. She insisted on living in

Figure 16. Elise Wiedmann Löw-
Beer, taken by Edith Tudor-Hart,
England, 1940s. Photo courtesy of
Roger Pollak

Vienna; she did not want to be part of Brno's elite society or have her children singled out as they would have been in Brno or Svitávka, where, in Fritz's words, "the name Löw-Beer meant much the same as Rothschild in Vienna or Paris, or Rockefeller in New York." Paul told me he was grateful to his mother for this wise decision. In Vienna Elise was close to her older sister Charlotte (by 1919 a widow with no children) who had a flat on the same floor of their building, as well as a friend called Tante Olga.

Paul said of his mother that early on she had lively friends, but she totally effaced herself for Rudolf and his rigid schedule. She expressed no interests. Ala added: "Elise never took time for herself, not even to go to the hairdresser." Fritz wrote that "she seems to have had the unfortunate idea that she had to run her household as Rudolf was running the factories: as economically as possible. I do not know whether Rudolf himself was stingy in that respect and gave her only a small sum for household expenses." Rudolf and Elise didn't entertain, and Paul and Helene were never able to invite over other children. Elise's ability to maintain her privacy and anonymity shows that she wasn't just a pushover.

Elise had a predilection for hoarding. This habit was likely brought on during the First World War, when, Paul said, there was less to eat in Vienna than during the Second World War, and it was very hard on his mother. Elise had to get used to thrift even though she was driven in a company car and received weekly deliveries of food from the countryside. She began to store large numbers of cartons. Years later, when the Nazis came to her flat, the officers spent some time looking through the cartons for incriminating material, only to discover they were all empty. One of them cut himself on the cardboard, and Elise offered to bandage his cut. The act completed, they left politely, albeit taking the car keys and her papers with them.

The Sisters' Family

The Wiedmann sisters came from a cultured, well-off Viennese family. Their father, Heinrich (1843–1916), was born in Bielitz, where his father Salomon (c. 1805–83) owned a textile factory. Heinrich was the eldest of five brothers and a sister. Three brothers died young, and the fourth, like Heinrich, had only daughters. Heinrich began working in Vienna at the age of fourteen. Fritz writes that he "seems to have been a self-made man. He began his career as an office boy at Gebrüder Gutmann [the Gutmann Brothers] in Vienna and gradually rose to become their *erster Prokurist* [chief financial administrator]." He also married Berta Steiner, the Gutmanns' niece.

The Gutmanns were another remarkable Moravian family. Next to the Rothschilds and the Wittgensteins, they were the richest and most prominent Jewish family in Vienna.[3] The Wiedmanns were less wealthy than the Löw-Beers, but the Gutmanns were much wealthier. Beginning in the coal business, the Gutmann brothers Wilhelm and David had come to acquire 50 per cent ownership, shared with the Rothschilds, of the largest iron and steel works in the Austro-Hungarian monarchy. The Vítkovice (Witkowitz) steelworks are located in the city of Ostrava, on the border between Moravia and (Czech) Silesia, north of Brno, but the Gutmanns and Wiedmanns lived in Vienna, and the industry was managed

Kinship Diagram 8. Heinrich Wiedmann, Berta Steiner, and the Gutmanns (partial)

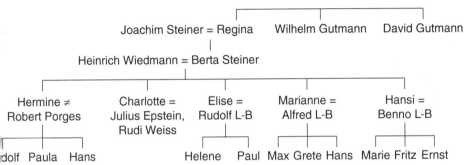

from there. Berta was the daughter of Wilhelm and David's sister Rebekka Regina Gutmann, born 1828 or 1830. Regina married Joachim Steiner from Prostějov (Prossnitz), Moravia, and gave birth to five children before dying young in 1866. Berta (1853–1942), her eldest child, was left responsible for her siblings until the Gutmann brothers stepped in. They arranged her marriage to Heinrich Wiedmann when she was seventeen, thereby ensuring her a good income and cementing the loyalty of Heinrich, now a family member. Years later, Heinrich and Berta's grandson, Rudolf Porges, also became a manager at the steelworks.

Wilhelm received a hereditary knighthood in 1878, as did David, each becoming Ritter von Gutmann. They converted to Christianity, and their aristocratic descendants became linked through marriage to the Prince of Liechtenstein, the de Beers, and the Montefiores.[4] There was a complete break between "their" family and "ours," even though they are no more distantly related than some of the Löw-Beers who attended the family reunion. Despite their wealth and renown I have never heard the Gutmanns mentioned in the family.

The Wiedmanns lived first in the Schutzengasse, Vienna 3, and later in a villa that Heinrich built on Böcklinstrasse in the Prater district, which they shared with the family of his widowed sister Pepi Latzko, whose son Wilhelm was to marry Heinrich's granddaughter Paula. They were assimilated, more so, said Paul, than the Löw-Beers. However, unlike the Gutmanns, they did not convert.

The family was interested in the arts and patronized music and the theatre, enjoying what the imperial capital had to offer in its final decades. Marianne wrote that her father "frequented the opera, the Burgtheater, and also enjoyed operettas. Nestroy was his favourite playwright. At his morning toilette, he would often sing the current hit!" They invited stage actors and opera singers to their home. As Hans said of Marianne, she grew up when Vienna was at its peak.

Both Hans and Paul recalled Heinrich as jovial. Fritz wrote that "Grosspapa Heinrich was a merry old gentleman ... Grossmama Berta was small, energetic and rather severe." Fritz added: "Grandfather Heinrich, who died [in 1916] of diabetes ... was kind and warm-hearted. I was quite fond of him, but he simply 'disappeared' after his death and I do not know what kind of a man he really was. I suspect that Grandmother Berta, who had quite a forceful personality, dominated him."

Paul said that while Berta was very kind to her grandchildren, she was severe with her daughters. Marianne was her favourite. Elise and the children visited Berta only twice a month and always with Rudolf. Rudolf used a pedometer to discover the shortest route from house to house, and the children were not allowed to play or dawdle along the way.

Berta (my great-great-grandmother) died in an old persons' home in Vienna during the Second World War.

Heinrich and Berta Wiedmann had five daughters, of whom Elise was the third and Marianne the fourth. A son died in childhood. The eldest daughter, Hermine, married a gynecologist, Robert Porges. They had two sons, Rudolf (1891–1914) and Hans (1898–2001), and a daughter, Paula (1893–1988), before they divorced.[5] Divorce, wrote Fritz, "was still rather scandalous in those days." He added: "There was a slight aura of scandal surrounding Hermine, and years later my mother made a veiled remark to the effect that Hermine had been unfaithful." Fritz recalled playing with Hans Porges "in Grossmama Berta's *Gartenhaus*." Hans too became a gynecologist and attended the births of a number of Löw-Beers in New York.

The Porges family was one into which Wilhelm Gutmann had also married. Wilhelm's second wife was a Latzko, as was the wife of David Gutmann. Hermine's daughter Paula also married a Latzko, Hermine's first cousin Dr. Wilhelm (Willy) Latzko. The couple divorced, and for all the years I knew her Paula was single. After the war, she lived in New York but spent the summers in Switzerland as a companion to her aunt Marianne, a gracious lady with glossy white hair and pearls.[6]

The Wiedmanns' second daughter, Charlotte, married Julius Tobias Epstein (1858–1919), a banker in Brno. Fritz remembered "a belly with a gold watch chain across it, an upturned moustache, and he was rather pompous, I called him 'Bumberus' at least in my thoughts; however, he brought chocolate cigars or cigarettes which made him quite acceptable to me. I scarcely remember Charlotte in those days, but she became my favourite aunt later."

"Charlotte was the only one of the sisters interested in art, literature and the 'outside' world in general," wrote Fritz. Another cousin called her more sharp-witted than her sisters. "Charlotte," Fritz continued, "was dangerously ill with a streptococci heart infection for two years or so, which disappeared when she formed a relationship with Rudi Weiss ... who was about 25 [actually 29] years younger than she." Rudi was the reputedly unattractive younger brother of my grandfather Hans Weiss. In effect, Rudi took up with the widowed older sister of his own older brother's ex-mother-in-law.

All this detail shows the bounded social circle in which these people married. The Wiedmann sisters appear to have been somewhat freer of patriarchal constraints than the Löw-Beer sisters; of course, they were somewhat younger and came from a bigger city. The unconventional relationship between Charlotte and Rudi proved stable, and they lived openly together. Rudi invested Charlotte's money and watched the stock market. They eventually married in order to facilitate visas to the United States, and they stayed together in New York until Charlotte's death in 1954 or 1955. When Eva described her exiting her building in Manhattan and pushing away everyone in front of her with her cane, it provoked a dim memory of my own of a sharp old woman with a cane.

On Charlotte's death Rudi took up with an elderly Jewish woman from New York named Toni, whom I remember from their visits to Switzerland. Toni wore ugly orthopaedic shoes, couldn't go on walks like the Europeans, was "not an intellectual," and seemed in all respects anomalous. Poor Toni was not liked by "the family" and was doubtless unaware that Rudi may have maintained a discrete relationship with Marianne. Rudi seemed, to me, to keep closer ties with the Löw-Beer/Wiedmann family than he did with his Weiss siblings, but like my mother, he was connected to both. Unlike his accomplished siblings, of whom more later, Rudi appears to have had no job or skill other than being a charming conversationalist. Paul said Rudi was put in nominal charge at Sagan in the late 1930s (after Hans Weiss emigrated) but couldn't really manage a factory. Rudi liked much older women. When I asked Paul whether Rudi had had a wife before Charlotte, he replied with a smile: "Perhaps she also died."

We can see all the people of my great-grandparental generation mentioned in the death notice of the first of them (after Theodor Pollak) to pass away (Figure 17). The last sentence asks people to refrain from sending condolences.

Figure 17. Death notice for Benno Löw Beer. Image copied from Geni

Chapter Seven

The Double Cousins, before the War

The three brothers and three sisters who married one another had eight children between them. They were double cousins to each other, all born Löw-Beer, and the five boys among them members of the firm from birth. All eight were born within a single decade, after the turn of the century and before the First World War (between 1902 and 1911); all lived through the radical transition in European society I refer to by the shorthand term "modernity" and through the Second World War. All experienced the shift from proximal residence to dispersal and readjustment in new settings and circumstances.

The period from 1901, when Alfred and Marianne wed, through 1938 was one in which the family was, as Dani put it, a community unto itself. As Fritz wrote, "the 3 L.B. families formed a nucleus, and all other people were more or less peripheral." It was tightly bound and hierarchical. But as the eight double cousins came of age, they moved apart in distinctive ways. How the double cousins navigated their lives is described in this and the following chapters.[1]

Residences

Family life and the intensity of relations in childhood were shaped by the pattern of residence. The original factory was in Svitávka, a village 39 kilometres north of Brno. During the summers Pauline lived in a dwelling attached to it. Residence for her sons became an issue as they married.

Kinship Diagram 9. Double Cousins

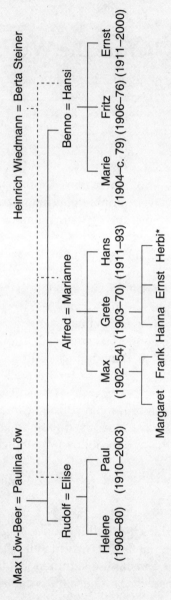

* This generation only includes children born before the family fled Czechoslovakia.

Once he came of age, the division of labour was such that Benno managed the factory in Svitávka. He was therefore the only brother to live there year-round. Alfred managed the factory in Brno and lived there. In 1902 he and Marianne had a flat on the Jakobsplatz, in the centre of town; a year later, they took up residence in a flat attached to the Brno factory on the Czechnergasse. In 1913 the villa on the Parkstrasse (Sadová) came on the market, and, as Marianne wrote, "within 24 hours we decided to buy it. Shortly after moving in, the war started. They were exciting times." The Parkstrasse house is now a museum known as Villa Löw-Beer. Benno and Hansi took up the flat on the Czechnergasse.

Rudolf, says Fritz, "lived 9 to 10 months of the year in a comfortable but by the standards of those days not very large apartment in Vienna but in 'my time' (i.e., after about my 20th year [1926]) ... he spent only short weekends in Vienna and the weekdays in Brno and Svitávka." Elise chose to spend most of the year in Vienna, where their children were schooled.

Hence the primary residences of each of the brothers and their respective children were in three separate places. However, they also built residences in Svitávka, where they gathered in the summer. Fritz describes it this way: "When my father [Benno] became engaged, he went to Rudolf and told him that he wanted to build a house for his bride. Rudolf opposed this at first, of course, but consented after a while. Being always interested in technical matters, he even designed the house himself, and a contractor from Brünn, Nebehosteny, built it ... This was the 'Grosse Villa' where I as well as my sister and brother were born. It was built on a piece of land encircled by water, the *Mühlgraben* [mill race] and the Svitávka [stream] on three sides, the fourth was closed partly by a 10 ft. high stone wall with glass splinters on top, partly by a wire fence. Next to the Old Factory a bridge was built across the *Mühlgraben* with a wall and a wooden gate in front of it. Some fairly old trees, mostly birches and horse chestnuts, were incorporated in the front part of the garden. My father ordered some wagonloads of various trees from Dresden for the rest of the garden. There was even a gingko tree (gone now) ... also *Kastanien* [chestnuts] with tables and chairs [beneath them] ... Alfred built the 'Kleine Villa' (which would be

Figure 18. The Grosse Villa in Svitávka. Photo courtesy of Roger Pollak

considered rather large nowadays) … as a summer home and the garage might have been built in 1908 when my father seems to have bought his first car which was also the first in 'the family.'"[2]

The Grosse Villa (Figure 18) was begun in 1900, well before Benno's marriage in 1903. Art historians Dagmar Černoušková and Iveta Černá describe it built "in the spirit of an Art Nouveau château building with Baroque and Neo-Classical elements … by the Moses Löw-Beer company … over the years 1900–1902. Within viewing distance, in an extensive park, the father of Grete Tugendhat, Alfred Löw-Beer, had the so-called Kleine Villa built in the year 1906 according to a project by the Brno builder Josef Nebehosteny [1852–1921]. Both buildings are registered on the Central List of Cultural Monuments."[3]

The Grosse Villa was not modest.

Benno and Hansi lived in the Grosse Villa, which Rudolf and Elise shared with them. Alfred and Marianne spent summers in the Kleine Villa. After Benno's death, Alfred's oldest son Max came to manage Svitávka and lived in the Kleine Villa year-round with his wife and children.

The two buildings were close to each other, and much activity was conducted in common. The family added fruit and vegetable gardens, greenhouse, beehives, bowling alley, garage, and later tennis courts and a large swimming pool. The villas remain standing and are used today, respectively, as the Svitávka city hall and a dentist's office and residence, as described in later chapters. Because the villas were part of the firm rather than privately owned, family members who lived in them could not ask for restitution after the war.

Childhood in the Garden

The cousins played together in the garden at Svitávka. Two of them, Max and Grete, had between them five children who also played there before the Second World War, especially Max's children Margaret and Frank, who lived in Svitávka year-round. Fifteen more children were born to the double cousins after their dispersal and came to know each other in lesser degrees of intimacy. My mother, born in Brno in 1924, was the oldest of the twenty offspring of the eight double cousins. The youngest is Jane, born in 1951 in Montreal.

Their proximity in age and the common interests of their parents meant that the double cousins saw a good deal of each other growing up, especially in summer, when the entire family convened in Svitávka.[4] For the children, Svitávka was something like a magical garden, although at times it could feel more like a hot house or even a place of captivity. It formed an inner family ring, as Fritz called it, and forged a strong identification among the inhabitants. As Fritz wrote, "the garden was practically an island not only in a topographical sense; we were also not supposed to leave it ... Of course, 'the Family' had no social contacts with anyone in the village at all." Those outside the inner ring could resent it. Years later, in New York, Fritz was "greatly surprised to learn from Hans Porges ... that he had never been invited to Svitávka. He had ... felt very slighted and had never quite overcome some bitterness."

As a child Fritz lived there year-round. "My schooling started when I was 5, and it was entrusted to 'Oberlehrer Mayer' from Boskowitz.

There were two primary schools in Svitávka but my parents considered that we could not enrol in either. One was the regular school of the village, and it was Czech-speaking. For one of us to go to a Czech school was quite unthinkable, quite apart from the fact that we would not have been sent to school together with the children of our workers and peasants. The second school was private and run by the firm for the children of our German-speaking 'Beamten' (functionaries). The single teacher, a lady, was, of course, paid by 'us' (the firm), and it was understandable that we were not enrolled there. So Oberlehrer (head teacher) Mayer (or Meyer) came from Boskowitz, or sometimes, we were driven there for our lessons. Grandmother's horses were used for this purpose, and occasionally I was allowed to drive them. Oberlehrer Mayer lived in the ghetto, which still existed at that time, and in his house I 'experienced' above all, smelt, for the first time a W.C. without the W. This has given me a lifelong aversion to that sort of primitive 'facility.' I remember also some rare sleighrides, sometimes we rode on toboggans tied to the sleigh."

Of Pauline, the matriarch, Fritz wrote that "she seemed very dignified but also radiated benevolence. She lived in an apartment … in Brünn … in winter and in the 'Alte Fabrik' in Svitávka in summer. We … had to go to say 'good morning' to her every day after breakfast. There we would get some pastries, usually meringues, which we called 'Windpusserln' [wind kisses] which, for some reason, were never made at home. Grandmother chatted with us for a while and then let us go … play." Pauline died in 1919.

"The Wiedmann grandparents, Grosspapa Heinrich and Grossmama Berta, also came to Svitávka … fairly often," wrote Fritz, "and they stayed in our 'Rotes Zimmer' [red room]. We had two guest rooms, 'rotes' and 'grunes' Zimmer but, in those days, no guest bathroom. Each guestroom had running hot and cold water though." In his memoir of 1962, Frank, from the following generation, says: "Grossmama Berta I can see sitting on the white bench under the chestnut tree or in her room in the Grosse Villa dispensing chocolates.[5] Tante Hansi appears in front of the Villa by the tree surrounded by violets. I never felt at ease with her. I wonder if I realized then that she was the mother of Onkel Fritz. In a way the servants Blažek, Tešar, Horák, Toni and Rezi were much more real and immediate. They were my daily companions together with Slečna ['Miss,' Czech for Fräulein]. She was the one on whom any minor unhappiness could be unburdened and who never revealed any annoyance or impatience with me."

In this world of dense kinship Frank referred to his father's cousin Fritz as his uncle. The senior relatives were more remote than the servants, to whom the children had strong attachments. In addition to the nannies, the chauffeurs were salient figures, and the cars themselves were memorable. Fritz wrote: "In 1910 father bought his Benz car which I remember very well because it played a big role in my life. I also drove it a few times in about 1924. Blažek was father's chauffeur. He had a daughter and a son, Tonds, who was my principal playmate for years, even though my parents frowned on this friendship. Rudolf bought his first car, a second hand, chain-driven, red Mercedes in 1911 or 12, and this was followed by his Minerva in 1913. The Minerva was still there and in use in 1939. There was another chauffeur, Slaviček. Alfred took over the red Mercedes and then bought a new one (not red) in 1914. His chauffeur was Sipek."

Fritz added a handwritten note to the typed letter. "The Minerva was dark green. By the time it was 25 years old cars had changed enormously ... It was very high and open in the back." In her memoir of 1972, Helene wrote: "It didn't bother my father [Rudolf] that the car was 25 years old, and that wherever we went through the villages, crowds would come to look. The car worked perfectly. It couldn't go very fast but sitting on the high bench in the back the wind blew in our faces so it seemed we were racing along. In the front the glass gave a bit more protection. I loved that car more than any other." Mr. Slaviček gave her driving lessons, but the gearshift was difficult to manage.

Relations forged in this enclosed world were intense. Fritz wrote of Helene that "she is a little more than 2 ½ years younger than I but still nearest to me in age with the exception of my sister Marie who is 2 ½ years older, and she was my play fellow and love during those summers in Svitávka over 55 years ago." He looked forward eagerly to her arrival and remembered "my somewhat incredulous dismay when someone, I think it was a 'Fräulein' (governess), told me that we were too closely related to marry each other."

"Helene has told me that I was always the leader in [our] games," wrote Fritz to Joan, "and she is undoubtedly right, although I had not been conscious of this before. But the eight children were really divided into three groups. There was Max, born in 1902, over four years older than I, and Grete about 2 years younger than Max. Marie, about 1 ½ years younger than Grete, usually tagged onto her. Then there was I with Helene and finally Paul, Ernst, and Hans." As Helene herself recalled, she "often went with Fritz who planned elaborate games. Normally he pretended he was Benno, his father, and I was Hansi, his mother. Or else I was Rudolf – bossed always by Benno (not like in real life) ... Later, no longer interested in me, he took more exciting trips through the woods with Paul."

Helene offered an extensive and loving depiction of Svitávka in her recollections presented to Marianne on her ninetieth birthday, 2 September 1972. "I remember the two terraces at the Little Villa: the one at the front would often be occupied by Aunt Marianne and Uncle Alfred, the one at the side used for breakfast on all sunny mornings, as well as for shelling peas, cleaning mushrooms, and plucking red currants ... On September 2nd one went to the Little Villa to congratulate Aunt Marianne on her birthday. Of all these, there is one which I remember particularly. Ernst Latzko conducted us in Haydn's Children's Symphony! In addition Gretl [Grete] put on a play, or was it a poem, where we all took part – I think it was called the 'Four Seasons.'"[6]

Helene continued: "The main action in Svitávka took place out of doors – especially for us children, where we all met in different combinations and situations. The garden enclosed a whole world of opportunities. I remember as a small child experiencing each part with wonder and delight ... The 'big sandpit' was our usual meeting place. Fritz once built a glorious fort there – it was at the time of World War I – and organized a grand war game. Nearby was the croquet lawn, which I especially loved to play when I was a little older. And there sat the nannies. Of all of them I remember particularly Fräulein Schmidt, she stayed with us the longest and was also the nicest."

"Temptations of different kinds were in the kitchen garden," Helene wrote. "Next to the huge beds of seasonal vegetables were several kinds of strawberries, then came the cherries – soft ones, hard ones, light, dark and sour – and then the red currants. We only had a few apricots and peaches trained on the wall. Later came the *Ringlos* (greengage), the sugar-sweet 'real' ones, then the *Zwetchen* (prune) whose trees were scattered all over the garden as well. By the time the pear and apple season arrived we were back in Vienna ... Red and green hazelnuts could be picked, cracked and eaten at once, from the many bushes about."

"At the other side of the 'Big Villa' lay the tennis court," Helene continued. "We were soon introduced to the game by our mother [Elise] who was a good player ... She was the only person I knew who neither possessed nor used white tennis shoes. She believed that the colour white should not come in contact with the ground, even in the form of shoes. She wore elegant light brown leather booties, with no heels when she played. How I envied the other children's white shoes! ... The best player was Aunt Marianne. If I remember correctly, Uncle Alfred was a keener player, but not as consistent. I don't know which of them was the faster runner. Aunt Marianne was shorter and round but had amazing agility of movement. Also she knew exactly where to place the ball."

"Further away behind the 'Little Villa' was the playground," Helene recalled, "and behind it, the swimming pool ... Mother used to exercise with us on the bar and the rings ... She could pull herself up on the rings, and do a handstand on the horizontal bar ... The pool was the meeting place before noon. The two older gentlemen, Rudolf and Alfred – I can't remember Benno anymore – would come then as there would still be an hour before dinner. They would both dive in headfirst and both swam well, but behaved quite differently. My father would do his laps methodically, but Uncle Alfred played ball and other games with us children, and even came a little earlier to make sure there was enough time ... Aunt Marianne found swimming difficult to learn, but enjoyed it more. She went from side to side wearing a belt made of cork."

Helene also mentions bowling and basketball, a rowboat, and bicycling through the countryside. She describes the participation and leadership of Max Pollak, Eveline's son. Helene was taught to ride a bicycle by Mr. Tešar, the caretaker of the Grosse Villa, as later Margaret and Frank were taught by Blažek, the chauffeur. Helene is the only one to refer respectfully to the employees as "Mr."

Helene continued: "I loved the surroundings of Svitávka, both the immediate and the distant. At first we went with the parents on Sunday afternoons – started by car and then walked through especially beautiful countryside. Later, I loved going walking with Paul, either directly from Svitávka, or through short journeys by rail." Sometimes "we had to run like mad to get to the train and not be late for supper … We loved the pine woods with their spicy scent and the glorious clearings in between, often covered in glowing wild roses. We seldom met anyone in these woods. In the fields there were farmers working. The fields also had a charm and beauty … When I was almost grown up and had holidays in Svitávka, I would go nearly every day on a walk with Aunt Marianne … These small excursions are among my happiest memories."

Joan said her mother's love for Svitávka was lined with guilt. As Helene added in her memoir, "something which I have neglected to mention was very important. That was the enormous contrast between our estate and the village, 'the Outside.' When one came out of the cool, green shady park with its tall, old trees shut off like an island between the two Svitava river branches, over the bridge, through the gate into the dusty, hot village, it was as if it was another world. The people were mostly barefoot and shabbily dressed … Many of them greeted us in a humble way." In her childhood, Helene knew no Czech and could not communicate with the village children, although she had friendly relations with the chauffeurs, who knew German. By adulthood, she could get along in Czech, and in the next generation Margaret and Frank had a Czech-speaking nanny and attended the local school.

Fritz concluded: "I do remember a good deal about people and things as they were up to 1914 but I saw them of course only with the eyes of a child. There are many 'pictures' which somehow became imprinted on my memory, like overtaking a streetcar … with Papa driving his Benz car on the way into town or being overtaken by a motorcyclist on the road to Vienna and a while later overtaking him in turn, and Papa saying: '*Jetzt kann er Staub schlucken* [now he can swallow the dust],' me falling into the swimming pool in Svitávka and dimly hearing Tešar, the janitor, calling for my hand, and many more." Yet this life was not without disruption. Fritz wrote: "We had lived in Svitávka all the year round until 1914 (or 15?), when our schooling made a move to Brno necessary ... I hated Brno ... Papa was already ill at that time. In the summer of 1916 he was taken to a Vienna sanatorium and we, the children, never saw him again. He died on October 22nd aged 42."

Finances

The firm was run as a partnership, with Rudolf as the senior partner. All recognized male descendants were partners, and each partner received a share of profits. Each partner was also liable in case of failure. "That's why women weren't made partners; to protect them," Paul told me with a sweet but ironic smile. The women acquired at the discretion of the men. Women inherited money, daughters apparently receiving a sum invested for them at birth and a dowry on marriage. Rudolf bequeathed money to his granddaughters on their births. Paul said that in fact the women usually had more money, presumably liquid assets, than the men.

Rudolf decided each year what proportion of money to reinvest and how much to distribute to the partners. At first Paul told me that Rudolf never consulted the others, but later suggested he must have asked them what they needed. Any part of the profits a partner put back in, he would gain interest on. The income was first divided into three parts – one for each of the brothers and their respective descendants. Paul would get a portion of his father's share. Sons were partners from birth since this practice lowered the income tax.

Each partner was expected to work in the company. Family members did not receive salaries, and no formal differentiation was made according to how hard they worked. For many years Hans, Paul, and Ernst were too young to work for the firm, yet they received their portion. Alfred's son Max, who was working full time, resented this arrangement, a resentment furthered by the fact that, as his father had two sons, he received a smaller share than Paul. Rudolf eventually acknowledged and adjusted the payments. There was evidently a tension between the ideal of working for "the family" and earning for oneself.

Hans described the situation somewhat differently. He confirmed the boys became partners at birth. On the books, they each received part of the profit. But it stayed on the books; they weren't paid out. Hans received a portion of Alfred's share. His older brother Max did receive a larger amount because he started working for the firm earlier. The proportions were set every year and not based on a fixed share. Rudolf received the largest amount, because he worked the most, and Alfred somewhat less, with Benno's sons receiving less again, based on a distinction between working and non-working partners. Hans said this formula didn't create friction until after the war.

Hans explained that if it hadn't been for the war, the firm would soon have had to be completely reorganized as a "limited" company with shares and stockholders, paid management on salary, and a board of directors deciding on dividends to pay annually to stockholders. This restructuring never took place. During and after the war, the assets were simply those they had taken out of the country. These were largely in Rudolf's hands, and until his death he decided who received how much. As one granddaughter put it, she didn't know how Rudolf handled or divided the money, but "he was the one who made it and he was the one who brought it out."

At some point the situation shifted from one of annual distribution to full division. Paul and Helene as Rudolf's children were the main heirs. Hans said that he and Max accepted the formula, but Benno's sons, Fritz and Ernst, may have complained. Max and Hans also drew on a trust that was managed from Alfred's death by Marianne.

Grete's inheritance was tied up in the house in Brno, so she had less financial claim than her brothers or cousins. Until the reunion in 2017 I did not know that some people thought Grete might have received more than her share. How, they asked, were she and Fritz Tugendhat able to build another beautiful house (though not as luxurious) in St. Gallen in the 1950s? Everyone knew that Fritz was not a good businessman and unlikely to have the means. Who then provided the capital? Presumably it was partly financed by Marianne. It was clear that after Alfred died she would live with Grete, and she had her own suite that was built into the house.[7]

Rudolf also created a trust fund for needy relatives who, after his death, could apply to the trustees for assistance. Among others, he had in mind the descendants of his sister Eveline. Ellen Pollak showed me a letter from her father John dated 1983 that included a note from his father, Bruno, in turn, and a letter that Bruno had received in January 1954 from a General Trust in Zurich that was handling Rudolf's will. They wrote that Rudolf had "formed a trust during his lifetime, with the purpose of caring for a large circle of members of the family." Among the beneficiaries listed were Bruno and his wife and three sons. The advisors managed the fund and could determine whether and how much support to offer. The letter continued: "Should an emergency force you to take advantage of the trust, we ask you kindly to turn to us." John Pollak added that he hoped "no such emergencies will ever occur that any of us will have to revert to this trust," and he indicated that Paul Löw-Beer was then the family trustee. Ellen's brother Roger once met with Paul's successor, Peter Löw-Beer, around 2005 on behalf of the widow of their uncle Bobby and received some assistance.

It is clear that Rudolf continued both to conceive of the family broadly and to keep some of the money centralized.

Adulthood

If the previous generation was faced with the task of fitting into the family and firm and the expectations of the patriarch, the generation of double cousins was more concerned about emerging from it. While experiencing great family pressure they also had somewhat more individual autonomy than the previous one, which was enhanced by the spirit of modernism and the diverse intellectual, aesthetic, and political movements that were swirling in the interwar period. The cultural focus shifted accordingly from Vienna to Berlin, where, as young adults, Helene, Grete, and Paul each independently spent some time. There were greater possibilities and expectations for discovering oneself. For some, this new focus was expressed as coming to terms with class and inequality, for others with what they saw as a kind of authentic expression of being.

Three of the cousins developed communist leanings; however, no one spoke to me about the crash of 1929 or the effects of mass inflation and unemployment. But then, I did not think to ask.

The double cousins shared a common social background and historical circumstances as well as an intense family identification. Yet for reasons of character and contingency (sibling order, gender, a parent dying young or living long), they also diverged. Each cousin pursued their individual lives with family ideals and expectations in mind. They looked at one another to see what they each were making of themselves. There was identification and mirroring but also competition and some deliberate turning away. The regard was evaluative, judgmental: *You have money, intelligence, and ability; what will you do with it?* This thought was less with respect to the others, than a directive to the self: *What can I do with the opportunity I have been given?* And later, *what can I do in the face of flight and rebuilding a world elsewhere?* People were expected to make the most of themselves; some were lauded, others scorned; some were complacent, some intrepid, some anxious.

The references could be quite personal. Hans and Paul maintained a deep lifelong friendship. But they, along with Ernst, all very close in age, were also competitive, as manifest on the tennis court. At a family reunion in Kärnten (southern Austria) in 1983, Hans and his wife Edith picked up Jackie and me from the train station. As Hans drove fast and aggressively over the mountain roads to the hotel, Edith remarked that he always became more macho around his family. There was a sense that everyone had to strive to be better than the others, and the competition was stiff.

Each cousin dealt with their legacy in their own way. I offer brief sketches of six of them here. Rudolf's son Paul is the subject of chapter 9 and Grete of the following onés. I regret that I cannot give everyone equal attention.

Helene (1908–80) was older than Paul by two years, and the siblings were close their whole lives. Helene described a happy childhood, but Paul told me that she had suffered a good deal, especially from her father's disinterest. Neither parent showed much physical affection, and a loving nanny was replaced by a standoffish one who preferred him and treated Helene badly. Paul described Helene as a gifted child, "irascible, funny, insanely tall, and fat. At age 12 she weighed over sixty kilos, but in puberty that changed, and she became lean." Indeed, she developed an unhealthy focus on food and dieting that lasted throughout her life.

Of all the cousins, Helene was initially the most independent. She attended university in Vienna, earning a PhD in psychology under Charlotte and Karl Bühler, and published a book on the psychology of foster mothers and foster children. Moving to Berlin, she researched and co-authored a book on the treatment of children with disabilities.[8] Later, she did a degree in occupational therapy. Paul described her mind as analytic and logical.

In Berlin Helene married, and not just outside the small community of Jewish industrialists. Kakutaro (Kusi) Inoue (c. 1900–67) was a Japanese student and journalist who also worked for the Japanese chamber of commerce in Berlin and may have served as translator for a Japanese man who was getting Jews visas. Rudolf took a great liking to him. The marriage was a good one. Helene told Paul that the cultural differences were irrelevant and that she always knew what Kusi was thinking, much as she had with Paul.

Her daughter Eva said that "Helene belonged to a communist cell in Berlin and once participated in a protest which was fired upon and which terrified her. She headed a youth group ages 7–10, which included both Jewish and non-Jewish children, some devastatingly impoverished. She had two aliases, first Hilde and later Erika. She applied for a party card, but it never arrived, so technically she was never a member of the Communist Party. [Later] in England she found homes for refugees and lectured on what was going on in Germany ... [F]earful by nature, this demonstrated her degree of conviction, her 'agape' and finally her courage." Kusi's activism was kept secret.[9]

Max (1902–54) and Hans (1911–93) were the sons of Alfred and Marianne. As the oldest of the double cousins, much was expected of Max. He and his sister Grete (a year younger) were the best in their respective classes, yet, as Marianne wrote, "when Max came home with a report card full of 'excellent,' except in gym – only 'good,' instead of praising him for his accomplishments, his father berated him." Later Hans felt the pressure as well. Hans said of himself: "I was like a Spartan." He said that he had a very strong Protestant [sic] work ethic and punished himself to study. He needed to be excellent. "If the family is so prominent, I have to be better than everyone else; how else to justify our position?" At school, they asked: "Are you the stupidest of the Löw-Beers?" The pressure to work hard was even stronger within the family. Hans recalled how one day, when his father discovered him lounging on a sofa, Alfred said: "Take your hands out of my pockets!"

Max was sent at age eighteen as an apprentice to a woollen mill in Bradford, Yorkshire. On his return, he managed the factory at Svitávka.[10] He married Edith Dub (Dubová, Czech for "oak"; 1904–88), said by their daughter Margaret to have been "the most beautiful woman of the Jewish community in Brno." They went on honeymoon to Egypt and began married life in the Kleine Villa in Svitávka, where Edith quickly had to learn to manage a household and servants, and to serve as a kind of lady bountiful in the community. Margaret was born in 1928 and Frank (František) in 1931.

In a two-hour oral history recorded by the Vancouver Jewish Historical Society, from which I draw extensively,[11] Margaret remembered "everything as just idyllic." Max went to the factory in the morning, came home for lunch prepared by their cook, returned to the factory around 2:00, and came home again for dinner. On weekend expeditions they picked flowers, berries, or mushrooms and in winter went skiing. Max and Edith often went on holidays, leaving the children in the care of their grandmothers in Brno. Margaret's childhood in Svitávka was less constricted than that of her father. She went to the local Czech school and had friends in the village, with one of whom she continued to correspond throughout her life.

Margaret said the family had no idea what was going to happen to them. She was not conscious of being Jewish, and no one at that time was practising. Edith and her brother were "very good looking, both non-Jewish looking." Edith was upset that Margaret looked like Max and tried pressing on her nose so it wouldn't be hooked. That was "probably anti-semitic," admitted Margaret.

Max himself felt under-recognized. He resented having to work in the factory and live in a house belonging to the firm, as well as the fact that he was not sent to university like Hans and his cousins. Among other things, it meant he was less exposed to political ideas and perhaps explains why he appeared less socially engaged than Hans or Paul.

Where Max was said to be unhappy and neurotic, Hans was described as a "golden youth," and he told me that his father admired his success with women. Growing up, he had to light Alfred's cigarettes. But while his father "looked like a general and tried to behave like one ... it was all show. In reality he was a soft person" and soon ceased to have authority over Hans. Hans was, however, afraid of Rudolf, whom he described as having "absolute authority." Rudolf decided what his son and nephews should study. Hans was sent to learn chemical engineering. Rudolf decided that Hans should work for the firm in cement and sugar, whereas he would have preferred to conduct research outside the firm.[12]

Hans came of age attuned to the social and political realities of the times. In the new republic, the issues were in the first place ethnolinguistic. Hans was sometimes attacked by Czech-speaking boys on the way to school. When stopped by a policeman, you had to say that Dvořzák was a better composer than Beethoven. Hans was conscripted into the Czechoslovakian army, an event his mother called a "disaster." Rudolf declared he was performing a sacrifice on behalf of the entire family. Hans minded less; he became proficient in Czech and later told his daughter that the army taught him discipline and hardship.

Hans had a bar mitzvah; the rabbi was his teacher in school. Otherwise there were no religious observances in the family, no Jewish holidays or traditions. Only on Yom Kippur his father didn't go to work. They celebrated Christian holidays. Hans called his cultural milieu German; that was the language in which Kafka and Brod wrote. The wealthy Jews were tied up in German-speaking society, and he never heard Yiddish spoken. Alfred forced him to go to a German athletic association. The difficulty lay not in being Jewish – Hans said he experienced no anti-semitism at school – but in being so rich. They were "one of the three wealthiest families in

Czechoslovakia." Hans played in a German tennis club, most of whose members were Jewish, against the explicitly Jewish Hakoa and Maccabi clubs. Of his high school class almost half were Jewish, and they came from all social classes. Most of them were gassed.

Hans pursued his higher education in Brno, studying as an undergraduate at a German-speaking university and for his doctorate at the Czech-speaking Polytechnic. There were many Jewish students from Romania, Hungary, and Poland, places where Jewish entry to university was restricted (*numerus clausus*). In the chemistry labs, there was strict separation of students from the "far east" from those of the "homeland," in effect, anti-semitism. Hans tried to break through this prejudice and insisted on working with the Jews, although he was classified with the Czechs. He met a Polish student, Srul Bernstein, who taught him about Jewish life, and they became lifelong friends. As a result, he came to identify with Jewish causes more than did his siblings, although, like the rest of the family, he did not consider Zionism a serious option.

Hans was member of a liberal student organization in university. There were Nazi groups and Zionist ones as well. Like his age-mate, close friend, and double cousin Paul, Hans moved to the left and came to consider himself a communist, though he never joined the Party. Nor did he tell his parents that Srul was a communist organizer when he found him a job in the firm. After the war Srul settled in Poland but became disillusioned and moved to Israel. He and Hans visited each other several times between Israel and Canada.

Hans offered a picture of the business shortly before the war. He estimated there were some 2,000 to 3,000 employees in the woollen factory in Sagan and 900 in the Czechoslovakian factories. Paul thought perhaps 300 of these were in Svitávka, where in the last years Max introduced spinning from virgin wool, imported mainly from Australia. In Brünn there was the finishing plant, where they treated the surface of the cloth with chemicals to give it toughness and sheen. The dye plant was in Svitávka. Hans described the technology as simple. The textiles were marketed from Brno mainly within Austria and Czechoslovakia. There were no real exports except for sugar; some went to Italy and the rest to the home market. There were cartels for the cement and sugar; they held 14 per cent of shares of the cement market for Czechoslovakia.

The firm financed a school in Svitávka for the children of the workers. Marianne oversaw it for some time. The firm owned the workers' houses. There were unions in the textile plants but not in cement or sugar. The latter was seasonal work. The beets were weighed before washing. They estimated the percentage of dirt. If Hans ended up with more beets than he paid for, he got a bonus. The beets were contracted from small farmers as there were no big landowners in Czechoslovakia following Masaryk's land reform. Svitávka itself had very small farms, around an acre each, with a few cows. The family also owned a farm. Mr. Stanek, the farmer, brought Marianne eggs, milk, and pork sausages. Hans helped harvest potatoes and hay. The farmers used horses to transport produce to the train station. Svitávka was lucky to be on the Prague-Brno rail line.

Hans was sent to Denmark to buy machinery and to England to learn techniques in the cement industry.[13] In 1938 he returned to Czechoslovakia, just as people were leaving it. He was placed in charge of the sugar factory and stayed right to the end. They sold the factory to the Slovak fascist party, the Hlinka. An armed guard entered, greeted him with a salute, and told him to discharge all the Jews. Rudolf, Max, and Grete had already left, and only Hans and his parents remained. Hans helped them acquire false identity papers.

Marie, Fritz, and Ernst suffered from their father's early demise and their mother's preoccupation with her own health, Marie perhaps most of all. While Hansi was alive, Marie remained at her beck and call. Marie was born in 1904 in Svitávka; her profile on Geni.com does not list a date of death (a niece places it c. 1979), indicative of her marginality.

Fritz and Ernst could not have been more different from their sister. They had access to money from a young age, and they did what they liked with it. They dressed in hand-tailored suits and drove fast cars. Fritz (1906–76) was an aesthete. Sent by Rudolf to a textile manufacturing or design school in Leeds, he nevertheless resisted working in the firm. Instead, he became an expert in Chinese art. He accumulated a remarkable collection of Chinese lacquerware,

Figure 19. Fritz Löw-Beer in April 1929, aged 22. Reproduction from Monika Kopplin et al., eds., *Im Zeichen des Drachen: von der Schönheit chinesischer Lacke. Hommage an Fritz Löw-Beer* [*In the Sign of the Dragon: On the Beauty of Chinese Varnishes. Homage to Fritz Löw-Beer*] (Linden Museum Stuttgart, 2006), 12. Image accessed through Villa Tugendhat, http://www.tugendhat .eu/en

which he housed in a flat in the Grosse Villa redesigned for him in 1934 by Rudi Baumfeld and where he lived with his wife, Mimi Pollak (1915–2011) from Prague. Fritz paid meticulous attention to craftsmanship, and his collection achieved wide renown.[14]

Ernst (1911–2000) studied law in Prague and then became head of the administration, sales, and export department of the Löw-Beer firm. He commissioned a beautiful modern house in Brno, also designed by Baumfeld (and Norbert Schlesinger), in 1935, which he was able to inhabit for only two years.[15] Ernst lived there with his first wife, who had a son, known as Petit Choux.

Ernst and Fritz lived well but seemingly without foresight. They bought luxury cars up until the very end; Ernst's son Peter was shocked to see that the date of a bill of sale on a Bentley was that of the Anschluss: 15 March 1938. The cars left an impression. Seeing their last name when they checked into a hotel in Brno a decade later, in 1948, the clerk asked Hans and Edith: "Are you the people with the big Mercedes?"

How they all departed and started new lives elsewhere is the subject of the next chapter.

Departures and After

The family did not leave en masse. Each adult or couple had to secure papers enabling their respective departures. Exits were sudden or delayed, according to circumstances.

When the Germans entered Vienna in 1938, Rudolf happened to be in Moravia, and he did not return to Austria. In Vienna, Paul was forced to do humiliating things like clean the cellar of a café. It was left to him to help his mother leave. Elise had to be coaxed out of the apartment; among the things she packed were some beautiful old books. Paul needed a form saying they had paid the high exit fee and Jewish taxes, and then had to pay a bribe to have it confirmed. They drove to the bridge leading to the sugar factory directly on the Czech side of the Danube and were met by the director of the factory (which was still theirs) to help them clear the Austrian border; the Czechs had nothing against them. Meanwhile, Paul's wife Ala used her Lithuanian passport to cross into Czechoslovakia by train. Paul picked her up in Brno, and they drove to Svitávka, where Ala had never been before. A few days later, they took the train to Prague and from there a flight to England, which they reached by July. Hans Weiss helped them acquire visas.[1]

After selling the sugar factory and trying in vain to sell more, Rudolf left for Switzerland. He did not feel safe there, so he and Elise went on to England, where they spent the war. Rudolf travelled on stateless papers and wasn't happy when his Austrian citizenship was eventually returned. Paul explained: "He was a very cautious gentleman and found that statelessness is a good thing if you have a lot of money." Rudolf was too old to be interned, but Elise, in her late sixties, was incarcerated. She disliked the prison and wore long black gloves because she worried about germs, but she bloomed during her subsequent internment on the Isle of Man. She emerged bubbling, happier, and younger-looking than before. Paul's daughter Kitty repeated what has obviously become a family story: having coped for herself without Rudolf's overbearing presence, Elise emerged a new woman. She had to share a bed with a Nazi but declared she never slept better.

Rudolf and Elise moved to Lugano after the war, where the climate suited them and they felt more at home.[2] They lived out the rest of their lives in the Palais Hotel, with spells in the Kur Hotel in St. Moritz in the summers. Kitty recalled her childhood stays in St. Moritz, during which her father and grandfather talked continuously about the remaining factories in Austria. Rudolf remained full of anger at having lost the other factories, his life's work, and refused categorically ever to set foot in Austria again. Marianne also stayed in the Kur Hotel during the summers, and other relatives, including Marie (Benno's daughter), Helene, and Grete, visited. The adults played a card game called tarok.

Rudolf died a few years before Elise, after which, according to Fritz, "as his widow at the age of 80 ... she changed very surprisingly for the better," rather like the description of her release from the internment camp. I have a dim recollection of being taken as a young child (perhaps aged six) to visit her in the hotel in Lugano. Elise was short and slim, with a good deal of hair piled on top of her head, and greeted me affectionately. I was used to receiving chocolate from older female relatives (and have become addicted), but this was the first time I received a tube of coin-shaped Droste chocolates. On later reflection, it seems very surprising to receive Dutch chocolate in Switzerland. I think Elise must have been a good soul. It was astonishing to learn as an adult that she had suffered from syphilis. I cannot remember whether I also met Rudolf; more likely my memory comes from the photo where he sits with the magnificent ear trumpet that was supposed to assist his hearing (Figure 20).

Figure 20. Rudolf Löw-Beer, Lugano, c. 1940 or 1953. Photo courtesy Roger Pollak

On the day of the Anschluss in 1938 Max was in London on business. He phoned Edith to join him with the children immediately. They left without saying goodbye or telling guests that a scheduled party was cancelled. Escorted by Edith's parents, they drove to Prague, where they had never been before. Edith and the children boarded a plane and landed at Croydon. The children were put in boarding school, a rare coed one (Bedales, in Hampshire), which, Margaret said, became famous later when Princess Margaret's children attended. The move was tough. Not only were they uprooted, leaving everything familiar behind, including their language, but, as Margaret put it, in Czechoslovakia they had been "on top."

The break was not absolute. Max and Edith made trips to the continent, and the whole family went skiing in Davos in December, which was the last time Margaret saw her maternal grandparents. That summer they went again on holiday to Switzerland, where Max was treated for recurrent digestive and neurological [sic] problems and Edith took cooking classes as she realized she could no longer be assured of servants.

The family's permit to stay in England was limited, and they contacted various embassies for visas. They were lucky to be one of only a thousand families let into Canada, probably because Max showed he had $75,000 to start a textile factory. They arrived in Montreal, August 1939, a week before the war began. Hans, perhaps the last out of Czechoslovakia, followed shortly. Grete could not get into Canada.

In 1940 Max took his family across the country to Vancouver. There were already textile factories in eastern Canada, so the west promised greater opportunity. Exile and war did not stop the family from enjoying themselves. They got off the train in Banff and went by horseback, riding high enough up in the mountains that they could enjoy skiing in April.

Margaret remembered their arrival in Vancouver, sitting with huge quantities of luggage as her father went off to take an apartment at the Ritz Hotel. Margaret was twelve, Frank nine, Max thirty-eight, and Edith thirty-six. Vancouver was ideal as Max wanted to be as far from Europe as possible and because the climate enabled him to grow rhododendrons. In addition, he and Edith were anglophiles. They bought a beautiful home in Point Grey. Edith's mother was able to send their belongings from Svitávka, including home movies, before being sent to Theresienstadt and murdered in Auschwitz.

Max was unsuccessful at starting a business and became interested in growing fruit. One day in 1954, as he was pruning a pear tree, he fell and was paralyzed from the waist down. Despondent, he took his life, at the age of fifty-two. In truth, he had long been unhappy. He was jealous of his siblings who were more confident and better liked.[3] In addition, he thought he had not received his fair share of inheritance. Grete had received money to build the Tugendhat Villa, whereas Max had resided in the Kleine Villa that was property of the firm. Unlike Grete, he was a partner; that would have been his reward. But of course, the firm ended abruptly. He did receive money and invested it, and the family lived very comfortably. Margaret said: "I can't complain." But Max evidently did complain, regularly, in letters to his mother. At his insistence, Rudolf and Marianne gave him more money. Another

Kinship Diagram 10. Descendants of Max and Hans Löw-Beer

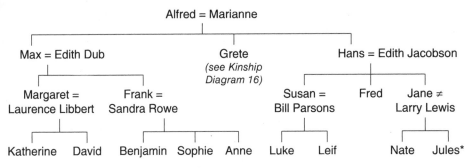

* Spouses of this generation and children in the next are not included.

cousin suggested that Hans and Grete may each have given Max portions of their inheritance as well.

Max and Edith needed the money to maintain their lifestyle. They were very conscious of their social class, as were their children. Edith collected Chinese ceramics (about which she had learned in Svitávka from Fritz) and engaged in voluntary activities concerned with the arts. Bizarrely, she donated some of her and Max's clothing to the Vancouver Museum. Frank went to Stanford, then trained as lawyer at Oxford and practised in Vancouver, where he ran for the Liberal Party in the federal election of 1974. One of his hobbies was playing polo. Margaret married an Oxford classmate of Frank's who came from an eastern European Jewish family. In 1975 she became a practising Jew in a liberal London synagogue, whose rabbis, as Margaret characteristically put it, had "world-class credentials."

There is a line in Frank's memoir of childhood written in 1962 where he recalls his sister "as that same serious and straight little girl I see even now when she concentrates over an investment portfolio much as she used to over a poem she was memorizing."[4] Their wealth and interests could not have been more different from ours in Montreal. If they looked down on us, we had our own, reverse snobbery and were both titillated and appalled by the polo playing. The affectations are now over. Their children have grown to be very nice and unassuming people. Having survived the deaths of her father, brother, and two husbands, Margaret lived "with great vigour and determination," as her children put it in an email announcing her death in Vancouver in October 2020. Margaret had been among the family members most interested and helpful in seeing an accurate family history produced.

Hans remained in Montreal, where he and his wife Edith and their three children Susan, Fred, and Jane became a significant part of my life.[5] They helped my mother when she arrived, and we followed them to the same suburb. I knew Hans as Uncle John. Edith confusingly shared the same name as Max's wife; both were Edith Löw-Beer. We referred to them respectively as Edith-from-Vancouver and Aunt Edith. The two women were very different. Edith-from-Vancouver was part of the European world, whereas Aunt Edith really was from Montreal, born and raised there. Although of Jewish background, she and Hans became practising Unitarians. Unitarianism afforded an open approach, one that transcended rather than negated Jewish identity.[6]

Breezily at home and confident in Canada in a way the rest of us were not, Edith was looked down upon by some family members for not speaking German. She was often vague and impressionistic – in a family that was so good with language and valued facts and clarity. But Edith wore her wealth lightly and unpretentiously, and was an extremely warm, charming, and authentic person. In these respects she was similar to, and modelled herself after, Marianne. She was an excellent cook and hostess, and like many women, engaged actively in "kinship work," keeping a benevolent eye on us and maintaining connections with all the scattered relatives. I remember her cheerful honk and wave from the car after she deposited groceries on our front porch during three months of imposed quarantine when my brothers and I successively had scarlet fever. Edith became a beloved centre of gravity; her eightieth and ninetieth birthdays in Montreal were major events, with family members flying in from Europe. In later life, she became a philanthropist and engaged in various civic causes.

Hans explained that Rudolf had remained in charge of the firm until the last minute. After the war he administered the family investments from Lugano; no one would make a financial decision without speaking to Rudolf first. Yet Hans found himself in Montreal with no advice from anyone and had to make decisions on his own. He received some financial help but wasn't dependent on Rudolf. Later, he consulted regularly with Marianne and advised her on investments.

Hans said he always looked down on selling. Only producing had prestige; it was honourable to create something, while retail was beneath them. To justify his admission to Canada he was expected to start a business and help the war effort. He began a factory in the small town of Granby, making wooden propellers and trainer planes for the military, and was proud of his ability to shift production to children's furniture and canvas deck chairs after the war.[7] Hans was practical and adjusted well to circumstances. In 1948, while visiting Czechoslovakia to arrange Alfred's reburial, he got word that the factory had burned down. After much agonized decision, because he wanted to be his own boss, he joined his father-in-law's office equipment company. He took it over in 1953.

The need to prove himself lasted; Hans attributed the stroke he suffered in the late 1980s to the fact that he had pushed himself so hard all his life. I recall my father remarking after a dinner at their house how glad he was not to be in business and have the worries and responsibility Hans had expressed at the table. And yet his Canadian business was very successful. In the end he made a large fortune through retail. At the time he spoke with me, he had some 1,800 people working under him and declared that Rudolf would not have had the personal skills to run such an organization. Hans tried to be progressive and felt torn between being the owner and boss and wishing equality for the workers. He taught his children that with money comes responsibility to look out for others. On retirement Hans sold the firm and established a charitable foundation that Edith and their daughters continued to manage after his death.

※

I assume Marie spent the war in England; afterwards she settled near Rudolf and Elise, where her main companion was her dog, Dino. Fritz describes her "alone in a little house in Lugano," overlooking the lake and reached by funicular. She lived independently and presumably happily in her own lights and was hospitable to nephews and nieces. Marie was disparaged by the rest of the family as tedious and eccentric. She was overly concerned with her health, practising yoga and eating yoghurt before they became fashionable. I remember her visiting in St. Gallen and being merely tolerated as she eagerly tried to be part of things. I only ever heard one unqualifiedly positive remark about her, and that was from an in-law who said she was the only genuinely nice person among the Löw-Beers.

On Max's departure, Fritz was in charge of the factory in Svitávka for the following year. Together with Mimi and Ernst, Fritz escaped by train 24 March 1939 for England. Ernst was accompanied by Maritza, remembered as blonde, made-up, and bejeweled. Maritza declined to cross the Atlantic, and so together with Fritz and Mimi, Ernst boarded the SS *Athenia* for Montreal. The next day, 3 September, only hours after England declared war, the *Athenia* was torpedoed by a German submarine. Ninety-eight passengers and nineteen crew members died, but the three survived, albeit in separate lifeboats.[8] Apparently, the purser made off with the family jewels, but safely reunited, they boarded the next boat to Montreal.

In the lifeboat of the *Athenia* Ernst swore to himself that if he survived he would forget his past life and start over. In Montreal, looking for a place to stay, he knocked on a door that was opened by a young woman of anglophone Protestant background. He and Ann Lecky eloped, and she was disowned by her parents for marrying a Jew. Fritz and Ernst and their wives managed to get papers to the United States and moved to New York, where they were naturalized in 1946. They may have bribed a state senator for the papers.

Ernst's law degree having gone down with the *Athenia*, and being a financial whiz, he became a successful broker on the New York Stock Exchange. Ann and Ernst had three children, Joan, Peter, and Margot. At Ann's request they simplified their last name to Lowber. Ernst was described as a snob. Once, the family travelled to Europe and drove to Vienna in their huge white and red Chrysler that horrified the Europeans and embarrassed Joan.

Fritz managed to have his Chinese collection shipped from a museum in Amsterdam where it had been on display. And Mimi's mother was able to send their furniture from Svitávka to New York before she herself was deported and murdered in Auschwitz. Mimi and Fritz had two children, Anthony and John. Mimi earned her MD in Rome, where she and Fritz lived from 1952 to 1962. On return to New York, she became a psychoanalyst. Fritz himself never worked, except for a period as a dealer in Chinese art in New York until the Chinese government stopped the flow of artefacts.

Fritz declared he had been frightened of emigration and, as John said of his father, "in some sense he never truly adapted to the reality of life in the United States, or in Italy ... He remained fixed on the past." This perspective is perhaps evident in the letters I have drawn on. Fritz also maintained a long correspondence with Grete about art. Dani described Fritz as a pure formalist, uninterested in either the representational content or the context of a given work. Grete didn't agree with his views but found them interesting; they shared a deep appreciation for quality. Fritz's approach to art is indicated by a recollection of Hans's daughter Susan. Fritz took her to the Met and spent the entire afternoon concentrating on a single painting (a Breughel), telling her never to look at more than one piece per visit to a museum.

I don't recall meeting Fritz or Ernst, though Ernst's daughter Joan remembers a visit we made to New York when I was very young. My mother and Ann liked each other very much, and Ann visited us on her trips to Montreal once she had reconciled with her parents. I recall my mother saying with awe that a blouse Ann purchased cost more than our family budget for a week. Fritz gave my mother a wedding present of a Chinese vase.

Neither brother's marriage lasted. Mimi divorced Fritz to marry another psychoanalyst. With his second wife, Jeanine, Fritz visited Grete in Switzerland. When served the classic and absolutely delicious family dish of apricot dumplings (*Marillenknödel*), Jeanine declined, memorably remarking: "*On ne mange pas des boules avec des fruits dedans*." Marianne never forgave her. On Fritz's death Jeanine sold most of his collection to the Linden Museum in Stuttgart, which subsequently held a special exhibition on "the beauty

Kinship Diagram 11. Descendants of Benno and Hansi

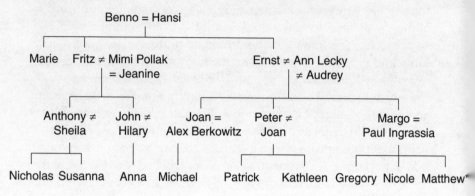

* Spouses and children of this generation have not been included.

of Chinese varnishes" to commemorate the hundredth anniversary of his birth.[9]

Ernst married, quite literally, the girl next door. Audrey was roundly denounced by the family as a gold-digger and derided for her crass behaviour. Ernst's children despised her. On a visit to Vienna Audrey insisted on staying at "the best hotel." When they dined one evening at a different hotel, she pouted because it could not be the best. She flashed her ring and bragged she had wanted a big diamond or none at all. Such vulgarity astonished the Europeans. Audrey walked out on Ernst when he grew decrepit, taking half his fortune. Ernst too was materialistic. Joan recalled that "when he died, I had to dispose of c. 10 pairs of custom hand-made shoes [and] I don't know how many suits. In his later years I had to write out his bills. He had a bill for $1,000 from Nordstroms. I asked him what he had bought for $1,000. He said socks – a dozen silk and 2 dozen cashmere!"

Fortuitously trapped in Cambridge, Massachusetts, during the course of an ice storm in 2018, I received hospitality from both Johnny and Peter, sons respectively of Fritz and Ernst, and first cousins to one another. I had first met them at the family reunion in Brno the year before. They remarked how their fathers had remained attached to Europe. Ernst periodically showed his children the album of professional photos of his house in Brno, proudly declaring it the first house in central Europe with air conditioning. Ernst made a good deal of money in New York, while Johnny said of his immediate family that they were not rich. This view is certainly relative: Fritz didn't work, was able to send Johnny to private school, and had a flat overlooking Central Park. A cousin recalled it as gloomy with cabinets full of jade artefacts.

Sons and daughters identify with their parents but also differentiate themselves. Where Fritz was an aesthete, his son Anthony was fascinated with finance. Given stocks as a boy, Anthony began to play the market and quickly apprenticed himself to his uncle Ernst. After a career as an investment banker, Tony's retirement project is rescuing pit bulls. By contrast, Ernst's son Peter spent one summer on the stock exchange and despised it. In midlife he quit a job in computers to drive a taxi part time and the rest of the time work pro bono in support of undocumented immigrants. Peter's sisters likewise are down to earth. Johnny was briefly an academic sociologist and then went into public interest law. He has his father's love of sports cars, but is a much softer and more engaged person than I imagine Fritz was. His Brooklyn brownstone is filled with books and art as well as furniture rescued from Svitávka.

The members of my family are nothing if not judgmental. While the brothers had been fond of each other, Ernst looked down on Fritz for not working, while Fritz looked down on Ernst for working in finance. Meanwhile, both of them continued to wear hand-tailored clothing. By contrast, Helene was ascetic. Paul was embarrassed by his materialistic New York cousins and made gentle fun of them, but he welcomed them warmly when they visited Vienna and showed off their success. Despite enormous differences in outlook, as Paul's daughter told me, "the family feeling was very, very strong."

Helene and Kusi left for London in the early 1930s, although Helene returned periodically to Berlin. They found themselves in England at the beginning of the war. Considering their options, the couple decided to move to Japan. They were en route via the Panama Canal when Japan joined the axis and the canal was closed. The ship docked in Florida, and somehow they got into the United States. Helene had stayed in touch with Gerti Weiss. Her best option was a student visa, and so she asked Gerti's husband, Kurt Lewin, the famous psychologist, who had acquired a position at the University of Iowa, to register her there. She thought that, as at a European university, all you had to do was enrol; you didn't have to show up for classes. She went to New York to help Kusi who was interned on Ellis Island and was surprised to receive a phone call from Kurt telling her that Iowa had expelled her on the grounds of absence. From Montreal Hans put up the bail for Kusi's release, and Helene enrolled at New York University. An irony is that my mother had intended to study with Kurt Lewin, her goal equally derailed by Pearl Harbor. Hanna and Helene had similar interests and were very fond of one another.

Helene and Kusi settled in New York. Kusi worked as a correspondent for *Asahi Shimbun*, a major Japanese newspaper, and established a newspaper for the local Japanese community. A strange thing then transpired. Helene was very thin and had stopped menstruating at age sixteen or seventeen, a fact Paul attributed to the bad psychological treatment she had received as a child, but due more directly to radical diets and anorexia. She was told that she could not bear children. In her mid-thirties she began psychoanalysis; suddenly, she began to menstruate, and she became pregnant, giving birth successively to two healthy girls, Eva and Joan. Both daughters later trained in psychotherapy; Joan says she is – quite literally – a child of psychoanalysis.

The family left New York abruptly for Switzerland in 1957 because Helene couldn't bear being questioned by the FBI about communist connections. The girls remember being pulled from summer camp. They went to St. Gallen, where Grete and Fritz had returned in 1950. The family rented a tiny apartment two floors above a bakery. The girls envied Grete's expansive new house. Joan told me she loved that house, as did I. After six months they relocated to Geneva, where Kusi had better opportunities than in a provincial city like St. Gallen. There were visits between the cousins. Helene was exceptionally fond of Grete, and the feeling was reciprocated. But Marianne, who loved to eat, took Helene's reluctance to do so as a provocation.

There are many ways that people who are born with money can respond to it. They can live well and enjoy their wealth, as Marianne did. They can save, invest, exhibit generosity, or spend excessively and flaunt their privilege. Or they can respond to it with disquiet and even guilt. Both Paul and Helene were concerned that their privileged position in life did not come directly from their own merit. They responded by trying to act in the world for greater justice. Helene also withheld things from herself.

Helene was distinctly, one could almost say actively, uninterested in money. The only money she spent on herself was for psychoanalysis. She was completely unmaterialistic, a trait perhaps she took from her mother. The family lived very simply; in both Washington Heights and Geneva they inhabited small apartments, with no original art on the walls or even a set of silver cutlery. But Kusi invested their money well, and at some moments they drew on it. Eva once asked her mother for a very expensive silk raincoat. When Eva told her the price, Helene leaned over and announced she was going to faint. But then she said: "Well, since I didn't faint, you can have it." Helene and Kusi were each described as gentle, and they gave their daughters a good deal of freedom. Money was spent on the girls' education and trips, including ski holidays. They generously supported Kusi's family, in difficult straits in Japan after the war. Once they went to Japan and travelled first class.

Although Helene was the first Löw-Beer woman to gain a PhD and publish books, she never worked full time. Paul said she was too modest to build an academic career. Her daughters felt that not all family members credited her achievements. She volunteered eight-hour days as an occupational therapist at a hospital in New York, and in Geneva she belonged to a charitable organization called *Les Filles d'Esther*, visiting Jewish psychiatric patients at Bel Air Hospital. Having money, she refused to take a paid job that she said could go to someone who needed it. Helene tried to eat organic, whole grains, vegetables, and no sugar, but as she aged, and especially after Kusi died, she became very frail and possibly malnourished because her body was unable to assimilate nutrients. Osteoporosis and lung problems resulted from the regimes of fasting and detoxification to which she once subscribed; she suffered some twenty bone fractures before she died.

Eva and Joan are only a few years older than me, but of my mother's generation. They were closely attached to Paul and Ala as well as to their parents. Joan told me that while she was growing up, "family" meant her nuclear family plus Paul and Ala. They were all too conscious of family values. Eva earned a PhD in order, she said, only partly in jest, to show the family how easy it was. She left a tenure stream position in classics at UCLA to train horses, a love of hers since childhood. Joan became an opera singer and later a child psychotherapist in Manhattan. Both rebelled against their mother's austerity. Having grown up in small apartments where the neighbours complained of noise, Eva moved to Connecticut where she could have a large house and her own horse.

An Ending

Alfred and Marianne stayed in Czechoslovakia until all members of the younger generation had left. As a strongly pro-German liberal and once head of the German Liberal Party in Brno, Alfred was convinced he would not be arrested when the Nazis invaded. But Alfred delayed his departure for other reasons as well, as intimated in the poignant letters sent by Marianne in the course of her own escape.

On 20 February 1939 Marianne writes from Brno to her son Max in England: "Only now in this difficult time, do we know how good we had it, how worry free we lived, or could have lived. The future for all of us is unknowable. I wish nothing so much as to live together with you and to remain in contact with your children. But …" At the same time, she manages to pack and send him a *Doboschtorte*[10] and a bottle of Slivovitz. Alfred adds a brief note, wishing Max a good life and mentioning the officials with whom he is trying to settle affairs.[11]

On 3 March, Marianne writes Max again, gently chiding him to temper his requests to Alfred. "He cannot cope with so much." Max evidently wants his and his wife Edith's personal possessions sent from Svitávka. Among the items is Edith's fur coat (which, Max's daughter Margaret strangely notes in her translation of the letters, was eventually donated to the Vancouver Museum). Marianne adds that Fritz Tugendhat was leaving the following day for Switzerland.

Marianne herself left Brno on the 15 March, driven by a chauffeur to Prague and managing to get past a German convoy they met en route. She had a false ID that her son Hans had purchased for her, and there was a family story about stuffing a ring into a sausage. The troops occupied Brno that same day, and Alfred was immediately arrested and placed in a cell in police headquarters. He stayed there from 7:15 am until 6 pm, when he was released. On 16 March his passport was confiscated, and he was forced to sign over his property to the Reich. From Switzerland, Alfred's daughter Grete spoke to Alfred by phone and found him very depressed and saying that he would remain at home. On 17 March Hitler paraded in Brno.

Grete wrote Max on 20 March: "Yesterday I could no longer get through, so phoned Richard Schwarz [Fritz's sister's husband, who with his young family were all subsequently murdered] who told me all relatives are OK and that he saw Papa that morning. Today at lunch time Mama telephoned me. She spoke as if I was about to give birth and that she might not be able to get there in time. Could I please send her a telegram when it happens? After much thought and advice from Ernst Wolff,[12] I have decided to send her the following telegram tomorrow: 'Gretl has a kidney infection urgent that you come – Fritz.' The business of my having a child could easily be ascertained, while I really *have* had a kidney infection recently, and might be able to get a doctor's certificate for this. Whether this is just mother's idea, or if she really knows that in such a case one is allowed to leave, I really don't know. Of course I have to leave it to her as to what she does with the telegram." Grete then disagrees with whatever plan her brother Max has suggested and urges him to "pursue contacts with August

Löw-Beer [in England]. He seems to have connections in the diplomatic world where he might have more success than you. In addition, he also knows the middlemen who can be bribed." She adds: "This problem with the parents really was preventable."

From St. Gallen on 4 April, Marianne wrote Rudolf: "I arrived here yesterday at 6 pm. The trip was made worse through my own fault. I set off with tickets that had expired and found myself in the train to Eger [on the German border] without money and without tickets. In Pilsen the conductor allowed me to extend the time – Hans had bought the tickets on March 16th in Prague but they had only a 10 day validity." This letter indicates she spent many days in Prague. "However, at the border the German conductor refused to recognize the extension and forced me to pay the section from Pilsen to Eger. I then went to the ticket office but got absolutely nowhere without money, even with the offer of my watch and wedding ring as forfeit. As it was Saturday [1 April] most shops were closed but I eventually found a jeweller who agreed to give me 20 marks for the watch and 10 for the ring. The ticket cost 29.10. I still had small change and so telegraphed to Gretl. As a result I received a telegram on the train from Dr. Ernst Wolff to say I should get out at Freiburg as every visa to enter Switzerland had been declared invalid and he would not be able to get me permission to enter until Sunday afternoon – when I arrived in Basel he was able to get permission to stay only 8 days. The next day he contacted the British Consul in Zurich and was informed that there was nothing doing about a visa for Britain. But the Consul in Basel was prepared to write to Prague to make some effort."

Marianne explained the delay: "In Prague I needed an exit visa and this was very difficult to obtain. Partly caused by the egoism of the children. Fritz insisted my passport be kept back until they were out of the country; this made for the delay and awkwardness for Alfred. He on the other hand insisted that I must have left before he would attempt to leave."

The man to whom Marianne submitted the passport for the exit visa returned it a week later without the visa. And then, "that evening, miraculously the man appeared with the visa without even having the passport. A week was lost through this delay. So here I am but in a terrible state of worry and fear, which you can probably tell from my handwriting, about Alfred ... It should never have got so far for Alfred to be in this position." She mentions other friends waiting in Prague for exit visas. Her contact in Prague, Dr. Sobotka, "behaved very well, he promised me faithfully that he would get Alfred out. But what can he do at the border? And who knows if Alfred was able to go to Prague, we know nothing here. Today we heard that the couple Stern committed suicide – she was a year younger than Gretl."

The same day Marianne wrote Max: "Dearest Children, Thank you for your kind words. I can't really be happy as long as I am in constant fear and worry about Alfred. I can therefore not give any indication what our intentions are ... It seems stupid to make plans before Alfred is out. On Friday, when I spoke to Dr. Sobotka for the last time, he said a Czechoslovak passport in Alfred's name would be available Saturday and so Alfred should have been able to travel on Monday, Tuesday at the latest. Something must have gone wrong ... The middleman who obtained the exit visa for me and the three others, and who had promised the passport, via a police employee, somehow failed and the passport didn't materialize. Every day that passes is terrible." She added that she had permission to stay in Switzerland for only eight days and mentioned the fate of others. "So many sad things have happened ... These days I cannot think of anything else except that Alfred will be saved. He is the hostage for the whole family." She closed saying: "Edith, I hope your clothes are with your mother, as nothing can be taken out of our house. She could send them on to you."

A week later she wrote Max: "You must certainly have been informed by Rudolf as to what has happened – Alfred must have been seized at the border." She mentions various contacts she has tried to help find him but says she wants nothing done "without discussing it first with Rudolf. Through trying to escape, Alfred's position has worsened. In any case, the political situation may bring war at any time – then he is there and I??" She was still without a visa for England and says: "Hans Weiss [Grete's ex-husband] suggests I fly without visa and he will wait with me in Croydon at the Home Office to get the visa there ... I am of the opinion that because of the huge loss of time Alfred's position will be much more difficult to solve. He has sacrificed himself for all the others ... Gretl [Grete] was active politically as well as philanthropically and so everything of theirs has been confiscated."[13]

Here is what was subsequently learned of Alfred's last days. On 17 March, he travelled to Prague, where he unknowingly overlapped with Marianne. He purchased false papers, with a passport under the name of Schweiger, and then headed by train towards Switzerland. He never arrived. On Marianne's behalf, Hans Weiss hired Sir Paul Dukes, a well-known British former secret agent, to find him. Dukes travelled to Germany and Bohemia to investigate, publishing his findings as an adventure story in *A Memoir of the Gestapo* (1940). Dukes learned that Schweiger's body had been discovered 11 April on the railroad tracks just outside the town of Mies (Czech Stříbro) on the train line between Prague and Nuremberg. On 23 June 1939 Dukes managed to have the corpse exhumed from the local cemetery and was able through the clothing to identify Alfred. The body had been run over by a train, but the question was whether Alfred had been shot first by the Gestapo or killed secretly by the people who had provided the false papers in order to conceal their own activities, or whether he had committed suicide. From Duke's reconstruction, the death was likely accidental. Alfred had been stopped at the border on 10 April. The passport was a good forgery but the exit visa a bad one, and he was instructed to spend the night while the local Gestapo contacted Prague to investigate. During the night he slipped out, planning to regain the train at a spot past the border officials. Exhausted and terrified, he seems to have fallen on the tracks, knocking himself unconscious, and was run over by the next train. The Gestapo had no idea of his true identity.

In 1948 Alfred's son Hans, who had managed his own escape around the same time, returned to rebury Alfred in the Jewish cemetery in Brno, where Alfred's parents Max and Pauline also lie.[14]

Years later a story surfaced (I heard it in 2018 from historian Jakub Pernes in Brno) that Alfred had committed suicide to draw the attention of the Gestapo away from his sons who were travelling on the same train. That story is certainly false, as Alfred's sons were not with him. But Pernes does not accept that Alfred's death was an accident. There was no bullet hole evident, yet he could have been shot before the train ran over him. Mr. Zoubek, the mayor of Svitávka in 2018, suggested that as Alfred was well known as one of the richest people in the country, perhaps he was the victim of a thief.

Fritz Löw-Beer writes: "So the L-B family really came to an end in 1939. It simply fell apart." The pieces relocated to London, Vancouver, Montreal, New York, Caracas, and eventually Lugano, St. Gallen, Geneva, and Vienna. But as already glimpsed, they reimagined and reconstituted themselves in new ways.

Chapter Nine

The Patriarch's Son

Paul exemplifies the Löw-Beer legacy, and his life merits telling in more depth. Paul (1910–2003) was the only son of the eldest son and destined to be the main heir, although he was eight years younger than his double cousin Max. Of the five male cousins Paul was perhaps the one least damaged by their upbringing, albeit the son of the patriarch himself. He was the warmest and also the one who could be said to have had the most continuous life, insofar as he returned to live in Vienna after the war and managed the few remaining factories on the Austrian side of the border. Nevertheless, his life was more complex than most. Paul and his wife Ala were active, ethically fine and upstanding people, but they kept two large secrets.

I did not know Paul well, but I interviewed him in 1988. He was very pleased to talk, a bit shy but eager once he got going, with a boyish grin that broke out often. He replied slowly, thinking first. In 2018 I spoke with his daughter Kitty and more briefly with his son Martin and grandson David. I also rely heavily on the master's thesis on Paul's life written by Traudl Schmidt for the University of Vienna in 2005.[1] Traudl is the wife of the brother of Kitty's ex-husband Arnold Schmidt, and she knew Paul for many years. She interviewed him extensively shortly before his death, when Paul was ninety-two. Therefore, I have more direct information about Paul than I do about his sister or their cousins. And after reading 100 pages, much of it in Paul's own words, I came away with a sense of what a full life his was.

Paul's personality was virtually the opposite of Rudolf's. Traudl Schmidt describes him as modest, calm, and having a real interest in people. Her characterization of a kind of whimsical irony rings true and brought to mind the expression on his face when he spoke to me. Here was a man capable of drawing from an accumulated experience of life and yet also open to new experience.

If Max's daughter Margaret enjoyed the feeling of being "on top" in interwar Czechoslovakia, and Hans felt the pressure of having to live up to it, Paul was embarrassed by the family's position. He was glad his mother chose to live in Vienna and raise him out of the limelight. Paul found Svitávka "awful" and not the idyll people claimed to remember. He felt guilty knowing that his father, in effect, owned the whole town. As children the cousins had no friends there, only each other. They would sometimes peer through the garden fence at the children on the other side, without shoes, in the dust. When he was young, his father brought him to work during the summer. In her memoir Helene says that at the age of eight Paul spent a few hours a day in the section where samples were woven and the following summer in the office. As a girl she was not taken. Paul hated it, both because the work seemed pointless and because he was treated as somehow special. He recalled being "deeply impressed how absolutely my father's behaviour was accepted. The distance he had from everyone was enormous." Rudolf, he said, was a good professional but also a complete authority. His commands were quickly passed down. He didn't like long phone conversations, and once he had said what he had to say, he would simply add "Finish" and end the call. "The class difference was embedded in the structure and consciousness of people like solid masonry." It bothered Paul deeply.

The ambivalence persisted. During our conversation in 1988 Paul said he was embarrassed to revisit Svitávka as an adult. He was afraid he would either be booted out – or else asked to buy up and revive the factory. Rudolf's interactions with the staff and workers made a lasting impression, which, Paul said, eventually had decisive consequences for his politics. His critique of capitalism evidently grew more from his distaste of these interpersonal relations than from the material exploitation of the workers.

Paul attended a Gymnasium in Vienna from 1920 to 1928. It was run by the Piarists, a Catholic order, but he referred to it as secular and federal. There were many Jews, the percentage rising at each grade, such that in the Matura (graduation) year they were in the majority. Paul described himself as conservative at the time, but he once organized a strike against an unfair maths teacher.

On weekends when Rudolf was in Vienna, he and Elise took Paul and Helene to the opera and theatre. Paul told Schmidt: "We had a strange financial arrangement in the family, one that hurt me because I never learned to handle money. I never got pocket money, but I lived with the awareness and the certainty that there was a lot of money. I could have money for anything I needed or wanted and was never denied anything. But I never actually asked for anything either. In elementary school I wore sailor suits and never a tie. There is a class photo of the Matura, where one student is in a shirt and no tie, and that was me, because my mother considered ties unhealthy."

Paul's relationship with Rudolf was complex. He told Schmidt: "I had the difficulties of being the son of a great father." He described his boyhood perception of Rudolf as "enormously domineering and impressive." He resented Rudolf and rebelled against him, and yet they were close. Paul told Schmidt: "He realized that I was not well suited for business, but that's not how the Oedipus complex works, and I went into business."

In fact Rudolf passed on to Paul what remained of the factories after the war. Apparently, the terms of his will were that the factories went to Paul and the money to Helene. But as Kitty said, he must have left "a little" money to Paul as well. It is possible that Paul borrowed from Helene when the business needed it. Paul's cousins also retained rights in the Austrian factories; Hans told me that he sold his part to Paul.

Paul is someone who was widely loved and admired by family members. He was said to have had an "extraordinary personality," to retain a "fantastic memory," to be "interested in everything." As his grandson David wrote, "Paul kept the family together. He was interested in people. And he knew a great detail about a lot of family members, what, with whom, and how they were doing, etc. In that sense, he really was the centre for our part of the family, and it has been difficult to connect ever since he is gone."[2] In 2000 Paul drew a large number of family to Vienna for the celebration of his ninetieth birthday, during which they went together on a visit to Svitávka.[3] I did not have the time or means to fly to Vienna, nor a strong enough attachment. But when I spoke with Paul in 1988, I liked him enormously. I recall Paul and Ala walking arm in arm, tall, thin, and elegant, a perfectly matched couple. They exuded warmth and intelligence. At the time we met, Paul said he continued to read current research in chemistry and was on his way to do business in Milwaukee. He expressed regret that his younger son Peter refused to learn chemistry but declared that Peter was taking over management of the business. Paul himself wanted time to write.

Paul loved botany from childhood. Rudolf declared it impractical but gave him a microscope, and Paul wrote a highly praised school paper that Kitty described as "almost a dissertation." Paul began studying botany at the University of Vienna in 1928, but at his father's request shifted to chemistry, which Rudolf anticipated would be useful for the factories. He graduated the first course in 1930 and went on to Humboldt University in Berlin. There, through three turbulent years, he engaged with two people who came to have a very strong influence throughout his life, his future wife Ala (1910–97) and his best friend Berti (Engelbert) Broda (1910–83).

Ala (Alice Rachel) Rabinovitch came from Lithuania. Her native language was Russian. Vilnius was a seat of Talmudic learning, but Ala's family were doctors, and she too studied medicine, once she overcame fainting at the sight of blood, and became a pediatrician. When Paul and Ala met, she was a Communist Party member and in love with a Russian man, Emanuel Margolis, who was recalled to Moscow. Ala's sister, Beate, actively prevented Ala from following him. Paul consoled Ala, which led to their relationship and, eventually, a happy marriage. Paul explained that he didn't have to ask Rudolf's permission; at that time people just lived together.

Paul and Berti first met as fellow chemistry students in Vienna. Berti had mixed Christian and Jewish Moravian roots but grew up Christian in Vienna. Berti's life is recounted in a compelling book by his son.[4] The book mentions Paul and Ala several times; later I will add one salient fact that is missing from it.

Paul became politicized during many discussions with Berti. He also took advantage of the large library of the Labour Association that was across the street from the family apartment in Vienna. He called the library the "turning point"; there he read Marxist literature, starting with the *Arbeiter-Zeitung* (*Workers' Paper*), the organ of Austrian social democracy, which was then very left-wing. He also had many conversations with his father. Paul argued that only under communism would workers take a real interest in their work, since it belonged to them, whereas Rudolf declared that such a system could subsist only under duress. Paul, son of the capitalist patriarch, became a communist. Rudolf, as I noted in chapter 5, feared the communists more than the Nazis. But he tolerated Paul's attraction. As Paul said, "my father had a problem – he liked me."

Communism was far from a political force in Austria at the time. Paul thought to himself: "Such a little sect doesn't interest me; I want to see what happens in the big world." The big world was Berlin. So he set off in the fall of 1930 to continue his studies in a setting where there was a large Communist Party. Berti went along, and they shared accommodation for a time. He described Berti as a strange person, someone who did not develop close personal friendships, though he did become Paul's best friend, and they both continued to study chemistry. Paul also found the cultural life of Berlin a huge attraction after "provincial" Vienna. "I was twenty years old and became a communist during my first year of study in Berlin. Pretty soon after my arrival I joined the KPD [Communist Party of Germany] even though I was a foreigner."

Paul participated in heated discussions and learned how to conduct factional infighting, but never joined violent clashes or street fighting. Above all he spent time with an agitprop group, *Das Rote Sprachrohr* (The Red Megaphone), led by Maxim Vallentin, who became director of the Gorky Theatre in the German Democratic Republic (GDR) after the war. "Because I was neither musical nor had an acting talent, I only played a little piano and accompanied a song every now and then, but I was a source of money for them, because I was a bit richer than the other members. The 'Red Megaphone' was the agitprop group of the Central Committee of the

KPD, one of the most interesting and artistically superior among the agitprop groups, of which there were at least five or six ... Maxim Vallentin was a completely obsessed director ... He made great artistic demands and rehearsed an incredible amount."[5]

Paul and Ala became part of a close-knit group of intensely debating and politically active students that included Ala's older sister Beate as well as Berti and his girlfriend and subsequent wife, Hilde. Hilde was a German Jew partly raised by a Christian family. Their activities came to the attention of the authorities. In May 1933, while working on their dissertations at the Institute of Physical Chemistry, Paul and Berti were abruptly arrested.[6] Berti appears to have been the leader of the Communist Students' Union in Berlin.[7] "We were taken to a general police prison, the so-called *Alex am Alexanderplatz*. It was a huge shock because of the atmosphere of fear that we experienced." The Gestapo interrogated and tortured people whom they suspected of being communists, but because Paul and Berti were foreigners, they escaped beating. "The interrogation was fruitless, and we were not forced to name anyone. I do not know what I would have said under torture, but I was not tortured ... The police prison was crowded. The veteran police officers there were decent to us, but again and again men were brought in and showed fellow prisoners their blue and bloody backs. They had been tortured by the Gestapo. In the fourteen days we were in prison, only a few were released, and many were sent to concentration camps. But we were Austrians and relatively well connected and that saved us from torture and concentration camp. Thanks to the intervention of my father, we were released after fourteen days and expelled from Germany."[8] What Paul does not recount here, but is part of family lore, is that he wouldn't leave prison unless Berti was freed as well. Rudolf, albeit furious, bailed out both of them.

Berti returned to Vienna, while Paul went to Prague "because," as he said, "I did not feel like going home." Paul loved Prague, where he continued his studies and received a doctor of engineering degree at the German University there in 1935. He extended his studies to a doctorate of philosophy in Vienna in 1952. As a foreigner Ala was not admitted to medical school in Prague, but she was able to continue in Würzburg, and she and Paul visited each other. Paul recalled that "once she was commissioned by the KPD to visit a certain family in Berlin to warn them. So she drove from Prague to Berlin, but as a good observer she noticed immediately that the people who stood around the given address did not look sympathetic. She turned back immediately. The family she should have warned had already been arrested, and the police were waiting for people like Ala to turn up. Her powers of observation often saved Ala in her political work."

In fall 1935 Paul returned to Vienna, where the Comintern instructed him to enter the family firm and take a leading position. He became director of the cellulose factory. "A short guest performance," he called it, since it lasted only until the Anschluss. Ala joined him in Vienna. As she told me in 1988, "I had the pleasure of fleeing Hitler twice" – first from Germany and later from Austria. She and Hilde completed their medical degrees, enduring uncomfortable conditions and anti-semitic harassment.[9] Paul "introduced Ala at home, and she became very friendly with my parents and was well received, especially by my father; he could be very charming with people whom he liked." In 1937 the Comintern instructed Paul and Ala to move from their simple apartment to a fancy one; Rudi Baumfeld, the same architect who worked for Paul's cousins Fritz and Ernst, designed the flat and the furniture.

Paul and Ala married in 1937 but kept it secret so as to retain her Lithuanian nationality. Ala's sister Beate, however, married in Austria precisely to gain citizenship. She had taken German citizenship on her first marriage but needed to get out of Germany. "Beate was an intense, adventurous woman and did some very dangerous things for the German Communist Party. She stayed in Germany long after most of her friends. One night she even got into the Ministry of Aviation and copied documents there. Another time, overnighting in a rented room, she discovered her landlady was the wife of a high Gestapo man and was able to peruse the documents he kept at home, thereby saving a number of people ... After the war, the German Communist Party contacted her in Vienna to suggest naming a street in Berlin after her ... Beate always told us a lot but often exaggerated so that you never knew what to believe."

Paul and Ala spent the war years in England. Kitty was born on 2 September 1939, the day after the war began. Ala's contractions started en route to Cambridge, where pregnant women were being evacuated from London. Cambridge was also the choice because the Brodas were there. Ala's mother was visiting from Lithuania for the birth, and she stayed on, thereby saving her life. Ala's father was shot in the Kovno ghetto in Kaunas, and many other members of her family were murdered. Rudolf and Elise settled in Baker Street, while Paul and Ala, with Ala's mother, moved to St. John's Wood in a little flat on the third floor of a house with many Jewish families. They were often evacuated; Kitty remembered bombardments and terrible noise.

Paul said that during the war they experienced the English at their best. "In the midst of the bombing they stayed disciplined, calm, and companionable. 'Have a cup of tea,' they would say. As a seafaring people, they had the comportment of crews of ships in need. None of us will ever forget that." But as "enemy aliens," the Austrian Jews struggled to acquire work permits. In 1942 Ala found employment as a doctor and Paul in a small pharmaceutical company.

In London they associated with the Austrian Centre, an organization to assist refugees and provide cultural activity, with a newspaper, music, theatre, and heated political debate over Austria's future. Paul contributed to the Free Austria Movement, gave a lecture about post-war reconstruction of Austria, and supported future Czech-Austrian cooperation. The Austrian Centre was known as a hub for communist activity, and both Paul and Ala came under observation. An item in the Public Records office reads:

Paul LOEW-BEER (1)/ Rachel Alice LOEW-BEER (2), aliases Paul LOW BEER/ Alice LOEW-BEER, Ala LOEW-BEER, Rachel Alice RABINOW-ITSCH: (1) Austrian (2) Russian/Austrian. Paul LOEW-BEER was an Austrian chemist and businessman who arrived in the UK as a refugee from Czechoslovakia and Austria in 1938. He had strong communist links in Austria in the 1920s and 1930s; and from 1940 to 1946 was actively involved and influential in a number of UK-based communist dominated or influenced Austrian migrant organisations. LOEW-BEER

returned to Austria in 1948. Despite his strong international communist links and prominence as a businessman and financier there is no
clear evidence in these files that he was ever a Soviet Intelligence agent.
These files contain few independent references to their joint subject,
Alice LOEW-BEER, a Doctor who evidently shared her husband's communist sympathies.[10]

In 1946 by plane, and in 1948 by boat when Kitty was eight,
the family travelled to New York to visit Paul's sister Helene and
Ala's sister Beate, who were each then living there. In 1948 they
stayed for three months, and Kitty was sent to school. She didn't
know what her father did all day and suspects in hindsight that
there might have been something secretive. Beate and her husband
Heine Spitz had certainly lied to immigrate in 1938, declaring they
were not and had never been communists. After Paul's death, Kitty
discovered that her parents had tried unsuccessfully to emigrate to
the United States as well.

Beate and Heine spent time in Albuquerque. Paul wrote: "The
heat there was good for Beate's severe rheumatism. Beate was a very
active member of the apparatus ... They drove around the region ...
Beate claimed to be studying Karl May [the popular German author
of Westerns]; much of *Winnetou* takes place in New Mexico and the
geographical descriptions were supposedly accurate. Why they did
that I did not know, probably as a camouflage ... Heini worked in
a hospital and had many contacts ... As they lived near Los Ala-
mos they were suspected of atomic espionage, probably rightly so.
Maybe they were used as couriers."

Subsequent to the second New York trip, Paul and Ala returned
to live permanently in Vienna. They bought a sloping former vineyard in Neuwaldegg, on the edge of town, from which it was easy
to go walking in the Vienna Woods. When Paul purchased it, the
property had two houses. The lower one was small and inhabited
by an elderly couple who had been Nazis involved in implementing aryanization. Paul let them stay until they died. Afterwards,
he enlarged and rebuilt the house; Kitty's daughter and her family now live in it. Paul and Ala moved into the upper house. In
2018 that house was inhabited by Kitty's son and his family. Kitty

herself lives in an architect-designed house that she and her former husband built at the top of the property. The houses are situated in a garden with fruit trees, fishpond, and swimming pool. The arrangement is reminiscent of Svitávka and the garden joining the Tugendhat and Löw-Beer Villas.

Despite a good offer from the pharmaceutical company in London and the possibility of British citizenship, Paul returned to Vienna to take responsibility for family business that remained on Austrian soil. The cellulose factory had been run by Swiss partners during the war and was returned to the family. It was just an empty shell, and Paul sold it in 1950. The textile factory in Fischamend, just outside Vienna, had once held their best spinning machines. At the end of the war the Nazis partially destroyed it, but Paul was able to produce textiles for a few more years. Paul bought out the shares of his male cousins. Hans said he was willing to sell because at the time Fischamend was in the Russian zone.

In 1951 Paul founded a chemicals company in Vienna, which developed complex organic compounds, and later he added the factory in Fischamend to it. They produced products ranging from naphthenic acids for detergents, Vitamin B, and rust protection for cars, making money on some products and losing it again on others.

Paul was probably deeply ambivalent as both a communist and a factory owner. When Martin was young, he came to his parents one night and asked his father how he could be both. Paul replied: "You are a clever boy." Martin's son David said that Paul tried to work it out through the way he organized his factory and the treatment of the workers. Moreover, he hired many communists, people who would have had difficulty finding work otherwise, and this policy helped him justify being an owner.

Schmidt calls Paul "a very generous, pragmatic, thoughtful man … [who] showed that a 'humane' capitalism in a company with engaged employees could be economically successful." Giving employees the chance to share or realize their ideas was more important than maximizing profits. "He led his operation in an almost patriarchal form and understood it as one big family with whom he had a particularly close relationship, for which he was responsible, and who repaid him with loyalty and love." She concludes provocatively that "his style of management probably did not differ very much from that of his father." In 1989 Paul sold the detergent department to Unilever and the rest of the company to the employees.

Ala worked full time as a physician. She had wanted a job in a hospital, but as Jews were still unwelcome, she worked for some thirty years as a pediatrician for foster children, inspecting a series of children's homes. Schmidt adds in a footnote that Paul and Ala often provided financial support and distributed fruit to the children. Later, Ala volunteered as a doctor in prisons. She never had a private practice.

Paul and Ala lived relatively modestly. They began post-war domestic life in Vienna with a cook, maid, and gardener, but cut back on servants over the years. After their death the contents of their house were estimated at 6,000 euros. They appreciated art but didn't purchase any. Paul supported many people, including some of Ala's kin in the United States and Lithuania, and a woman who ran a left-wing bookshop in Vienna. Paul was warm as well as generous. When his son Martin divorced, Paul took his grandson David on a trip to Copenhagen, just the two of them. Ala is described as a loving maternal figure by her nieces. Kitty, however, remarked that her mother "never had time for any of us." A daughter-in-law recalled that she could never sit through a family lunch without being called to the phone by someone in need, seemingly more concerned with those less fortunate than with her own family.

Beate and Heine returned to Austria and revoked their American citizenship just in time. They were denounced two weeks later by the double agent Boris Morros as Soviet spies. It was announced in the *New Austria*, 1 September 1957, that they currently lived "in Vienna in the house of an Austrian industrialist."

There was an additional reason for Paul's return to Vienna and to factory ownership – the Party told him to do so. This disclosure is the first secret. Paul was not simply a communist but also for a time an agent, albeit a minor one. The Party wanted like-minded people at all levels of society. And what better cover than that of a wealthy industrialist? His good friend Berti – who also resettled in Vienna – had been an active spy for the Soviets, linked to the Cambridge Five and passing on documents concerning developments in nuclear physics during the war and after.[11] Recently released KGB files indicate that men like Berti acted willingly and without financial compensation, out of a mixture of idealism and a rational thinking through of consequences. It was imperative that if the Americans had the bomb, the Russians had to have one too. They believed they were helping to maintain a balance of power and preventing the unilateral use of nuclear weapons, hence decreasing the chances of nuclear war. They also believed in the principles of communism.

The Cambridge Five included Kim Philby, Donald Maclean, Guy Burgess, Anthony Blunt, and John Cairncross. When Maclean defected in 1951, his American wife Melinda took their children to live in Geneva. Their sudden disappearance from Geneva in 1953 was widely reported in the press as a mystery and investigated by the police. They soon discovered Melinda living with her husband in Moscow but never found out how she got there.

In 1953 the KGB asked Paul to convince Melinda Maclean to join her husband and to pass her some money. "I did that, completely stupid, with money that they gave me. After detailed instruction, highly conspiratorial, I withdrew it from a bank in Switzerland. I came in a straw hat and dark glasses; if anyone looked suspicious, it was me. In any case, she got the money from me.

"The only thing we really did for the secret service was to organize their trip. First, we had to find Mrs. Maclean ... We had to inform her and get her consent to help her travel to Russia to her husband. It was hard to meet her, but Ala had an incredible memory and a lot of imagination. She had seen her picture, and she could figure people out. She learned that the children attended the International School in Geneva and that their mother always picked them up from school. So Ala went, recognized her immediately, and simply addressed her and informed her that she could leave then and there to join her husband; she just had to take the children by train and get off in Schwarzach – St. Veit in Austria. I would pick her up there. That actually worked: she got off the train, and I drove them in the Wachau to a specific place where a path goes down to the bank, and there was a car from the Russian secret service already waiting for them. The people were indignant because I was a little late; they were very nervous, for no good reason. The Macleans went off in the Russian car. She was a very nice woman with very sweet children. In this way I worked for the secret service."[12]

The next time the KGB asked Paul to do something he refused. Paul told Traudl Schmidt that even before they emigrated to England, he "wanted to stop working for the secret service, but it was not so easy." The Party had to give permission for everything, even to emigrate. "In the fifties, I still had contact with the KGB. At a certain point, I said to them, 'I don't want anymore, I want to say goodbye to this club,' and they said, 'Okay.' That probably went so easily because I was someone from whom they could not expect anything more; I had no public position and was not in any structure from which they could expect information. I never heard from them again. I did not think getting out would be so easy and was quite astonished and relieved. I suppose they were relieved too since they never had anything from me to report, and so had been disappointing their superiors. Otherwise, it would probably not have been so easy to extricate myself." In any case, Paul concluded, Vienna was no longer a centre of information or as full of spies as before. "For me, my farewell was painless. Likewise for Ala, although she was much more valuable because she was much more gifted, with that incredible personal memory."

In fact Ala had long-held doubts. By 1933 she knew from her former boyfriend Emanuel about the oppression in Russia, but she kept this information to herself, thinking it would have broken the relationship with Paul, who was then convinced about the cause.[13] Kitty remembered that during the Rosenberg trial, Ala said to her that "in other places terrible things are also happening." Emanuel had returned to the Soviet Union, where members of his family were subsequently killed. He survived; some twenty years later, he and his wife visited Paul and Ala in Vienna, where Ala declared he had become petty bourgeois.

Martin thinks his father left the Party in 1956. Paul was extremely upset at the revelations about Stalin, and Martin recollects Paul showing him books by Solzhenitsyn when they appeared. Paul himself said the events in Hungary weakened his attachment, "but they did not destroy my illusions. The real break came in 1968 with the events in Czechoslovakia, where everything in the world looked different – to me; not in reality, of course." In late life Paul acknowledged the Soviet Union had severely compromised communism, but he was also very pessimistic about capitalism and critical of neoliberalism.

Ala was present in 1939 when Hilde gave birth to her son, whom Hilde and Berti named Paul after Paul Löw-Beer.[14] The couple subsequently divorced, and Hilde later married Alan Nunn May, whom she met after his release from prison for espionage. Berti had known him before, but Paul Broda concludes that his mother's successive marriages to two spies were a coincidence. In 1956 Paul and Ala visited Hilde and Alan in England.

Berti became a distinguished molecular biologist and physical chemist at the University of Vienna. He fell out with the Party when he openly criticized Lysenko.[15] Berti was part of the family when Kitty and her brothers were growing up. He came often for meals, at least every Saturday.[16] In 1960 Berti wrote his son that Paul and Ala were the only people in Vienna with whom he felt he could really speak his mind.[17] Berti died in 1983.

Kitty reflected that because Rudolf had forced Paul into a certain career, it was important to him that each of his children should choose their own lives. Kitty gained her MD and a PhD in immunology, eventually becoming a practising and research-oriented psychoanalyst. Martin studied in Germany, partly under Habermas, and became a philosopher. Family members call him brilliant, a philosophical genius, and possessor of sarcastic wit. A German colleague described him as friendly, disorganized, and attractive to women because he appeared so serious. Martin taught in Berlin and Frankfurt, but he suffered from depression and later Parkinson's disease. Ironically, he said, the Parkinson's removed the depression, and his mood was never better. No longer able to earn

Kinship Diagram 12. Descendants of Rudolf and Elise

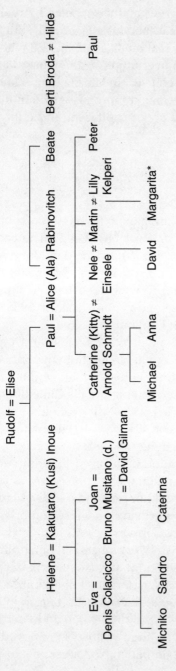

* Spouses and children of this generation have been omitted.

even the small amounts he had received from teaching, he was supported by Paul.

Peter was described as very likeable, funny, leftish, and intelligent. Paul thought Peter was best suited to managing the factory, and he became an executive. Peter was ambivalent and envious of Martin's intellectual achievements and the approval he received from Paul. Being good with money just didn't seem to count. Paul tried to compensate him: when they sold the factory, he put the money in Peter's name, with the understanding that Peter would share it with his siblings.

Ala died in 1997. Paul then revealed their second secret: Peter's biological father was Berti Broda. When Peter was young, they had consulted a psychoanalyst who advised them not to tell him. But throughout Peter's childhood something had seemed off, and Peter had wondered why Berti often wanted to do things with him. In retrospect, Kitty could also see that there had been something romantic between Ala and Berti. Evidently, Paul had accepted the relationship; Berti had been a fixture in the household.

This parentage was a secret that Berti also kept. Paul Broda depicts his father as lonely and longing for another child. In writing his book, Paul Broda drew on his parents' letters, and he spared nothing, not even their critical remarks about himself. It seems evident that he did not know he had another brother.

Peter did not take the revelation well; whether because of it or for another reason, he hid all the money over which he had legal control. Millions of euros disappeared, probably around ten million, though I heard speculation up to fifty million. The family had not lived lavishly, but they had been, as another cousin said of them, *very* rich. Martin and Kitty had been assured by Paul that there would be plenty of money, and they counted on it. Peter evidently thought that as the one who had worked in the firm, it should be his.

Peter's actions were completely unexpected; everyone who knew him was shocked. Paul tracked down Peter in London and asked him to reconsider. In response Peter nearly threw him down the stairs. Peter's actions are likely not only about the money itself but also about feeling betrayed and unacknowledged. His siblings sometimes run into him in Vienna, but he doesn't speak about his motives.

And so, that is the fate of the remaining Löw-Beer fortune, inaccessible to Rudolf's direct descendants.

❧

There is a final twist in Paul's life that I found completely unexpected but very moving.

On arriving in Vienna after the war Paul joined the Jewish community. Schmidt said Paul was "never religious, but always generously donated to the religious community, lived consciously in the circle of his family, and above all had Jewish friends and co-workers." With respect to Israel, he simply did not think Zionism was a viable political solution. Paul himself had a bar mitzvah; his sons and grandsons did not. He and Ala celebrated Christmas, with a tree and presents. Kitty says her parents wanted them to be like other children.

Kitty told me that the family were not practising Jews. Her ex-husband is not Jewish nor have her children married Jews. So I was surprised to see menorahs in her kitchen. Kitty responded that two days before Paul died (in 2003, at the age of ninety-three), they held a Passover ceremony at Paul's request. David's mother Nele, albeit divorced from Martin, was close to Paul. As David wrote me, "neither Martin nor Kitty knew how to celebrate Pessach. My mother, being the only one not Jewish, knew it, and we made the dinner with all the symbols, songs, etc. I guess it was the last time Paul went down for dinner." Martin's daughter Margarita, who had attended a Jewish elementary school, asked the four questions.[18] Paul gave a *brocha*, a Jewish blessing, over Martin and Kitty. He was very happy. At his funeral the chief rabbi spoke, and Kaddish was said. David remembered shaking Peter's hand and said it was probably the only time he had seen him over the past many years. Paul and Ala are buried prominently in the Jewish cemetery in Vienna.

PART III

Grete and Her World

Each man is in each instance in dialogue with his forebears, and perhaps even more and in a more hidden manner with those who will come after him.
– Martin Heidegger, "A Dialogue on Language,"
in *On the Way to Language*

Chapter Ten

Grete and Her Family, in Former Times

I turn at last to the final double cousin, my redoubtable grand-mother. For her daughter Ruth, Grete had something unattainable. That is her attraction for me as well, but what is unattainable is also beyond description. Over the next three chapters, I reach towards it. In this one, I explore family life in the Tugendhat House, including my mother's story of her childhood and her nanny Irene Kalkofen's story. I draw in as well the families of Grete's two husbands – my two grandfathers, Hans Weiss and Fritz Tugendhat – since they were all part of Grete's world.

Grete often began sentences in English with "in former times," a phrase I took to mean before the war. To my great regret, I cannot remember what followed the phrase; hence I cannot draw on conversations with her. Instead, I rely on talks with my mother and other relatives, publications on the Villa Tugendhat, and a long interview with Irene, conducted in April 1989.

Grete was born on 16 May 1903, fifteen months after her older brother Max and eight years before her younger brother Hans. As a child she lived first in the family quarters adjacent to the factory in Brno, moving into the expansive house on the Park-strasse about 1913.[1] She spent summers in Svitávka. Hans said that Grete was always best in school and, unlike Max and himself, punctual and precise. People respected her and agreed that the family genius went from Rudolf to Grete. Indeed, affirmed Hans, Rudolf adored her. Grete was gifted, strong willed, *têtu* (stubborn), and decisive.

Grete studied philosophy or political economy at the University of Vienna, possibly the first Löw-Beer woman to attend university, but she left after a year, age nineteen, to marry Hans Weiss (1900–80). Her brother, Hans Löw-Beer, said the marriage was not arranged and that both parties were the kind of people who did what they wanted. Hans Weiss's son, my uncle Peter (1938–97), concurred. He said his father was the sort of person who planned his life; he never just floated but did what he wanted, so the marriage wouldn't have been imposed. Peter thought it had been a love match – though one between people who soon found they weren't compatible. My mother emphasized how much Marianne and Alfred liked Hans and thought they "partly chose him," and her sister Dani too thought it might have been partially arranged. Grete had been in love with Fritz Tugendhat, some seven years older, but as he never declared an interest, presumably out of shyness, she accepted Hans Weiss when he came calling. Hans was handsome, with a forthright, impressive demeanour, and Grete wanted children.

In any case, it was a marriage that helped cement relations in the firm. The wedding took place in 1922 in Brno, after which Grete went to live in Sagan, where, since his father's death the previous year, Hans managed the large textile factory, co-owned with the Löw-Beers. Sagan (now Zagan) was a small town in what was then German Silesia and is now Poland.

Interlude I: The Weiss Family

Hans Weiss was young but already in charge. He wanted to go to medical school but first enlisted in the First World War, on the German side. His university career was cut short when his father died; as eldest son, he was called to run the business and look after his siblings.[2] Peter later reflected that Hans had been the right person in the right place at the right time. He was competent and had lots of opportunity. He modernized the factory, introducing better technology. Hans viewed himself as very "modern" and rebelled against his father's ways of handling the factory workers, albeit the family was already characterized as liberal and progressive. He was one of the first people to start a crèche for workers' children. At the same time, the system was paternalistic; workers brought him their problems, and he was even made a kind of local justice for a while. Having this power at a young age, said Peter, he didn't miss it later when his business was no longer successful. He was neither a communist nor afraid of communism; he told Peter that "you're much too sensible to believe in that."

Grete entered a household full of intellectual ferment. Peter described Hans as a practical man, but he respected intellectuals and was interested in what they had to say. He supported his siblings in their pursuits and was a friend of Kurt Lewin, then developing his reputation as an innovative psychologist. Peter thought Kurt might have been Hans's tutor. In any case, Hans brought Kurt home, where he met and subsequently married Hans's oldest sister Gerti (1896–1986), who also became a psychologist. On a holiday at Timmendorf, on the Baltic, Kurt filmed my mother as a toddler as she tried to sit down on a log, recording a child's spatial perceptions. The film has been widely shown. My mother saw a copy as an adult and suggested that, while it was not professional, Kurt may have been the first psychologist in the world to make a film to demonstrate something. It was Hanna's first subjection to public representation.

In recent years I have been approached independently by three intellectual historians, each investigating one of three other siblings of Hans – Anni, Paul, and Lene. I learned in 2016 in an email from Steve Silberman that Anni Weiss (1897–1991) played a major but hitherto unrecognized role in the identification and treatment of Asperger's syndrome.[3] Working with Hans Asperger in the children's clinic at the University Hospital in Vienna, Anni was among the first to take careful notes and to understand children whose condition came to be called Asperger's.[4] She left for the United States in 1934 and became a student and an Associate of Child Guidance at Columbia University's Teachers College.[5] She was followed in 1937 by Georg Frankl, a psychiatrist from the same clinic. They married in New York, possibly to ensure his citizenship, and found work with Leo Kanner at Johns Hopkins University. Kanner drew on their ideas and clinical work but did not offer them permanent jobs, and they left for the University of Kansas. Silberman argues that Kanner took credit for conceptualizing autism, overlooking Anni and Georg's more human perspective and their appreciation of the continuum of neurodiversity.

Paul Weiss (1911–91) became a mathematician who did important work in Cambridge with Paul Dirac and Max Born in the 1930s. Interned in Canada during the war, he then taught in the United Kingdom before moving to the United States in 1950, teaching at Syracuse and, from 1958, Wayne State.[6] He married a zoologist, and they had an unorthodox lifestyle with three children and a house full of animals. I have a vague memory, probably false, of alligators in the basement. Paul was friendly with my father and came to my wedding. In later life he visited my uncles in London and would stay for months, often lying in the bathtub until noon.[7]

The third sibling of interest to an intellectual historian was Hans's youngest sister Lene (Helene, 1898–1951), who became a student and something of a scribe of Heidegger's. It was through Lene that Grete developed her interest in Heidegger, but this story is reserved for chapter 13.

My mother described the Weiss sisters as "intelligent in a slow ponderous way." They seemed to want their doctorates more than marriage, she said. Lene never married; Anni married late. Anni spent her last years in a retirement home in North Carolina and was over ninety when she died. My mother never went to see her, and I never met her. Gerti and Kurt left Germany in 1933. Kurt accepted a position as a refugee scholar at Cornell, moving to the University of Iowa in 1935 and MIT in 1945, where he died of a heart attack two years later. He is known for the development of field theory and group dynamics in social psychology; tasked to support the US war effort by persuading Americans to change their eating habits, he also developed applied psychology. Gerti became a professor at Simmons College. Their son Daniel died as a young man, and their daughter Miriam became a psychology professor as well.

Growing up, the children of Hermann's brother and Mumma's sister lived next door in Sagan, and the double cousins were in and out of each other's houses. They were all musical, competing between their respective Steinway and Bösendorfer grand pianos. Elly (1897–1950) emigrated to the United States with her two sons.

Figure 21. The Weiss family, 1920, at the twenty-fifth wedding anniversary of Hermann and Mumma. From left to right in the back are Anni, Rudi, Lene, Hans, Gerti, and Paul. Hermann died in 1921, a few months after the photo was taken. Photo and information courtesy of Robin Weiss

Lotte (1902–c. 1981) married Paul Dussauze, who was executed in 1944 as a member of the French resistance; she spent the rest of her life in the Marais quarter in Paris. Käte (1906–87) married Dr. Franz Stiassny from Brno, and they emigrated to Israel, where their children live under the name Yagil. "Our" family kept in touch with Lotte, whose address proved attractive, and my mother had visits from John Weil (1929–2010), one of Elly's sons, a distinguished chemist.

Marriage and Remarriage

Grete and Hans had two sons in quick succession, each mysteriously dying a few days after birth. The third pregnancy was that of my mother. Grete returned to Brno to give birth as Marianne insisted that she be under the care of her obstetrician. Hanna was born on 29 November 1924 in the house on Parkstrasse and turned out fine. The birth certificate, issued by the Israelite community of Brünn, adds that she was "legitimate." Grete became pregnant again; however, the marriage did not survive. Grete and Hans each wanted more children, and there was talk of genetic incompatibility, though this issue was never resolved. As my mother said, "the question was, why did I live?" Moreover, Hans had another woman on the side, and Grete was in love with another man. Grete later said that she had known from the beginning that the marriage with Hans was a "disaster" (a favourite word in this family).

In 1927, pregnant and with a small child, Grete moved to Berlin, renting a flat on the Uhlandstrasse, close to the Ku'damm in what was a thriving and prosperous part of the city. The building must have been subsequently destroyed in the war; when I looked for it, I found an ugly lingerie store. In May 1928 Grete gave birth, and the new baby also died. Grete and Hans divorced amicably the same month, and Grete received a licence to remarry six weeks later.[8] Fritz and Grete wed in Berlin-Wilmersdorf that summer and honeymooned in Oostende in Belgium. They returned by airplane, which seemed very romantic to Irene. Grete's younger brother Hans recalled that he and Hanna were taken along and remembered dancing with Grete there, though this incident was probably the following summer.

The second marriage proved a good one. Grete believed you could only truly love one person in your lifetime, and as Dani affirmed, Fritz was Grete's great love, "absolutely." Grete idealized Fritz, while most people saw her as the dominant member of the pair, largely because he was quite taciturn. Fritz was an outstanding amateur photographer who experimented with a Leica and developed pictures of very high technical and aesthetic quality. They provide an incomparable record of the family and the Tugendhat House; a few are reproduced here.[9]

Interlude II: The Tugendhats

The Tugendhats were already closely entwined with the Löw-Beers, but less wealthy. Like Hans Weiss, Fritz was the son of the owner of a textile factory linked to the Löw-Beer firm. The Villa

Tugendhat website says that "the Tugendhats did not have their own companies but were the co-owners of the Brno wool factories Feldhendler & Co. and Max Kohn, having been involved in trade with cloth for several generations." Hermann Tugendhat (1834–1902), Fritz's grandfather, came from Bielitz in Silesia (the city from which Heinrich Wiedmann also came, where Eveline L-B moved on marriage, and where Elise Wiedmann married her first husband).[10] Hermann moved to Brno where he became head of a firm named Tugendhat & Meiler. In 1865 he married Marie Löw from Boskovice (1843–1912). Marie was first cousin to Pauline, Grete's father's mother; the great-grandfathers of Grete and Fritz were brothers.[11]

Between 1866 and 1882 Hermann and Marie had twelve or more children, of whom at least eight reached adulthood. Their first son, Emil (1867–1928), was born in Brno; in 1893 he too married a woman from Boskovice, Marie Fleischer (1869–1942). They had five children: Hans (b. 1894), Fritz (1895–1958), Robert (1897–1978), Franziska (1898–1981), and Lise (1900–42). Other Tugendhats preferred to marry out. One of Emil's brothers moved to France early in the century, and another brother, Benno (1877–1942), married a French woman. Emil, Benno, and Benno's son René are described as active in the Brno social scene. Emil was vice president of the Administrative Commission of the Trade and Commerce Chamber, member of the Pension Fund Committee of Industrialists, and honorary member of the Czech Tennis Association. René (1909–87) ended up in Buenos Aires under the last name Rennie. Emil was described as a "great guy," but it seems that he was also secretly abusive at home.[12]

In 1896 Emil was appointed to the woollens company Max Kohn and by 1919 had purchased it, along with his sons Hans and Fritz. Hans Tugendhat was sent to Leeds for a year to learn the technology. When Fritz returned from the First World War, he too was put to work in the factory, although he wanted to study medicine. Emil's brother Benno was a partner from 1905 in the Feldhendler company, which was engaged in sorting rags and spinning wool.[13] When Siegmund Feldhendler died, the company became fully operated by the Tugendhats, and in 1923 Hans and Fritz became public shareholders. The company was seized during the German occupation. Recall that the Max Kohn company also had a share of the cement factory that was co-owned by the Löw-Beers (see chapter 5). Hans Tugendhat, said his widow Minnie, was very impressed by Rudolf. "Rudolf was his role model and even his 'god.' Well," she added, "he was everyone's God." Minnie herself described Rudolf as polite and pleasant.

Fritz and his older brother Hans worked actively at the woollens factory. But the brothers did not get along. Hans was bossy, and Fritz wanted to escape. Grete disliked her brother-in-law and felt he kept Fritz down. The third brother, Robert, was more independent. He was an inventor, emigrating before the war with his wife Trude and her daughter Dorlie to Australia, where he founded an electrical equipment firm and shortened the family name to Tugen. The Tugens prospered and were active in the peace movement in Australia.

The House

During her time in Berlin Grete attended soirées at the home of communist art historian Eduard Fuchs. His house had been designed by Mies van der Rohe for the art collector Hugo Perls in 1911–12. In the summer of 1928, shortly before they married, Grete and Fritz made an appointment with Mies. Grete wrote: "From the very first moment we met him, it was clear to us that he should be the one to build our house, so impressed were we by his personality ... [A]bove all, the way he talked about his architecture gave us the feeling that we were dealing with a true artist."[14] Architectural historian Wolf Tegethoff concludes that "it is irrefutable that it was the then still unmarried Grete Löw-Beer [that is, divorced Grete Weiss], introduced by Eduard Fuchs, who first reached out to Mies van der Rohe." He calls her the "driving force and *spiritus rector* in choosing their architect."[15] Grete was twenty-five at the time. Her brother Hans described her as far-sighted and holding the pursuit of beauty as a worthwhile aim in life.

Grete was ready to return to Brno, where Alfred offered her the plot of land above his house. They moved back in September 1928, renting a flat on the Parkstrasse near the building site. Grete didn't think twice about living next to her parents; it was the thing to do then.[16] Mies visited that September and expressed his enthusiasm. As recounted in chapter 1, he submitted the plans on New Year's Eve. In March 1929 Alfred officially gifted the plot to Grete; she applied for the building permit in April, and construction began in June.[17]

Grete, Fritz, and Mies came to a common understanding of what they wanted. Thereafter Grete left Mies on his own. "She felt he should express himself completely," observed Hans. Dietrich Neumann writes: "Mies had been given the creative and financial freedom to create a classic 'Gesamtkunstwerk,' that is, a 'total work of art,' where everything from the building itself down to the furniture, curtains and door handles was selected and designed by himself and Lily Reich. Mies carefully chose the material for the solid honey colored 'onyx doré' wall and made a special trip to Paris to find the right kind of Macassar wood. The radical innovation in the spatial-functional arrangements was equaled by the use of new materials and the application of recent technologies."[18] Neumann mentions the chromium plating, opal glass, and white linoleum, which "had the photogenic effect of a space whose floor and ceiling seemed of equal brightness."[19] The replacement of load-bearing outside walls with floor-to-ceiling glass "must have struck many contemporary visitors as shockingly new."[20]

The glass, onyx, ebony, and chrome produced a play of reflected light, creating what Dani and Ivo call an effect of immateriality. Great attention was paid to the quality of both the materials and the craftsmanship. As Dani brilliantly put it, "the furniture, including desks and tables, were of irreducible simplicity in form and owed their appeal to the perfect proportion, exclusive materials and beautiful finishes. The value that was previously conveyed by decorating details was transferred entirely into the material."[21]

It is not quite true that no personal requests were included. Grete asked for direct access to the children's rooms, and Fritz requested both a darkroom and a film projection room. Grete also insisted on sun awnings.[22] However, when Fritz questioned the tall floor-to-ceiling doors, Mies said they were central to his vision and non-negotiable. Mies and Reich consulted with Grete and Fritz as they designed the furniture and décor. Irene said that Fritz made a big wooden model of the house at the factory. "They made furniture out of cardboard. It was like a doll's house." The family moved in during early December 1930. Grete was listed on the land register as the owner.

Mies came to inspect in February 1931. He and his associate wore Homberg hats and trench coats, reminding my mother, after the fact, of the FBI.[23] Grete's cousin Paul, who liked the house, said the older generation never indicated how they felt. I heard no mention of Rudolf's opinion, only that he always held Grete in high esteem. As for Alfred, he was not very enthusiastic, said Hans, but he let his daughter go her own way – she was a very strong personality and knew what she wanted.

Dani told me that when her mother commissioned the house she had a sense she was contributing to modern architecture. Yet Mies was still relatively unknown, and the Barcelona Pavilion, designed over the same period, was not yet finished, still unacclaimed, and did not influence Grete.[24] Paul added that Mies himself didn't know then that "he would never go on to do a better piece of work."

In reply to the question of whether the Tugendhat House was habitable, Fritz wrote that the inhabitants "can feel free to an extent never experienced before … [W]henever I let these rooms and all they contain take their effect, I am overcome by the feeling that this is beauty, this is truth … Anyone seeing these rooms will sooner or later come to the conclusion that here is true art."[25] And Grete wrote: "Mies is trying … to restore the primarily spiritual sense of life to its proper place." She added: "I find [the rooms] large and austerely simple … in a liberating sense. This austerity makes it impossible to spend your time just relaxing and letting yourself go."[26]

One can agree with Dani's account of an affinity between the principles of Mies's design and the thought of Heidegger, as noted in chapter 1. In a conversation in 2018 Dani called their shared concept *das Geistige in der Kunst*, a phrase she says is untranslatable. It was a specifically German concept, coming from idealist philosophy. It is not "spiritual," but something like the sublime, yet not quite. She grasped for another untranslatable German word, *das Wesen*, the being or essence of the work.

A German colleague, commenting on the house that Wittgenstein built his sister in Vienna, remarked that architecture is philosophy put into form.[27] For Grete and Fritz, the philosophy was one of truth – a truth of clarity and unconcealment, of things in themselves. For Mies, a window is not a hole in a wall; it is the boundary between inside and out. However, the relation of Mies's house to Heidegger's subsequent idea of dwelling (*Wohnung*), in which one drops façades and finds a place to live in safety as oneself, is at best an ironic one. For Heidegger, the *Wohnung* is precisely *not* an open modern house but the rough forest hut or cozy Bavarian farmhouse. And perhaps it is a place of dwelling made safe by the expulsion of those unlike oneself. As my son Simon put it, Grete's house can be understood as a critique of fascism and German primordialism, a hyper-rejection of things connected with the past and a vision of a future devoid of national sentimentalism. Thus the affinity between the architecture of Mies and the philosophy of Heidegger is something that Heidegger himself likely would have rejected. Where Mies exemplifies the modern, Heidegger turns to a romanticized pre-modern past.[28] The former, where things are at stake, as they were for Grete, pushes one to think; the latter enables one to sink into the comfort of the known and unquestioned.

The Bauhaus eventually produced a counter-reaction. In a conversation in 2018, German architect Niels Gutschow called the Bauhaus "ideology" that form should follow function "totalitarian," insofar as it declares what is the *right* way to design or decorate and that everything else is wrong. Gutschow detests the accompanying idea that one should educate others to good taste, but he is equally if not more opinionated than those he criticizes. He likened the idea of opening the living space to light and sun, and making the division between inside and outside invisible, to the invention of the bikini and to nakedness, that is, to exposure.

This view is entirely contrary to my grandparents' way of thinking. Indeed, in turning to metaphor, Dani said the house was like a garment for her parents. The house substantiated and was adequate for what they stood or strived for. It was clear rather than either cozy or uninhibited, and it certainly did not violate the inhabitants' privacy. "It structures my mind," Grete said. When people challenged how one could live in a house like this, Grete said it helped her thinking. While the house could be restful and comfortable, it also posed a challenge to its inhabitants to live up to their ideals; it kept them challenged.[29]

For Dani, writing in 2002, "the message of this house is absolute perfection."[30]

Irene

Irene Kalkofen (1909–2004), the children's beloved governess, provides an invaluable witness to life in the house. During our talk in London, she spoke almost non-stop for over eight hours, as we lubricated ourselves with sherry and a bottle of rosé over the dinner she served. Irene explained that she had been working in a children's house in Berlin but was looking for another job. She recalled going for an interview in Grete's flat. It was April 1928, and Grete was eight months pregnant. Her friends Käte and Lene were there as well, vetting the applicants. Irene found Grete "so beautiful" and Hanna lovely as well. "Grandma [Grete] said, 'I'm expecting a child. You'll have to be there for the baby. I'll look after Hanna myself.'" Grete added: "I'm going to remarry; can you come with us to Czechoslovakia?"

Grete gave birth to a beautiful baby. They were happy to see it was a girl, thinking it would live. However, "she died on the third day. Exactly as the other two."[31] But Irene was kept on.

In June the family went to the seaside at Timmendorf, on the Baltic. Marianne joined them from Brünn, as did her sister Charlotte together with Rudi Weiss.[32] From Timmendorf Grete and Fritz made excursions back to Berlin to converse with Mies and look at other houses he had built.[33] In September they moved to Brno.

Irene herself was only eighteen. She had had an unhappy childhood. Towards the end of our conversation, Irene revealed that her mother had been unmarried, and her father died when she was four months old. Her mother kept her a while, and later gave her to an orphanage. She did well in school and received a scholarship, but started work at sixteen. They were, as she said, working class. She dreamt of becoming a doctor, but the choices of career were only office worker, nurse, or seamstress. She stopped before her last year of training in nursing because people told her she was too young to take exams and should do some private nursing first. Also, she wanted to see the world. "Well, I got as far as Czechoslovakia."

I think my mother had a happy infancy. There are lovely photographs of Grete and Hanna together. Hanna had memories of feeding chickens in Sagan. But Irene said that Hanna was disturbed at the divorce. At first Hans came to see her in Berlin, and then he didn't come any more. After Grete's stay in the hospital, Fritz visited, and Hanna was jealous. Irene recounts a tantrum in the middle of the Ku'damm and needing a policeman to get her up. Hanna said she wanted to be a boy, and Irene said: "We'll play you are a boy." She had her hair cut short and told people her name was Peter Oliver, after Olivaer Platz, where they would go to play.

Once they visited Sagan. "A man walked behind Hans, carrying his attaché case; it was very posh." Hans had purchased a painting by Daumier, *Un homme et son enfant*, which he lent in 1930 – insured for $5,000 – to an exhibition at MoMA and in 1934 to the Orangerie. He either lost or had to sell it later.[34]

Irene went to Brno with the family. In the winter they skated in the Augarten; in the summer they went to Westende, a quiet seaside resort in Belgium. The Czech government refused to extend Irene's work permit, and so on the return trip, the family left her in Berlin. Irene then had a very bad time. There was no work for nurses after the stock market crash, and she was ineligible for unemployment benefits because she had been abroad. In the end she found a job as maid for a nosy invalid, Miss Pferzenheim. Grete had written a very nice reference, but as Miss Pferzenheim couldn't understand why Irene hadn't stayed in Czechoslovakia, she thought Irene had forged the letter.

In the meantime Grete hired Hedvika Jurečková (Schwester Hedwig) as a nurse for Ernst, born 8 March 1930, and Daisy Cachelin, a Swiss governess, for Hanna. Hanna disliked the nurse, who was eventually let go, but Daisy let her play full time. On Irene's return, Daisy moved to the house of the Walter Löw-Beers but continued to come to Hanna on Thursdays to teach her French, and Hanna became fluent. They stayed in contact. During the Kennedy presidency Daisy worked as governess for the Pat Kennedy/Peter Lawford family, and while visiting my mother in Montreal at this time, she recounted first-hand stories about Jack's dalliance with Marilyn Monroe.

Irene received a letter from Grete saying that Miss Pferzenheim had written to ask if the reference letter was genuine. Grete said they could take her back, thanks to a friend who was the labour minister and could get her a permit. Grete even asked Hans Weiss for a letter saying that as a German citizen he demanded his daughter be raised by a German nanny. Grete added that they had a little boy, but so delicate and sensitive that he only went to his mother. She warned that if he didn't take to Irene, it would be difficult. But Irene was confident and very happy to return. She arrived in Brno in February 1931, in the late afternoon. Fritz fetched her from the station. Hanna jumped up, hugged her, and danced around. Grete had just bathed Ernst, who let Irene help dry him. When he turned six, Ernst said to Irene: "I'm very happy I was so nice to you when you first came."

Ernst was born eight months before they moved into the house. Herbi followed on 24 February 1933. Grete devoted herself to them. Irene called Grete a good mother, even "too good." The children were always clinging to her. Yet when Irene returned from a two-week skiing holiday one winter, Grete was jealous at how they responded. When Grete herself was away, Irene was tasked with writing her every day about the children. Ernst didn't eat, and only Grete could feed him. But when Grete returned from a trip, she found he had gained weight and pronounced him too fat. Perhaps Grete was too possessive, especially with Ernst, but that was natural after losing three children, said Irene. As an adult Ernst himself told Dani that his relations with Grete had been difficult. As for Herbi, he was a self-sufficient child. He was happy to be with Irene but didn't miss her when he wasn't. In contrast to Ernst, he loved to eat. Hanna, Irene described, was "so strong."

Despite some critical remarks, Irene "venerated" Grete, "an unusually fine and understanding personality, and I owe her a lot." Grete loved Irene as well. Irene contrasted Grete with her own bad mother and with the mother in the English family with whom she worked later. "I dressed the baby in white and took him to the garden, where he was seated and fed chocolate cake. In an hour the maid was sent to me to fetch the child back. And that was what they called mother's hour."

Fritz, said Irene, was remote from the children, although later he changed and took them on expeditions. He usually didn't have much to say. She described him as very self-disciplined. "There was a lot of pressure to behave. But it was the times, and it was like that in all the better-educated families ... There was the responsibility to make something of yourself. They were all very gifted – and it would have been a pity not to use it." On the Tugendhat side, there was a young man who was a brilliant chess player, to the neglect of everything else. Ernst began playing at age seven and soon wanted to play all the time. Grete, Irene, and Fritz played with him, until Fritz decided it was no longer a good idea. "He said, 'No more games if I win.' But Ernst won, straight away. He was very good, and Fritz was very worried."

"Ernst was the perfect child. But he must have tried hard to be perfect. It's not normal for a child to be perfect from the beginning. But we thought we'd just let them grow. They led such a sheltered life. That also not so good." The children did not fight among themselves. "Hanna liked books and she always read to Ernst, he liked to listen."[35]

"We were not religious," said Irene, including herself in the family. "Grandmother [Marianne] would ring up to say, 'Don't send the children to school tomorrow, it's Yom Kippur.' But we wouldn't have known." Hans Weiss didn't want Judaism for Hanna, but Ernst was sent to Hebrew classes. The boys were not circumcised. From a young age Ernst thought about death and God. In a letter to Irene at age seven he wrote: "Liebe Schwester [Nurse/Nanny], I shall always be good so that you never die." During a visit to his great-grandmother in Vienna, Berta had palpitations and a nosebleed, and Ernst asked: "But when are you going to die already?" Ernst stopped eating lamb and chicken, accepting *Rindfleisch* (beef) only until he learned what animal it came from. He said: "If we kill animals to eat then we in turn will have to die." When Irene visited him in Berlin half a century later, he served artichokes because it had been Grete's favourite dish.

The children ate breakfast and lunch at the dining table with the adults and supper in Hanna's room, the food brought up in the lift.

During the last two years Irene was invited downstairs for supper. Grete's family, said Irene, "always ate simple, nourishing meals, nothing ostentatious. There was soup, meat, vegetable, a heavy or light pudding depending on season, plus fruit. The children had rolls, jam, butter, and milk or hot chocolate for breakfast." Meals at Max's or Marianne's, she said, were much more ostentatious. After lunch Grete always napped, a pattern she retained throughout her life. Irene and the children listened to records and danced in the library. Grete "was very strict and only liked classical music," but Fritz also had musicals in his collection.[36] The children had beautiful toys, including all the Dr. Dolittle animals.

Irene said: "We lived happily in the house ... [I]t was wonderful." "People always said it must be like living in an exhibition, but it wasn't like that at all. After all, we had the upstairs rooms, and the children had the terrace, with sand and water boxes." Irene could sit in Fritz's bedroom to read the newspapers. She felt it was her true home. She said: "I grew up in this family. I only became half-way normal when I lived with them." Grete "was a model and the children so intelligent and imaginative." In 1979, when they regained contact, Irene wrote Hanna that being in the family had been the happiest time of her life.

The immediate family sometimes treated Irene like the oldest child, but this familiarity was not true of others. "Every morning Grete telephoned Marianne, each of them still in bed. Each maid heard the conversation at their respective end. Once Marianne said to Grete, 'Don't forget that Schwester [Irene] is only an employee.' I knew I was hired help; she didn't need to rub it in." Marianne was very much "of the old school. Marianne's mother Berta was worse; on visits to Brünn she would offer the children a candy and then offer me one – but of cheaper quality. But Grete was never like that."

Unequal treatment was the reason that Irene didn't like summers spent in Svitávka, where she inevitably fell sick. Irene preferred it when the nuclear family took a holiday by themselves. She didn't like Hansi, who put on airs. And Mutzi (Marianne) too acted more that way in Svitávka. Grete liked Svitávka because she had known it since childhood, but in fact they spent only two summers there. One summer on the way to a seaside resort on the

Baltic, they stopped overnight in Sagan, and later Hans and Rudi came to visit them at the beach.

Sometimes they walked in the beautiful countryside and grilled meat over a fire. The one place the children were never taken was the factories.

The family kept mostly to itself. They rarely had house guests, said Irene, and had little to do with the Löw-Beers who lived on the other side of town, that is, the brothers who ran the other company. They came over perhaps once a year. Marianne came almost daily; Grete, said Irene, "was very, very attached to her mother."[37]

Irene had a very nice room in the Tugendhat House. When Grete's friend Käte visited, she took Irene's room, and Irene slept in Hanna's room, where there were two twin beds. Irene thought Käte was very beautiful and perhaps bisexual. The women planned a summer trip to her cottage in the Black Forest in 1936. Irene couldn't go along because there was a law within Germany that young women were not permitted to work for Jewish families. Indeed, the new German vice consul threatened to send her back to Germany on her own to "improve her thinking."

Irene looked out for herself. On an early family holiday in the Dolomites, Grete skied with Hanna while Irene cared for the boys inside, but one day Grete had bronchitis and told Irene to take Hanna out. "I seized my chance." Irene already had pants and boots, and she borrowed skis and took part in Hanna's lessons. Because she had been watching so avidly, she knew what to do and learned fast. She never became a good skier, but she could go anywhere and was not scared. She remembered a time they were pulled behind Fritz's car.

Holidays for Irene were a problem. She didn't want to go back to Germany. So she asked for time off for skiing. There must have been quite a discussion between Grete and Marianne, because Marianne said to her, you already go on holidays; we go summer and winter. "It's not *my* holiday with a child in each hand," retorted Irene. So she got her two weeks. And when Grete asked her what she wanted for Christmas, she said skis. "And I got them. It was a good thing I spoke up for myself, because otherwise I would never have got anything!"

Figure 22. Grete as a young mother.
Photo by Fritz Tugendhat, c. 1935,
Pinatype or Duxochrome; Archive
Daniela Hammer-Tugendhat

Irene described Alfred as a very nice man, friendly and hand-some. Marianne was vivacious, and they made a good couple. Marianne was always so elegant and also flirtatious. "Grossmama Mutzi was quite a number." When someone called her "Gross-mama," she replied: "Just call me Mutzi."

Irene said: "We all trembled when Rudolf came." And then they discovered their idol had been having an affair with Hansi all that time! Irene found Hansi vivacious, like Mutzi. "Grete," she said, was "like a Madonna."

Hanna's Childhood

My mother lived in the house from the age of five to thirteen. She did notice the house was different, unlike the third-floor flats she encountered at the birthday parties of school friends. She found it a fine place to live and never complained about it. She wrote that her parents were happy there and that perhaps "living in the house sparked my interest in art and other cultures." She recalled games of hide and seek. She played mostly in her bedroom, the terrace, or the garden but was allowed to be in the main room.[38] She couldn't remember if her parents ever played with her. "But it was never an argument." She was off to school through Saturday and that was followed by hours of homework. She read a lot.

Hanna was very attached to Grete and almost never criticized her. But in 1987 she told me that Grete had read John Watson, the founder of behaviourism, and believed in stimulus/response and complete exactitude. "She wasn't awful," said Hanna. "You have to look at things in light of the times. When I say she didn't talk much to me, perhaps it's true the house was 'unlivable.' I was sent to my room, not as punishment but that's where I was supposed to be. There were standards of behaviour, and they were enforced." In a letter to architect Dieter Roger in 1985, Hanna said she and her siblings agreed that her parents were particularly strict; they had very high expectations of the children. She even used the phrase "poor little rich girl."[39]

Grete's brother Hans, Hanna's beloved uncle, said that everyone was very conscious that Hanna came from the first marriage. Grete tried hard not to treat Hanna differently, but presumably she did. Hans described her as a very gifted pupil, who learned everything by heart and had an incredible memory.

Some of Hanna's playmates were Jewish and some not. They knew the difference according to the separation of children in the religion classes at school. Grete asked for Hanna to be excused from religious training. Her best friend was Gretl, blonde and much taller than Hanna. Gretl's mother had been Hans and Grete's nanny, Fräulein Schmidt. Then she married Dvořzák; despite the name, he was very German and a schoolteacher. When Gretl was young, they came to show her off to Marianne, and the friendship with Hanna began. Gretl came every Sunday, picked up by the chauffeur. They drove to the woods for family hikes, followed by lunch at home and play in the afternoon. They created theatre together, but, Hans said, Hanna ran the whole show. Hanna recalled that Gretl was permitted to go to live theatre and films, and she recreated them for Hanna, so Hanna, who was not permitted, made up her own plots to be even. Hanna decided early on that Ernst was going to marry Gretl. Eventually, Gretl's father became a Nazi. Hanna regained contact after the war. I have a vague recollection of hitchhiking on the Autobahn in the mid-sixties to stay briefly with Gretl and her husband in Hamburg. Later my brother Bernie did as well.

I asked my mother about servants. Irene lived upstairs with the family. On the ground floor there was Thea, the German-speaking maid, and Anna, the cook. Some of the time there was a second Czech-speaking maid named Christa.[40] The gardener was employed by Alfred and had a separate house, down the slope. Gustav Lössl, the chauffeur, and his wife had an apartment above the garage. He started the car with a crank.

Hanna had little memory of Svitávka. They did not spend long periods there but might drive down for a day or two. In the Kleine Villa, Edith's cook served home-baked rye bread with delicious goose fat or goose liver spread. One summer Grete rented a simple apartment in a farmhouse. Hanna recalled a lovely day spent picking and stomping grapes at a vineyard owned by a German-speaking farmer outside Brno. She also remembered a pleasant holiday in the summer of 1936 at Käte's summer house near Freiburg (the trip on which Irene could not go). Hanna had no memory of Boskovice except once visiting a hunchbacked old kinswoman.

Hanna often wondered what her mother did all day. Grete sat in the library; she read heavy stuff, philosophy, art history, and literature. This period was a great time for German literature – Rilke, Kafka, Zweig, Werfel. From 1933 Grete became active in the League for Human Rights and was often absent for hours, counselling refugees, primarily Jews from Germany. Grete served on the executive committee and helped emigrants establish houses and grow food. She held an annual bridge tournament in the house with up to 100 guests to raise money for the League. Hanna was dressed in an eighteenth century wig and the boys as pages. Fritz photographed each guest as they arrived, developed the photos, and had the children take them around to the guests and sell them to make additional money for the cause. Other years

Fritz used a hidden movie camera and showed the film before the guests left.

Hanna walked to school, going down through the lengthy garden, past Marianne's house, and then along the park and a district of broad avenues and fancy gated houses. On her way home, she often stopped to see her grandmother. She said in 1987: "I can still see her desk before me, where she kept the chocolate. There was a complete bear rug and a grand piano, which she played well. If I asked politely, I'd get chocolate." Marianne was not strict with her, and they were close throughout their lives. Hanna said Marianne lived the typical life of a wealthy lady of the time. In the morning she would call in the cook to discuss lunch and dinner. Then perhaps she called in the dressmaker. She lived for the theatre and ballet. Brünn had good cultural activities to which Alfred and Marianne were regular subscribers. Grete and Fritz went occasionally. Hanna was only very rarely allowed to attend the theatre and once was taken to see *Emil and the Detectives*. The family did things together on Sundays. Alfred rode horses, and Fritz hiked. Sometimes they ate at Grete's, sometimes at Marianne's.

A sense of domestic life at Marianne's in the 1930s can be glimpsed from the reminiscence of Hanna's cousin Frank, which he presented to Marianne on her eightieth birthday in 1962. His mother drove him into Brünn from Svitávka once a week in a green Tatra. He remembered the "small dining room, a sunny intimate room with a high ceiling … I felt honoured to be allowed to be present … Vati [Frank's father, Max] and Grosspapa [Alfred] were there … I was fascinated by Grosspapa's concentration alternately on his chewing and on his conversation and his periodic pointing to dishes of food which he required." Frank recalled fish in a white sauce followed by marron purée with whipped cream. "The other memory I have of that room is of Hans [Frank and Hanna's uncle] in his uniform getting ready to go back to the barracks with his bayonet at his side. The room I remember best is the Grosse Halle with the balcony around it … I can see Grosspapa coming in the main door and heading for the wash basin that was somehow discreetly hidden in the woodwork. At the far end in front of the fire was a bearskin rug on which I was sometimes allowed to lie.

Figure 23. Hanna, Herbi, and Ernst in front of the onyx wall, 1937 (February 1938 at latest). Photo by Fritz Tugendhat; Archive Daniela Hammer-Tugendhat

Once I was permitted to come down when you [Marianne] had guests, and I can see Onkel August [of the other L-B branch] who was seated near the door to the room where the Christmas tree had been put up. Was that the year that I was six [1937]?"

When Hanna began school, it was fine to place her in a German-speaking one. As Czech nationalism rose, Ernst was sent to a Czech-speaking school, which he attended for one and a half years. Grete and Fritz hired a private tutor and began learning Czech as well. As the political climate worsened, Grete grew anxious. In 1936 she and Fritz began learning Hebrew and went to Palestine for four weeks to explore whether they could make a go of it there. They were not moved by Zionism but went simply to gauge their options, concluding it would be too difficult to set up a factory. Later they considered Kenya. There was a personal as well as political push for emigration, as Fritz could not stand working with his older brother.

Hanna was largely oblivious and told me she never encountered anti-semitic remarks in Czechoslovakia. During these years her major challenge was Fritz's distance. Hanna considered Fritz her father, loved him, and wanted to be treated like her brothers. But when she addressed him as Papa, he would not respond, apparently believing it dishonorable and dishonest to acknowledge another man's child as his own. Years later Grete admitted to Dani that Fritz had been cruel to Hanna, but nothing was said to her at the time. Even now, I feel pain on her behalf and cannot forgive my grandparents their silence.

Chapter Eleven

Grete and Her Family, the War Years

The war brought Hanna into closer connection with her father. Hans Weiss and Grete were married for five years. Hans spent the next five single and then married Steffi (Stephanie Loevinsohn, Berlin 1906–65). His first question to Steffi was whether she wanted children. Ernest (1932–2006) was born in Berlin and Marian (b. 1933) in Zurich. Hans, as my mother put it, figured out Hitler early and left for Switzerland in 1933. In fact, the consequences of Hitler's rise to power were evident earlier in Germany than in Brno. Kurt Lewin and Gerti left in 1933 as well. Their daughter Miriam (1931–2014) later wrote of precipitating factors: a Jewish doctor was beaten to death in Sagan, and Gerti was expelled from her professional association because she was Jewish.[1]

Rudolf kept calling Hans back to tie up loose ends at Sagan. Steffi resented these demands and felt that Rudolf never treated Hans quite fairly, but Peter said that Hans would not have allowed Rudolf to intimidate him. Hans realized they wouldn't get permanent status in Switzerland and thought France would fall. So in 1934 they moved to England, where their sons Peter and Robin were born. Hans was interned for eight months in Scotland where, according to Peter, he had the time of his life; at the height of his powers, he organized the camp. Steffi was not interned. They became British citizens after the war.

At age eight, Hanna suffered from ear infections and was sent to a hospital in Vienna, where she had her eardrums pierced, and subsequently to recuperate near St. Moritz. There she was looked

Kinship Diagram 13. Hans and Gerti Weiss

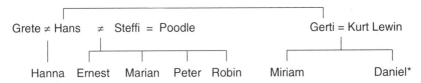

* Spouses and descendants of this generation have been omitted.

after by Hans and Steffi. Steffi was a swimming instructor and taught Hanna how to swim. Aside from that, Hanna saw Hans only on annual visits. These were very formal, and she hated them. Each year's visit was much the same as the last. But in March 1938, the visit had a different outcome.

It may have been coincidence that the visit coincided with Hitler's march into Vienna, but Hans explained to Grete that as he, and therefore Hanna, were German citizens, she was at more immediate risk of being rounded up than the rest of the family, who held Czech passports. It was decided that Hanna should leave with him. As my mother told me in 1987, "it all happened very fast." Being pulled suddenly from her family without explanation was a terrible shock, one that Grete later justified by saying that Hanna must have known about Hitler and why it was necessary. But Hanna at thirteen knew only vaguely about the political situation. "The family were predictable about everyday things – home from school, lunch, homework, Latin conjugations, 'Have you eaten, sit down, do your homework.' The normal thing for me to do was complain. This day I said I had lots of terrible verbs. My mother said, 'Never mind the Latin, we have important things to do.' I was stunned. 'Go with Irene and decide what clothes to pack. You're leaving with your father tonight.'"

Hanna added: "My life had been ordered until then. That was the first sudden – completely sudden – change. Father never stayed longer than two days or so." Hanna then admonished me: "These things are not to be published. I was thirteen and maybe I am wrong." May she forgive me. I think sufficient time has passed (she died over thirty years ago), and her account has sufficient authority.

Hanna continued: "I knew my father, but not intimately. The visits were always very artificial. Irene would say, 'Your Papa has come, wash your hands, change your dress.' I was three at the separation. The word for 'dad' was 'pápa.' My brothers called Fritz this. I was told to call Hans 'Papa.' I was told to wear my best dress. He always sat on the same red chair and got black coffee. It was a big curved beautiful chair set in the middle of the room. I had to stand there, and he would say things like 'Do your work well in school,' and 'What's your report card like?' Also, he smoked." This memory may be the source of my mother's lifelong intense dislike of smoking. "I saw him about once a year."[2]

They left together that evening; it was 13 March, the day after the Germans marched into Vienna. Hanna remembered the trip as an adventure. They travelled by train and must have circled around Austria. They spent the night in an unheated jail in Hungary. Hans offered Hanna a cigarette, and she couldn't stand it. She didn't know why they were imprisoned or why they were released the next day. Perhaps Hans made a phone call and got things moving; she imagined that Alfred influenced their release. Hanna said: "We crossed into Yugoslavia and I remember it well because my father said, 'Now we'll celebrate with a glass of wine,' and it was the first time I drank wine." From there they went by train across northern Italy and through France to England.

School in England had to be negotiated. Steffi took her to purchase uniforms. Marianne later said that Steffi had been horrible to Hanna, but Hanna denied it. Hanna liked Steffi and said Steffi was kind to her, though she never treated her as a daughter. It seems as if the responsibility for care was placed entirely on the women. In England Hanna was allowed to go to the cinema and remembered *The Scarlet Pimpernel* with Leslie Howard.

At her first school there were three German-speaking girls. Hans thought it would be better to separate her and so sent her to Cheltenham. Hanna said perhaps she had been spoiled but she couldn't deal with thirteen beds in a dormitory or the very bad but heavy food. She couldn't tie her school tie or play cricket, and for the first time in her life, she was called a dirty Jew. She had always been top in her class, but here they didn't value the things she was good at, like fluency in French. There were no men at the school, and so one night she crept out on the roof to have a look at the milkman arriving at dawn. She was caught and had her badge publicly ripped off at a school assembly. Her only friend was her distant cousin Friedl, the daughter of Walter Löw-Beer (of the other branch). They had been in the same school in Brno, although Friedl was older. Friedl later became a psychoanalyst and married the historian of antiquity Peter Brown, with whom she had two daughters. Hanna told me that they once visited Grete in St. Gallen after the war. "Grete," she said, "is like you, Michael, in that she is extremely critical of people. Rarely for her, she wrote that she was completely delighted with Peter Brown."

Hans thought of himself as a man of the world and someone who could get things done. He returned to Europe several times to help people leave and in the end barely made it out himself. He fetched his mother and Steffi's parents, helped several Löw-Beers acquire visas to England, and was the one who hired Sir Paul Dukes to discover what had happened to Alfred.

Hans was benevolent and attuned to his responsibilities, but he was not very interested in children, either his own or later, his grandchildren. He was described by his son Peter as self-centred in most respects and indifferent to the emotional needs of others, but a very interesting companion, a man of strong likes and dislikes, and a fund of stories about Germany. He tried to create a firm for refugee designers and artists. When it failed, some of his kin who had invested were angry at their loss. Hans himself retooled and began in the polishing industry. The Weiss family gained nothing or very little from the Sagan factory. The Germans sold it and gave the family no compensation. After the war Sagan was in Poland, and no reparations were possible.

Relations between Hans and Grete were never entirely broken off. Peter remembered a family vacation after the war when they briefly visited Grete in St. Gallen. When Peter said he thought it was odd to visit one's divorced spouse, Hans replied, not at all. Growing up, said Peter, the family silver had an engraved H and

G on it. Steffi never minded; given the five-year gap between the marriages, she wasn't worried. Presumably, Grete herself had rejected the cutlery; she had a new set engraved with GT. We have inherited part of the set and sometimes bring it out for company dinners. The cutlery is a nuisance because it needs polishing, and the individual pieces are much larger than ones people commonly use today, almost as if my grandparents were a race of giants.

Irene in England

Grete and the two boys departed for Switzerland immediately after Hanna left, "with one suitcase," as Dani heard it. Fritz stayed behind to pack and organize their affairs, making several trips before finally leaving on 4 March 1939.[3] Some of the furniture was brought to Switzerland and later made it to Venezuela and back. Fritz had established relations to manage a textile factory, perhaps via an investment on Alfred or Rudolf's part. It was in a place called Kirchberg, and the family lived in the nearest city, St. Gallen.

However, Fritz's position remained uncertain. Grete wrote her brother Max on 20 March 1939 that they had no news regarding work for Fritz in the Swiss city of Solothurn. "Naturally we are interested even more than before in going to Canada. I even asked Ernst Wolff's brother [Elias, in New York] whether he could help Fritz get a job there. I fear though that all these possibilities will be too late."[4]

Grete brought Irene to Switzerland, where she was able to stay only six weeks; the Swiss declined a longer visa, saying children their age didn't need a nurse. Irene returned to Brno. The family suggested she go to England. Hans Weiss posted an ad for her, and they received a reply from Rolf Gardiner, son of the Egyptologist Sir Alan Gardiner, who had spent much time in Berlin. It was the nicest letter, said Irene, and he wrote that they had many German friends. She prepared by reading Galsworthy novels. Irene left Brno on 2 July 1938 for the Gardiners in Shaftesbury, Dorset.

One fall weekend in 1938 Irene visited Hanna at her first school, Moira House in Eastbourne. "There was no central heating – and we had come from such a comfortable home … We both cried. We were both unhappy, but happy to be together." As she was living in Dorset, she didn't see Hanna again.

Irene hated her employers. They were nice to her, but Rolf was a Nazi. In April 1939 he gave a lecture in Berlin on folk music. On his return, as the maids unpacked his suitcase, he said: "Come and look, you'll like it." There was a dinner jacket with Nazi insignia on it.[5] They argued, and he said she had been badly influenced by the Jewish home she had been in. She couldn't say she was totally anti-Nazi, because she had to stay employed in order to acquire permanent residence. But "it was disgusting," and she wanted to get away. Another problem, much more mundane, was that she didn't know how to light the fireplaces. And whereas in Brno she had had her own very nice room, in Dorset she had to sleep in the nursery and therefore had nowhere to relax on her days off. She went to the room of the Swedish maid, which was tiny and had no heat.

Irene asked for a week's holiday, during which she looked for a new job in London. She went to a Jewish refugee colony in Hampstead and found work looking after two boys in Golders Green, returning to Dorset only to give notice. But she was an enemy alien in Britain. Some weeks later, the police sent her to the Isle of Man where she spent eleven months. "Well," she said, "it was an involuntary holiday; you didn't have to work." There were some 4,000 women, among them very well-educated Jewish refugees. Eventually, she was examined by a tribunal. They asked about her hobbies, and when she replied reading, what kind of books, were they communistic? They looked over her collection of Penguins, and she passed.

Irene emerged interested in working with children with bad war experiences. Grete had subscribed to a psychoanalytic journal, and Irene had read the issues. She reflected on her bad experiences with her own mother and tried to do the opposite. She got an interview with "Miss Freud" (Anna Freud), who was running a home for refugee children, and worked with her from 1941 to 1945. In London she sometimes visited Hans and Steffi after work, on her bicycle. They lived in a lovely house just off Hampstead

Heath. Hans had an office near Pall Mall. She found Steffi very nice but such a different type from Grete. Hans had wanted Grete to go hunting with him. "Can you imagine her doing this?" But Steffi was very sporting and the right wife for him. Peter described his mother as ebullient and vital, a good foil for Hans.

Irene said: "The children of Brno always lived in my heart." Ernst and Hanna wrote to her, but Irene replied only once, feeling devastated the relationship was over. Eventually, she lost contact, though she often talked about them with her friends.

At the end of the war Irene spent two years working in censorship for the American army. They wanted perfect German speakers. The army felt the need to re-educate the Germans, but it was the American soldiers, she observed, who needed re-educating. She was stationed near Stuttgart but visited Berlin to seek out her half-brother, only a year older than Hanna. She had held great hopes for him. He wasn't a Nazi but was put in the army very young, as an ambulance driver. She discovered that he had died of lung disease during the Russian campaign, before the age of twenty.

The reason Irene joined the army was that when she asked for more work with children, Anna Freud had replied that since she was German and not Jewish, they would reject her. On her return to England she was told she shouldn't have believed Miss Freud. So she worked for two years in a sanatorium for young men who had caught tuberculosis in the concentration camps. They were supposed to be under fifteen to get into England, but some were older. In 1989 she was still good friends with some of the "boys" and attended an annual reunion.

When Irene's doctor advised her not to lift patients, she shifted to bookkeeping for a Jewish refugee doctor from Berlin. One day she saw a copy of the magazine *Du* in his waiting room. There was an article about houses of the early twentieth century, and as she suspected, the Tugendhat House was among them. However, the article contained a mistake, describing the interior wall as marble, not onyx. This detail bothered her, and she wrote the magazine, explaining she had lived in the house for eight years. They recommended her to Dr. Glaeser, a curator at the Museum of Modern Art, which had a Mies archive.

When she worked for the American army, Irene could have chosen to move to the United States, but she said she saw the worst side of Americans. She did want to see Niagara Falls ("I'm very keen on waterfalls"), and in 1977 she accepted an invitation from a cousin to visit Manhattan. So she wrote Dr. Glaeser asking if he wanted to meet her. There was no reply. Her taxi to the airport was late, and while she was waiting for it, a letter from Glaeser arrived. She wouldn't have received it if the taxi hadn't been late. They spent a day together, and he took her to a posh restaurant where she had a martini and got drunk. She managed to tell him quite a lot, for example about the colours used in the house, not visible on the black and white photos.

Glaeser never contacted her again, but one day she got a letter from Montreal with the sender listed as Hanna Lambek. She hadn't known Hanna's married name. Glaeser had come to Montreal to interview Hans and Hanna, and he had provided Irene's address.[6] My mother subsequently visited Irene and enabled my visit as well. Irene also saw Ernst in Berlin, and he visited her in London. Once they went together to visit the house in Brno. I have included Irene's story here because Hanna and Ernst really did consider her part of the family.

Venezuela

In 1938 Fritz and Grete settled in St. Gallen. In 1939 my mother joined them for summer vacation and was, she said, the only person delighted when Hitler invaded France, since it blocked her return to England. Grete placed Hanna in the English-speaking section of the Rosenberg Academy from which she graduated high school. Her parents expected her to come first in every class. All was well except for a cycling accident on holiday in May 1940. Her chain broke as she was riding down what she recalled as "the steepest street in Europe," in Paudex, near Lausanne, with her brother at her back. A courageous man stepped in front of the bicycle to prevent the children going into traffic, but Hanna hurtled off the bike and had scars to show for it.

Grete was increasingly nervous as Hitler kept annexing territory, and when the possibility arose to go to Venezuela, they took it. This exodus was arranged through her best friend Käte. Käte was older than Grete and had married very late, when she was already over forty. Ernst Wolff was a Swiss citizen and an international lawyer and financier, with connections everywhere. Käte told Hanna she married him purely to help them leave. Wolff learned of three Corsican financiers who had purchased a textile factory in Venezuela but didn't know how to manage it, and thereby found a job for Fritz.

The family left for Venezuela on 13 January 1941. Ernst, aged eleven, wrote Irene in detail about the journey. Bringing thirty-five pieces of luggage, they went on a very slow and crowded train through France. Ernst slept up on the luggage rack, recording his first glimpse of the blue Mediterranean. The engine was uncoupled in Narbonne, and they worried they would miss their ship in Lisbon. But after an anxious night in a hotel, the train proceeded the next morning to the border, where they spent several hours at Spanish customs before a long bus ride to Barcelona, where they boarded another train to Lisbon. I remember my mother telling me as a child about emaciated people reaching up their arms for food whenever they stopped at a station.

In Lisbon they boarded the *Lourenço Marquez*. Hanna shared a cabin with Marianne. The ship took them to New York, where they had to stand on the dock for several hours in the freezing cold and were then interned for a day and half on Ellis Island. Fritz was interrogated at length before they were allowed into the city, where they spent ten days. Ernst describes in wonder his first experience of a cafeteria, details about the exhibits in the Museum of Natural History – "the most beautiful museum in the world" – and a place he calls Rocky Feller. They then embarked for Venezuela.

The family settled in Caracas, staying nine years. Grete and Fritz never really adjusted, but Marianne made friends in the emigrant community and took out Venezuelan citizenship. Ernst wrote: "Papa works in a factory, Hanna in an office, mother and Grossmama in the kitchen." Hanna was put to work right away and rapidly acquired Spanish. In a letter of 9 November 1942, Ernst writes they speak German at home, but he speaks Schwyzerdütsch with

Figure 24. Hanna, Herbi (partially hidden), Grete, and Ernst, St. Gallen, c. 1940. Photo by Fritz Tugendhat; Archive Daniela Hammer-Tugendhat

Herbi and English or Spanish at school. Ernst played violin and said his two best friends were German Jews.

Grete gave birth to Ruth in late 1942, a sign they were starting a new life. Hanna wrote Irene: "Mummy feels rather well and is very happy, so are we all. It is so wonderful to have a baby in the house again … Mummy thinks from the way she drinks that she will become a rather sensitive child, more like Ernst than like Herbi and me." Maria Daniela was born in 1946, conceived shortly after the end of the war. She was called Maria in deference to the new country, but once they returned to Switzerland, she insisted on being called Dani. Hanna spent a good deal of time caring for Ruth but had left by Dani's birth and knew her only from visits home.

Hanna worked first as secretary to an Austrian emigré and then from January 1943 to September 1945 in the textile firm known as the Lanex. Fritz managed the production side, while his partner, a

Kinship Diagram 14. Grete's Children

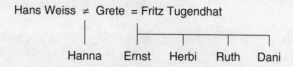

Dr. Bloch, ran the rest. The factory had about 100 workers. Hanna worked under Bloch's supervision, "mostly selling the 'casimires' (worsteds) Fritz makes, doing all the work, like measuring and cutting lengths, invoicing, and selling, myself." She prided herself on her competence and efficiency, and quickly became indispensable; she was accountant, cashier, correspondent, and stock-keeper. In May 1945 she wrote Irene that she was temporarily in charge of the commercial side of the Lanex. "I work all day in the factory now (before I spent the mornings at home, taking care of Ruth)." She enjoyed the work but was marking time, awaiting a visa to study in North America.

Hanna had an active social life, albeit in the face of disapproval from Fritz. One day, according to my cousin Marcia, who must have heard this story from her father, Hanna broke a bottle of perfume and was cowering below the stairs as Fritz called her a whore. Hanna went on weekend excursions with friends, and they founded a lecture club at which she gave a talk on Shakespeare. At dances she was chaperoned by Marianne.

Hanna hoped to study psychology with her uncle Kurt Lewin in Iowa, but, as she told the story, the day she was due to pick up her visa at the American consulate was 8 December 1941, the day after Pearl Harbor. The United States entered the war, and visas were abruptly denied. Unlike the others, with Czech passports, Hanna's German papers limited her movement. She received admission to McGill University in August 1944 but had to wait another year for the US transit visa. In September 1945 she headed to Montreal where her uncle Hans had settled. Ernst departed for Stanford soon after, and Marianne to visit her sons in Canada.

Before she left Caracas, Hanna spent some mornings getting "into the habit of cooking again, because uncle Hans's Canadian wife wants to learn how to bake 'Sachertorte,' etc. from me."[7] She wrote Irene: "Don't you remember that you promised to come and be nurse to my children? As I see it, I shall not have the money for a nurse ... but I could see us working together somehow ... I shall probably study psychology and kindergarten training. The difficulty is that in the university the interesting subjects are only given from 3rd year on, and I despite my age (nearly 21!) have to start as a freshman. I don't think I'll get to 3rd year, because I think I shall marry in the meantime." She detailed plans with a Venezuelan boyfriend who was going to the United States and added: "But of course nobody knows of all this, so don't mention it should you write to my family or see father [Hans Weiss, in London]." She hoped that going away might open her to other academic subjects, "as in school I have always been interested in everything, and anyway, being given the chance (thanks to the U.S. Consulate I had 4 ½ years of business life ... and a lot of personal experience here before getting that chance) I am taking it ... During my time working and living like a miser, I have saved Bs. 20,000 (equals about £1470) which is more than I need for travelling and study."

Gifted with her mother's seal and nutria fur coat and a typewriter from Fritz, she travelled by plane to Miami and thence to New York, where she briefly visited the families of Fritz and Ernst Löw-Beer.[8] At McGill she completed her bachelor and master of arts degrees but didn't study further because, she said, the psychologist Donald Hebb was more interested in rats than people.

Coda on the Tugendhats

Not all the Tugendhats were as fortunate as the Löw-Beers in leaving Czechoslovakia. Emil's brother Leopold (b. 1882) died in Auschwitz in 1944, Benno was shot, and Marie was murdered in Treblinka. Fritz's youngest sister, Lise, was murdered, along with her husband and two children, Tomas and Renate, in 1942.

Hans Tugendhat escaped. I interviewed his widow Minnie in Toronto, where she lived her last decades in a small but elegant house on Castlefield Avenue. Aunt Minnie (whom, as a child I privately

Kinship Diagram 15. Tugendhats

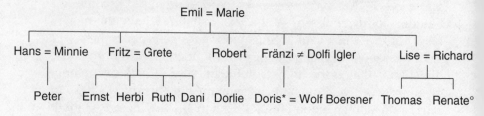

* Descendants of this generation are omitted.
° Lise, Richard, Thomas, and Renate were all murdered in 1942 by the Nazis.

called Minnie Minor, after the car), actually Wilhelmine Herrenritt, the daughter of a noted jurist from a Catholic noble family, was born in Brno and raised in Vienna. Minnie was very beautiful and had several men courting her. When her mother threatened to send her to a convent school, Hans, whom she barely knew, proposed marriage and she accepted. She said: "And it lasted. I don't want to tell you how long." Pause. "Shall I tell you? Fifty-three years. It could have been worse." This remark was very positive considering what happened. Hans, who was very conservative and had even told his family that he was marrying Minnie to "improve the blood," assumed that because of Minnie's status he would not be touched. But he was imprisoned in Spilberk Castle and contracted tuberculosis. Worse, the Nazis took away their adopted daughter, whom they never saw again, albeit they were able to keep their son Peter.

As for Minnie, as Hans Löw-Beer put it, "all Minnie knew at the time [of the courtship] was that Hans [Tugendhat] was a well-known industrialist. The rest never entered her head." In fact, Minnie wasn't entirely oblivious. She told me that if the last name had been Tugendhaft, she wouldn't have married him; it was "too Jewish." She said of Hans's mother, Marie: "She didn't look Jewish, but she was – one hundred percent." In any case, Minnie paid for her decision.

Hans, Minnie, and Peter arrived in Venezuela in 1946. As relations with Fritz were uncomfortable, and Hans resented now being under Fritz's thumb, they soon departed for Toronto. During my childhood they occasionally visited Montreal. Minnie was erect, cool, and elegant. Hans was politically conservative, for which he was much disapproved by the rest of the family. Peter stayed in Venezuela. Minnie often visited and brought a young stepdaughter of Peter's back to Canada. Prejudices are passed on. Dani said: "We all hated Hans." She seemed not to know how he had suffered during the war.

Hans and Fritz's sister Fränzi (Franziska) was an excellent sportswoman. Skiing in Davos, she met Dolfi Igler, a Viennese playboy. "Fränzi," explained Minnie, "had a weakness for blond men ... 'Father Tugendhat' [Emil] was very upset." Minnie was the only member of the family to attend the wedding. Minnie added that Dolfi came from a nice family but was the black sheep. When he turned out to be a Nazi, Fränzi abruptly left him, even though she was pregnant with Doris, born in 1928. Fränzi kept in contact with Dolfi's family, and Doris spent summers with them before the war. Dolfi, said Minnie, had a *"kshpuzi"* – an affair – with the countess of Thurn and Taxis. He died in a plane crash in Mexico in 1936.

Fränzi and Doris tried to emigrate to Australia to join her brother Robert, but something went wrong with their papers. When Fritz refused to help them reach Venezuela, Grete went behind his back and sold a diamond to cover their trip. Fränzi was eccentric. My mother described her as a character; my cousin Marcia, who was raised in Venezuela and knew her well, says she suffered from manic depression. But she was well liked. Doris married another refugee, Wolf Boersner. Wolf had been in a serious affair with Käte (divorced from Ernst Wolff), whom he left for Doris. It was, as Dani characteristically put it, a "catastrophe" for Käte. Grete never forgave Doris.

Fränzi is mentioned in a lengthy memoir written by Eric Löw-Beer (1910–95), the son of August, of the "other" branch of Löw-Beers.[9] Eric provides an account of life among his peer group of wealthy young Jews from the late 1920s. It is a round of parties, hunts, golfing, and fancy hotels. After some false starts in university, Eric worked for his father's firm, first as the agent in Paris and then from Brno, but always with time to attend dinner parties and the opera, and take holiday weekends in Normandy or at his parents' hunting estate. He described the last of Grete's annual parties in Brno without mentioning that they were held to collect money for refugees. His firm had become more international than ours; they got money out before the war and retrieved more property after. In the United Kingdom, Eric became a successful textile entrepreneur, cattle breeder, and gentleman farmer. His children had breakfast served on silver plates. Privilege and social capital appear among the central preoccupations of his life. It could hardly be more different from the seriousness with which Grete, Paul, Helene, or the Weiss siblings conducted theirs.

Chapter Twelve

Grete and Her Family, after the War

At the end of the war Rudolf and Elise moved from London to Lugano, as did their niece Marie. Marianne's two sons were in Canada and Hanna in Montreal as well. In 1950 Marianne accompanied Grete and Fritz from Venezuela back to St. Gallen, Switzerland. Paul returned to Vienna, and Helene relocated from New York to Geneva by 1958. So all three female double cousins were settled in Switzerland, albeit in the Italian-, German-, and French-speaking parts, respectively. Anna Löw-Beer's grandson, Eveline's grandchildren, Fritz and Ernst Löw-Beer, Charlotte with Rudi Weiss, and Hermine's daughter and son were all in New York. Herbi, Doris, and Fränzi stayed in Caracas.

The family may have fallen apart in 1939 as Fritz L-B wrote, but it might be more accurate to say it changed shape, from the enclosed garden and firm to a dispersed network whose members remained connected by emotional ties and financial interests. In this network St. Gallen became a central node. Living together for most of the year, Marianne and Grete were the twin axes, each engaging in extensive correspondence and attracting visits of family members from around the world. The two women were very different in temperament, and there must have been some strain, but they managed cohabitation well.

Mutzi

Marianne had been, since well before the war, the dominant personality among the women. Paul said that "if Elise wanted to stay anonymous in Vienna, not so Marianne – on the contrary, she didn't mind being at the centre of things!" Kitty described Marianne as Rudolf's complement – lively, a lot of fun, full of ideas: very present. Marianne was the person who knew how to handle Rudolf. She was fond of him and unafraid. When she asked him to help someone, he did. Hans said she "was in contact with everyone. She was the real centre, the head of the family, due to her personality. Small funds to help family members were dispensed by Rudolf, but Marianne was the one they came to and who administered the whole situation." For twenty-two years, from Rudolf's death in 1953 to her own in 1975, she continued, by virtue of age, generation, and personality to be widely respected, albeit without any actual power.

If we deferred to Marianne, we all loved her. Ruth and Dani called her Grossmama, but the North American relatives, including my brothers and me, called her Mutzi. My mother addressed her as *Abuelita* (Little Grandmother), in reference to their intimacy in Venezuela, where Mutzi had served as an indulgent chaperone, enabling Hanna to have more fun than Grete or Fritz thought proper. Mutzi was affectionate, good humoured, and open-minded. Her granddaughter Margaret described her as "a real matriarch," a delightful person who told her the plots of all the Wagner operas and loved to sing the songs of the day. She was also reputed for her excellent memory. Margaret visited every year.

How much of Mutzi's money came from personal savings and investments, from Alfred's will, or from Rudolf, I don't know, but she lived well. In the early post-war years she moved between St. Gallen and New York. Her name appears almost annually on steamship passenger lists between 1946 and 1956. On boats from Venezuela she is identified as Wiedmann del Lowbeer. She visited friends in California and her sons in Canada but spent most of her time in a hotel on Central Park West. She had relatives in New York on both her mother's and her father's side, as well as several Löw-Beers. She maintained a discreet love life.

Mutzi's visits to Montreal were always a big deal, with much anticipation and flourish. She travelled with large amounts of luggage, of which I inherited an enormous black suitcase covered with stickers of ocean liners and hotels. She stayed with Hans and Edith, and they visited her in New York. In the summers when we joined Grete and went to a resort, Mutzi sometimes came along; but if we stayed in a three-star hotel, she put up at a fancier one, with a more elegant restaurant. Her image is tied up for many of us with chocolate; she kept a box of the very best hand-made chocolates at her bedside, and one of her grand-nephews recalled the delicious dark chocolate she brought on her visits to New York.

Hans praised his mother's ability to organize a staff in Brno but also her flexibility in adapting to Venezuela and willingness to take on household tasks. She had much more business sense than Grete or Fritz, invested wisely, and advised Hans on his own business. He described her as a "real personality," who knew how to make conversation and made many friends on her trips to Montreal.

Mutzi was quite plump. She walked with a stick but was keen on country strolls. She sat with a smile on her face and drummed her fingers on the tabletop. She wore silk dresses and a few pieces of jewelry with large stones. Her birthdays were annual events, elaborate affairs with an abundance of flowers, tributes, reminiscences, wrapped presents, and many kin in attendance. Her eightieth birthday in 1962 was a special occasion; there was much excited planning while we were present that summer, albeit we were expected by Grete to return to Canada before the event. This decision was for lack of room in the house, but it also pointed to where we stood in the order of things.

On Grete's death in 1970, Hans said: "Mutzi rose to the occasion ... while Grete's children were all shattered." She told her son she wished she had been more self-sufficient and independent of Grete in later years. She continued to live in the house; my mother and other family members took turns staying with her.

When Mutzi died in 1975, at the age of ninety-three, a Jewish funeral was held. In her will she divided 19,000 CHF among five Jewish charities. There was a generous bequest to Käte and smaller ones to a few other people. The bulk of her money was divided

Figure 25. Marianne (Mutzi) Wiedmann Löw-Beer at her eightieth birthday, 1962. Photo courtesy of Roger Pollak

equally among her ten grandchildren, with a large addition to a grandson who was ill.[1]

In the words of a granddaughter, Mutzi "knew how to live her life" and was the happiest of the sisters. A grand-nephew observed that "Marianne didn't obey rules at any time."

New Starts

My parents married on 27 May 1948 in Montreal, with Mutzi in attendance. My father's immediate family were modernizing Jews who had moved to Germany from Galicia and entered the lower bourgeoisie in Leipzig, where he was born. In 1939 Jim and his sister Sonja were sent on the *Kindertransport* to England, where my father was eventually arrested as an enemy alien and shipped to Canada. He spent the early war years safely interned in logging camps, where he studied informally with some of the older internees and eventually was released, penniless, to continue his education. He became a mathematician, with additional interests in logic, linguistics, and the history and philosophy of mathematics. He spent his career at McGill; to protect my brothers and me from the draft, he refused all opportunities to move to the United States. After the wedding Hanna took him to meet her parents in Caracas. Though she had become fluent in Spanish, her fourth language, and loved Venezuela, this visit was her last.

Meanwhile, in October 1945 Fritz requested through a Czech lawyer confirmation of his Czech citizenship, pointing out, as was necessary, that he had been a loyal Czech both before and during the war, had sent his son to a Czech school, and participated personally and financially in the League for Human Rights in the fight against fascism. In 1947 Grete applied for the restitution of her house, while Fritz also applied for restitution of two rental properties he owned in Brno. However, from 1948 restitution became impossible, and "the Tugendhats obviously refrained from taking any further steps in the matter."[2]

In June 1950 Grete and Fritz left South America. Grete didn't want her young daughters growing up in Venezuela, where she felt the quality of education was poor, and Fritz had been shaken by a labour demonstration chanting: "Capitalists, go home!" It was impossible to return to Brno, and for Grete, Germany and Austria were out of the question. There was still the factory in Switzerland, and that was where they went. The factory subsequently went bankrupt, part of a more general crisis in the textile industry, but Grete lived twenty years in St. Gallen and raised Ruth and Dani there. On the way to Europe, they stopped in Montreal to see Hans and to attend my birth. I was late to arrive, surely a sign of things to come, and I can feel Grete's impatience.

Fritz and Grete lived for several years in a flat in St. Gallen while they built their new house. When Dani visited schoolmates in accommodations crammed with heavy furniture, she thought her parents were poor and was ashamed to bring friends over. Only when they moved into the new house did she realize what they had. She loved the house, which, she said as an adult, "was so avant garde." The neighbours disliked it, and the newspapers made vulgar criticisms. As Dani reflected later, St. Gallen was the worst place

Figure 26. Rudolf and Grete, Lugano, c. 1940 or 1953. Photo courtesy of
Roger Pollak

possible in Switzerland to have settled, the most narrow-minded
part of the country. The girls felt foreign, and their parents failed to
integrate or develop friendships there. Fritz never learned Swiss-
German, and it was embarrassing when Grete tried to speak it.
Eventually, they each passed the stringent citizenship test.

Ernst left Caracas for Stanford in 1946, but after graduating set
sail for Europe and Heidegger, with whom, as I describe in the following chapter, he had begun corresponding. Herbi had been sent
to boarding school in the United States, outside Boston. There he
met Katherine Logan (1933–2019), when they were both fourteen.
Kathy came from Montana, where her father kept a ranch. After
graduation in 1951 Kathy followed Herbi to the University of Chicago. They married in 1953, and Grete flew over from Europe to
Montana for the wedding.

A family story has it that Herbi preferred playing bridge to studying. Visiting in Chicago and assessing the situation, Fritz withdrew Herbi from university and sent him to Venezuela, where, without any support, he took on his father's failing business interests and subsequently worked very successfully in insurance.[3] When the Venezuelan textile factory did badly, Fritz had invested heavily in the production of an orange drink, an enterprise that also floundered. Mutzi was furious, saying Fritz had spent the money on a crazy venture. But Herbi made a success of things and lost his image as a "bad boy." He was far better at business than his father.

Herbi and Kathy had three children, my cousins Eduardo, Marcia, and Andy, who were also sent to high school in the United States. As children we met only when our family visits to Europe coincided, at a beach outside Barcelona, on the shore of Lake Biel, and lastly in the Bretagne. In 2018 Kathy recalled that Grete had paid for the hotels in Europe but they paid for the plane fares, via Lisbon. All these trips had to be arranged by letter and must have been planned well in advance.

Kathy co-founded in 1966 a successful English-language school in Caracas. The last years with Herbi were very difficult as he was drinking heavily and grew increasingly out of control. Herbi committed suicide in 1980. Retiring in 1998, Kathy eventually followed her children back to the United States, where each of them had settled.

In St. Gallen

Grete died on 10 December 1970, struck by a vehicle as she crossed a street in St. Gallen. She was downtown, doubtless engaged in Christmas shopping, perhaps ordering the box filled with foil-wrapped chocolate tree ornaments and bars that she sent us every year. In those days, Swiss chocolate was unavailable in Canada, and it was a delivery we eagerly anticipated. It is startling to realize that Grete died younger than the age I am as I write this book. I can think of her only as much older than me.

Grete, whom I called Granny, was someone I approached cautiously and held in some awe. I cannot say I knew her well. We visited every three years in summer, travelling on the lower decks of ocean liners.

We spent part of the time at a hotel on the seaside or at a lake or mountain resort, sometimes together with the Venezuelan cousins, and part of the time at her home in St. Gallen. If my father accompanied us, we also did a trip as a nuclear family. An early memory is driving with Fritz and Grete in the back seat of their red Ford convertible, with the top down, over the Gotthard pass from Italy to St. Gallen. I remember the fresh cold mountain air and a picnic in a pine forest on the descent. My aunts Ruth and Dani and my brother Larry and I shared the back seat, presumably without seat belts. It was August 1955. We were returning from Marina di Massa, an Italian beach near large marble quarries. My parents remained in Italy on a week's vacation for themselves. At that time Fritz and Grete still lived in the apartment.[4]

Fritz died on 22 March 1958 of stomach cancer. My mother received the long-distance call, an ominous sign in those years, standing at our black telephone installed on the kitchen wall and started to cry. She did not attend the funeral, but she took his death very hard and wore black for months, which I thought was odd as we were not Catholic.

The house Fritz and Grete built in St. Gallen was extraordinary.[5] I cannot dissociate it from the person of Grete, though I think I may have loved the house more. Both were exceptional; both, as she said of the house in Brno, "helped one think." The large open living space had a floor-to-ceiling window along its full length, facing onto a lawn and meadow beyond. The dining area had an expandable solid round table, on the Brno model, and elegant slung leather chairs. At the other end of the open room were beautiful bookshelves affixed to the wall, and in the spacious area between were Grete's desk facing the window, a sofa and Barcelona chairs set around a square glass coffee table, and a Le Corbusier recliner that my mother particularly loved. The furniture was elegant and precisely placed. At the dining end was the Macassar credenza from Brno, on which rested silver fruit bowls heaped in June with apricots and by August with small purple plums, both of which found their way into the dumplings we sometimes had for supper, covered with sugar and melted butter, and always accompanied by breathless discussion of which relative had once eaten how many. Above the credenza was a large Picasso. At the far end of the living space was a corridor to Fritz and Grete's bedrooms, bathroom, and a small private terrace. After lunch the door to this wing was firmly closed, and quiet was imposed on the household for two hours while Grete took her nap. Fritz was dead by the time we first visited the house; his room became the space where, during his stays, Ernst retreated to work and Grete imposed longer periods of quiet.

When the weather was nice, lunch was held in the enclosed but unroofed square courtyard at the core of the house. Klara, the gentle, sad-eyed maid, served and sat silently with us at lunch, but Grete and Mutzi also cooked. We had linen napkins, each rolled into its silver embossed ring and changed weekly. In mid-afternoon, once Grete was up, we returned to the table for home-made cake.

The front of the house was cool and dim. Off the entryway was Mutzi's suite that included sitting and sleeping areas and its own bathroom. The stairs to the second floor were faced with an abstract painting by Hans Hartung that looked like a black scribble but has stuck in my mind more than the other works. Upstairs, the hall was also cool and dim with high walls lit from windows along the top. Ruth and Dani each had large, interesting rooms, full of bright toys. Klara had a room at the far end, whose door I never saw open. Ernst had a rather simple bedroom, where I was permitted to sleep when I got older and he was not in residence. His wardrobe smelled of wood and wool jackets, and he had a small private sun deck that opened as a kind of shallow well in the roof of the house. A spry, assertive cleaning lady, Frau Imhoff, came at least once a week. Everything was spotlessly clean; the smell of the cleaning agent instantly brings me back to the house.

Fritz was an idealist, and Grete idealized him. But Fritz struggled in Switzerland. The business did not go well and eventually failed. He sold it at a loss and would not have survived financially had it not been for Grete's money.[6] As Grete's brother Hans put it, Fritz ran the factory technically well, designed the textiles, loved the honesty and tidiness in Switzerland, and felt at home there, but the business and marketing sides were foreign to him. He consulted with Grete, but they were both bad at business. What counted was intellectual and artistic ability. For Hans, only Mutzi had common sense, both feet on the ground.

Fritz was also in considerable pain as his cancer developed. He had never been talkative, and his silence grew. Fritz never shouted or used bad words, Dani said, but if he were angry, he would withdraw to his room, saying nothing. It was very important to Grete that he eat, so leaving the table seemed a kind of punishment to her, and the girls felt guilty. One of Helene's daughters remembered that Fritz never said anything to her when they visited. She was afraid of him and felt he was an angry person, bottled up, although she acknowledged it could have been due to the cancer. Another cousin found Fritz friendly but said he was in the background; Grete was the head of the family.

Dani and Grete were particularly close. There was something in common in their personalities and gifts, and they shared both a love of art and a taste in it. Grete instructed Dani as they travelled through Greece and Italy together. They loved ancient Greek, Medieval, and Renaissance art, but not Baroque; my mother had similar tastes but experienced the art less intensely. Grete also loved impressionism and Picasso. "She really tried with modern art," said Dani. "She was open and tried to like it. She bought a Poliakoff and a Hartung, but there was not a real relation."

Dani said of herself that she was too attached to Grete. She was twenty-four when Grete died and devastated by the loss. It was over Christmas, and they had planned to meet at a Braque exhibition in Munich. At the same time she was "trying to develop an autonomous life with this overwhelming mother." This goal Dani managed effectively, becoming a respected art historian in Vienna and bringing a much-needed feminist perspective to the field.

Dani's relationship with her mother was intensified through the house in Brno.

In Brno

In the meantime, the Tugendhat House had undergone its own history. Early in the war the chauffeur, Gustav Lössl, in whose keeping it had been left, began selling off pieces. The Macassar ebony wall, as well as the remaining furnishings, were removed no later than autumn 1940, before a German soldier and student of architecture, Louis Schoberth, examined the house. Lössl even planned to cut up the onyx wall to be sold as gravestones but luckily never got that far.

The Gestapo confiscated the house on 4 October 1939, and the German Reich appropriated it on 12 January 1942. They rented it to Walter Messerschmidt, the director of a wartime factory (*Klöcknerwerke*) through 1945. He raised the chimney, bricked up the milk glazing of the entrance hall, and as his daughter smugly recounts in the film *Haus Tugendhat*, divided up the main living area to create the feel of a cozy German farmhouse. In the interview she shows no concern over the appropriation or for the well-being of the owners.

Brno was liberated by the Red Army in 1945, under the command of Marshall Rodion Yakovlevich Malinovsky of the 2nd Ukrainian front, with the participation of units of the Romanian Royal Army. The cavalry division took over the house and caused considerable damage. A first repair was carried out shortly thereafter, under the auspices of Karla Hladká who set up a private dance school in the house from 1945 to 1950. From 1950 to 1980, as documented in *Haus Tugendhat*, the building served as a rehabilitation hospital for children with orthopaedic problems.

In 1967 the architect František Kalivoda proposed a proper restoration, and he invited Grete to Brno. That November Grete visited her house for the first time since 1938.[7] Appalled by the alterations, she wrote Kalivoda on 11 November 1968 that she thought it vital to restore "the large living area and the clarity of the composition" as well as the large windows. She added: "To spend huge amounts of money on making a museum out of it I would find unreasonable and irresponsible … I also fear that an empty house would seem dead and cold – this house, as much as it is art, is still a framework for human life like any other house."[8] At the invitation of the city, Grete went to Brno again in 1969, accompanied by Dani, and gave a speech in Czech on 17 January concerning the house's construction and materials. In a letter to Kalivoda of 24 November 1969, she was prepared to donate the house to the appropriate state body "providing that the house is returned to its original condition in order … that it be used for an architectural centre."[9]

In April 1970 Grete and Dani attended a second conference concerning the restoration. Grete offered to cooperate with Kalivoda on a book; unfortunately, she died that December and he shortly thereafter. On Grete's death Dani felt responsible for the house. Dani cites a letter of condolence from architectural historian Julius Posener: "We will never see the like of her. When I met her last year in Brno, I felt that she represented a class of people now becoming rare and, secondly, that she was unique. You, dear Ms. Tugendhat, appeared to resemble your mother very much at that time. Maybe you will carry on the spirit of this extraordinary woman."[10]

Dani admired Grete for going to Brno without bitterness. Grete's aim was to see the house properly restored, not to get it back. The one thing she wanted returned was the Lehmbruck statue. The city officials told her it had disappeared and perhaps the Messerschmidts had taken it. She hired a private detective, but he couldn't find it. They mistook Messerschmidt for Messerschmitt (the airplane manufacturer). But that mistake was irrelevant, as the family discovered much later, because the statue was in storage in the Moravian Museum, apparently all along.

Dani called her mother very realistic – but also idealistic and ethical. She was realistic in that she acknowledged that Czechoslovakia was then a communist regime and there was no private property. She was idealistic because she thought satisfactory arrangements could be made for restoration and access, and she wanted the public to be able to appreciate the beauty of the house. She was ethical because she saw this restoration was for the common good and the right thing to do.

Dani and Ivo subsequently devoted an enormous amount of care to the well-being of the house, one in which Dani had never lived, in homage both to Grete's vision and to the work of art that the house is. In this endeavour they were strongly supported by her sister Ruth. "After almost 40 years of struggling the House was finally restored and reopened on February 29th, 2012."[11] Dani and Ivo have written extensively about it, and readers should turn to their beautiful book and other scholarly essays.[12]

In the 1960s the house had fallen out of cultural memory. The sad thing, said Dani, was that Grete did not live to see the change in the appreciation of the house – it subsequently became a UNESCO World Heritage site (in 2001) and developed world renown, and her son-in-law did much of the restoration. She wouldn't have minded not living there.

Intensity

As the photo shows (Figure 27), there was something about Grete that made her a centre of gravity and moral authority. Everything was serious and somehow urgent, exact, immediate, and profound; one felt insignificant and shallow in comparison. That unpretentious certitude and unreachable importance has motivated this book.

From St. Gallen Grete corresponded with dispersed family members, passing news from each of them to others. She spent so many hours at her typewriter that the neighbours assumed she was a professional writer. Dani saved her letters, whereas my mother, in her efficient way, systematically tore them up after reading and responding. Hanna received a single-spaced typed letter, often of several pages, every week, and every week she wrote back. When I went off to college, I started receiving typed letters in English from my mother. They were very matter of fact, full of details of no interest to me, such as a running saga about a broken washing machine. I can't recall receiving a letter from Grete.

Grete's efforts at orchestrating communication happened face to face as well as by post. Virtually everyone visited St. Gallen, often annually, drawn there as well by the presence of Marianne. Grete was always organizing things, said Dani. Even on walks, she paired people whom she thought ought to talk to each other. Ivo and Zwi (Ruth's husband) once found themselves paired on the walk from the house to the small zoo and woods nearby, and they shared a good laugh about it, thereby, in effect, doing what Grete had planned for them.

Going on walks was important to Grete, both to appreciate nature and for effective communication. She had a heart ailment and needed level paths, not so obvious in Switzerland, but she

Figure 27. Grete, a characteristic pose. Taken at the second international
conference in Brno dealing with the refurbishment of the Tugendhat House.
Photo by Jindřich Secký, 24 April 1970; Archive Daniela Hammer-Tugendhat

knew places. Older relatives walked with their hands clasped
behind their backs, or in Mutzi's case, with a cane, sometimes
clasped behind as well. In nice weather Grete tied an ugly sun
visor above her glasses. She always knew what the weather would
be and was especially attentive to air pressure, feeling ill when the
föhn blew.

Grete, said Dani, had "an enormous feeling for quality." She
had few dresses but wore them for ten to twenty years, they were

such good quality. She would never buy clothing on the spur of the moment, for herself or her daughters, but only when they needed something, and only in good material; she would always feel the fabric. "She owned few things," said Dani, "but perfect ones." And she hated consumerism. Any product she saw advertised on a billboard she would refuse to buy. She wouldn't shop at Migros, the Swiss grocery chain, because, she said correctly, it was hurting the small shops.

Grete never talked money or politics with Dani. Grete had worked hard for the League for Human Rights but had seen the problem less as fascism than as anti-semitism. She remained doubtful concerning all ideologies or that politics could effect change. Grete tended to see things at the level of the individual, observed Ivo. What matters is that you as an individual try to lead an ethical life. "Conditions permitting," Ivo added.

Grete was judgmental, and others were vulnerable to her view of them. She disliked her brother Max and disputed his claim that he had been cheated of his fair share of inheritance. She loved her younger brother Hans but had a way of dismissing what he said. Hans admired the intellectual quality of Grete's household. His wife Edith joked that "Hans married me because I had glasses and he thought I was an intellectual." Hans thought highly of my mother yet saw her too as constantly trying to win Grete's approval. But Hanna also stood up for herself and, despite Grete's criticism, didn't change the relaxed way she raised my brothers and me. Hanna was vibrant, optimistic, and positive, but also driven. Her sisters said she had repressed how things had been for her.

Each of Grete's children faced the question of her approval of their partners. Grete, Ruth told me, "found no point of contact" with my father. They argued over philosophical matters in a manner Jim found non-adversarial (a description confirmed by Ernst), but each was sure of their respective positions. A bigger issue, I suspect, was his emotional distance. Grete also disapproved of Ernst's first partner, Margot. Ernst never settled with either Margot or Anna, the mother of his son Martin. Margot eventually married elsewhere, but in their old age and her widowhood, Ernst moved into a floor of her house. It is on the outskirts of Freiburg, in the direction of Todtnauberg.

Kinship Diagram 16. Grete's Grandchildren

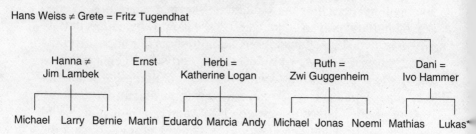

Hans Weiss ≠ Grete = Fritz Tugendhat

| Hanna ≠ Jim Lambek | Ernst | Herbi = Katherine Logan | Ruth = Zwi Guggenheim | Dani = Ivo Hammer |

Michael Larry Bernie Martin Eduardo Marcia Andy Michael Jonas Noemi Mathias   Lukas*

* Spouses and the following two generations are omitted.

Grete liked Herbi's wife Kathy. I had the chance to see Kathy in 2017 in Washington DC. She was smart and cheerful despite chronic obstructive pulmonary disease (COPD)–induced shortness of breath. When I asked her memory of Grete, she replied simply: "Grete was intense." She paused. "*Very* intense." Kathy also provided some insight into Herbi's relations with his parents. She recollected that he had once said: "I hated my father, but my mother damaged me more."[13] Nothing would have been more horrific for Grete to hear.

Herbi felt that Grete was never satisfied with him; nothing he could do was ever good enough. Fritz was withholding. At the age of seven, Herbi had soft-boiled eggs at a friend's house. His friend blew an empty shell at his father that hit him in the face, and the father laughed. When Herbi tried this trick at home, Fritz said nothing but only gave him a look of complete disdain. Herbi never got over it. He could not believe it when Grete told him on Fritz's death that his father had loved him the most.

For Dani it was of tremendous importance that Grete got to know Ivo. She told Dani he was "*ein gans besonderes Mensch*, a really special person." These words were very high praise from Grete. Once, when they were still childless and on holiday in the mountains, Grete sent Ivo a photo of Dani as a child that came with a single written comment: "since you like children."

How Grete came to know English and to speak it well I have no idea, but speak it with her grandchildren she did, as did her daughters with us. Only four years my senior, Dani and I played together as children. Dani remembers an incident when we quarrelled. Hanna took my side, but Grete retorted: "*My* children never lie." This recollection captures a feeling I had at the time: we were secondary. Reading Grete's remark now, it is as if she were saying to Hanna: "*You* are not my child." Back then, the attention that Grete gave her young daughters meant there was less room to give my brothers and me grandmotherly affection, a point I accepted. Grete was kind and generous, but somehow not very warm – very different from my mother and my father's mother, from whom I received unmediated love and physical affection.

Paul's daughter Kitty liked Grete very much. When Kitty was seven or eight, they went on walks together and had long conversations. Grete, Kitty remembered, taught her the importance of talking one on one, that to learn the truth about someone it has to be a conversation between two people. She said that Grete took her seriously. Another cousin, by contrast, found Grete intimidating and said she was glad she had not been Grete's daughter, precisely because Grete herself was so serious. She preferred Marianne, who was full of enjoyment and vitality.

Other family members shared Grete's quality of bluntness that inadvertently hurt those around them, and perhaps I do as well. This bluntness was in part a cultural style or mode of interaction. While trying to describe Grete, I came upon Iris Murdoch's account of the impression that Ludwig Wittgenstein made on her, which she took to be idiosyncratic. Murdoch wrote: "Both he [Wittgenstein] and his setting were very unnerving. His extraordinary directness of approach and the absence of any sort of paraphernalia were the things that unnerved people. I mean, with most people you meet them in a framework, and there are certain conventions about how you talk to them, and so on. There isn't a naked confrontation of personalities. But Wittgenstein always imposed this confrontation on all his relationships. I met him only twice and I didn't know him well, and perhaps that's why I always thought of him, as a person, with awe and alarm."[14]

Grete and Ernst could make similar impressions, albeit less extreme, and they were both kind-hearted. Helene's daughter Eva understood this duality: "I grew fond of Gretl.[15] She was a strange woman. I was 14 or 15; there was a cook weekdays but on weekends we had to cook. My mother wasn't good at it, so I cooked. I [made] ossobuco. But rather than stick to the recipe, I decided to cook it with mushrooms instead of tomato sauce. Afterwards in the kitchen, Grete said to me, 'I make it with tomatoes.' This was clearly a put down. But then she added, 'Did you make the salad dressing? It was delicious. Can I have the recipe?'" As Eva shows, Grete could recognize and redress the immediate effects of her speech.

The principle is one of saying things as they are and rejecting hypocrisy and circumlocution. This approach parallels Grete's rejection of ornamentation in design and adhering to the principle of "less is more." Bluntness is related to truth as what makes itself manifest. It is not that truth becomes manifest in or through art, and hence is somehow distinct from it, but that beauty is itself truth (or a form of truth) in its unconcealed material form. For Grete, as for Heidegger, art is not a matter of the subjectivity or genius of the artist; the artist and the work are the mediums through which truth reveals itself. However, it is a more complicated matter to see oneself as the medium or channel of truth in interpersonal relationships. Eva described Grete's attitude as a kind of naïveté. It is as if speaking the truth somehow makes it right.[16]

Grete tried to live ethically and to think what that meant. If for Wittgenstein and Ernst living ethically manifest through a deep sense of guilt or need for redemption, as far as I know, it was not so for Grete. Grete appeared to take every moment, every encounter seriously. As Dani's comment about the Poliakoff indicates, the art she purchased was not for show or investment but to be engaged. Her niece Susan recalled that when they listened to music in the evenings, full concentration was expected. Someone remarked that Grete's attitude was almost religious; indeed, that she had an interest not only in Heidegger but in Catholic mysticism. Although she was neither believer nor practitioner, perhaps she was religious in the sense of cultivating what could be achieved through submission to a kind of discipline. It is striking to read Ernst's published comments that religion affords a means to take accountability for one's life. He cites Kierkegaard that without religion "the seriousness of life … is dispensed with."[17] Put another way, their mode of being responded to a kind of post-religious longing for meaning or truth in a world where, Ernst argued, there was no absolute or transcendental grounding for ethics.[18]

I do not mean that Grete couldn't enjoy herself or laugh, but she was not noted for playfulness. Perhaps her children and some of her grandchildren share this deficit to a degree. Someone outside the immediate family spoke of the siblings' "incredible *serious-ness*," adding that there was no sense of humour in the family. A cousin observed that family members were "either very serious or depressed; a tough family."

Although many people described the atmosphere around Grete as highly intellectual, Dani found her less intellectual than emotional. "She was very, very emotional. She had very intense feelings." Eva specifically mentioned her appreciation for the intensity of Grete's emotion when her father, Kusi, died. Ruth described her in *Haus Tugendhat* as a lively and strong woman who could get terribly excited. However, as Dani wrote Hanna in 1984, Grete had continued to develop, becoming more open and less righteous as she aged.

Ruth and Dani felt they had to become something special even though it was never explicitly stated. Conversely, Grete extolled them. A problem for their cousins was living up to their reputations. Hans compared his daughters to his nieces. Eva wrote me: "My mother, Helene, idolized Grete and that meant also Ruth and Dani and maybe Hanna too – and so I hated them all," though she added this hatred didn't last. When I mentioned that I felt I would never be as smart as some of my relatives, Eva responded that I had been subject to a kind of myth "perpetuated especially around Grete and the Tugendhat children – a myth my [Eva's] mother and uncle subscribed to a little too zealously in my opinion."[19] As I have said, it was a family trait to single out someone for idealization at each generation. It was Rudolf, then Grete, then Ernst, Ruth, and Dani. Grete's children certainly never wished idealization upon themselves, but they could not help inheriting some of her intensity and seriousness.

After Grete died, Ruth and Dani were expected somehow to become the family anchors in Europe. But they studied, worked, and raised young children without servants, and they didn't have the time or resources to be as present as their mother and grand-mother had been. They were responsive and hospitable, but given that they too had been idealized, they inevitably disappointed rela-tives, some of whom felt insulted by their apparent lack of interest.

Grete died suddenly, leaving her children distraught. They all flew in for the funeral. When Helene announced she was coming, they asked her not to because they felt they could not attend to someone so frail. In a way it was a typical response; both person-ally overwhelmed and concerned for Helene's welfare, they put truthfulness over tact. Having loved Grete, Helene came any-way, managing to lose along the way the Dior crocodile leather handbag that Eva had insisted she buy. The siblings' anxiety was heightened by the fact that Jewish custom dictated the funeral be held immediately. A telling moment came when the rabbi rejected the flowers they brought as against Jewish law.

Mutzi continued to live in the house until her own death five years later, in 1975. Grete's children then came together again to sell the house. Each selected pieces of art or furniture. "Unlike other families," Dani told me, "there was no conflict"; the siblings encouraged each other to take things rather than trying to get them for themselves. Grete had left a letter saying she had no will because she knew her children wouldn't fight over property. She had only assigned one piece of jewelry to each of them. She left considerably less money than Mutzi.

Ruth and Dani used their inheritance to each purchase a house with several flats, in Zurich and Vienna, respectively. They wanted places where they could rent at low rates to friends and have a sense of community. In Vienna real estate was cheap at the time. Dani and Ivo knocked down a wall so they could occupy the two adjacent flats on their floor. Ruth and Zwi live in a smaller build-ing with a gorgeous view over Lake Zurich. Ruth maintains her psychoanalytic office in the basement. Zwi has his psychiatric and psychoanalytic practice in the city.

When Ruth and Dani's children were young, they alternated Christmas between Vienna and Zurich. One year they visited the house in St. Gallen. Dani was shocked at how radically the new owners had changed it, adding a half wall across the middle of the large room and shrinking the patio. "They destroyed it," she said decisively.

Hanna

My mother must have drawn on family money around 1952 to purchase our first house, a small bungalow in a suburb of Montreal, and a dozen years later, by which time my father had a decent salary, to upgrade to a modest two-story house and simple Danish furniture. Hanna was frustrated at not continuing with a PhD but gamely played the role of faculty wife. My parents regularly entertained. I enjoyed helping guide annual outings of the McGill mathematics department to Mont St. Hilaire. The cars assembled at our house and proceeded in convoy from there. We knew the mountain well as we hiked there almost every Sunday.

At some point in my childhood Grete invested in an apartment building in Montreal. As the tenants did not always submit their rent on time, Hanna was tasked with collecting it, something she detested. Grete must have realized what a bad idea the whole thing was and soon sold the building.

Around 1960 Hanna's father, Hans Weiss, divorced Steffi to marry Gerlinde Oberweiler (1931–2006), the childless German widow of a business associate. As she was known to everyone as Poodle and considerably younger than my mother, this turn of events seemed to me, on the cusp of adolescence, highly titillating. In 1961, en route to visit Grete, we stopped to see Hans and Poodle on holiday in southern France. Our ship, the *Cristoforo Colombo*, boarded in New York, was too large to dock at Cannes, so we disembarked on a motor launch dispensed across a stretch of blue sea. From Cannes we drove to the small hotel perched on a promontory with a staircase leading to a tiny beach. I discovered how good French cooking was and how tricky to negotiate the sea urchins on the rocky beach. Poodle herself was quite sedate. In 1965, diagnosed with terminal cancer and wishing to die at sea, Steffi booked an around-the-world cruise with her daughter

Figure 28. Hanna and Larry, Castelldefels, Spain, 1961. Photo courtesy of Ivo Hammer

Marian that unfolded as she had planned. Hans himself died in 1980; my mother paid him a visit shortly before, but for her it was nothing like the trauma of Fritz or Grete's deaths. Hans left what money he had to Poodle, and on her death she left it to Steffi's grandchildren.

When I was young, Hanna spent one day a week at McGill researching and writing a novel based on the story of Phaedra. My parents were both interested in Minoan and Mycenean life, an interest that propelled my own in archaeology. But Hanna was more practical than literary. She left the novel unpublished and turned to various civic causes, notably the Consumer's Association of Canada, where she became national vice president in 1971–74 and 1979–80, and president of the Quebec section, 1973–75. She was active lobbying government, addressing producers' associations, and giving large numbers of interviews. In particular, she lobbied against misleading advertising and for food safety standards and fair pricing of basic foods. She produced and hosted a television show aimed at consumers' rights that was eventually taken off the air because of her uncompromising stance towards even the show's sponsors.

Hanna came to the attention of William Tetley, cabinet minister in the Liberal government of Quebec from 1970 to 1976, and worked with him, drawing up the first provincial Consumer Protection Act and advocating successfully against advertising aimed at children. From 1976, needing a salary, she worked in the office of the Austrian consulate general, becoming vice consul in 1980. She drew on her multilingual skills, enjoyed working with the clients, and developed friendships with international members of the diplomatic corps, but disliked the snobbery of the successive Austrian consuls. She taught courses on consumer education at Concordia University and pursued a transatlantic romance with Laurent Schwartz, a well-known French public intellectual.[20] Her main cause became Amnesty International; she was very active from 1972 until her death.

Hanna's toughest challenge came with a diagnosis of multiple myeloma in January 1981. Told initially that she had only a few weeks to live, she lasted a decade, at times in intense pain from a fusing spine. During one particularly horrible period she ran out of morphine, and the pharmacists refused to give the drug to my brother Larry who went to fill the prescription on her behalf. She was intensely determined to live. Ala said: "Hanna has such a strong will that she even keeps her vertebrae together." The worst episodes aside, she continued to work and to participate in Amnesty, trying to bridge rifts between the anglophone and francophone branches in Quebec. Sympathetic to Québécois nationalism, she increasingly made French her language of public conversation;

to my consternation she started answering the phone in French. She visited her sisters annually and treated their children, as she did mine and my brother's, with grandmotherly love. She lived intensely in the present, not the past. Her visit to the Tugendhat House was not so important; her immediate family was. Ernst, Ruth, and Dani visited after Christmas 1990. Having waited for them, she sank into a coma and died in the first days of 1991.

Chapter Thirteen

The Philosophers: Helene Weiss, Käte Victorius, Ernst Tugendhat, Martin Heidegger

Several members of the family had relationships with Martin Heidegger (1889–1976). My grandfather's sister Lene (Helene) Weiss was his student and scribe for over a decade before the war, and my mother's brother Ernst Tugendhat was his unofficial student, and eventually critic, after the war. What linked them was Grete, who, while never his student in the literal sense, was inspired by his ideas and became deeply familiar with his work. Käte Victorius, a close friend of Lene and Grete's and virtually a member of the family, was his student as well. I cannot explain the attraction of Heidegger, either the man or the ideas,[1] nor can I explain how Heidegger himself appeared genuinely to care for Lene, Käte, and Ernst, despite being well aware that they were Jewish. What I can do is chronicle what I know of their relationships. Ernst became a significant philosopher in Germany,[2] and because I have known him the best, though not nearly as well as I would have liked, I devote the most space to him. However, his relationship with Heidegger would not have taken place without these three women.

I draw extensively on correspondence maintained in the *Deutsches Literaturarchiv* in Marbach. I am indebted to the archive and to Ernst and to Arnulf Heidegger for permission to peruse the letters.[3] Ernst gave his permission immediately, while Arnulf was at first concerned about the contents. He was not worried about anti-semitic material but whether there would be evidence of sexual relations. I found only one letter from Lene to Heidegger and

Kinship Diagram 17. Lene and Ernst

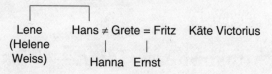

none from Käte, while Heidegger's own correspondence is discreet. From family sources I know that Käte was his lover; I feel certain that Lene was not. Here I peruse the letters to Käte only insofar as they pertain to Ernst and not for what they might indicate about their personal relationship. I am interested in Ernst's relationship with Heidegger, but do not attempt to fully address the philosophical ideas discussed in the letters.

I was accompanied to Marbach by Sonja Asal, who was of invaluable assistance in gaining access to the archive and in reading, transcribing, and discussing the material with me. Sonja introduced me to Ulrich von Bülow, the head of the manuscript division. He described a visit to Ernst in Tübingen. Ernst gave him some papers but pointed to a huge pile that comprised his diaries, which, he said, he would destroy. Von Bülow tried to get him to change his mind but in the end accepted it. Von Bülow told Ernst how Heidegger had arranged his correspondence such that Ernst was the only person who had a shelf dedicated exclusively to himself. This revelation piqued Ernst's curiosity, and he eventually went to Marbach and read the correspondence.

Lene

Lene Weiss was born in Sagan in 1898 but went to school in Hamburg from 1914 to 1918. In 1919 she began studying with Husserl and Heidegger. On her CV, written in 1942, she says she studied, with interruptions, in Marburg (1919–20), Freiburg (1920–21 and summer 1922–23), Marburg again (1924–26), and began her dissertation in Freiburg in 1930. In 1934–36 she was enrolled in Basel. She lists her philosophy professors as Natorp, Hartmann, Husserl,

Heidegger, and Schmalenbach, but singles out Heidegger for his decisive assistance and stimulation regarding her dissertation, which she "undertook on the basis of his interpretation of ancient philosophy and for which his own philosophical intentions were critical." She thanks Schmalenbach for taking on her supervision "in the kindest way."[4]

Lene recorded Heidegger's lectures during 1924–25 and many others up to 1934.[5] Together with Herbert Marcuse, Hans Loewald, and others, she formed a study group dedicated to preserving the lectures. Lene wrote verbatim as Heidegger spoke, and Marcuse typed up her text. Lene was considered an accurate notetaker, and Heidegger himself counted on Lene's records.[6] Lene shared her notes with Käte and Grete. Ernst subsequently passed them to Stanford University.[7] Ernst knew Käte well, but he couldn't recall meeting Lene except perhaps once when she was dying.[8] I suspect Lene left the notes with Käte who passed them to him.

In the summer of 1927 Lene found herself distracted. On 23 August she wrote Heidegger a handwritten letter from Berlin saying that as she was unable to focus on her reading or give the work the concentration it needed, she was taking a break to enrol in a two-year gymnastics course. She hoped that would produce greater clarity so that she could return to philosophy and practise it at a higher level. In the meantime she offered to help edit his publications.

The letter is written in a comfortable tone. I do not know how he responded or how long she stuck to the gymnastics course, but the notes take up again in 1928. In March 1929 she transcribed Heidegger's famous debate with Cassirer in Davos.[9] Lene had the hotel room adjoining that of Emmanuel Levinas, a fellow student at the time, leading one historian to speculate that they may have had an affair.

Lene appears to have suffered writer's block, and her thesis on contingency in Aristotle progressed very slowly. By the time she was close to defending, Freiburg no longer accepted dissertations from Jews. Heidegger wrote a strong letter of reference to Schmalenbach in Basel, under whom she defended in 1935. In her thesis acknowledgments Lene says she owes what she knows in philosophy to Heidegger.[10]

From Basel Lene went to the United Kingdom, where she taught classical languages at Newnham College, Cambridge, from 1937 to 1939 and again from 1942 to 1944. She taught philosophy at Newnham (1944–45) and at Westfield College, London (1945–48), finally receiving a proper post at Glasgow in 1948.[11]

My uncle Peter Weiss remembered Lene from his childhood in England as "a pleasant aunt, much as you'd expect a minor doctor in philosophy to be." She was modest and very "mean" with herself; once, in a French restaurant with a prix fix menu, she asked whether she could have "a phone call instead of the spinach." This request became a saying in the Weiss family.

Shortly after gaining her position at Glasgow, Lene developed breast cancer. She spent her last year in a sanatorium in Basel, where Käte had resettled from Venezuela. Hans and his family visited. Peter remembered staying with Käte; she gave the children toys to build towns with in order to analyse their personalities.

Peter said that Heidegger repudiated Lene because she was Jewish and that was why she couldn't complete her thesis in Freiburg. After the war, Peter said, Heidegger wrote Lene a letter of apology. I haven't seen such a letter, but it is evident from Heidegger's letter to Ernst, reproduced below, that in May 1948 Lene wrote a long letter to Heidegger. In October Heidegger wrote Käte that he had received the printed version of Lene's thesis and "found it very mature. In the winter, when I have some Greek texts in the city, I would like to study the work thoroughly. Greet her, please, and thank her for me when you write to England."

During her illness, Heidegger, just across the border from Basel, sent Lene friendly postcards. On 1 August 1950 he wrote wishing her "recovery and tranquility, and above all the inner freedom to what is required of us every day. Everyone has to bear his burden of breakdown." He adds: "We never know whether such paths will not ultimately lead to substantial experiences that we would otherwise miss." He says he would be "very happy to see you again" but that it is still difficult for him to cross the border.[12]

Here is his letter of 9 November 1950 in full.[13]

Freiburg i. Br. 9 Nov. 50

Dear Helene Weiß!

Today I spoke to Ernst Tugendhat after the first lesson of my private seminar, which I am trying to run in a small group, and first asked about you. I am glad for you that in these heavy weeks and days there are people around to help and care for you.

You may be certain that I have often thought of you in the past few weeks. Now that there is a little more air after strenuous work, I would like to send you this very special greeting and sincerely wish you the right [unreadable] peace and patience. For what is patience other than collecting oneself into purer endurance, which always brings us a gift despite everything that is difficult, namely the experience that pain remains the great gateway to being.

And if you know it, I would like to write to you especially the words of Hölderlin from the conclusion of the Hyperion: "that, like the song of the nightingale in the dark, divine first, the song of life sounds for us in deep sorrow."

Since the border crossing and stay restrictions have been eased, I would like to try to reach Basel in the next few weeks and visit you. But you must decide for yourself. You may ask Käte Victorius to tell me briefly if and when and how a visit is possible.

With kind regards & wishes for you also in the name of my wife,

Yours, Martin Heidegger.

Also greet Käte V. from us.

On 18 November 1950 Heidegger and his wife arrived in Basel, no more than a thirty minute train ride from Freiburg, and put up at the *Drei König* on the bank of the Rhine, Basel's fanciest hotel. A letter of 21 December 1950 confirms the visit. Heidegger writes: "May you be as fresh as on the days of our visit, of which I often think. Preserve the inner serenity and freedom, where the world around you is confused and darkened. The pain, however, gives its healing power where we do not expect it. I hope to visit you again soon in the new year. A quiet Christmas with those close to you & dearest wishes to you."

Heidegger writes Käte wishing her strength to care for Lene. He writes Lene again in March 1951 to wish her a Happy Easter. Lene took a turn for the worse, and Heidegger visited again on 16 March 1951. There is a postcard in May from Bremen, where he gave a lecture. This period "was a time after the denazification process when Heidegger began to appear back in public, supported by friends and former students."[14] On 30 August he wrote Käte that there was maybe something comforting in Lene's slow and knowing death, that by strange coincidence on the day of her death (5 August 1951) he had delivered his lecture "*Bauen, Wohnen, Denken*" ("Building, Dwelling, Thinking"), and that when the manuscript was written up it should belong to her memory.[15]

Despite his obvious kindness, Heidegger evaded responsibility in his response to an official enquiry. On 13 July 1966 he received a query from the war compensations office in Karlsruhe saying: "We would be very grateful if you would tell us whether the late Helene Weiss intended to do her doctorate ... in 1933 and whether the non-admission to the examination for the Dr. degree was based on racial considerations." The letter indicated that she had been enrolled at Freiburg from winter semester 1929–30 through summer semester 1934.

Heidegger replied on 27 July: "Frau Helene Weiss was one of my excellent students, who worked with me for over ten years. In the summer of 1934, I submitted her dissertation to the philosophical faculty of the University of Freiburg. It was considered on formal grounds – since, after a ministerial decree of the then Badisch Ministry of Culture, only a limited number of Jewish students were admitted to doctoral studies – to recommend a non-German university for the doctorate. I then sent Frau Helene Weiss to the University of Basel. The work was printed in an expanded form as "Causality and Coincidence in the Philosophy of Aristotle" in 1942 in Basel."[16]

Some people say that Heidegger rejected Lene, but evidently that is not quite the case. He refers to her in 1976 as "one of my oldest and most gifted students."[17] Lene felt she owed a lot to Heidegger, and she volunteered to give evidence in his favour during his denazification process after the war.[18] Not only did both Lene and Käte renew relationships with Heidegger, but Grete – who would have been well aware of Lene's experiences – did not dissuade her son from studying with him. Whatever Heidegger's anti-semitism, evasions, and bad faith, they were not fully evident to these people in the years immediately following the war.

Käte and Grete

Lene was good friends with a fellow student Käte Victorius, whom she brought to Sagan, where the women discussed Heidegger with Grete in the early 1920s. Käte was Jewish as well, born in Berlin to musician parents. My mother described her as "uncommonly free." Despite their very different attitudes towards sex, Grete and Käte became best friends and remained so throughout their lives. Käte lived in Berlin and also acquired a cottage in the Black Forest, possibly financed by Grete. Later she moved to Basel and subsequently, along with her husband and Grete and Fritz, to Venezuela, and immediately after the war back to Basel. When I knew her, she lived in St. Gallen, near Grete, and would come over whenever we arrived. In Berlin she taught relaxation gymnastics but later became a psychoanalyst.[19]

There are some thirty-two post-war letters and cards from Heidegger to Käte in the Marbach archives, but none written by Käte.[20] The letters are addressed to "Liebe Freundin," and sometimes he calls her directly "Liebe." Käte had earlier been Heidegger's mistress. She had one or two abortions as a young woman that led to an infection and hysterectomy. I don't know whether this happened before Heidegger or whether he could have been the father. His second post-war letter (29 June 1948), in response to some challenge from Käte, contains a kind of rationalization of his and his wife's attitudes. It would not satisfy anyone today, but it appears to have satisfied Käte insofar as letters continued. He professes a deep affinity with her and describes his communications with Ernst as well. He writes on 26 October 1948 that "E. T. plans to study philosophy in Europe; Germany would still be best; perhaps

Gadamer in Frankfurt would be a possibility [as supervisor], as trained classical philologist, expert on Hegel and overall a good thorough and prudent reader."

By December 1949 Heidegger's son Jörg returned from prison camp in Russia, and Ernst arrived in Freiburg. In May 1950 Heidegger writes Käte that he is sorry he can see Ernst so little. In December 1954 Käte is living in St. Gallen, and Heidegger asks her to greet the Tugendhat family. In June 1956 he writes: "Ernst Tugendhat was with me the other day; I really like his quiet and methodical (*gründlich*) style. I hope that he accompanies me more often on longer walks."

In the 1920s Grete read the lecture notes that Lene brought to Sagan. She tried to keep up with his work and shared *Being and Time* with Ernst in Caracas. Ernst told me that Grete never met Heidegger in person, yet that was not the case. Heidegger wrote his wife Elfriede on 4 October 1964 of talking briefly to Frau Tugendhat on the occasion of a lecture the previous day in St. Gallen and of being driven in her car from a reception. He also saw Käte there. In a letter to Heidegger dated 2 February 1966, Ernst refers to a conversation between his mother and Heidegger in Amriswil (near St. Gallen). When I asked Ernst whether Grete could have become a philosopher, he hesitated before saying: "Well, maybe." Another time he stated emphatically that Grete didn't write or do philosophy: "She was not creative in that sense. But she was an intense reader of it."

When Dani was in her mid-teens, she went through a period with nightmares, anxiety, and depression. Grete responded by giving her an essay of Heidegger's on angst and nothingness. It didn't help at all. Käte asked Grete: "Why don't you talk to her about sex and love rather than giving her Heidegger?" But Grete refused, and Dani turned to Käte for help. No wonder that Dani told me her mother had no feeling for psychology.

Ruth turned precisely to psychology, first studying developmental psychology with Piaget before switching to psychoanalysis. But once, Ruth and her fellow graduate students organized a seminar on Heidegger. They rented a villa on Lake Garda and spent a week earnestly discussing his ideas. The seminar was led by Grete.

Figure 29. Käte Victorius, in the Tugendhat House, early or mid-1930s. Photo by Fritz Tugendhat, courtesy of Daniela Tugendhat-Hammer and Ivo Hammer

Ernst often visited St. Gallen. Dani recalled that "Ernst was like a god" when he came. Heidegger was a particular bond between Ernst and his mother, and Ernst passed on greetings between them. Dani said it was "a complete catastrophe" for Grete when Ernst broke intellectually with Heidegger. "She couldn't accept it at all. It was *horrible*." Grete tried to understand but couldn't.

Dani added that her mother never grasped the political implications of Heidegger's philosophy. Grete gave her an article of Heidegger's on art. Dani found it complete nonsense, pretentious and empty. She couldn't understand how her mother could take such rubbish seriously. And especially after the war, when it was clear he had supported the Nazis. "How could she?"

※

"I know what conceited means, but I don't know why I am conceited."[21]

In an interview in *Sign and Sight* conducted with Ulrike Herrmann in 2007, Ernst says: "Everything should be thrown away shortly before your death. I don't want people to be tempted to publish anything ... I can't understand why people think that when someone's dead you don't owe them any more respect, and you can turn their private life inside out." Yet he did not reject my project, and at the times we met, just as in his published interviews, he responded with directness.[22]

In earlier chapters I've shown Ernst's remarkable character and philosophical turn of mind already in childhood. Here I move forward, drawing on several sources – conversations with him, published interviews, responses from several people who knew him in Germany, correspondence with Heidegger located in Marbach, and letters my mother and Irene kept. I spoke with Ernst in Freiburg in 2015 and 2017. In the last conversation I found him very lucid, with his memory sharp on some topics and events, and less so on others. Intentionally, I did not probe too deeply.

Ernst turned eleven on the trip to Venezuela in 1941. In later life he retained little interest in the years before that, resenting it when interviewers asked him about the Tugendhat House instead of his work. He once responded that "the house never played a role in my life, or if it did, then it was a negative one. It's a matter of complete indifference to me where I live. Perhaps that's a reaction to our family's glorifying the house so much."

Ernst said in 2015 that Fritz and Grete, especially Fritz, were difficult parents. Fritz was strict, and although Ernst excelled academically, it was never good enough. Yet in the film *Haus Tugendhat* he expresses great attachment to Fritz and says they had an excellent relationship. Ernst also recalls an incident when (at the age of five) he threw a turtle and accidentally broke its shell. Fritz then told him he couldn't have a dog since he didn't know how to treat animals. When Ernst was thirteen, he organized his father's tool collection as a present for his birthday. He was very proud of the accomplishment as he wasn't a handy person. Instead of showing appreciation, Fritz ordered him to put things back the way he had found them.[23] Fritz, concluded Ernst, was very impressive to his children.

Ernst became a devout Jew in Caracas. He requested a bar mitzvah, declared he wanted to become a rabbi, and requested his parents stop celebrating Christmas. There was both an Ashkenazi and a Sephardic synagogue in Caracas, but his parents were not interested in religion and didn't attend. Judaism was something that, Ernst said, had "just stopped" by his parents' generation; they didn't even consider it. The bar mitzvah was held. In the 1950s he asked his parents to hold a seder in St. Gallen; Fritz reluctantly went along and read from the *Haggadah*.[24] Ernst himself then gave up Judaism. His world became more fully one of philosophy.

In letters to Irene from Caracas, Ernst was very enthusiastic about Venezuela. He attended school first in Spanish and then at an establishment run by Presbyterians.[25] In May 1945 Hanna wrote Irene that "Ernst is still very young, but he has finished the American high school here, and the logical next step is an American college … In character he resembles Fritz very much. However he has not Fritz's mechanical aptitude and is very theoretic. Both my brothers are boy scouts and love it and spend one afternoon a week on horseback. Herbi … is very gifted but lazy and prefers to do nothing to serious work of any kind. He is practical and also business-minded."

Ernst read Heidegger at the age of fifteen. "At the time I often studied philosophical texts with my mother, more out of friendliness to her. It was terribly important for her to do things with me."[26] When I said it must have been difficult to understand *Sein und Zeit* at that age, he replied: "Not at all." "The confrontation with *Being and Time* was formative for me, and very early … That really got me into philosophy."[27] Ernst decided then that he wanted to study with Heidegger, but Fritz insisted he go to university in the United

States first. He was still only fifteen when he went off to Stanford in January 1946.

Ernst was very happy at Stanford, sending Grete long letters describing his courses. He studied classics, finding the philosophy department wanting at the time. He learned to read Greek and Latin, and read Aristotle in the original. The language was not so difficult, he said; Aristotle wrote in a very straightforward way. Jackie asked whether he thought one had to be able to read Greek to be a philosopher. He said no, but added: "Maybe I used to think so." In any case, reading Greek provided a sound basis for his dissertation on Aristotle.

From 1947 Ernst received letters from Heidegger thanking him for sending CARE packages.[28] The letters are typed on onionskin with a few corrections in ink and signed in handwriting. The first one from 7 April 1947 reads: "On March 31, I was handed a care package in which your name was given as a donor. Thank you very much for the great help; it's the first one I have received from America. But I especially thank you for the helpful attitude expressed through this gift. I assume that you also deal with philosophy. You can rest assured that your kind care will benefit my philosophical work. I hope that later there will be an opportunity to give you a return by sending one of my pieces of writing."

Ernst sent at least eight packages during 1947, including one from Caracas. In his response of 1 December Heidegger writes that he is sharing the contents of a package with students and former students. He adds: "Time and again, I want to emphasize to you that it is not just the material help that moves me and for which I thank you, but the benevolent mind behind the gift." On 30 January 1948 he mentions his younger son, sent to the army at nineteen and coming home at the age of twenty-seven. Heidegger sends, as he had promised, a book with two newly published essays.

On 24 March 1948 Heidegger responds to a letter from Ernst that must have for the first time spelled out the personal connections.

He writes: "Of course I remember your aunt very well and I would like to know how she is doing and what has become of her work concerning the second part of the third book of Aristotle's physics. I am still concerned with those problems that I dealt with in the first Marburg Aristotle seminars. I last saw Käte Victorius at my Schelling lecture in 1936; at that time I learned from her that she herself was working on Schelling's treatise on freedom. In the meantime I have not learned more." Perhaps Ernst served as go-between; by 7 May Heidegger was writing Käte directly.

Heidegger writes Ernst not to worry about delays in his studies and that philosophy takes time and requires life experience, unlike, say, mathematics. He offers advice on what to read and says: "Above all … I would advise you to embark on a thorough study of Kant; my essay on 'Kant and the Problem of Metaphysics' 1929 could give you some pointers."

Some letters deserve to be reproduced in their whole.

Todtnauberg, 6 May 48

Dear Mr. Tugendhat![29]
Meanwhile two packages and the package with the wonderful ski suit arrived at the same time. The latter is particularly welcome; it will remind me of you and your parents' goodwill while skiing in the Black Forest, which you too may visit at some point. I was happy to learn about the progress you have made in your studies and about where you stand with your questions.

Last week I received a letter from Käte Victorius from Basel, which made me very happy. It is nice to learn about how years ago a young person experienced my own philosophical quest and how the spark of living thought [des lebendigen Denkens][30] got lit in her and has remained a constant fire.

I very much hope that, as you proceed on your path, you will be struck by a passionate kind of thinking and that it will encourage you to work indefatigably and to achieve ever-increasing clarity.

Might you consider the plan to study at some point in Europe, the birthplace of Φιλοσοφία?

We are always delighted to receive the CARE packages, also because our younger son [Hermann], who has returned from Russia, still needs nursing. The older son [Jörg] is still 300 km northeast of Moscow. But we hope that he will still return this year.

With the best wishes for your studies I send my warm greetings.

Yours, Martin Heidegger

Todtnauberg, 20 May 48

Dear Mr. Tugendhat!

Again you have gifted us two CARE packages. We thank you wholeheartedly for your great kindness. Your help has meanwhile become so sustained that I would like to ask you to hold back with your shipments.[31] We owe it to you that over the whole of last year things have been going so well. We would be very grateful if you could remember us around winter, which is the time we will be expecting our eldest son to return after three years of imprisonment in Russia. Assuming that you approve, I have gifted one of the packets to a very worthy person, a colleague, who is suffering from a very pernicious case of anemia and who can only be kept alive through particularly good food.

Meanwhile, I received a long letter from your dear aunt Helene Weiß in London,[32] in which she describes her academic work to this day. The letter and the brave, intensive way H. W. has continued on her path made me very happy. It seems to me that her work on chance in Aristotle, which she mentioned last, will turn out to be very important. But I also sensed from the letter that it is not easy to find a place of work in England that would do justice to her academic and pedagogical capabilities. H. Weiß is planning to meet Käte Victorius in Switzerland this summer. And what do your plans look like? I am waiting for a letter in which you tell me about that. I will be reachable up here the whole summer. My wife and I send our greetings, and please give our regards to your parents, with gratitude.

Yours, Martin Heidegger

On 27 November 1948 Heidegger advises Ernst: "It is natural and good for you to postpone the study of philosophy to a stay in Europe." He says Ernst can count on his help when he comes and should not make plans without his advice. He wants to send Grete and Ernst his interpretations of three poems by Hölderlin via Käte but says he "does not yet know how to make it accessible to her; because such things are still very complicated for us. The other day I received the printed dissertation from your aunt, also by way of a detour. The work has matured; I think she will still have the time to make her impact on us, a rarity."

He adds that his younger son, home now for a year, is slowly improving but they don't know when Jörg will be released. "That makes everything very painful."

On 11 February 1949 Heidegger thanks Ernst for Christmas packages. Jörg is still a prisoner in Russia. Heidegger has managed to get the texts to Käte, and she has forwarded them to Ernst. On 19 April he writes: "First of all, I thank you for ... the renewed great help that you and your revered parents have given us in the meantime. I will never forget you and your parents. We are now better off nutritionally, so I ask you again, in this regard, not to be worried about us." He adds: "It would be nice if you could start your studies in Germany in fall. I assume that could last for a long time, otherwise you would not achieve what is needed; slow inner growth." He offers advice about various professors and institutions, and says: "I look forward to getting to know you personally."

Ernst said: "I came to Germany as soon as I could and studied the whole time in Freiburg." He arrived in late 1949. Heidegger was prohibited from working officially with students and contact was limited, but Ernst would go out to Todtnauberg, sometimes with other students as well. They would hold "discussion groups," with MH sometimes hidden behind a curtain. In 1951 Heidegger was "rehabilitated," and Ernst took three courses from him. "I visited him in Freiburg from time to time, and we'd go for walks together. I was always 'scared stiff'; I felt totally unprepared. Then he sent me a card telling me when I should come with the words: 'No need to prepare.'"[33] Ernst felt quite insecure and did not yet take himself seriously as a philosopher (after all, he was only nineteen), although he had a high opinion of himself. By 1956 he wrote Heidegger an interpretation of a difficult passage in Hegel that differed from what Heidegger had said in class.

Ernst was never formally Heidegger's student. He did not find Heidegger charismatic in person and said that "as a person he was never very important for me."[34] He wrote his dissertation on Aristotle's metaphysics under the supervision of Karl Ulmer. The thesis was considered important, with a good argument, but written in heavy Heideggerian language. For the habilitation, no supervisor was needed; it only had to be signed off by the full professors across the university.

As Ernst began teaching in Tübingen, he gradually developed intellectual independence, while always remaining respectful and polite. Heidegger evidently responded in kind. In a letter to "Dear and admired Herr Professor" dated 11 November 1960 from Tübingen, Ernst thanks Heidegger for sending him an offprint of "Hölderlin's Earth and Sky" and offers in return an essay on Pindar. He acknowledges that his "projected habilitation thesis (on 'truth' in twentieth-century philosophy) is proceeding very slowly due to teaching duties and my feeble strength." Although the subject concerned Heidegger and Husserl, Ernst was gaining some distance and was less deferential to Heidegger and his use of language.

By winter 1964 the critique was in earnest. On 1 January Ernst sent, with some hesitation, a copy of the lecture he proposed to give in Heidelberg. The substance "turned out to be more negative than I had expected and is without doubt overdrawn. I nevertheless found the courage to send you this lecture, because I trust you will sense that what is important for me is not critique, but the matter itself. Maybe I got lost, but because I want to find out, I had to present my thesis in such an extreme [verschärft] way. I hope that they may be able to show me in Heidelberg, but preferably that you may show me, where I may be overlooking some very substantial things." He ended by asking to meet in person.

On 24 January Ernst thanked Heidegger for his initial comments and explained that he "proposes a 'slight modification' to Heidegger's essay On the Essence of Truth through which the thinking of Unconcealment can be thought as an openness for critique."[35] The next letter reported on the reaction to his lecture, 3 February, in Heidelberg. On the one hand, they found his critique "more or less irrelevant," while "on the other hand ... the audience took pleasure in you being criticized." Ernst was disheartened that they did not take his attempt to create an intermediate position seriously. He enclosed a draft for comments and added: "I also hope to have made clear that the primary intention of my work is understanding and not, as stressed in my lecture, criticism." Ernst politely declined Heidegger's invitation to stay with him.

After their meeting on 16 February, Ernst wrote on 24 February: "I will never forget this conversation. I have received a tremendous motivational push." He then gave a semantic analysis of *aletheia* in Greek texts, arguing that "your usage of *aletheia* is as misleading when referring to un-concealedness, as is your usage of the word 'truth' [*Wahrheit*]." He concluded: "You do not leave the 'specific problem of truth' undecided, but rather eliminate it."

Ernst's arguments evidently made an impact. On 2 March Heidegger replied, as summarized in the archives: "Heidegger insists that he himself has not excluded 'critical' reflection; it has been *undertaken* for decades up to the present day, but not yet presented as a 'theory.' Tugendhat's 'critical consciousness' and 'specific truth' appear to be concerned with ontic assertions and are not valid for ontological, still less for letheiological ones." From the letter itself: "I say today *aletheia* [written in Greek] does not mean 'truth,' nor only 'revelation/manifestness,' but a clearing of concealment. That's what my whole thinking is about."

In a further letter of 19 March, "Heidegger discusses whether the use of the term *aletheia* should be restricted to the propositional truth of assertion, or whether it can be legitimately extended to designate the realm in which such truth is grounded ... If 'truth' is understood in the conventional, 'specific' sense, then it is misleading to refer to the clearing (*Lichtung*) as truth, and this usage should perhaps be abandoned ... The question, again, is whether ordinary understanding can provide the measure of philosophical thinking. Negative response to the suggestion that his correspondence with Tugendhat should be reworked and made public."[36]

Heidegger is saying that staying with the common sense meaning of truth is to remain in the realm of reasoning. Sonja Asal pointed out that these letters to Ernst on *aletheia* mark Heidegger's turn, when he radicalized his idea of truth as something that opens to those who are receptive to it.

Ernst stood his ground. On 6 April he wrote that they appeared to misunderstand each other in writing on matters where they had presumed mutual agreement in conversation. He ended on what could be conceived as a conciliatory note. "I would love to ask you about the connection of Being and unconcealment [*Sein und Unverborgenheit*] and what the question of Being as Being [*Sein als Sein*] actually means. I think I have not understood that at all yet."

The archivists' summary of Heidegger's response of 12 April 1964 reads: "Suggests that T should present his views on 'natural truth,' perhaps in the introduction to his work ... Suggestion that T restrict his habilitation thesis to a study of Husserl, which is badly needed – especially because Husserl's work is still seen in terms of his final phase. H insists that what is essential in his own work has yet to be published; he is still working on a theme going back to his 1958 lecture on 'Hegel and the Greeks.'"

Ernst replied on 22 April that it was too late to restrict his thesis to Husserl. "The intention of the thesis is not meant to be a purely historical one, but a first step in asking the question how the problem of truth can be formulated anew today and especially in this respect one cannot leave out your thought." And further: "Your communication that the essence of your work has not been published, surprised me. If you were to publish these major studies, you could facilitate a different, concrete understanding of your later thought." Ernst concluded: "My goal is, of course, a truthful and balanced one. That, without a doubt, much of it will turn out wrong or too little differentiated is what worries me. But I tell myself too that the details, once they have been uttered, may be corrected by others and that one should not, fearing untruth, renounce asking about the truth where truth appears most important to one. This too we have indeed learnt from you."

On 1 January 1965, two days before departing for a term in Ann Arbor, Ernst wrote of struggling to revise sections of the thesis on Husserl.[37] He noted that the first part of Heidegger's lecture from summer 1925 had been "missing in my aunt's notes and was found only recently by Frau Victorius." It was a pity Heidegger's lectures from this period were never published. "When reading this lecture from 1925 I felt I was stepping back into the old workshop from which I believe I come."[38]

Ernst wrote that at Michigan he would be giving courses on Aristotle and on phenomenology. "One point I will want to make is to show that B&T [*Being and Time*] is not to be understood as existentialist philosophy." He added: "It means very much to me that you are continuing to participate in my development, and that you have received so positively my diverging thoughts and intentions is very surprising to me. I do not know whether I have the power to produce something reasonable and have repeatedly considered opting out of philosophy."[39]

On 9 May 1965 Ernst wrote from Tübingen where he had just returned from Ann Arbor.

> I find it difficult to concentrate on my habilitation thesis after the impact and the diversity of life there. But there is no way around completing the thesis – in one way or the other – by the beginning of July. It is even urgent as I will, as you may already know, be receiving a job offer from Heidelberg. I am very happy about this … With my phenomenological and positivist attitude, I hope to be able to bring the necessary antidote to the local Hegelianism … I have returned with a high opinion of Anglo-Saxon philosophy … What is done there may be narrow and without historical reflection, but this "analytical philosophy," which cannot be reduced to "logical positivism," is marked by a methodological rigour of accountability and discipline of argument which has not been seen since Husserl's *Logical Investigations*.

On 2 February 1966 Ernst wrote that the defence of his habilitation was scheduled for 9 February and that he would move from Tübingen to Heidelberg in April. He included a draft of his inaugural lecture. On 7 February, in what is a critical turning point, he questioned whether the word "being" is misleading:

> This is connected to the question the answer to which is very important to me: to what degree do we have to understand the "ontic" givens, which are the basis of "ontology," as beings [*Seiendes*] or, rather, as "sentences" (units of meaning); how one problematizes world depends on how one decides in this matter: does one understand the world primarily as the openness of the presence of being [*von Seiendem*] or as the openness of the understanding of meaning, and how the two are related. I hope that a conversation could help me clarify this.[40]

Ernst ended the letter by passing on warm regards from himself and his mother to Heidegger and his wife. Heidegger marked the above passage in the margins.

Ernst defended his habilitation and took up a professorship at Heidelberg, something that confirmed his abilities. As he said to Herrmann, "in the years beforehand, all those years as an assistant at Tübingen, I didn't believe in myself. I read job vacancies in the papers, but I never found anything I felt I could do. I had no faith in myself as a philosopher." He now knew he had something to say.

On 17 June his letter from Heidelberg began, "Dear and admired master [*Meister*], You can imagine the joy your letter gave me." Heidegger had not attended the inaugural lecture, but his presence "would have been too much of an honour." Ernst reported that "I think the impression my lecture made on the audience was rather strong, even if not many faculty attended." Ernst commented on the curriculum and level of the students in Heidelberg and added: "I have been nicely accommodated in the apartment in Gadamer's new house and I could not have wished for a better solution, with a view of the upper sections of Ziegelhausen and the surrounding wooded hills from my desk. In the department too, the conditions are good, particularly after Henrich reorganized it. And the most important thing is that contact with Gadamer and Henrich, as well as with the others, seems very fortuitous. We all hope that you will be able to come soon."[41]

Ernst added a response to personal comments from Heidegger concerning the lecture. "Yes, my mother came, although she was taking a risk with her still unstable heart, but it went well. I was very moved that in that context you thought of my father [dec. 1958]. He always feared that nothing would come of me and this event would have meant much to him."

While Ernst and Heidegger evidently remained on good terms, the critique was strong. If truth is understood as "unconcealment," what is the possibility of discriminating truth from falsehood? As Ernst wrote in his essay "Heidegger's Idea of Truth," "Heidegger's thought is not so homogenous as it makes itself out to be, and we seem today to have gradually achieved that remove from him which permits us, instead of taking sides for or against, to critically differentiate what does not appear to lead further from what should not be abandoned."[42]

Ernst has said repeatedly that he owed his departure from a Heideggerian mode of thought to his time at the University of Michigan when he was thirty-five, though clearly the ground was already well prepared. He began to read Wittgenstein and analytic philosophy. "I continued to adhere to questions posed by Heidegger, but I was no longer fascinated by them. Heidegger tried to apply his metaphysical concepts to Aristotle. I on the other hand wanted to show that Aristotle had actually headed for a philosophy based on an analysis of language all along."[43]

Chapter Fourteen

Tugendhat, after Heidegger

Ernst is famous in Germany not for following Heidegger but for reintroducing German philosophy to the analytic tradition. Relatively free of Heidegger's influence, he went on to have a highly productive and influential career, albeit one interrupted by personal problems.

Stefan Gosepath, a student of Ernst's in the 1980s and currently professor of philosophy at the Freie University in Berlin, where Ernst himself served as professor from 1980 to 1992, usefully divided Ernst's intellectual career into four phases: first, a Heideggerian one; next, a turn to analytic philosophy and a primary concern with language; then, what is called in Germany "applied philosophy," during which he addressed questions of ethics and politics; and finally, a period when he grew interested in anthropology, religion, and mysticism. As Stefan noted, Ernst has never been a static thinker, always moving along. However, I think it's fair to say that despite some retractions, these phases overlap rather than fully displace each other. Ernst was already concerned with propositional language in his doctoral thesis; conversely, he was never an exclusively analytic philosopher. The phases are roughly coordinated with his employment, first in Freiburg and Tübingen, second in moving from Tübingen to Heidelberg, third in the departure from Heidelberg to Starnberg and then Berlin, and fourth in retirement from teaching, spent largely back in Tübingen.

Recalling his time at Heidelberg, one former student said: "Gadamer's lecture had 200 students and one could understand him. Habermas had 400 students and one couldn't understand him [because of his speech defect]. Löwith's course attracted 600 students and only those in the first rows could understand him, because he was so short, his head barely above the lectern. But of them all Tugendhat was the real philosopher. He was special, great, and he came back from America with new ideas." Another student said: "Only Tugendhat represented a kind of Wittgensteinian counterpoint to the Hegelian dominance in the seminar."[1] Ernst taught Wittgenstein and advocated the displacement of ontology by the philosophy of language.

At Heidelberg Ernst was dean during the height of student unrest in 1968, and he described it as wild. He was more on the side of the students than the establishment. "The student movement led me to reconcile myself with Germany. In the early years I always felt like a foreigner. But I fully identified with the student protests. I was put off by the strange reaction of a large number of my colleagues. They wanted their peace. And yet it was quite a striking experience for me. I was treated as a normal human being!"[2]

Moved by the politics and frustrated at not working empirically on social problems, Ernst accepted an invitation from Habermas to leave Heidelberg for his institute at Starnberg and embrace sociology and history. He decided later that this move had been "an absurd idea," since "I work in a very precise manner. Strictly speaking, I cannot say anything on matters relevant to society because these are far too complex for me. I only speak about things that are part of individual identity."[3] However, in 1977 he wrote my mother how happy he was at Starnberg with Habermas and younger colleagues. Together with two sociologists, he was studying the development of justifications of legal norms over the past 200 years. They were anticipating a visit from Charles Taylor, and he was revising for publication his lecture course on self-consciousness covering Wittgenstein, Heidegger, and G.H. Mead. He wrote that his speech analysis book was highly respected in Germany and that Cambridge University Press sought an English translation. He also mentioned love affairs, "catching up with puberty" and, in effect, anticipating the emotional turmoil to follow. In

February 1980 he wrote that he was preparing a lecture in honour of Gadamer's eightieth birthday on whether the ancient concept of true happiness could still stand. He commended an undergraduate philosophy paper my brother Bernie had written.

Traditional and Analytical Philosophy: Lectures on the Philosophy of Language was eventually published in English by Cambridge University Press in 1982, seven years after the German edition. Habermas praised Ernst for tackling systematic questions head on and described the book as "concerned with nothing less than the transformation of Aristotelian teaching on the existence of being into terms of formal semantics ... The basic question of ontology for the meaning of being as such is replaced by the semantic question of the logical form of statements." The book "set new standards for reasoning" in Germany, and Habermas's one regret was that he could not dissuade Ernst from dedicating the book to Heidegger.[4]

Ernst accepted a professorship at the Freie University in (West) Berlin, hired along with Michael Theunissen to build up the department. Theunissen taught continental and Tugendhat analytic philosophy. Ernst was an outspoken public figure, active in the anti-nuclear movement and speaking about the Holocaust on the Roma. Yet he was very strict about the boundaries of philosophy. Apparently, he wouldn't let a contract lecturer give a course on Chinese philosophy because it didn't count as part of the subject.

Ernst has professed irritation that he is better known for having lived in the Tugendhat House than for his contributions to philosophy. Living in Berlin in 2016–17, twenty-five years after Ernst left the city, I can attest that this assessment is quite untrue. He is well and positively remembered as a philosopher: people lit up when I mentioned his name.[5] It happened on several occasions that the person reached out and touched me, and I received a good deal of undeserved attention as a result. I also encountered at least one person who considered him a narcissist. Even in the family, while loved and admired by so many, one nephew hated him for breaking up family occasions by getting drunk. Yet perhaps his bad behaviour had a kind of innocence to it.

No one responded more fully or positively than Israeli philosopher Avishai Margalit. Sitting at lunch at the Wissenschaftskolleg one spring day in 2017, someone brought up the question of restitution. Avishai said that many people have started digging into their histories in order to seek restitution for artwork. I said my family was not seeking restitution and that our artwork was a house.

"Where?" asked Avishai.

"In Moravia."

"Why not take it back?"

"Well," I began, "it was built by Mies."

"You are a Tugendhat?!" exclaimed Avishai. He seemed genuinely touched, even stunned.

Avishai knew Ernst as an equal rather than as a student. He called him a great philosopher and said there was no one with more integrity. Seeking a metaphor to describe Ernst, he began speaking about Max Scheler. When Scheler converted to Catholicism, the Bishop of Köln asked to meet him. He said how pleased the Church was that he had converted but that they were a little concerned about what he was up to at night. To which Scheler replied: "I am just a needle of the compass not the node."

"In Berlin," said Avishai, "there were many needles; Ernst was the node."

Philosopher Thomas Wentzer put it this way: "For Ernst, *everything is at stake.*"

Both men described Ernst as incredibly serious, a true philosopher. Two additional acts impressed Avishai. Ernst was the sole voice at the time to stand up publicly for the Roma. And as a professor he gave half his salary every month to split among his assistants.

Avishai likened Ernst to Wittgenstein. Both men were seeking redemption, and they each did so by trying to live an unencumbered life.[6] Neither man was concerned with appearance but looked only for what was true. Ernst never sought acclaim; he was and is "the real thing." He was not a snob, nor did he interfere in other people's lives, trying to correct them. When I told Avishai that Ernst had determined to stop doing philosophy, he replied: "Maybe he is trying to punish the world."

Avishai then told me something I had not heard before. When Ernst was young, and before he settled in Freiburg to study near

Heidegger, he went to Israel to meet Martin Buber, attracted by the concepts of the "I and Thou."[7] Ernst did not gain a high opinion of Buber and so went to Heidegger instead (albeit Heidegger is notorious precisely for ignoring intersubjectivity and the view of the Other). Ernst later corrected this story, saying that while he met Buber, he had never wanted to study with him and that was not the reason he went to Israel. He did acknowledge the parallel with Wittgenstein. But it was clear, as this picture would indeed require, that he was not terribly interested in the comparison and that Wittgenstein had not served as a role model for him.

Avishai invited Ernst to a Passover seder in Berlin in 1984. Ernst shook with feeling when they took out the Haggadah, which was a dual German-Hebrew one that Avishai assumed he remembered from his youth. I doubted the family had used one; perhaps it was the version he had asked his parents to read from in the early 1950s.

Ernst's manner of being found an affinity with Avishai's Viennese mother-in-law; they both had the *yeke* (German-Jewish) trait of bluntness, said Avishai, in which you speak the truth and expect the same from others. Avishai's family, who came from Tsarist Poland, were not like that. "It's not that you lie, but that you don't insist on saying everything."

At the time Avishai knew him, Ernst was beginning to suffer serious manic episodes. This illness was a further comparison with Wittgenstein: both were tortured; both had brothers who committed suicide. What they each feared, said Avishai, was not death but going mad; people for whom the mind is everything fear that above all. In Avishai's view, much of Wittgenstein's work can be seen as shaped by thinking about what going mad would mean.

Avishai revealed that Ernst returned to Israel sometime during the 1990s with the intention of staying. He planned to rent a modest flat near the bus station in Jerusalem. Avishai's mother-in-law told him bluntly it was a mistake for him to move to Israel. He admired her and subsequently wrote her many letters. Avishai also received letters – manic, crazy ones, in which every bit of space was used.

Avishai explained that Ernst had wanted to build a bridge between analytical and continental philosophy; that meant a bridge between Frege and Heidegger. It had been his goal from early on, ever since his undergraduate days at Stanford, and one can say, said Avishai, that he achieved it. But building bridges doesn't make you famous, he added; philosophy as a discipline values strong arguments over bridge building.

Whereas some people emphasized Ernst's clarity of expression, Avishai thought that despite his huge talent, Ernst's ponderous language and lack of style inhibited his uptake. He had a tacit rivalry with Habermas, who was the more confident and popular, his charisma heightened by the speech impediment. Ernst did not get the credit he deserved, and much of it has come by way of mouth rather than in print. Another person observed that while Ernst appeared to be in Habermas's shadow, deep down he was the better philosopher. Ernst himself told me once that Habermas had some strange ideas that were easy to take apart.

Ernst's directness could be received as cruel. He was notorious for telling his students and assistants that he didn't understand what they were saying. Nor was he deferential any longer to his seniors. People repeated the story that even to Dieter Henrich, his old friend, Ernst once said, in public: "I don't understand you," thereby indicating that he thought what he had said was nonsense. Ernst would indicate his opinion by putting his hand on his brow or, in later years, simply cupping his hand to his ear. Sometimes his opinion was evident on his face.

Ernst was said to be critical of everyone. When, as a fairly well-established anthropologist, I gave him a copy of a book I had edited, he remarked only that I had the concept of anthropology wrong.[8] Ernst always purported to be puzzled when he was told he had been too critical or that people were afraid of him. When Stefan told him the impression he made, he responded with pop eyes and said "I?" with incredulity. He perceived his comments not as harsh but as honest. It was best to be direct and truthful. Indeed, *truth* or truthfulness was a paramount value – and not coincidently the subject of Ernst's parting with Heidegger, on rational grounds and eventually on ethical ones.

In the published interview with Ulrike Herrmann, there is the following exchange:

> ET: I find it a lot easier to criticize than to pay tribute to someone. Jürgen Habermas once said to me: "You don't just criticize, you try to kill."
>
> UH: Many of your students and assistants suffer from a "Tugendhat Trauma." Your remark "I don't understand" whenever somebody gave a presentation is legendary.
>
> ET: That was simply the case; there was no strategic intention behind [it].
>
> UH: That's precisely why it was so deadly.
>
> ET: I may have inherited that from my mother. She was just as naïve.

Indeed, these descriptions remind me vividly of Grete.

Ernst sometimes attacked other philosophers in print. When he criticized Theunissen, his colleague in Berlin, Theunissen stopped being his friend.[9] Despite Ernst's digs, Habermas continued their friendship and didn't reply in print, possibly at the urging of his wife, who thought friendship was more important than philosophical disagreements.

Ernst was equally critical of himself, saying in each book that he had things wrong in the previous one, disappointed he could not find an absolute truth. As his sister Dani put it, "Ernst is a deeply ambivalent person, yet he can't accept ambiguity in ethics or in his life. He wants clear answers: everything must be either true or not true." That's why he dismisses art – and exactly why she loves it. For Dani, art can show contradictions, even within a single painting.

Ernst was recalled as a powerful, charismatic lecturer whose talks were widely attended. His impact came from his directness. Stefan said that Ernst lectured only on what he thought at the time. Everything he said came straight from him and was never just the digest of other people's ideas. Philosophically, he spoke against obscurantism, but also against simple dualisms, and was willing to look at what Heidegger actually said and critique it on logical grounds.

Privately, Ernst was not as confident as he appeared, and his philosophical ideas were changing. In 1987 he wrote me for advice on developments in anthropology concerning the study of ethics. He felt he had to give up his previous concepts and was uncertain where to find new ones. Unfortunately, I was then too immature to provide an adequate response, and in any case, developments in the anthropology of ethics only took off somewhat later.

Ernst wrote my mother that his philosophical edifice had collapsed, and he was thinking of forgoing the invitation to deliver the John Locke Lectures. He asked Hanna for her advice: to cancel would be very embarrassing, but to talk nonsense in Oxford over six lectures would be worse. He felt, he said, that his concepts were failing him.

I don't know how Hanna replied. But in the end, illness prevented him from preparing and delivering the lectures. He thus forsook a great honour and lost the opportunity to establish his reputation in the English-speaking world. In retrospect he told an interviewer that he "got bogged down in the 80s. I only gave two to three lectures in Berlin that made sense – but not many more."[10]

Ernst did give passionate public speeches in support of the Roma, asylum seekers, nuclear disarmament, and Palestinian rights. He was concerned that philosophy was too abstract and could contribute little to concrete problems in the world.[11] When people asked how he could criticize Israel, he replied: "Because I am Jewish." As a Jew he was ashamed of Israel's politics. Ernst said of his life in Germany: "I personally didn't experience any anti-Semitism. But that's not an objective statement, it may be a coincidence. What I do witness is philo-Semitism, for instance when Germans tell me they aren't entitled to voice the same criticism of Israel as I ... Many Germans would not have the courage to do so."[12]

During the 1980s Ernst began to reproach himself for not having perceived the significance of Heidegger's association with Nazism and for having come to study with him in 1949. "My 'gesture of reconciliation' now seems scandalous to me vis-à-vis the victims. Because I didn't suffer under Nazi rule. I didn't even experience the emigration as a personal loss. For me as an

eleven-year-old, the ship voyage to Venezuela was an adventure ...
That I as a Jew came back to Germany prematurely – that eventually struck back at me."[13]

⁊ᔕ

Significantly, the year Ernst began at Berlin was the year his brother
Herbi died. Some months earlier, Ernst had visited Venezuela, for
the first time in sixteen years. His report to my mother, written
2 February 1980, was very positive. Herbi was over a depression
linked to alcohol and had stopped drinking. Ernst had "the feeling
that we got closer, for me that was very important, also because I
strongly identify him with Dad." He was impressed by Herbi's son
Eddie and loved their country place.

A few months later Herbi and Kathy visited Ruth and Dani, but
on their return Herbi began drinking again; it was his only way
to curb depression. Shortly after, he took his life. Ernst wrote: "I
believe that it brought Herbi to despair that he could not keep it
under control. He was someone who could not admit weakness
either to the outside or to himself." He reflected: "You know, I
believe, we have always seen only the one side in him, his defiance of the claims of the family; yet at the same time he submitted
to them. He must have had a tremendous need for self-affirmation. And I believe, deep inside him, Papa's reproach must have
gnawed at him that he was a failure ... It is so terribly sad." He
adds: "Kathy and the children are responding admirably. Happily,
no one blames anyone. Kathy says we all did what we could and
we must respect his decision."[14]

Despite this objective report, Ernst took the death very hard. He
did feel guilt and recognized that Fritz had been harsh, more so to
Herbi than to himself. In 1984 he wrote Hanna: "Papa was probably difficult for us all, maybe for you and Ruth the most. He could
not give himself, and we loved him all so much."

Ernst and Herbi represented opposite poles in the family values
and strengths, and yet Ernst at least wanted to be more like Herbi.
In 1987, on a flight from Lisbon to Caracas, Ernst experienced that

he "incorporated Herbi into myself, Herbi now lives as a part of me – the effect of this was that for the first time I didn't see Venezuela with the eyes of our parents but with *his* eyes, and I tell you: I love this country, I no longer only love the landscape, but I love the *people*." Kathy's life was complicated by this romantic identification. Ernst was drinking heavily, and eventually she had to ask him to leave.

In Germany, Ernst had a relationship for seven years with a woman who had been told she could not have children. When she became pregnant, she determined to keep the child, even though Ernst did not want to be a parent. Ernst did feel a strong attachment to Martin, born in 1983, "a wonderful child," but refused to live with them. He acknowledged paternity and provided financial support but was again wracked with guilt. It was hard for Martin, who also felt slighted by the rest of the family.[15]

Mostly Ernst lived alone. Stefan Gosepath was invited once or twice to Ernst's apartment and found it "a great honour." He sat down and eventually realized the chair was an original Bauhaus.[16] Aside from a fancy but outdated stereo, Ernst lived frugally. In a radio interview Ernst said he subsisted on cauliflower. He would cook a single cauliflower and consume it over two days, and on Sundays he ate *Weinerwürstchen*.

In the 1980s Ernst often behaved badly. He came to parties, arriving exactly on time and expressing surprise at being the first. He sat in a corner and began to drink; Ernst said he couldn't relax without wine. The young people, especially women, at his feet were attracted on account of his reputation, his politics, and his being Jewish. He was very drunk by the end of the evening and had to be escorted home, often by a woman. Ernst said that in the early years he had had no time for women and was making up for it. In the morning he'd forget about the woman and the people he had been drinking with. They didn't count for serious philosophy the next day.

He did develop intense relationships but they never lasted, he said, because "my need for independence is too big." He travelled often to South America, sometimes giving speeches repudiating Germany. He wrote that he hated Germany and no longer wanted to speak German. It became increasingly evident that his behaviour was a manifestation of illness. Charisma slipped into mania. Someone who attended Ernst's last lecture in Berlin called it mad. Ernst announced he wanted to give a prize he was receiving to his dental assistant. The terrible thing, said my informant, was that people laughed.

In 1987 there was an acute episode when he was on holiday. Dani and Zwi flew to Majorca where they found him in a wild state. Dani recalled sitting on a balcony and hearing the beefy Germans in the next room saying: "We're going to get that goddam Jew." Ernst left the next day for America, feeling betrayed by Dani and Zwi for taking away his autonomy as they tried to put him on medication.

The mania recurred in California and then Peru, where he drove too fast and was refused accommodation at hotels. From Lima, Ernst sent a twenty-five-page single-spaced typed letter to his three sisters. He subsequently calmed down, but his preoccupations remained. In October 1991 he wrote my brother Bernie: "I shall marry a woman … whom I have known for 4 years in Venezuela, and our relationship became serious when I was with her in Chile before coming to Montreal last December [to visit Hanna just before she died]. The second great change, connected with this first, is that I shall leave Berlin definitely and move to South America. That I could do that so soon, I only learned in January when I found out that the time of retirement can begin already with 62, and I shall reach this age in March. You may know that I had already made an unsuccessful attempt of going to South America 4 years ago, so this is in line with something that I have been thinking about since quite some time."

Leaving Germany in 1992, he gave away his books to students. Many were signed copies from famous people – Ernst said he had no further use for them. The one thing he probably didn't part with was his typewriter. As for his mother, and for mine, the typewriter was a key instrument. "I can only think when sitting at the typewriter. I've got small sheets of paper, half the size of a normal page. The page number is on the right, the date on the left. I order them chronologically."[17] He never switched to a laptop. Michael Hesse in an eighty-fifth birthday tribute in the *Berliner Zeitung* joked that the typewriter was so old it might have been the one Ernst began his career with.[18]

In South America, Ernst continued to lecture and write. Together with two Chilean philosophers, he produced a book for children, *Manuel y Camila se preguntan: ¿Cómo deberíamos vivir? Reflexiones sobre la Moral (Manuel and Camila Ask Themselves: How Should We Live? Reflections on Morality)*.[19] He is widely known in the Spanish-speaking world, and many of his books have been translated into Spanish. In fact, Ernst was more comfortable in Spanish than English. South America was attached in his mind to Herbi and to a kind of freedom. But later, he reflected that the decision to move "was irrational. It was probably an aggression against myself, which I exteriorized. I suddenly had this hatred of Germany, I wanted to undo it."[20]

Ernst returned definitively from South America in 1999 and settled in Tübingen, where he had written his habilitation. He was friendly with his former colleagues, the Fahrnbachs, and they looked out for him. He was becoming hard of hearing, depressed, and drinking too much. Eventually, he returned to Freiburg, moving into the top floor of the home of his earliest partner, Margot Zmarzlik. She was widowed and quite frail herself. On my visits, I found him calm, hospitable, and generous. A colleague characterized him in this way: "High seriousness, unplayfulness [*Unverspieltheit*], nothing of postmodern arbitrariness, extreme sobriety, mercilessness [*Schonungslosigkeit*] not only towards others, but also towards himself, total incorruptibility, always ready for self-correction, unsentimental, and what is even more difficult, unpretentious, nothing of acting or pose."[21]

The Tübingen period was one of relative quiescence but also productivity. His book *Egocentricity and Mysticism*[22] is not only a clear analytic work but a refraction of his own disquiet at preoccupation with himself, the necessity for something that transcends the "I." As he says in the Herrmann interview, "I do have philosophical ambitions, and I'm happy when I'm successful in what I do, even if in fact I condemn such an attitude. I try to downplay my own importance, but in point of fact I experience how important I do consider myself." Of his precocious statement to Irene as a child that if we kill animals, we ourselves will have to die – a remark which she rightly loved – he now said how arrogant he had already been to think he could keep someone alive.

Ernst couldn't rationally believe in God, but he considered mysticism a good alternative. Distinguishing himself from Habermas's position on religion, Ernst said in 2007: "I've certainly got a need for belief."[23] These questions are evident already from his childhood. His son Martin called him a religious man born into a non-religious family. The mysticism – which he is clear he has never been able to practise himself – can be seen as an expression of Heidegger's "wonder of being, *dem Staunen vor dem Sein.*" Or, as Ernst himself said, of Wittgenstein's amazement that this world exists at all.[24]

Together with *Anthropologie statt Metaphysik,*[25] these books develop the idea of a philosophical anthropology that addresses Kant's question "What is humankind?" and begin an answer by means of Aristotle and the use of predicative sentences. In these books Ernst achieves two goals that had long been with him: overcoming Heidegger and offering an original integration of aspects of analytical and continental philosophy, bringing the precision of the former to the existential questions of the latter and conversely, situating language within the broader human condition.

In 2005 Ernst received the Meister Eckhardt Prize, a big deal; the previous winners were Rorty and Lévi-Strauss. Dani attended the lecture in Berlin, as did Habermas.[26] In it, Ernst distinguishes mysticism from religion; whereas the latter is "incompatible with intellectual honesty today," the former provides a means of self-relativization, overcoming the contradiction between subjective self-importance and objective self-unimportance. The mystical state is not one of pure bliss but also of mourning the misfortune of the world.

Ernst carefully selected a Palestinian school as recipient of the 50,000 euros prize.[27] He also published essays in *Der Zeit* against the war in Iraq and a piece on human rights, and gave a commentary to an exhibition on the Nakba that Ivo transcribed and plans to publish simultaneously in multiple languages, including Hebrew and Arabic. Ernst calls Zionism an outdated nineteenth-century idea and says that Arabs and Jews will only get along if Zionism is dropped.

With respect to Heidegger, Ernst was no longer ambivalent. He refused the offer to write a book on *Being and Time*, saying: "That would do him too much honour. It's not only the way he behaved in the Nazi era, but also what he said after 1945 – awful. I think there was something dishonest about him. In human and political terms for sure, but also in philosophical terms."[28]

In answer to a question in the 2007 interview concerning how he had spent his life, Ernst replied that he had focused exclusively on philosophy and had been a workaholic. Asked if he had a role model for that, Ernst replied: "My parents perhaps. My father was very calm, very strict, he exuded authority."

Whereas Fritz and Grete appear to have been serious all the time, Ernst took breaks, even if these were impelled by illness. From the serious business of philosophy and of being a Jew in Germany, he segregated time to drink, only to wake next morning and go straight back to work. He tried escaping to South America, on one occasion even to the furthest reaches of the Amazon. But in the end he was, and is, the man of integrity that Avishai Margalit described.

Ernst said in a letter to Heidegger I quoted earlier that his father did not expect him to come to much. His mother, on the other hand, had great expectations for him. He had to live up to them, and he did so. However, I think it is evident from the earliest accounts of his childhood that despite these exacting parents, he was always his own person – reflective, genuine, and concerned with existence. His reasoning led him on a path towards and then away from Heidegger, one that became a crisis for his mother and, in an entirely different way, for himself.

Idealization, I have said, is a family predilection and perhaps a family pathology. I have been deeply complicit myself, idealizing the family, idealizing Grete, idealizing Ernst. There is much

Figure 30. Ernst in Freiburg, 2017. Photo courtesy of Jacqueline Solway

positive to be said about the family and about both these people, and I hope to have said some of it. But there was a terrible irony in their otherwise exemplary lives. Not to hurt others has been a central concern in Ernst's life. That is evident already from his childhood. But with Fritz, Grete, and Ernst's stringency came unrecognized cruelty.

Ernst said in 2007: "When I think I only have a short time to live, I'm horrified. Not because I want to go on living at all costs, but because I feel I've 'frittered away' my time and should have lived very differently."[29] This statement is deeply ironic insofar as he has said that the central question for philosophy – and for humans – is how to live. It is also typical of his self-criticism and lifelong commitment to intellectual honesty. In any case, the life he has lived has been exceptional.

PART IV

The Family Regrouped and Represented

Silence is so accurate.

– Mark Rothko

Chapter Fifteen

The Reunion

In February 2016 we received notice from the Israeli lawyer tracking down family members in order to process the claim to money belonging to my great-grandfather's sister Cilla Hože and her son Max, who were murdered by the Nazis. The money could be released only once all descendants had signed an agreement. The amount proved to be a fairly large sum, but by the time it was divided *ex stirpes* (equally among members at each generation), I received only 1/180th before returning 20 per cent of my share to the lawyers. The money was trivial but, as noted in chapter 5, the fact that the lawyer brought into communication family members who had lost contact with one other and, in some instances, did not even know of each other's existence was consequential. A flurry of friendly emails ensued, and they led in turn to the proposal for a family reunion, an event that took place in May 2017.

My aunt Daniela was a key figure in planning the reunion. Dani is an art historian and has lived and taught for most of her adult life in Vienna. She is a passionate, forceful, and effective person and has been the family member most intensively involved with the fate of Grete's house in Brno. She accompanied Grete there in 1969. Later she published extensively on the house, including the major scholarly book that I have cited in earlier chapters. She was active in ensuring that the house be restored according to historically precise and highest standards. In this endeavour she was closely assisted by her husband, Ivo, himself a professional architectural restorer, and by her sister Ruth, two years older and a resident of Zurich. It is Grete's two youngest children, the ones born in Venezuela, who never lived in the house, who have taken the most responsibility for it.

Dani, Ruth, and Ivo worked extremely hard on behalf of the house. Over the years their efforts put them under a lot of stress, especially when politics in Brno grew complicated and brought restoration to a halt. At one point, concerned that the house would collapse if nothing were done, they decided to request return of the property to the family. The idea was that we would find a foundation to take over the house as none of us could afford to own and care for it ourselves, not even collectively. Ruth was approached by a Swiss lawyer who offered assistance. He appeared very professional, but when things changed in Brno and we decided to drop our claims, the lawyer became furious at losing both the fortune he had anticipated as his share and the symbolic capital derived from association with the house. He turned on us and sued the family for a large sum of money. The case was resolved in our favour, but not without a great deal of emotional expense on the part of my aunts. In any case, the house did get magnificently restored, and so visiting the house and celebrating its rebirth provided an additional incentive for the reunion. As it turned out, this visit coincided with interests percolating in Brno.

❧

Already that February Paul's daughter Kitty emailed from Vienna proposing a family reunion "to visit the places our parents and grandparents came from." Dani wrote that she had raised the idea with Mojmír Jeřábek, then director of the City of Brno's Foreign Affairs Office. "He found this a great idea too and thinks that perhaps the City of Brno could invite the whole Tugendhat and Löw-Beer family as an act of reconciliation … What do you all think about this?? (Of course, if the City of Brno really decides to invite the family it would mainly be a symbolical act, perhaps they would invite us for a dinner, but surely you would have to pay your trip.)"

In September Dani updated us:

Dear family,
Important news!!
The City of Brno has decided to invite three important Brno families: the Löw-Beer, Tugendhat and Stiassny. Brno organizes in 2017 for the third time an event called Meeting Brno; they try to reconcile with the Germans and the Jews. Our friend Mojmír Jeřábek … has launched the idea of inviting our families. The event will take place in May 2017 … The city is planning … to pay for the stay in Brno; if the city will also pay the flights is uncertain.
I think this is a wonderful occasion for a family meeting which some of us already mentioned.
You will soon get an invitation from the City of Brno.

love,
Dani

This message included an attachment from the city that explained the context and set forth an impressive and ambitious program of events,[1] including what they called the Löw-Beer, Tugendhat, and Stiassny Family Reunion. It was set up this way because the city had three houses on show, Grete's, Grete's parents', and that of the Stiassnys, an unrelated family of Jewish industrialists who had commissioned a beautifully designed and innovative house. The original owners had fled in the late 1930s.

The reunion was one piece of a much larger and extremely ambitious plan proposed by the city. As I discuss in the next chapter, our presence was to be an act of reconciliation, a mark of the former Jewish presence in Brno, and one piece of a broad multi-year program of cultural activities recognizing an ostensibly pluralist milieu. These aims were noble but mostly ignored by family members, whose main interest was in meeting each other. It was also a matter of revisiting a parental home, showing it to our children, and introducing them to one another. For some, it was about celebrating the restoration of the Tugendhat House or the villa of Alfred and Marianne. Others were more interested in their own former houses or in the factories. We seized the opportunity to bring together a widespread diasporic family and to indulge in a certain amount of nostalgia and appreciation for the achievements and notoriety of our forebears. We were all very excited.

Among many positive responses, Peter, a grandson of Benno, wrote: "I love the idea. I had completely lost track of Low-Beers until Erez [the lawyer] got in touch. The last reunion in 2000 for Paul's birthday was a lifetime memory for me. My dad's (Ernst Low-Beer's) last wish was for me and my family to go to Paul's 90th. I am sorry he missed it – he passed away in April 2000."

For Peter, the reunion had to do with acknowledging his deceased father. I felt much the same about my mother.

On 19 October 2016 we received an update. In addition to the City of Brno, the municipalities of Svitávka and Boskovice had become involved. Dani ensured that the hotel was suitable and that within the packed schedule of cultural events proposed by the city there would be time for family members to simply converse with one another. She also mentioned a public forum to be chaired by Mojmír with herself and a few others speaking. She wrote: "For us (Ruth and her family, Ivo, our sons, and me), it is very important to talk about the recent past, the problems in the whole process of the restoration of the Tugendhat House, etc. We are all happy about the invitation, but we don't want to create the impression that everything is and has been pure harmony."

Two things were evident. First, the reunion was planned jointly by Dani and the city. But second, if the city's agenda was one of reconciliation, Dani also wanted points of tension acknowledged. The family should accept the invitation with pleasure but also remain concerned about the condition of the house and critically aware of how our presence might be interpreted.

Finally, Dani asked whether she had forgotten any names on her circulation list. This request had interesting consequences.

When city officials asked Dani how many family members might attend, she estimated no more than fifty. We turned out to be well

over twice that number. One person attributed the large attendance to the ostensibly special nature of the family; as she put it,
"you wouldn't find this in other families." There were two contributing factors. First, many of us encouraged our adult children
to attend and quite a number of them brought small children of
their own. Second, although the event was conceived as encompassing the descendants of the three brothers, Rudolf, Alfred, and
Benno, as well as relatives of Fritz Tugendhat, the genealogical
scope expanded. The lawyer's letter had reminded us that the
brothers had sisters who were equally part of the family. Cilla's
descendants had been murdered, and Anna's had died, but one
of Eveline's descendants, along with her husband, attended. More
consequentially, members of another branch of Löw-Beers heard
about the event and started signing up. The common link is via
my great-grandfather's great-grandfather, seven generations back
inclusive of me and nine generations back inclusive of my brother's and my grandchildren – a long chain indeed.

One participant wrote a few weeks before the event: "I'm coming to Brno but was missed off the list. My aunt Rosemary Low-
beer forwarded to me. I'm daughter of the late Barbara Low-beer
and granddaughter of Eric & Ruth Low-beer. Really looking forward to meeting you all."

I was nonplussed as I had never heard of the writer or any of
the people she mentioned. I did know of the Aron-Jakob firm (see
chapter 4) and of the three brothers and their wives who had gone
to England at the beginning of the war. The author of the message
and the people she mentions are descendants of one of these brothers, August Löw-Beer. Descendants of the other brothers attended
as well. They have the Löw-Beer name, albeit with a variant spelling. Most are British, but there is a branch who had emigrated to
Brazil and spoke Portuguese as their mother tongue. Three Brazil-
ians attended. There were also three people from a branch of the
Aron-Jakob line that had separated from the rest two generations
after Aron-Jakob and were not part of their firm. The attendees'
grandfather, a professor in Vienna, had converted to Christianity, married a Czech woman, and survived the war in a village
of northern Bohemia.[2] They emigrated to Germany in 1969 and

mentioned family members who had left for the United States in 1945, including an engineer in Princeton, with whom they kept in touch. It was unclear how they kept their last name during the war.

Some members of the Aron-Jakob and Moses lines knew each other. The bridge was Daniel, of the Aron-Jakob branch, who was writing a family history and had approached a few members of our branch in doing so. His father had attended Oxford along with Alfred's grandson Frank. There had also been a friendship between Daniel's parents and Benno's grandsons. Years earlier I had met Daniel's uncle Gerry, and more recently my cousin Michael Guggenheim had introduced me to a woman from the branch. Yet Michael's mother Ruth herself said at the reunion: "These people are no more closely related to me than Peggy Guggenheim" – Guggenheims with whom she and her husband have no relation. Our genealogical link to members of the Aron-Jakob branch is also as distant as we are, via our great-grandmothers, to the von Gutmanns (see chapter 6) – of whom most people at the reunion hadn't heard and who doubtless ignore our existence.

The broadening of the group was exciting but not without a few awkward consequences. The city had to cover the expenses – food, lodging, local transport, and guides – for more than twice the number anticipated.[3] They were very gracious about this unanticipated expense, even in the face of some guests who mistakenly anticipated that their travel to Brno would also be covered. This sense of entitlement was not one that most of us held, but it underlay the event in the sense that there was the question of whether the hospitality stood somehow as, or in lieu of, compensation for lost property, property "Aryanized" by the Nazis and nationalized by the communists. Our numbers also meant that the gathering was less intimate than it could have been.

As the reunion approached, the emails increased. Eveline's great-grandson Roger Pollak heroically produced a massive genealogy to which photos of attending members were attached. Ivo sent files that included his technical articles about repairing the surface of the house. John Low-Beer circulated his father Fritz's letter. I hurried to finish and circulate a piece of my work (a draft portion of chapter 3), and Daniel circulated a draft of his book. So we arrived as primed as could be.

First Day, Friday, 19 May

When Jackie and I reached the hotel, we were overwhelmed by all the relatives sitting on the terrace. There were both my brothers, Larry and Bernie, Bernie's wife Linda, three sons and their partners, and four young grandchildren. There were my mother's sisters, Ruth and Dani, Dani's husband Ivo, and their children, partners, and grandchildren, and additional first cousins, children of Herbi and Ernst. There were my second cousins from Toronto, Vancouver, and England, many with partners, children, children's partners, and grandchildren. Then there were descendants of Grete's double cousins – of Paul and Helen, and of Fritz and Ernst. The two oldest living family members, my mother's brother Ernst and her first cousin Margaret, were absent. Dani confessed she hadn't slept in days and said this reunion was a once in a lifetime event.

The formal program began with a ceremony at the city hall, a lovely building with a broad interior courtyard into which at one upper corner a carved dragon lunges. Up a broad staircase are elegant reception rooms, where some twenty city officials awaited us. The mayor spoke of the significance of Jews for the textile industry and the development of Brno's modernism. He declared it time to welcome us back and spoke as well about the importance of embracing difference in Europe today. The city wished reconciliation with all the minority groups who had been driven out – Jews, Roma, and Germans.

The officials presented Ruth, Dani, and Ernst (in absentia) with documents of citizenship. I jumped to the incorrect conclusion that it was Czech citizenship. It was honorary status in the city, but very moving, nonetheless. Dani responded in German; she thanked them and said we were 90 per cent happy with the restoration of the house. Bernie spoke in English, recounting a visit several years earlier. As he and his immediate family followed a tour through the house, the guide said there were no family members remaining. Bernie interjected: "Here we are!" The guides should have known because family members have visited over the years, and Dani and Ivo were actively involved in the renovation. Bernie's point was that the city could and should do better.

Kinship Diagram 18. Hanna's Descendants

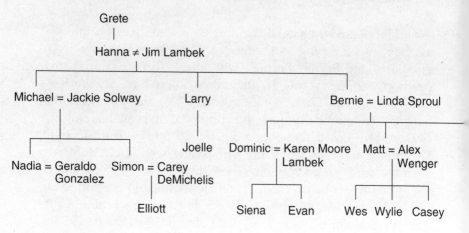

Following the reception, we attended a concert that opened the broader Meeting Brno program. The mayor reiterated the themes of his earlier speech to a large public audience. The Brno Philharmonic played pieces by Erich Wolfgang Korngold, born in Brno, who wrote scores for Hollywood movies, and by Felix Mendelssohn. It was no accident that both composers were Jewish. The violin soloist was excellent as was the entire orchestra.

We returned to the hotel, very hungry, for a buffet dinner for the extensive family. Pulled between relatives I knew more and less well, I sat first with my brother's children and grandchildren, and then with a first cousin I hadn't seen since childhood.

Second Day, Saturday, 20 May

Chaired by Dani's son Lukas, branches of the family were invited in turn to introduce themselves. Jackie and I and our children found ourselves in a cluster that included everyone descended from Grete. People spoke for each sub-branch. I said a few words about Hanna and also about her father, Hans Weiss, whose other children were not included in the reunion. Bernie introduced each of Hanna's living descendants. In this way, we appeared in groups that corresponded to the segments of the genealogies that had been drawn up on large poster boards with photographs attached. One group of three were Tugens, descendants of Fritz's brother Robert who had emigrated to Australia and shortened his name.

Some people spoke about family members who had died, including the painful mention of suicide, which has not been infrequent.

Rudolf's granddaughter Eva spoke of persecution. She added that although Rudolf had been possibly the most disliked member of the family, it was he who had led and saved the company. He had inherited a business in debt and made it prosperous: by 1938 there were nine factories debt free. The rebuilding required that he be tough. Her speech summarized the history I recounted in chapter 5, and it was told partly to offset the weight in the program placed on Alfred and Grete. This tension is intrinsic to the nature of a family understood as nested branches.

After two hours of introductions there was a lecture by Daniel. Daniel speaks, after Thomas Keneally, of "Schindler's ark," relevant because Schindler's final factory was appropriated from buildings left behind by Daniel's grandparents. Daniel's manuscript includes a compelling description of his grandfather's standoff with German soldiers at the edge of his property, which corresponded to the border separating Moravia from Bohemia.

Daniel spoke for about twenty minutes, comfortably making some questionable assertions. He interpreted the open concept of the Tugendhat House as a deliberate negation of the enclosed space of the ghetto. But neither Fritz nor Grete had ever lived in the ghetto, and it was not their point of reference. Daniel described the house as not easy to live in. As I noted in chapter 1, this view was a common attitude at the time it was built but not one to which the actual inhabitants subscribed. At risk of initiating disharmony, I spoke up and said that Daniel's perception was based only on reports of visitors to the house. My mother had found it very livable, and whatever neuroses emerged among family members,

Kinship Diagram 19. Decendants of Max Löw-Beer

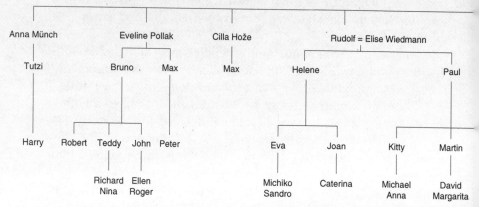

* People in the last line are one another's siblings. Spouses and subsequent generations are omitted.

they did not originate in the architecture. Others supported the point, saying that it had been Grete and Fritz's home, built to their taste, and they loved it.

Daniel suggested that Max was able to build up his business due to political connections, in some implicit contrast to the Aron-Jacob firm in whose line he himself stood. He told me later that Max's business grew more quickly and earlier than the other. He also thought our branch was wealthier than his, and Alfred the richest of all. I have no evidence for these claims, and the last is certainly wrong.

The story of Alfred's wealth circulates, I suspect, because Alfred underwrote Grete's house, and it is the subject of some envy. I heard speculation that Grete received more than her share of inheritance. One person went so far as to say they had grounds to sue for part of the house, only to add that, of course, they would never do so. The irony is that we (Grete's descendants) feel certain our second cousins are much wealthier than we are. This friction illustrates what I have come to identify as a pattern of how the branches and sub-branches imagine each other.

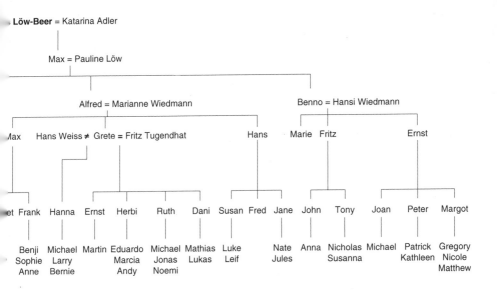

Daniel begins his manuscript with the question, What's in a name? The name of course is Löw-Beer, and that is what anchors the connection between his branch and ours. It is a connection reproduced through men, and it links together distant branches, each of which has other relatives to whom they are respectively genealogically much closer but through whom they are not linked by name. Daniel seemed to ignore the highly distinguished Placzek descendants of Karolina Löw-Beer. By contrast, he depicts the members of our two branches as a close-knit family during the 1920s and 1930s. Relations were friendly, but I doubt they were close. Among other things, this approach ignores the ties through mothers and wives that pulled people in different directions.[4]

As noted in chapter 2, starting with the patronym has particular consequences; it is, in effect, the name that produces "the family." Of course, Daniel is not alone in doing so; the existence of patronymic family names speaks for itself. And this family once did have a strong patrilineal bias, shaped not only by the name but by partnerships in the respective firms. But patriliny was never the exclusive mode of connection, and since the war it has largely given way to bilateral ties, that is, to roughly equal weight on relations constituted through men and through women, where one identifies as much with one's mother's family as with one's father's, and where women and men inherit equally from both parents. Indeed, the equivalence between women and men was evident in the way we stood up as different branches, some descending from a woman and some from a man, and a few of us connected to the rest of the family through successive generations of women.

By her name Grete Tugendhat both affirms and challenges the patrilineal narrative. She affirms it insofar as she takes on the name of her husband, and it is this name that is bequeathed to the house. But she challenges it insofar as she becomes, in a way, the iconic figure of the Löw-Beers, more cited and more celebrated in Brno than the men because of the legacy of the house. It is the house that makes the family famous, not the reverse, and it is the house that Brno is ultimately interested in, as a source of tourist revenue and a piece of symbolic capital. Grete is the central figure in this story. She hired Mies, identified strongly with his work and defended it, and in the end she was the one who recognized that the house belonged to the world – the public – and not exclusively to herself or her heirs. Moreover, as the anthropologist Marcel Mauss observed, a gift contains a part of the giver, and Grete is recognized as embedded, in a sense, in her act of donation and in the house itself.[5]

Accordingly, the next period of the day was devoted to watching and discussing the film *Haus Tugendhat* (in its English version), directed by Dieter Reifarth in 2013. As noted earlier, *Haus Tugendhat* documents the house from original conception and construction through the period in which the family occupied it, appropriation by a Nazi family, service as a dance school, and then as an orthopaedic rehabilitation centre for girls in the communist period. There are poignant interviews with Czech women remembering their childhood years in the house. The film details the rediscovery of the Macassar wall panels in the university refectory and former Gestapo bar, illustrates the commercials filmed in the house, as well as the meeting there between Václav Klaus and Vladimír Mečiar that dissolved Czechoslovakia. It includes reflections by art and architectural historians, recollections by Irene Kalkhofen, and an interview with Ernst, which confirmed, in a way, his presence among us. Those of us from the diaspora were not interviewed, which was probably a good thing.

Dani had sent me a copy of the film a year earlier, and many of us had seen it before. Those who watched it for the first time praised it, and there was lively discussion. In private I voiced my unhappiness with Irene's depiction of my mother as a jealous child, quite unlike her adult personality and without mention of the good reasons for feeling that way. Ruth and Dani thought Irene was mistaken to say that Marianne rang Grete to keep the children home on Yom Kippur. I think Irene was right on this score, but it illustrates how the voices of survivors (including mine) inevitably come to dominate those of the deceased. As Hilary Mantel put it in a discussion of historical fiction, the dead can only be interpreted.[6]

We were told there would be a march in the afternoon and could choose whether to participate. Dani had agreed to the mayor's request to speak on behalf of the family. When she fell ill, I rashly volunteered to take her place. I had no clear sense of what it was all about. Why was it called a pilgrimage of reconciliation? Who was to be reconciled with whom, and what did our family have to do with it? The fact that some family members were boycotting added to my unease, but I felt it was something we owed the city. Jackie and our daughter Nadia helped me figure out what to say.

As we joined the last few hundred metres of the march, we were subject to photographers and journalists. We passed a number of protesters holding placards and shouting at us. When I asked who they were, I received various answers, dismissing them as either communists or fascists. Perhaps some were Jewish. Some called the marchers Nazis. I did not have an opportunity to speak with the protesters and felt myself carried along by events.

The annual march commemorates the expulsion of German speakers from Brno in 1945. As documented in the next chapter, the point is not to absolve German speakers but to acknowledge their suffering at the hands of Czechs who forcibly expelled them. The march culminated on the grounds of the Augustinian Abbey, where Gregor Mendel once conducted his famous experiments with pea plants. People gathered around a raised platform with a children's choir. The mayor, standing ramrod straight, acknowledged the former cosmopolitan life of the city. He spoke against populism and was supported by a representative from a city in Germany.

My turn was next. I was asked to speak in short sentences to make it easier for my cousin Lukas who translated my words into German. A city official then translated from German into Czech. As Lukas said, we speak different languages because of the expulsions. I was brief, saying that while it was important to remember the past, the march should also remind us of the insecurity faced by current refugees. People clapped at this statement. I praised the mayor and tried to be polite and grateful. I said my mother had not encountered anti-semitism until she reached England.

As we left, we approached a stone that serves as a permanent marker of the events of 1945, and we each lit a candle, placing them among the many others that burned there. My son voiced the opinion that we may have been co-opted, but I felt relief and that we were all on the right side of history.

The family was then bused to the architecture centre, a beautiful modern building, where we heard a talk on Jewish life in Brno by Jaroslav Klenovský, curator of Jewish monuments in South Moravia. He said there had been some 12,000 Jews in Brno before the war, of whom over 9,000 were deported.[7] He described three synagogues, notably the Great Synagogue, three stories high, built in Moorish style in 1853 and burned down immediately on German occupation. The Jewish cemetery, started in 1852, now contains some 9,000 tombstones and 12,000 burials.

We walked from the architecture centre to the Stiassny Villa directly below it. It is an elegant building set in large gardens, used by the city for receptions. Despite the modernist exterior esteemed by Alfred Stiassny, the inside, with the exception of Alfred's bedroom, was fussier and old-fashioned, according to his wife's taste.

Figure 31. Speeches at the Pilgrimage of Reconciliation. From left to right, Lukas Hammer, Michael Lambek, Mayor Petr Vokřál. The tall young man in glasses is Jaroslav Ostrčilík, founder of the march. To the far right is Mojmír Jeřábek. Photo likely by Michal Růžička, courtesy of Meeting Brno festival

Jackie observed that these beautiful houses reveal the commitment of their owners to life in Brno. The houses were not only symbols of modernism but substantial commitments to a place and a kind of life, and materializations of it. Today that life is gone, but the houses remain in place. Their restoration speaks to other values than the ones for which they were constructed; they become icons of a forfeited past rather than an inhabited present – but with hope for the future as well.

Third Day, Sunday, 21 May

The next day was devoted to visiting the Tugendhat and Löw-Beer Houses. As we approached the former, many wondered whether it could live up to its reputation. From the street the proportions are striking – long and low with a gap through which one can see across the city. The façade is unobtrusive, the front door hidden in a small curve, like a shell. The translucent glass produces shifts in the tone of the entrance throughout the day.

Iveta Černá, the curator, and her staff hovered on the terrace to welcome us. Iveta had wanted to guide the tour and was unhappy when Dani and Ivo announced they would do it themselves. But she came graciously to greet us. We placed our feet on a machine that wrapped the soles of our shoes in plastic and were instructed not to sit on the furniture or to touch anything. Dani and Ivo wanted to show we were being respectful; if we didn't follow the rules, the management could forbid us privileges in the future. Our numbers also meant we had to go through the house in turns.

I followed a group led by Dani down the narrow travertine staircase to the main room. The space is expansive and open, yet also complex. The onyx wall – a giant slab floor to ceiling – is magnificent, with both mirroring and translucent qualities in certain light. Dani remarked that had it not remained, it wouldn't have been worth restoring the house. The formally arranged furniture – Barcelona chairs and glass coffee table – sit between the onyx and the giant wall of windows. The chairs are replicas. Some original pieces were taken with the family when they left; Dani, Ruth, and Herbi's children each have some. They offered to sell them back at a modest price, but the city refused, wanting the furniture to look new, not worn. As a result, the appearance is not exact; in particular, the leather upholstery is dyed a more vivid green than the original.

Behind the onyx stretches the study. To one side is the glass-walled conservatory, green with plants; to the other, the curve of Macassar ebony that envelops the dining area. Cruciform chrome-covered steel pillars support the structure. The windows overlook the garden and provide a view across Brno; they descend into the floor at the push of the button. The maids must have spent a good deal of time polishing the chrome and washing the windows.[8]

Dani explained that Mies started planning the house before he began the Barcelona Pavilion. The influence was in that direction, not the other, although the Barcelona Pavilion was finished first. Both constructions make use of vertical panels, clean lines, exact proportions, and an interpenetration of inside and outside. The latter could be achieved more fully in the Barcelona Pavilion as it was not designed as a house to be lived within.

Dani is always insightful and passionate when she talks about art. Here she focused less on the original design than on the restoration. For her, the visit celebrated the successful conservation, a goal for which she had worked for years. At the same time, she observed details that the restorers had not got quite right and aspects of the display of which she did not approve. Some family members thought she was being unduly negative, but Dani and Ivo's focused attention continues the perfectionism of Mies and Lily Reich, for whom every detail was extremely important. That is what makes the house the fabulous piece of architecture it is.

The pieces of the curved dining wall had been damaged, but they were restored and, in Dani's estimation, put back very well. The grain of the wood is much more subtle than the pieces that had replaced them before the originals were rediscovered. The outer panels are new and not as fine as the inner ones, but as an endangered species, ebony can no longer be harvested.

A source of dismay for Dani was that the dining table was displayed fully extended, big enough to seat twenty around it. That would have been extremely rare during the time her parents lived there. They did not entertain much, and mostly it would have been set at its smallest diameter, an intimate table for the immediate family. To Dani, the extended table looks ostentatious and signals that the curators are making a statement about her parents' lifestyle. Presumably, from the curators' perspective, the table is extended to show the marvellous structure – how a circular table can be extended outwards once and even twice. The dense pearwood set on steel columns is a remarkable feat of design. Grete had a similar extendable round table in her house in St. Gallen, and Dani too has one in her flat in Vienna.

The disagreement here is over the subject or object of representation. Is it a house or a home? Does the display concern the architect and his work of art, vacant of inhabitants – or the family who commissioned it and the life they lived within? How do you balance between the two?

In the basement is a room for storing winter clothing. It contained a rack of fur coats. But Grete had owned only one fur coat plus a stole for the opera. What were all these coats doing here? When I was accosted by the filmmakers, I asserted angrily on camera that the coats should be removed. I added that we needed some say in how we were represented. The fur coats imply rich, vulgar, ostentatious Jews, an anti-semitic stereotype. The house *is* ostentatious in its way, but it is a kind of aesthetic, even ascetic, luxury meant for the appreciation of the inhabitants, not for show. The couple lived quite privately and had parties only once a year. Grete was always well but simply dressed; her style was understated, her jewelry elegant but not showy. They lived Mies's maxim: less is more.

That afternoon Iveta knelt on the steps by Ruth and said she would remove the furs. It was as if no one had asked her to do so before. But in fact Dani had made the request many times. A few days later I realized another disturbing fact: the furs were the only item in the house indicating personal property of the owners. There were no personal items in the bedrooms, no clothing, toiletries, or other personal effects, only the furs. What kind of statement was that?

Ivo explained further details of the fixtures and the restoration. In the basement he showed us Fritz's dark room as well as the elaborate system for heating (with coal), cooling, filtering, and controlling humidity, as well as the narrow room into which the windows drop and their counterweights are held, like an elevator shaft. He told us that Fritz and Grete loved returning to their house. They could draw curtains to create more intimate spaces, and they often sat in the evening at the small table at the foot of the stairs that had a warm light coming from behind a translucent glass pane. It was as if life in the house, in all its detail, was somehow mythical in significance.

❦

By the end of the morning, Dani and Ivo had each given the tour to four groups. We then gathered on the lawn for a professional full family portrait. The result proved to be a photograph in which every member of the family is visible against the backdrop of the house (see the back cover).

After lunch, we reassembled at the Löw-Beer Villa that stands in a row of elegant edifices facing Lužánky Park. This property was the house of Alfred and Marianne, newly opened as a museum about the textile industry and the Brno bourgeoisie of the period. The entrance today is through a ticket office and gift shop. The central hall was a surprise. It is a very large room that rises more than two stories to a skylight. The skylight, which could be opened, is built in two layers, protecting the floor below. In other words, this house too is open and light-filled, although the proportions and feeling are very different from those in the Tugendhat Villa. At the far side, partly concealed by the balustrade, a wooden staircase ascends to the second floor. Here an open gallery runs along the four sides of the atrium, looking into it from above. The structure is quadrangular; the bedrooms open off the four sides of the gallery.

The atrium extends in the back to an elegant terrace with steps into the garden with a circular fountain and the extensive grassy slope that leads up to the Tugendhat House. The young adults and children spent much of the afternoon there. The rest of us toured the house and exhibits, comprised mainly of placards and wall-mounted photographs. The museum not only capitalizes on the tourism that comes to the Tugendhat House but also serves the practical function of displaying information that could not be placed in the Tugendhat House itself without destroying its space. If the Tugendhat House displays itself, contextualizing it becomes a main function of the Löw-Beer House. The central figure is once again Grete. There is little about Alfred and Marianne or their two sons. Naturally, this focus was disconcerting to the children of the sons, who had expected to see more of their direct antecedents commemorated. One placard declared the Löw-Beer House to be the sort of thing Grete was rebelling against. And yet the house was not in the least dark and cramped, but airy and spacious. If it was once cluttered with furniture, that is no longer evident. Perhaps the apartment of Fritz Tugendhat's parents looked different.[9]

Rows of folding chairs were set up in the central hall. We were entertained first by Ruth's son Jonas and his partner Andrea, talented musicians playing the accordion and violin, respectively. They offered lively tunes, subsequently described by the Czechs as traditional Jewish music, which, despite some Klezmer, it mostly was not. They were followed by a string quartet, introduced by a woman who said that some years earlier she had asked Ruth her mother's favourite pieces of music. And so, again, Grete was present as we listened to Schubert's expertly performed *Death and the Maiden*. Ruth and Dani were visibly moved by this further homage to their mother.

In the late afternoon we walked up through the garden back to the Tugendhat House, entering through the broad steps on the back terrace. Folding chairs were set up around the grand piano for another of Grete's favourite pieces, this time a Beethoven sonata for piano and cello, again expertly performed. Now we were guests of the city rather than visitors to the museum, so no one asked us to cover our shoes. More than one relative sat on the Mies replica furniture, and I tried a chair too. Herbi's sons, who have some of the original dining chairs, said they were impractical and tipped too far back. Even Dani agreed.

As we sat in the late afternoon light, I looked at the onyx wall, trying to experience its magic. It did not lead me to the past but reflected the happy chaos of the present. The windows were down, and the house felt lived in. Over a hundred family members and numerous city officials and museum guides mingled on the terrace below the house. We were treated to drinks and a buffet dinner, served from the basement, which we took outside to eat. The late spring weather was perfect.

Fourth Day, Monday, 22 May

We were taken through Brno to look at modernist architecture, though it proved hard to appreciate from the bus windows, and most of us were too busy talking to each other to listen to our guide.[10] Our first stop was the trade centre. Its buildings, constructed just prior to the Tugendhat House, remain remarkable innovative pieces of architecture. The 1928 Exhibition of

Contemporary Culture was financially supported by Alfred Löw-Beer and Emil Tugendhat, among others.[11] Mies visited the site and was surely impressed.

We stopped briefly at the site of the old Löw-Beer factory, established by Max around 1861, but could not enter the decrepit buildings. The guide said that Grete had lived there until age eleven. She is again the central figure, though as his descendants remarked, her older brother lived there too. Situated between factory buildings, the house must have been noisy.

The one remaining synagogue in Brno is modern on the outside, orthodox in design within, bright and unfussy. We were given another talk about the history of Brno's Jewish community. On 17 March 1939, the day Hitler entered Brno, the main synagogue was incinerated by the Germans with the help of Czech fascists. The guide said that at present there were some 300 Jews resident in Brno, most no longer practising and many coming from Slovakia. The most active members of the congregation tend to be recent converts.

Our presence felt a bit odd as it is doubtful that any of our ancestors had ever set foot in the place, though some of them may have attended the main synagogue on occasion. Most living family members were clearly not used to entering synagogues, and the men perched the proffered yarmulkes awkwardly on our heads. The sense of our inauthenticity was enhanced when we noticed a brochure on Jewish life in Brno that had on its cover nothing other than Tugendhat House. There is surely a paradox that the family comes to stand for an identity in which it showed little interest.

After lunch at a garden restaurant, we heard a lecture by Kateřina Tučková, the author of *Fabrika*, a novel about the early industrialists, and program director for the Brno festival. She recounted the history of the local textile industry, pointing out that the first manufacturers were Christian. They were Germans of Reform Church background, younger sons who had not inherited their father's business and were encouraged to relocate to Brno. One of them sold material to Napoleon's soldiers who needed winter clothes before the battle of Austerlitz, held just outside Brno in 1805. That detail corrects the family myth that this transaction was how the Löw-Beers started.

Kateřina explained that the first generation of manufacturers lived at their factories, while the second generation moved into nice villas, as Alfred did. She described the civic roles of the wealthy textile manufacturers and affirmed that Christian and Jewish owners mixed socially and worked together developing cultural institutions in the 1890s (see chapter 16). The wider point is that class was critical and formed a divide between German and Czech speakers.

Returning to the hotel, I discovered Helene's daughters eating a late lunch on the terrace. They were on their own schedule and explained that they had used the morning to visit the cement factory that the family had owned together with the Hožes, whose inheritance we had just received. Having looked around the factory, Eva was unimpressed and decided it was not worth trying to recover. Some weeks earlier Eva had asked Dani to have the cement factory put on the itinerary of the reunion. "Dani thinks I'm only interested in money," Eva told me, "but it is about justice."

An hour later we attended the public forum, held in the city hall. The beautiful chamber was packed with citizens of Brno, with the overflow watching the proceedings on screen in an adjacent room. Dani and Ruth sat on one side of the stage, Daniel and Anna Šabatová on the other. Šabatová is the public defender of rights (ombudsperson) of the Czech Republic and was selected by city officials in consultation with Dani. The meeting was chaired by Mojmír Jeřábek.[12]

How, Mojmír asked, did it feel for the family to be back in Brno? Ruth and Dani expressed gratitude and said how overwhelming it was for us to meet so many relatives. Ruth also spoke about her ambivalence. As she had said on Czech television in 2012, "our family didn't just leave this house in Brno and go for a walk."[13] Dani pointed to parallels between the family's flight and the present refugee crisis. She put the political situation bluntly: "When you start seeing people as Others, you lose your own humanity." Dani also mentioned the decades of work to restore the house and

Figure 32. The public forum. In the front row are Naomi Low-Beer, Jacqueline Solway, Joan Musitano, Michael Lambek, the husband of Anna Šabatová, Ivo Hammer. Directly across the aisle are Brno Deputy Mayor Matěj Hollan and Mayor Jaroslav Zoubek of Svitávka. In the second row are David Libbert, Bill Parsons, and Susan Low-Beer-Parsons, and behind Bill, Bernie Lambek. Photo by Michal Růžička, courtesy of Meeting Brno festival

how painful it is when her efforts are seen as interference. Daniel idealized interwar Czechoslovakia when the communities had lived harmoniously together. His father, Tom, named after Tomáš Masaryk, had evidently retained strong sentimental attachments to a place he had left as a child. Daniel emphasized the importance of the Schindler factory, recognition of the Löw-Beer name, and the need to commemorate the factory and the houses of his grandparental generation. He pointed to the importance of family stories, as compiled in *Arks*. Anna Šabatová expressed shame that growing up in Brno she had known so little, and she emphasized the importance of specificity over historical abstraction: people never thought about who had lived in the houses. And now the city owed us respect, acknowledgment, and self-representation.

Figure 33. The public forum, Mojmír Jeřábek, Ruth Guggenheim, and Daniela Hammer-Tugendhat. Photo by Michal Růžička, courtesy of Meeting Brno festival

Mojmír then asked for comments from the floor. Not many hands went up, but those who spoke were very positive, welcoming us back. One person mentioned the social benefits given the factory workers. Asked to conclude, Vice Mayor Hollan asserted that morally the houses were ours and that they would take our critical comments seriously. Dani told me afterwards that Grete had not necessarily agreed that the house was hers any longer. History brings change, and property is not private forever. Evidently not all Löw-Beers felt the same. There was an embarrassing moment in the forum when a member of the Aron-Jakob branch interjected that whenever one asks a question of Czechs, one gets the response that "things are complicated." He hoped the Czechs would learn to take a new attitude. His patronizing statement likely concerned property claims.

In fact, Daniel's uncle Gerry had acquired a Czech passport in order to reclaim his parents' house. Once it was in his hands, he sold it. When he failed to share the proceeds with his siblings, his brother Tom sued him. The suit stopped when Tom died unexpectedly. Perhaps the tensions were overcome, as Gerry's daughter Naomi attended the reunion, and everyone seemed to get along.

Outside the forum, discussion concerning restitution simmered in the background. Ivo explained that at one point the city had wanted to return the Tugendhat House to the family, but the Czech state refused. The city in turn rejected the family's idea to invite a foundation to manage it; this idea became moot when we could not locate such a foundation and once the city took the right steps to restore the house. What is of concern now is to place someone from the family in a position to help oversee the house, with respect to both material issues, like the leaking roof, and symbolic ones, like how the family is represented. Despite the openness of the forum, there remained a contrary sentiment in Brno that "foreigners" shouldn't interfere.

Fifth Day, Tuesday, 23 May

Our last day was as full as the others. We drove first to Svitávka and then to Boskovice, retracing in the opposite direction the roots of our ancestors from the ghetto to the city. If the social and economic distance was extensive, the distance in kilometres was short. The countryside is lush, with rolling hills and productive fields. We passed signs for tourist attractions, including karst caves and the Boskovice castle and its Jewish quarter. Driving through the quiet village of Svitávka, we entered the park and pulled up at the large villa. The villa has a fine entrance with the date 1902 carved above. Inside, a curved staircase rises to a large hall on the main floor and from there a grand staircase to the second floor. The dark wood is reminiscent of the Löw-Beer House in town. The villa is owned by the municipality and serves as the town hall. It looks stately, but when I first visited in 1988 I wrote: "I'd be very embarrassed to admit my ancestry here. No matter what the proletarian housing looked like, the difference would have been enormous. Like lords in their manor surrounded by their serfs. Extremely distasteful."

We received welcome speeches from the mayors of Svitávka, Brněnec, and Boskovice. They were very hospitable, having prepared for us cake and coffee, individual gift bags containing books and mugs, and later an excellent buffet lunch. We were invited to wander the villa and grounds but not before they presented us with the best gift – a film they had made. The mayor of Svitávka said he was ashamed the factory was so rundown, but he was clearly proud of the film. It seemed odd to begin with a film about the place we had come to see rather than to see the place itself, but we all settled down to watch.

As the film began, I realized that I had already discovered it on the internet. It begins with a scene of a Nazi rally, followed by a shot of a train steaming across the countryside and a suitcase thrown from its window. It then shifts to the present with the premise that a group of children have discovered the suitcase in the attic of the villa. A kindly grandfather figure tells them the story of the people who once lived there. The film returns to the past and shows Grete Löw-Beer as a young girl with her family. They arrive in a nice car, drink and eat on the terrace, and stroll in the garden. There are several old images of the factory buildings and lovely shots of the two villas.[14]

I thought the film quite charming, but some relatives were upset that it did not explain why the family left or state explicitly that Alfred was killed. Moreover, the film asserted that no family members had ever returned. One cousin almost broke into tears as she stood to voice her complaint. The mayor said he welcomed corrections and apologized for the omissions. He acknowledged that it was obviously incorrect to say that no family members had returned – especially given our presence then and there.

I was somewhat embarrassed by what appeared ingratitude on our part. Indeed, the first scene had alluded to the Nazi terror. I liked the fact that descendants of the factory workers had dressed up and performed as the former owners and their family. It seemed a nice piece of mimesis and another way in which the family is being represented, a kind of popular alternative to Mawer's literary attempt in *The Glass Room* or the scholarly one of the curators at the Löw-Beer Villa in town, or even this book.[15] It is intriguing that the family was still the object of so much interest in Svitávka, and the reversal of hierarchy enacted in the film resonates with me as an anthropologist.

It was also evident that the film had been designed for children, which accounted for the upbeat music and the way the story was constructed. But because it purported to be educational, the omissions were all the more troubling. Our life in the community had become a kind of fairy tale. By contrast, the mayor has mounted an impressive exhibit of family documents in the villa. He acknowledged that he was only an amateur historian, but he clearly had gone to considerable effort and hoped to develop a museum. Some of the photographs are misidentified, but they were only replicating the same mistakes made in Brno.

The mayor explained that he had worked in the factory during the communist period, and his father had worked for the Löw-Beers. I asked him to tell me honestly what the Löw-Beers had been like as employers. He insisted they had been great, providing schooling, housing, and health care for the workers. I asked several local people what they "really" thought of the Löw-Beers – and they all had similar positive things to say.

The smaller villa is now the home and practice of a family of dentists. A spontaneous visit during Paul's ninetieth birthday had frightened the inhabitants about their rights to the property. The dentist's wife had prepared this time, greeting us politely and giving us an hour to visit the house. Beyond the entrance hall is a central room with a stained-glass skylight. We saw two fully equipped dentist's rooms, but were not given access to the residential portion or the lovely side terrace, which the owner declared private. The swimming pool that was once behind the villa no longer exists.

The villas are each quite beautiful, and the whole place retains a kind of serenity. It is known locally as "little Paris." The smaller villa had been Alfred and Marianne's summer home, but once their son Max was grown, he inhabited it full time with his wife Edith and two children, Margaret and Frank. Hence it was Max's grandchildren who showed the most interest there. They had arranged to meet one of Margaret's old school friends. She stood outside the house with a granddaughter as translator and graciously answered questions. Her parents had owned the village pub; she herself had become a nurse. She was very clear when I pressed her that the workers had liked the Löw-Beers.

After lunch a few of us wandered over to the factory. We crossed the small channel and approached an area with several decrepit buildings four and five stories high. A young man in overalls appeared; introducing himself as the current owner, he cheerfully offered to show us around. He unlocked the oldest building and took us upstairs, where we found the factory floor that once housed industrial looms and spinning machines now crammed with rows and rows of old automobiles, mostly of former Czech and Russian make. There were several floors of cars, which he had brought up by means of the remaining freight elevators attached to the outside of the buildings. The young man, who is not originally from Svitávka, was hoping to open a museum of vintage cars. On the empty top floor, we found some abandoned bobbins with threads.

Returning to the park, we found that at Daniel's request one bus had left to inspect the Aron-Jakob villa and ruins of the Schindler factor at Brněnec. The other bus took us directly to Boskovice. The visit there was disappointing. We had insufficient time to appreciate the former ghetto as we straggled along behind our guide. We saw the largest of the three synagogues, built originally in 1638. It is covered with restored floral frescoes in a style said to be Ukrainian or Polish Jewish. In 1942 it was converted to a storehouse for confiscated Jewish artefacts. There is no longer a Torah scroll, and the building is now a museum. We peered into an underground mikvah and visited a museum in an old house.

The cemetery is impressive, extending across a hillside on the edge of town. The ground is quite uneven, but the place is cared for and the grass had been cut recently. There are hundreds of tombstones in various states of disrepair. The stones of Moses (1793–1851) and Katharina (1801–83), founders of our line, stand side by side (see Figure 4). I spotted the stone of a woman named Husserl, presumably a relative of the philosopher, who came from nearby Prossnitz.

That evening, the City of Brno invited us to the castle for a final dinner. The terrace offers a panoramic view of the city, and one can spot the Tugendhat House on the far side. The vice mayor said he had been honoured to host us and invited us to encourage family and friends to visit. My cousin Eduardo thanked the city on our behalf, and Bernie thanked Dani and Ivo. Bernie joked that we could hardly advertise Brno to our family, as the family were all here.

Next morning we departed. Our Canadian cousins and a few Europeans went to stay at a castle in Austria they had rented for a few days. They had both the money and the comfort in spending it to do so.[16] About a week later, two Löw-Beers found themselves by chance in adjacent seats at a theatre in Prague. For the next couple of weeks there was a flurry of emails, with people sharing photos, and several polite messages from the officials in Brno, including an online survey requesting our evaluation of the event.

The positive feeling is captured in this reflection that unites the family with the architecture and speaks to the continuity of generations. My daughter-in-law Carey writes: "There has already been so much said about how nice it was to spend a day in the gardens of the Löw-Beer and Tugendhat villas, about the kids playing in the fountain, the beautiful music moving seamlessly from inside to outside. The long hours of sunshine and togetherness breathed life into those spaces and illustrated their capacity to hold life beautifully. I only want to add a small note … Did you notice the size of the steps on the wide outdoor staircase that leads from the main floor [of the Tugendhat Villa] to the garden – where I was sitting with Siena during the concert …? Each step is not more than a few inches high. The absolute perfect height for a young person to sit comfortably without their feet dangling." Siena is my nephew Dominic's daughter. She is the oldest child of the youngest generation.

⁊ᷓ

Throughout our time in Brno the buses that transported us had a large picture advertising the Tugendhat House pasted on the outside, embedding us, as it were, within a representation of ourselves. This image serves as a metaphor for the entire visit and perhaps for this book.

We were offered many representations through which to see ourselves. For virtually the entire visit, we were being filmed. The cameras followed us around, and individuals were invited to speak directly to them. The cameramen assured me that they were independent, not in the direct employ of the city. In addition, there was the formal family portrait, taken by a professional photographer, and a red-haired journalist who followed us assiduously. At least one participant suggested that the city appeared to be walking a fine line between celebratory documentation and surveillance, especially because we were never formally asked for our consent. We cannot control the representations made of our visit and do not have the right to do so.

There is an elaborate politics concerning who has the authority to represent and who is subject to representation. It is partly a matter of how we and the houses are represented by others, outsiders who use us to various ends, but partly how we represent ourselves or select who among us should be our representatives and which family members or achievements are of sufficient value to be represented. What gets included and what is excluded, inadvertently or intentionally? Moreover, each representation introduces its own form of distortion; the young adults declared it "weird" to be the subject of museum displays.

In producing the event that we found ourselves in, the city was using us to further its advertisement of the house. But the city also saw the event as part of a broader program of reconciliation, an opportunity to acknowledge the family and to redeem itself for past shabby acts. Relations between the family and the city have been uneven. Now, the city was being extremely generous. And yet some family members remained uncertain about the consequences of having accepted its hospitality. Were we opening a conversation or settling affairs, a final handshake in a long goodbye?

At the time, the sentiment in the city was to maintain a positive relationship with us. One of the filmmakers suggested there should be an event every year or two. In its questionnaire the mayor's office also raised the possibility of future reunions. Of course, it depends on who is in power in Brno.

Some family members were sceptical. One of the younger adults said: "While we were in Brno, I was most interested in what the state was getting out of the meeting and also the various political uses to which the visit might be put." She wondered whether the reunion was offered to forestall possible grievances over property appropriated by the state. And perhaps "the family was being presented as evidence of the state's completed multicultural journey from exile to embrace." I myself don't think the city was quite so instrumental.

To the extent that we were represented as Jews, there was a general feeling, even some anger, that not enough was said about flight, extermination, Czechoslovakian collaboration with the Nazis, or the fact that some Czechs readily appropriated abandoned property. On the other hand, we could hardly be seen as "representative" Jews, especially not of the murdered.

From no side could anything be said politely concerning the exploitation of labour that contributed to the Löw-Beer fortune.

Family members were doing their own recording. Some took notes, and many more took photographs, which they later posted or circulated. One could read our trip as a kind of pilgrimage to an ancestral home. The family is not religious, but perhaps it worships itself. And the Tugendhat House has become something of a sacred shrine. With time, the ancestors, as irascible or difficult as they were in life, also become sacred and the last living members of the generations born "over there" treated as venerable elders. Is that because of what they lived through, or how they lived, or how we imagine it, or is it merely because they are old or dead? There is something impressive about the strong personalities, the determination to excel, and the cultured habitus they display. Daniel depicted Margaret living behind glass windows over the Pacific, swimming daily in the ocean, and whipping up Viennese cakes and boletus omelettes. Margaret's determination was subsequently manifest in fall 2020 when, aged ninety-two and fed up with the pandemic, she leapt off her high-rise balcony.

While there was a sense of what anthropologist Victor Turner called communitas – fellowship and equality in the time-out-of-time of the reunion – lines of difference within the family were also apparent. Family members represented their respective branches, speaking on behalf of particular deceased relatives and serving as the ultimate authority on their own experience. Dani and Ivo spoke a great deal in public and to the family, as did Daniel. Members of our branch were nonplussed by the way Daniel appeared to speak for all of us and embarrassed by remarks we found off-key. Conversely, perhaps he was put off by Dani or me, or by the focus on our line of Löw-Beers. My immediate family, who know me only too well, felt that I was competing with Daniel to tell the story. The whole event could be described as an agon of representations.

Had it not been for the Mies house and for Dani's engagement in its restoration, there would have been no invitation to Brno and no reunion. Dani and Ivo focused on the house as the main object of concern and appreciation. Daniel tried to balance the Tugendhat House with the Schindler factory, as though these were equivalent achievements that unified and exalted the family. For the Czechs, Grete was a central figure everywhere, not only in her own house but displayed prominently at her parents' house and in the film produced in Svitávka. She has become a key character in the local narrative. Alfred's descendants questioned why more attention went to his daughter than to his sons; a granddaughter of Rudolf found his achievements under-represented; and Ellen felt that

Rudolf and Alfred's sisters were ignored. I too exhibited representation envy, alert to moments where my mother was erased from
the list of Grete's offspring.

These concerns challenged the idea that we were "one" family.
As I noted earlier, at each generation a family segments, and each
branch sees itself in relation to branches of comparable location
and scale. But equally, the relevant level of scale depends on context. People who are all Löw-Beers in one situation are members
of the Moses Löw-Beer family in contrast to the Aron-Jacob family in another, or the descendants of Rudolf, Alfred, or Benno in a
third. The further back the split, the larger and more inclusive the
branches but the weaker the solidarity among the members.

Other lines of connection and contrast crosscut the logic of segmentation. Over the course of the reunion, there was some talk
of insiders and outsiders. Those who returned to Europe after the
war were insiders relative to those who remained in the Americas
or Australia. Generation was another salient distinction. Whereas
the pre-war heritage holds a powerful if ambivalent attraction for
members of the older generations, for younger ones it is a curiosity
to which they do not fully relate. One of my second cousins said
his mother was lucky to be born in Canada; her European cousins
don't seem able to escape the past as easily.

Since I spent most time at the reunion speaking to people my
age and older, I asked my adult children about encounters with
their age peers and observations of the reunion. Many of the
young people spent the evenings getting to know one another outside the formal program. Framing the reunion as a homecoming
hardly resonated for them. My son Simon said: "I was socialized in
Canada and I am not Czech, don't speak the language, etc. There is
little of me that I feel is reflected in the life of that place, and there is
little in the life of the place that feels like me." He added: "I feel dis-
connected from that period of the family history … It's not as if I'm
part of a German-Jewish community, the textile industry, etc. I am
generations, oceans, cultures, economic classes, languages, even
centuries removed from the people in those places. What are left
of my ancestors' lives in Moravia are houses far fancier than ones
I will ever live in and factories where my ancestors exploited the

labour of the proletariat. I have a great deal of difficulty relating to those ancestors." Some of his European age cohort were also sceptical. One young woman asked: "Why should I care about this?" But in the end, according to her mother, she loved it.

Carey observed that the struggle over representation did not seem to concern people of what she called the "second diaspora generation" nearly as much as it did those of older generations. Among the younger generation, "parental and grandparental devotion to The Family and to The House were viewed variously as affectionately perplexing, politically problematic, and in some cases pathological." One cousin jokingly explained his father's "newfound obsession" with the family legacy as a midlife crisis. Nevertheless, this generation was interested in what the state was up to, and it was a subject of speculation over drinks. They showed a range of responses to the city's gestures of inclusion – some enthusiastic and appreciative, others uncomfortable or sceptical, and others outright rejecting the overtures.

For Simon, "adding to the strangeness ... my family history is presented to me, quite literally, in a curated form designed for a curious but uninformed outsider ... If my family narrative and history was not a product presented for public consumption, I would not worry so much about the nature of that narrative and representation. Given that it is a product for public consumption, I feel I have a stake in controlling that story. Mitigating that last concern, however, is how much the older generation care about the presentation of the family. This makes me less likely to add my two cents. I don't want to step on that hornets' nest."

Simon observed that the dense program of lectures, classical music interludes, and modernist art tours was hardly an agenda for most family reunions, and it said something about our family in particular. Whether the program was more a product of the Czech officials than the family, "the activities of the reunion seemed to help reproduce a particular kind of identity – we're a family of forward-thinking international academics, with sophisticated taste in art." He suggested that "performances" of aesthetic appreciation have been a way to mediate social belonging. The family identified with neither Yiddish-speaking nor observant Jews, nor as gentile Czechs or Germans. It needed a place to anchor a vision of itself as "modern, enlightened, bourgeois, and international/cosmopolitan." Performing as an intellectual himself, he cites Marx's remark in the *18th Brumaire*: "The social revolution of the nineteenth century cannot take its poetry from the past but only from the future."[17] For Simon, "the family saw itself as part of a new enlightened age, and the house is a vision of the poetry of the future. The house represents a (perhaps lost) future."[18]

Simon based his argument on an essay by Hannah Arendt in which she distinguishes aristocratic, bourgeois, and mass culture. The "aristocratic" (actually, ancient Greek) exemplifies unmediated appreciation of the aesthetic, while the bourgeois emulates the aristocratic; in a claim for recognition and status "the bourgeois cultivate an aesthetic sense and collect art pieces to show that they too are cultured." Simon suggested that the family's relation to the house and modernist architecture could be an expression of "a desire for this unmediated, genuine relation to the aesthetic ... This dynamic ... is inextricably tied up with being Jewish and being denied recognition from the goy world, while also wanting to differentiate ourselves from the Jewish past." It is not a matter of emulating the aristocracy but of identifying as people of "genuinely good taste." This view was evident in a remark attributed to Grete that Mrs. Stiassny was "ostentatious." As Simon ironically put it, "their bad taste gives them away. They're the bourgeois collecting art for status; they were not truly unmediated like us." Grete and Dani's appreciation of the aesthetic was and is completely genuine and unmediated; the problem arises for those of us (like me) whose aesthetic sensibility is less acute.

In the end we were all left asking ourselves: In what way are we "Löw-Beers"? Do we identify with some idealized fantasy or is there some substance? What kind of attachment to this legacy do we have or want to have? Is it a material or a symbolic inheritance, or perhaps a sentimental one? Does a common legacy bind us in solidarity with one another as a family? And what are the implications for continuing relationships – of friendship no less than "kinship" – with one another or with Brno?[19]

MEETING BRNO 2017

The aim of the cultural festival Meeting Brno is to monitor and remember history of the biggest Moravian city which thanks its face and importance to Czech, as well as German and Jewish community. Topics reflecting history will blend with current topics in many artistic performances and discussion forums.

FESTIVAL PROGRAMME

Discussions forums:

* Three discussion forums taking place on the Masaryk University platform will deal with topics such as radicalisation, similarity vs. difference, toleration vs. aggression.

Guests: leading Czech, German and Austrian intellectuals, political representatives, writers

Literature:

* Reading of a German resident writer who will be staying in Brno during May as a resident of the joint programme of the House of Arts and Meeting Brno festival.
* Writers discussion – Oto Filip, Milan Uhde and Kateřina Tučková will discuss the issue of expulsion of Czechoslovak Germans starting in 1945 in literature process.
* Literature workshop with a resident writer, Austrian writer and Kateřina Tučková.

Theatre:

* Brno theatre Feste has been dealing with pressing social problems for a long time. For the festival they prepare an original play with participation of Czech and German actors who will perform moments of the regional history directly in Brno's streets.

Music:

* In 2017 it will be 60 years since the death of an important Brno native of Jewish origin, the composer Erich Wolfgang Korngold, laureate of

several Oscars in the field of film music. A conference about the benefits of his work will be opened in Brno with a concert by the Brno Philharmonic at the beginning of the Meeting Brno festival.

Visual arts:
- Exhibition of a German resident artist will be held in the House of Arts.
- Exhibition of old photographs showing certain places in 19th century and in the first half of 20th century will take place in the former German House at Moravské náměstí.

Film:
- There will be documentary films on holocaust, expulsion or radicalization in general. Two documentary films will be prepared for this purpose – the first about important Brno Jewish industrialists and artists, directed by Petr Lokaj, and the second one about Erich Wolfgang Korngold, directed by Martin Polák (Czech TV Brno).

Walks for public:
- Jewish Brno trail
- Central Cemetery trail (to the graves of our Czech and German ancestors)

PILGRIMAGE OF RECONCILIATION 2017
Pilgrimage of Reconciliation from a mass grave in Pohořelice will take place on Saturday, May 20, 2017. It will be closed by festive speeches and a cultural programme at Mendlovo náměstí (18:00 – 22:00).

Accompanying events:

JEWISH TOPICS

Meeting of Brno Jewish families' descendants
Invitation of descendants of Jewish factory owners and important personalities who participated in the boom of the City of Brno: programme

prepared by Foreign Relations Department of the City of Brno, representatives of the Tugendhat, Löw-Beer and Stiassny families have already been addressed.

Foundation of a Documentary Centre on Holocaust of South Moravian Jews

Introduction of the vision of the Documentary Centre on Holocaust of South Moravian Jews. We seek to build it at the site of the former Jewish synagogue, burnt in 1939.

Jewish Brno trail

Installation of 10 panels with benches to guide walkers through the most important places and history of Jewish Brno.

A statue for the 5th platform of the railway station where the Brno Jews were transported from.

GERMAN TOPICS

Festive mounting of Dr. Guido Glück commemorative plaque

Commemoration of an exceptional personality – a German citizen of Brno who saved a Jewish man from the transport at the end of the 1930s.

MEETING BRNO – LONG-TERM PLAN:
* Promote awareness raising of once multicultural city and values emerged thereof
* Promote a dialogue among cultures, religions and representatives of various attitudes in the spirit of tolerance and mutual understanding
* Offer the public through artistic performances experiencing of serious social issues such as migration or religious or social collision
* Documentary Centre on Holocaust of South Moravian Jews
* Transformation of a former Tugendhats' factory into a museum of textile history (namely the Tugendhats' factory at the Vlhká street is important, so that apart from the Tugendhat Villa there is also an

evidence of where the capital was coming from for construction of
UNESCO monuments that the city builds its marketing strategy on)
- Commemorative plaques to important Jewish and German
  personalities
- Documentary films (development of a documentary on Brno native,
  physicist and mathematician of genius Georg Placzek directed by
  Petr Lokaj, etc.)
- Publication
- Building a Central European network of artists, intellectuals, cultural
  managers and other personalities of social life through monthly
  residential programmes

CONTACT
Kateřina Tučková, Ph.D.
Programme manager of the Meeting Brno festival
www.meetingbrno.cz

Chapter Sixteen

Reconciliations in Brno

Jews as Germans

"Our Neighbours Are Missing"

Fifteen months after the reunion I returned to Brno, curious to learn from the organizers and other citizens what they thought about the event. In 2017 these people were in the background for me, eclipsed by all the relatives, known and unknown, I was so intensely engaged with. Why had they invited us, and were they satisfied with the outcome? What did we and our heritage represent for them? I learned how deeply representations of the family were imbricated in local concerns about historical experience, in the dominant narratives of that history, and in the contested politics of the present. This knowledge was a healthy displacement of family narcissism.

I was privileged to be accompanied by David Henig, a fellow anthropologist and born in Czechoslovakia. David translated when it was necessary, informed me about historical events and political circumstances about which I was quite naïve, and provided astute commentary on my own practice. David himself is Jewish through his mother's mother. His great-uncle was a victim of political oppression, imprisoned from 1976 to 1985 for the "crime" of listening to jazz. The harsh sentence, David recognized, was a manifestation of the anti-semitism then dominant.[1]

Before our arrival, we set up a few appointments. The filmmakers Roman Zmrzlý and Radovan Kramář, who had followed us during the family reunion and condensed many hours of taping into an excellent forty-minute film, were among the most eager. Indeed, they wanted to follow us and record our activities, much as I was trying to understand theirs. Their eagerness was a mixed blessing. They stimulated questions and added their own perspectives, but I worried their presence would be intrusive and distort some of the more delicate interviews I wanted to make. We settled on a compromise where they would accompany me part of the time. We learned from each other. They told me of Daniel Low-Beer's ambition to turn the factory in Brněnec into a Schindler and Löw-Beer museum, and the impediments he faced.[2]

The filmmakers' attention reinforced the fact that throughout the visit I was not only interviewing but being interviewed. Queries came from almost everyone we spoke to, and my research was subject to an interview by the mayor's publicist that appeared on the City of Brno's website. Representations upon representations.

I began by asking Roman and Radovan about their interest in the family. They explained that the invitation to film us the previous year had come at short notice. They were surprised by what they learned and, as they put it, how big the debt was. They found meeting the family to be very emotional and decided to begin a longer documentary of their own.

Roman, who was thirty-six, said that people of his generation were starting to revisit history. He had had an interest in the architecture for years, but no one had talked about the families who once lived in it or knew the stories of how they escaped. The whole thing was being forgotten. For Radovan, the reunion had additional importance. He was twelve when the regime changed, and it was only then that his parents told him of his own Jewish ancestry. He said what I was to hear repeatedly, that before the Second World War Brno was a multicultural city. Lots of people went missing, their absence replaced with silence. The regime was good at keeping things disappeared. "History is always subject to reinterpretation," he explained.

Radovan described how the Year of Reconciliation, celebrated in Brno in 2015, resonated for him. "What part of me was this, what part of my identity?" His Jewish grandmother had been adopted into a Christian family as their illegitimate daughter. They had a son who died in Stalingrad, but she was frightened, encountering the SS every day. Some family members had fought for Germany, some against. There were lots of mixed people like Radovan. When he and his wife bought a remote country house, they discovered a swastika etched in the plaster. He didn't remove it because he saw it as a sign that he owned the house now and had triumphed over the Nazis. I was taken aback and urged him to destroy it; on his return after the weekend he said it was gone.

Roman and Radovan were working on a feature-length film provisionally titled *Absence*, with support from the newly established South Moravian regional film fund. They draw on footage from the reunion and new material such as the interviews with me and ones they have conducted with Dani and Ivo and with Daniel, but our family is only a part of it. Roman explained that one of the themes is "how you see us"; in other words, how "we" – the descendants of the exiles and emigrants – see "them" – citizens of Brno. This film is part of the larger project for Czechs like Roman and Radovan of coming to terms with their own past. "Absence" refers to the fact that "our neighbours are missing." The Löw-Beer family's large but brief presence in 2017 made that absence all the more evident.

People are absent – yet the houses are present. Brno's architecture from the 1920s and 1930s depended on Jewish architects, they said, housing the workers moving into the city during that time of prosperity. Radovan himself lives in a building designed in 1928 by a Jewish architect.

All this serves as a reminder how much the memory of family – perhaps of any family – is mediated by architecture.

"A Well-Developed Sense of Historical Pessimism"

In the story of *Absence* Jews have a presence, but not nearly so central a one as North American Jews like to imagine. This disparity is in part because Jews were not the only ones to disappear from the city and in part because "being Jewish" was not the most salient aspect of the identity of many pre–First World War and interwar Jewish citizens of Brno. Some converted to Christianity, while others simply let their Jewish practices slip away. Many were "German" in the sense that concept had in the late years of Austria-Hungary and the early years of independent Czechoslovakia. It was a linguistic and cultural attribution, not an ethnic, religious, or racialized one. It was based largely on how one lived, on "practice," as anthropologists might say, rather than on a naturalized or idealized "essence."[3] As Jakub Pernes, a young historian working as a curator at the Löw-Beer Villa, put it, the more salient distinction in that period was based on language not religion.

It was not simply a matter of upwardly mobile Jews trying to assimilate. Sociologist Csaba Szaló told us that in the 1920s quite a number of Hungarian Jews came to study at the new Technical University established in Brno. They were excluded from study in Hungary because of prejudicial acceptance rates (*numerus clausa*) against Jews, but in Brno they were counted as Hungarians rather than Jews. For Szaló, from a cultural point of view, the Jews of Brno were Germans. He argues that there was no category of "Jews" as such but rather hyphenated identities, Hungarian-Jews, German-Jews, and so on, and that it falsifies history to treat them as a single category.

Szaló and others argue there were no strict boundaries around identities. Nevertheless, some sense of Jewish identity remained as did some anti-semitism.[4] People of my family's class continued to socialize and marry largely among themselves rather than with German-speaking Christians or with Czech speakers. Occasionally, they married Hungarian-speaking Jews. There were instances of Jewish-Christian intermarriage in Brno; in my family one was between Hans Tugendhat and Wilhelmina (Minnie) Herrenritt, who came from an elite bilingual but mainly German-speaking Catholic family.

Until the early 1930s Brno was characterized by complementarity and competition between its German-speaking and Czech-speaking citizens. This duality was the salient internal difference, and it played out in both the economy and the domain of what came to be called culture. Mojmír Jeřábek, now director of the Czech Centre in Vienna, located this conceptual distinction with Romanticism, which from the beginning of the nineteenth century proceeded by classifying things: Czech language and German language, our culture and their culture. There followed the idea that one must defend and celebrate one's culture. Each community had to show they were equal or better.[5]

Although in ordinary life many people were bilingual and mixed freely, when it came to "culture," each group wanted to distinguish themselves. There was both a German *corso* and a Czech *corso* along which members of the respective communities strolled. The streets were adjacent and parallel to each other in the city centre. As Brno became a prosperous industrial hub in the second half of the nineteenth century and Czech speakers grew in number and confidence, they built a "Czech House" to symbolize – and literally house – their "culture," a building with reading room, theatre, restaurant, and spaces for social gatherings. Completed in 1873, today the beautiful *Besední dům* houses the Brno Philharmonic.[6] This building is where the family attended the first concert of the Meeting Brno festival.

German speakers of course wanted a cultural centre as well. They selected a site on the road circling the inner city that imitated Vienna's Ringstrasse. Construction of the *Deutsches Haus*, or *Německý dům*, began in 1888 and was completed in 1891. It was a large building whose "rough cast red bricks and high Gothic gables" referred to the architecture of the old Hanseatic cities and evoked "Pan-German ideas."[7] The building housed the German Association, library, restaurant, beer halls, lecture rooms, and a large ceremonial ballroom that after the First World War, when the Czechs dominated the municipal theatre, showed German theatre and opera. The *Deutsches Haus* played a significant role in the cultural life of the city until it became a site for Nazi rallies. It was destroyed in 1945.

The German speakers were citizens of Brno and Moravia, but they also felt a kind of "Germanness." Why did they identify as German rather than Austrian? Prior to the First World War, people were citizens of Austria-Hungary. Austria-Hungary was an empire, a political entity rather than a cultural, national, or ethnic community. There was no conception of being Austrian per se. Once the empire collapsed, Austria was a new phenomenon, a state rather than an ethnos, and the German speakers of Brno were citizens now of Czechoslovakia, not Austria.

Both before and after the First World War, most Jews participated in German culture. As Mojmír explained, although they did
not have nationalist sentiments against Czechs, they participated
in the German House. In fact, it was a Jewish factory owner, Friedrich Wannieck, who rescued the building project after a crisis on
the Viennese stock market threatened the financing. Alfred Löw-
Beer was a member as late as 1932, and possibly served as chairman of a cultural group.[8]

Nevertheless, the collapse of Austria-Hungary was decisive.
The new hegemony of national identities created a clash between
national citizenship and language. German speakers, whether Jewish or Christian, could no longer be identified or imagined simply
as citizens of a diverse empire. In 1920 the city of greater Brno was
created, incorporating the outlying villages in which many factories were located. As David Henig explained to me, this new entity
was part of a nationalist politics: changing the ethnolinguistic composition of the city to create a Czech-speaking majority. Already in
the First Republic there was talk among Czech speakers of "the
German question." The Jews faced their own question of how to
identify with the new nation-state of Czechoslovakia; whether, in
effect, to "become" Czech or remain German. They soon had to
face the fact that speaking German and participating in German
high culture was no longer sufficient for being German.

With the rise of Hitler some German speakers in Czechoslovakia tried to distinguish themselves more explicitly as Germans
in an ethnic or racial sense rather than only a linguistic one and
hence to distinguish themselves from other German speakers, like
the Jews. This differentiation became evident in women's fashion
as girls started braiding their hair and women wore white socks.
The *Deutsches Haus* became a bastion of anti-semitism. As German
nationalism increasingly adopted essentialist and racial dimensions during the 1930s, Jews were forced to recognize their difference, increasingly caught between rising Czech nationalism and
German anti-semitism. On one side identified by Czechs with Germans and on the other side despised by Germans, Jews were in a
situation that became untenable. Perhaps 1936 was the watershed
year when people identified as Jews began plans to emigrate.

For those who stayed on or who returned from the death camps, fate remained cruel. The regimes that succeeded the German occupation found it convenient to continue identifying Jews as Germans. This association happened both during the crucial period between 1945 and 1948, when Czechoslovakia's president, Eduard Beneš, encouraged scores to be settled, and during the communist period from 1948 and with renewed force from 1969. The hatred for the German occupiers was passed on to the Jews, and just as no one who was identified as German could ask for property back, neither could anyone of Jewish background who had spoken German. The communists were very nationalistic; they wanted an ethnically homogenous Czech population and continued the expulsion of the Germans that began in 1945. The tragic irony and great historical injustice was that the most extreme victims of the Germans came to be identified with their murderers.

If Jews were identified with Germans when it came to citizenship and property, they were also subject during the communist regime to powerful symbolism as "Jews." They were singled out as bourgeois enemies of the people, suspected as the intelligentsia of being too independent minded. During the 1950s it was dangerous to identify as Jewish. The secret police had a list of people they considered to be Jews. Jews reported greater anti-semitism on the part of Czechs (that is, those identified nationally and linguistically as Czech) after the war than before.

Many of the surviving Jews tried to leave. There were several waves of emigration – in 1945, 1948, and 1968. Some 250,000 people left Czechoslovakia after 1968. Many were highly educated and productive members of society, and many had Jewish roots. As Mojmír deftly put it, they had by then "a well-developed sense of historical pessimism."

Organizing Meeting Brno

The reunion and the events around it are, in turn, a retort of optimism, an attempt to uncover what was positive in the history, acknowledge what was negative, and counter the xenophobia characteristic of the present. The organizers were a diverse group.

What they have in common is an understanding that the question of how to live today in the Czech Republic depends on knowing and acknowledging the past.

The theme for Meeting Brno 2017 developed by Mojmír and his colleagues was the commemoration of pre–Second World War cosmopolitanism that included Germans and Jews. They wanted to acknowledge the contributions of citizens of that period to the life and well-being of the city – contributions that are most evident in Brno's industry and architecture. They also wanted to acknowledge the complicity of Czechs in their disappearance and in maintaining silence. Our reunion was one piece of the festival, and we were only a small, if significant, part of the public they wanted to reach. The question of Germans and Jews was central to the reunion in ways the family had not imagined.

Deputy Mayor Matěj Hollan recalled that the decision to invite our family emerged on an Italian beach where six of them (including Mojmír, Kateřina Tučková, and Petr Kalousek) were attending the Rimini Meeting for Friendship among Peoples, an annual cultural event since 1980 on which Meeting Brno is partly modelled. It was important to show that Jews had seen themselves as part of the broader German community, and the celebration of our houses would contribute to that. This commemoration, they felt, would provide a better understanding of Brno as once a bicultural, bilingual, cosmopolitan city. It was not a matter of restoring the past but of reminding people what their city used to be and who used to live there. Without understanding the place where you live, said Hollan, you can't develop. Of course, as David pointed out, "cosmopolitanism" is an idealized projection; the situation of the First Republic might be more realistically described as one of coexistence.

As Hollan explained, the overall motivation was to acknowledge that something central to Brno's identity had been violently uprooted. Brno used to be a Czech and German place, where people functioned together. It is no longer the same, and citizens feel the absence. The organizers wanted the family to feel it is our city too, to feel welcome. They were pleased that some of us remained in touch after the reunion. If any of us were to return to live or do business in Brno that would signify an act of closure to our expulsion.

The family has come to represent for contemporary residents of Brno the cosmopolitan, culturally "German" elite of which Jews were a part and to represent, as well, people who were victims of both Germans and Czechs. There is rich ambiguity here concerning the identities of perpetrators and victims that came to a head in the Pilgrimage of Reconciliation and helps explain why my two aunts, so close to each other in many respects, came to differ on whether we should participate in it.

The March

At the end of the Second World War, newly reinstated President Beneš legitimated a popular backlash against German and Hungarian speakers with a state decree that stripped them of citizenship unless they could prove loyalty to Czechoslovakia during the war. Acts of violence were committed, property was confiscated, and people were expelled. The effects of these actions have remained contentious to the present day.

In Brno the most brutal event was a march of expulsion on 31 May 1945. Some 20,000 people identified as German, mostly women, children, and the elderly, were forcibly marched towards the Austrian border; more than 1,700 are said to have died of exhaustion along the way. Able-bodied men were kept as forced labour, interned in six camps around the city, and subsequently expelled, tortured, or murdered. People were ostensibly removed as former enemies and oppressors, but the situation was confused. For one thing, those expelled included some German-speaking Jews who had only just returned to Brno from extermination camps or hiding spots. For another, many of the guards who forced people out had been collaborators. They had worked in a large arms factory that the Third Reich had expropriated and were better fed than workers in other factories and had access to weapons. At the end of the war, they turned suddenly. The impetus to expel German speakers was not only one of punishment or revenge but the opportunity to publicly switch sides and to seize their property.

Meeting Brno is timed to coincide with the annual Pilgrimage of Reconciliation, an event that commemorates the forced march. The pilgrimage was initiated in 2007 by Jaroslav Ostrčilík. Jaroslav is a member of the Green Party and a vegetarian; he is quite young, sports a man bun, and has a firm gaze. He explained over lunch that the march was originally his personal project. It ended at Pohořelice, close to the Austrian border, where the original forced march had stopped. In 2015 the city took it on as part of the Year of Reconciliation they were organizing. Petr Vokřál, the mayor, and Matěj Hollan, a deputy mayor, had just been elected, and the Brno city council adopted the Declaration of Reconciliation and Common Future, expressing regret over the events.

Jaroslav, who is not of German background, says: "We need to remember that half the city disappeared within the course of one summer. And most people today don't know about it." It had been a taboo subject; no one talked about it – it was as if it had never happened. Kateřina Tučková said that growing up she never heard talk about the expulsion of Germans or about Jews. She became interested when living in a quarter of Brno that seemed curiously empty. That led to research and the writing of a novel about a young German girl who was expelled.[9] As a consequence, she was asked by the mayor to work with Jaroslav on the 2015 march. Their aim was to apologize to all victims of the war, not just Czechs. The response was so positive that they created Meeting Brno as an annual cultural festival to address themes from Brno's past and continue to oversee the march.

Kateřina explained that the city provided 50 per cent of the budget for Meeting Brno; they sought the rest from various sources, including foundations and embassies. She affirmed that "culture" helps with integration – one can begin to understand and experience others through art and music. The main goal of Meeting Brno, Kateřina said, is to learn from and address history – and show it is not simply past but actual, happening now. History is not just an academic question, something one studies in school, but rather has emotional salience. The things lived through and suffered by our grandparents are still alive. We need to show coexistence, to understand our history and educate people, so it doesn't repeat.

Beginning in 2015, the direction of the march was reversed, leading *from* Pohořelice and the Austrian border into the heart of Brno, to the Augustinian Abbey. The abbey contains a dormitory that once served as a prison where Czech patriots were executed by Germans and subsequently German collaborators were tortured by Czechs. Buses deposit the marchers in Pohořelice in the morning; they arrive back in Brno on foot around six in the evening, covering some 31 kilometres. The reversed direction provides a message, not only one of penance but that "we can bring the missing home." The innovation was also practical; it is easier to gather people at the end for speeches. The number of marchers has risen to 150–300 people; more gather for the speeches. Some are descendants of those on the original forced march and attend from Germany and Austria.

Jaroslav is not religious, and the march is not specifically Christian, but he modelled it on a Christian procession – it is explicitly called a pilgrimage – and drew on the symbolism of candle lighting. Fundamentally, it is an acknowledgment that people were hurt, not only by Germans but by Czechs themselves. Kateřina says the German question has been "a shadow on our history," but now Czechs are able to talk about it and to admit there were some non-guilty victims on the German side. Some were just ordinary people.

The march is controversial insofar as it apologizes to Germans and as it singles them out from Jews, Roma, or others victimized by Czechs. One elderly critic told us that the marchers forget that in 1938 when Germany appropriated Sudetenland, many thousands of people had to flee. Protesters included both ultranationalists (even neo-Nazis) and communists, a collaboration that mirrored the actual coalition in the Czech parliament. Both factions claim the march is revisionist history, and some even justify the original expulsion, claiming it was conducted to save Germans from being lynched in Brno. Some protesters worry that the marchers support property claims of the Sudeten Germans or are being naïvely used by them. However, property is not the issue for the marchers; as David observed, by speaking of "reconciliation" rather than "justice," the march is operating in an ethical rather than a legal key. As Roman told us, this event was the first to say "We are sorry."

As another person put it, "the nationalist idea that 'we are the only true victims' is so tiresome."[10]

The march has contemporary resonance insofar as it offers a kind of resistance to populism and to President Zeman, who was elected by playing the German card and inciting fear among Czechs. The mayor was identified as leader of the efforts at reconciliation and was honoured with two German prizes, but his team said he risked his political career over his support of the march.

Towards the end of our conversation over beer in Prague, Kateřina and I surprised each other. She told me it was crucial that the descendants of the Jewish inhabitants had joined the march. She said: "For us, that was the greatest moment of the entire festival – that Jewish and German and Czech people came together in the march!" On her part, she was dismayed to learn that for the family the march had not been central; many of us had paid it no attention or hadn't understood its significance. Indeed, I had read it as an invitation to welcome new immigrants. In retrospect, I was lucky that people appreciated my remarks. Our mutual surprise highlighted how different was the horizon of historical experience the family brought to the reunion from the historical horizon of the organizers.

For Meeting Brno, our presence was not simply affirmative of mutual understanding; it took the weight off criticisms that the marchers are deferring to German interests. If Jews can acknowledge German victims, what is wrong with Czechs doing so? But the situation is made more complex by the hesitation of the small Jewish community currently resident in Brno to participate. The community is described as very closed. I was told they hadn't cooperated with our visit, keeping a low profile, and worrying that they could be attacked. One young woman was unable to join Meeting Brno, said Kateřina, due to community resistance. However, in some contrast to this picture, the very next day I saw a young Czech woman sitting at ease in a café in Brno, wearing a chain with a prominent Star of David.

In a sense, our family was "brought home" in the way the march intended. But while we dropped into the city from our foreign locations and basked in the attention we received, some local Jews do not feel at home; attention is precisely what they fear.

Houses with Strange Names

The idea of inviting Tugendhats spread to include Löw-Beers and Stiassnys, and to commemorate three important houses. "The names of the houses were strange to us," said Mojmír. They were unspoken, more or less prohibited during the communist period. Mojmír himself had not been aware of Grete's visit in 1969. The house was then simply a children's hospital; no one thought about how it came to be built or who had owned it.

The Löw-Beer Villa

We met with Jakub Pernes, a curator at the Löw-Beer Villa. Jakub is a historian eager to supplement the villa's collection with as much family memorabilia as he can find. They have none of the original furniture, most of which was stolen by the Gestapo officers who lived in the house. After the war, the national administration listed all the household items, considering both the property and the owners as "German." By the time they made their list, which included a billiard table, few items of value remained. The administration sold them at very low prices; they were never offered to the family. An antique wardrobe given to the Museum of Brno was subsequently "lost."

Jakub is sad that unlike the Tugendhat Villa, there are no interior photographs and no memory of whose room was whose. He showed us the pair of rooms he thinks were Alfred and Marianne's, based on a small wall safe (found locked and empty) placed discretely in one corner. Like other bourgeois couples, Alfred and Marianne had separate bedrooms, but unusually, theirs were separated by only a glass door. The two large rooms overlook the fountain and garden.

Jakub added something I had not known, namely that beginning with Max, the Löw-Beers, both men and women, had invested individually in real estate in Brno, including apartment blocks and commercial buildings. None of this property is mentioned with respect to compensation.

Jakub thought the original owners, the Fuhrmanns, sold the house to raise capital for their factories. But in an email to me in

2005, Michael Fuhrmann, describing the owner, Moriz Fuhrmann (d. 1910), as a "self-made textile industrialist," wrote that Moriz's son Hans sold the house when his bride Valeria found it not to her taste. Valeria was a granddaughter of Rabbi Baruch Placzek and Karolina Löw-Beer.[11] Interestingly, another grandchild of Baruch and Karolina, George Placzek (1905–55), was a noted physicist for whom the City of Brno held a memorial symposium in 2005 at which then mayor Richard Svoboda declared: "Everything that Brno has until the present day celebrated and of which we remain proud is the joint work of all three cultures [Czech, German, and Jewish]."[12] This statement is a useful reminder that we are not the only accomplished family (though Karolina's descendants could be called "ours" as well) or the only one to be validated by the city.

In the Tugendhat Villa

Our next appointment was with Iveta Černá, curator of the Tugendhat House. Because the garden fence between the houses was locked, we had to go around by the public staircase and streets. Iveta's office is in the chauffeur's flat appended to the main villa over the garage. The office shares the view across the city and sits above the room of the security guard. The guides have a lunchroom next to Iveta's office. They were giving eight tours per day with a maximum of 15 people each, thus 120 visitors per day. The house was fully booked through November and no longer needed advertising.

Iveta greeted us warmly. She was trained as an architect and art historian during the late communist period. She has worked at the villa since 2002 and described all the paperwork they completed to acquire UNESCO World Heritage status and subsequently European Union funding for the full restoration. There was a seven-year delay due to the poor quality of the architectural submissions. But the benefit was that when in the third competition they found a good team, they had a thorough proposal ready for the European Union. Iveta acknowledged Ivo's contribution and the conferences he organized. The history of the restoration is long and complicated; accounts can be found in Dani and Ivo's and in Iveta's books. Iveta also paid tribute to Grete: without a client who was able to formulate what she was looking for and appreciate what she saw, there would have been no house. And without the house, she said with more exaggeration, there would have been no Mies.

Iveta then provided us an engaging personal tour that highlighted the unique design elements. She explained the elaborate filtration of air, passing over cedar oil and then through cedar chips. The door handles to the bedrooms, borrowed from a design by Gropius, stand out from the doors in ways that make them easy to use. The kitchen window opens flat against the wall. The chrome bars beneath the big glass panes were heating ducts that removed condensation from the windows. In Fritz's photograph [on the front cover], Iveta observed, you can see that Ernst has placed his feet on them for warmth. The electrical outlets are indented into the floor. She pointed to a box in the liquor cupboard where they kept Havana cigars in anticipation of a visit from Mies. She said the reconstruction revealed a lot of secrets about the house, technical parts they hadn't realized, and each detail was restored with exactitude. The restoration, she said proudly, is considered one of the best in the world.

A bust of the Lehmbruck statue stands in its original place, but it is an imperfect copy made of bronze. The curators are bitter we didn't give them the original and do not understand why. In fact, we had good reason. It was the one single piece that Grete had specifically asked to have returned to her. Moreover, city officials had apparently lied to us, denying knowledge of its whereabouts, whereas since 1962 it had been stored in the Moravian Gallery along with miscellaneous objects taken from "Jewish houses." One day Dani heard a curator casually mention the statue and realized its presence. Relations over the fate of the house were tense at that point, and so Ruth, Dani, and even Ernst determined to get it back. The curator took nine months before she would even let them look at it. When Dani sued for restitution of the statue as well as the furniture stored there, the director of the Moravian Gallery surreptitiously asked the state to declare the objects inalienable. However, Dani's suit was successful. She contracted an agent from Sotheby's to remove the statue to London, where in auction it sold for five times Sotheby's estimate, the value probably increased by association with the house. I happened to be living in London at the time and was present at what felt like a horse race, the bidding went so quickly. When the Moravian Gallery was outbid by a private collector, a Czech newspaper reported that typical greedy Jews had absconded with Czech heritage. We felt we had requested only a very small portion of our inheritance and that, in any case, the statue was not an intrinsic part of Mies's design but a mobile piece of art Grete had selected independently. After the lawyer's cut, the proceeds were divided equally among Grete's five children. My brothers and I each received one fifteenth.

Iveta's interests lie more in the technology than the lived experience or social aspects of the house, and she is a bit tone deaf to the house as a home. She really doesn't understand my grandparents' mode of living. Of a pull cord in the bath, she remarked incongruously that they could call for champagne. During the tour I was in suspense whether she would take us into the fur storage and how many coats we would find. There were three; Iveta said the coats were donated but didn't explain their presence. Roman, who was filming, embarrassed me by reminding Iveta that I had been angry about the coats the previous year. Iveta asked: "Are three coats still too many?" And I said yes.

Iveta mentioned some conflict over the rights to photographs. On its website the museum accused Ivo of copyright infringement and, as Dani and Ivo told me later, of offending the Czech people. The museum threatened to sue their Austrian publisher to prevent editions in other languages. They also banned the sale of the book at the gift shop. Dani and Ivo then accused the museum of defamation. At the threat of a lawsuit, the statements were removed from the website, but there was no apology and the book was still not on sale at the villa.

Ivo thinks the accusations stem from a mix of jealousy, bad conscience, and a little anti-semitism. The petty acts illustrate the inability of some Czechs to come to terms with the fact that Dani and Ivo are not simply "family," whose quirky ideas can be indulged or dismissed, but experts in art history and conservation, respectively, and know exactly what they are talking about. They caused further irritation by bringing in foreign experts. The Czechs receive their input grudgingly, as challenges to their competence. Iveta's superior, Pavel Ciprian, who managed the city museum in the castle, had been opposed to the family reunion, considering us "shit-disturbers," and was said to have asked defensively: "What can those foreigners tell us? Why should we listen to them?" On the other hand, Ciprian was happy the Tugendhat House was making money for the city museums.

Iveta emphasized that before the conflict over permissions, relations had been extremely good and that they were always open to the family's suggestions. She stayed several times in Dani and Ivo's flat in Vienna and slept on Grete's bed, an heirloom that Dani had placed in her spare bedroom. (I have slept on it as well.) Iveta told me she had a dream in the bed that she gave birth to my mother, thereby illustrating the degree to which she has come to identify with Grete and hence to consider the house as her property or, as she told me, her child.

In sum, although the house is supposed to exhibit the cosmopolitanism of the city, it also evokes Czech nationalist insecurity. Moreover, the quarrels are evidently not simply over material property or competence but over rights to representation. They manifest deep emotional attachments on all sides. The house raises the question of what is "ownership."

Mojmír Jeřábek is one of the officials to unreservedly credit Dani and Ivo for their role in conserving and protecting the house, and he understands why they can't remain silent when they observe a problem. He has often served as a mediator and observed that occasionally the family's requests are unreasonable but mostly not. Immediate tensions have to do with maintenance, for example when the awnings warp or new cracks appear. The worst problem has been rainwater accumulating on the roof, which Ivo has pointed out repeatedly for several years only to have his concerns dismissed.

As we left, Iveta pointed to the red roof of the Arnold Villa, just visible behind the trees. After the war, it was used as a kindergarten. The city has applied to a Norwegian fund to turn it into a research centre for the Tugendhat Villa. It may house Meeting Brno as well. As it belonged to Alfred's sister Cilla Hože, who was murdered, I said it must remember the Holocaust. Iveta replied that it would be billed as a "centre for dialogue." Dani and Ivo have since proposed it be renamed Vila Hožeová (Haus Hože) rather than Arnold (the architect).

A point of tension, as Roman observed, is that the houses are depersonalized, with no signs of people having lived in them. They have become public spaces, displays of themselves or venues for concerts, private parties, and official meetings. Iveta herself explained firmly that the house qua exhibit concerns Mies's architecture, not the family.

One evening when Roman and Radovan wanted to film an interview with me in the garden, we found the property closed for a private function, booked well in advance. Elegantly dressed men and women were escorted down to the lower terrace for drinks and dinner. The filmmakers were irritated and took me round to the garden of the Löw-Beer Villa where we could glimpse the party through the fence. They invited me to express outrage on camera, whether at being excluded or at the commercialization of the property, which I declined. Earlier they had described Iveta as very professional, but now they said she acted as if she owned the house. During the family party the previous year she had asked: "What do the family want? We spend one million crowns annually on heating alone. The family wouldn't be able to afford it." That is true (although the house also makes money), but as one person concluded, she is not interested in understanding the history because she doesn't share it. Our respective horizons are not contradictory, but they are dissonant.

In the Grosse Villa: Svitávka and Beyond

The next day Roman drove us to Svitávka to interview Jaroslav Zoubek, the mayor. I was initially unhappy with the idea that we would film Mr. Zoubek, but he was more than willing and quite at ease in front of the camera. David found the translation challenging but observed that Zoubek was used to pausing between sentences in order to give a translator time.

Mr. Zoubek ushered us into his office in the Grosse Villa, where we sat together comfortably in a corner away from his imposing desk. Zoubek clearly loves the building. The office retains the beautifully patterned wood panelling of the original room. The original blinds still rest over the windows. And when he is exhausted or upset, Zoubek sits on the wooden staircase to restore himself. He speaks to visitors about the house and family "from the heart" and without charge. As he points out, this building is quite different from the Villa Tugendhat. There is a more organic kind of memory work here.

The mayor proudly pointed to a large portrait of Fritz Löw-Beer, completed only a week earlier. It is a likeness of Fritz in relatively old age, taken from a photograph. He hovers over some vaguely Chinese artefacts, and two sports cars are visible in the background. Another oil painting features Josef Nebehosteny, who built the Grosse Villa as well as the railway station and other important buildings in Brno. The next portrait Zoubek commissions will be of Rudolf.

In early adulthood Fritz was the primary resident of the Grosse Villa and renovated several rooms into a modern apartment. Mr. Zoubek explained that the company was so prosperous that Fritz didn't need to work and could spend time on what Zoubek called his hobbies. He said proudly that Fritz had owned a Mercedes with air conditioning, one of only forty-eight made at the time. Zoubek was visited by a British aristocrat writing a history of Bentleys; Fritz and his brother Ernst each ordered one in 1938 but were only able to enjoy them briefly before they fled. Zoubek thought that Alfred drove one of the Bentleys to Prague to use as a bribe to get an exit visa. In any case, the trail of the missing car ended in Prague.

Zoubek's motivation for welcoming the family the previous year was less political and more personal than those of other officials. He had been working on his museum of the family for the past eight years, calling it a labour of love. He was bemused and somewhat disappointed that he was telling us about our deceased relatives rather than the reverse. He insisted incorrectly that Grete was born in the Kleine Villa; in fact, it was built after her birth.

Zoubek explained that Svitávka had been an agricultural village. With the arrival of the Löw-Beers it became a prosperous town, with rail connection to Brno. Ninety per cent of the inhabitants worked in the factory. His grandfather had been a foreman, his father a maintenance worker, and his mother a clerk. He himself worked as a foreman in the factory from 1983 to 1992. When he joined, the machinery was still original; the Löw-Beers had deployed the latest technology such that the factory was able to function another sixty years after they left. Under communism, there was no investment in technology, so they were undercut by more efficient production elsewhere. In fact, Rudolf himself had reduced his investment in technology by the mid-thirties, but Zoubek's point was to make a contrast with the communist period.

The factory at Svitávka slowly carried on for a few years after 1989. Now the buildings are collapsing, and the machinery is gone. The town experienced 20 per cent unemployment when the factory finally closed (by 2002), but things had started to improve. People were moving into Svitávka from Brno, as Jakub Pernes told us he has done, commuting by car or train to Brno for work.

The Grosse Villa became a municipal building. During communist times it also contained a school and a canteen. Zoubek's ambition was to restore the villa to its pre-war condition and use it for cultural events. He managed to get some European Union support and was trying to attract more for the reconstruction of the park. The Kleine Villa contained a medical clinic during the communist period; under privatization the municipality had first rights of purchase but to Zoubek's great regret missed the opportunity. People now resent the dentist family's wealth.

Privatization was a theme that arose in many conversations. It began in the early 1990s, a heady time in which there was an explosion of activity and everything seemed possible, a sense, as someone put it, of total freedom but no clear goals. The results were not what those who had fought for the end of political repression had hoped. Entrepreneurs bought up state properties, including factories, stripped them of their assets, and declared bankruptcy.[13] Some became very wealthy. The wealthiest either left the country or became right-wing politicians. And if the businesses that continued most successfully were ones purchased by foreigners, it only exacerbated resentment and contributed to xenophobia.

It is evident that questions of property and restitution are tied to those of nationalism. David observed that in all the talk about foreign property, people rarely mention the seizures made by Czechs themselves between 1945 and 1948. To regain property and citizenship post-war you had to demonstrate you had supported Czech forces. Among the displays Zoubek set up is a 1949 letter verifying with evidence from Czech embassies in the United States and elsewhere that Löw-Beer family members had supported the free Czechs against Germany. Other letters from the family ask after the factories and the workers. Nevertheless, some people accused the family of being "Germanizing." On display is a letter dated 1946 in which a chauffeur testifies that the Löw-Beers had spoken German not Czech. Zoubek said that in 1945 Rudolf himself decided that it was over. Nor did Paul try to take back the factories. Paul and Fritz each revisited Svitávka in 1968, but the security guards wouldn't let Paul look around.

Because of bad memories left by the authoritarian communist regime, it appears difficult in the Czech Republic today to come up with publicly acceptable left-wing critique. When it appears, critique has more to do with human rights than with questions of labour. People dismissed my pointed questions concerning exploitation. We heard again that the Löw-Beers had been good bosses. But more than that, the Löw-Beers were praised for being entrepreneurs. People asserted that far from exploiting citizens, the firm contributed to Brno's overall prosperity. A city official in Brno said the capitalists had earned their wealth; they took risks and worked hard to become successful. They paid the workers good wages – and after all, anyone could have tried to start a business. The Löw-Beers started out poor: look at Boskovice and the other poor Jewish towns. She respected them for their enterprise and believed in being self-made. Here we are praised in light of neoliberal ideals.

As sociologist Csaba Szaló put it, exploitation as a concept plays no role. They say of capitalist entrepreneurs simply that they were clever. What had once been a negative stereotype – smart in business as a Jew – has become positive.

Zoubek had papers showing that when union representatives came to Svitávka to ask workers to join a strike, they refused. The union in Svitávka was independent, and people were doing quite well. "Everyone was paid fairly, according to the job they were doing – unlike under communism where everyone was paid the same no matter what the work." The Löw-Beers were socially responsible; they built homes for the workers and a school for their children. Zoubek compared it to the famous initiatives of the Bata Shoe Company in Zlín. Before Christmas the Löw-Beers sent gifts to the schools. Their own children went to the local school. Zoubek was speaking of the 1930s; he had no knowledge of earlier times.[14]

I pushed Zoubek about conditions in the factories. What were the working hours? "A good question," he replied. "People had to work Saturdays; it was like that everywhere. But definitely not sixteen hours per day[!]" There was no child labour; workers began around the age of sixteen. He didn't know about support in case of industrial accidents but thought there had been some workers' insurance and that accidents were infrequent. He concluded that the working conditions were above the standards of the times. People were rewarded for what they could deliver, and the firm had a reputation for that.

There are other forms of exploitation besides labour. Fritz had a series of girlfriends in Svitávka. A woman recently suggested to Johnny that he might have a half-sister, but the dates proved the claim wrong. I gingerly raised the question of sexual exploitation, and here, to my surprise, Zoubek dropped his idealization and agreed; the girls' families did feel this way. The theme is not simply a contemporary one, he asserted, but was well understood at the time.

Some people are ashamed of what happened to the factories. They say that first the communists and then the neoliberal entrepreneurs extracted the value that their predecessors created. They benefitted from it but also wasted it. Such people don't understand that freedom also means taking responsibility. The point extends from industry to the entire cultural life of the city: the vanished cosmopolitanism and multilingualism, the creative and architectural energy that made Brno a centre of modernism in the 1920s has been lost. There is even nostalgia for Austria-Hungary and the artistic and intellectual excitement of fin-de-siècle Vienna, with which neighbouring Brno, then across no fenced border, was associated. In the interwar period, which our family has come to signify in Brno, there was, as someone put it, much human power to build things. Now, people told us, the rich are neither well educated nor clever; they don't try to do anything. There has been a swing from an extreme form of communism to an extreme form of capitalism.

Multiple Perspectives

The Mayors

Something I came to realize was the precarity of our relations with the municipalities. What happens depends on political events and who holds office. The mayoral elections did not look promising. Jaroslav Zoubek had won the previous election based on the Löw-Beer theme. But now he found himself challenged on the same grounds. He said there were people in Svitávka who assumed he was personally benefitting from his interest in our family. They were saying he was getting millions of crowns to help us get the property back.

There was certainly a hope in Svitávka that attending to the family's past could somehow financially improve the present. But tourists are few, and moreover, the mayor must have drawn liberally from the city budget to welcome us in 2017. Zoubek's attachment to the Löw-Beers is deep and somehow personal, but not financial. He had a long and friendly correspondence with Fritz's son John and was justifiably proud of his exhibition. If he were to lose the election – as he thought he might – he would donate the material to the provincial archives. He said people didn't understand that he was simply acknowledging the family's contribution to Svitávka. Indeed, the town recently won an award for the most beautiful city hall in the Czech Republic. However, the dissent illustrates that not everyone in Svitávka is pro–Löw-Beer.

The situation of the young deputy mayor in Brno, Matěj Hollan, was bleaker. Hollan had been a supporter of the entire Meeting Brno program; he was a genial and active presence at the reunion and went drinking with the younger family members in the evenings. But we had no idea what a sympathetic and outspoken figure he is. Hollan is an activist, working on issues like hunger, homelessness, and human rights. He had been vice chairman of *Žít Brno* (Living Brno), an informal local arts movement that developed a satirical response to the former mayor. When the mayor tried to censor them, they decided to enter politics. In the elections of 2014, *Žít Brno* won some seats and held a balance of power, supporting Petr Vokřál of the ANO (YES) Party as the new mayor. Hollan was rewarded with a post as a deputy mayor. But having missed the opportunity to transform itself into a political party, *Žít Brno* provided Hollan little support in the current campaign.

Most salient was Hollan's stance on immigration. He said publicly that if the national government were to accept refugees, Brno would take ten to twenty families. This cautious statement provoked hysteria. The national spokesman of ANO called him a traitor, and his Facebook page and email were flooded with threats, even to hang him or kill his children. His opponents said immigrants would rape Czech women. Hollan observed that the discourse had become the language that was used against Jews in the late 1930s. He wants Brno to be an open place where people are not apprehended by race. But, as his colleague said, idealists are judged harshly. Hollan himself had few illusions about his political chances but refused to compromise.

Although everyone we encountered welcomed our presence, it was evident that they sat atop a surge of xenophobia. Our presence was appreciated all the more to help counter it. Hollan located the roots of the xenophobia in the years of totalitarian rule. Milan Uhde, a distinguished intellectual and former dissident with whom we spoke, placed it in a longer trajectory. "Czechs think they are the only ones to have suffered, that they are saints. 'We have suffered – and so no one can tell us anything.'"[15]

Our visit was linked for Hollan to his own family history. His mother's family were German speakers who declared themselves Czech in the 1930s. A great aunt worked for a year as a servant in a Löw-Beer House, which Hollan visited during the reunion with a descendant of the employer. He added a personal story about the Tugendhat Villa. His grandfather and great-grandfather were heroes on the eastern front. On their return in 1946, the authorities offered them the villa to live in. As they were both builders, they realized how expensive it would be to heat and rejected the offer for that of the abandoned house of a German family.

Our meeting with the mayor of Brno was preceded by lunch at an elegant restaurant hosted by Mojmír, without whose original suggestion, organizational skill, diplomacy, and connections – everyone agreed – the family reunion could not have happened. Mojmír professed himself very happy with how the reunion had gone, the number of people, the atmosphere, and the smooth unfolding. The logistics had been complex and made more so by how many of us attended, producing last minute challenges to provide enough food, buses, and so on. It was the biggest event Mojmír had organized in fifteen years working for the city. One of the main achievements, he said, is that people will never again be able to say the former inhabitants of the house and their descendants don't exist.

The meeting with the mayor was quite formal, with Mojmír in attendance as well as a photographer and a publicist. The conference room was hot, and I was nervous and ill-prepared. Petr Vokřál was friendly and dignified. He was in a stronger position than Hollan, a savvy politician, albeit one whose position was not fully understood. Vokřál was recognized for being effective, but his generally progressive intentions at the local level were offset by his position in the populist national political party ANO led by Andrej Babiš, reputedly a former KGB agent and someone who had gained his considerable wealth through questionable means during privatization. Vokřál himself was a successful businessman of good reputation and considered "one of the few intelligent people in ANO." Although deputy head of the party, he chose not to serve in the national government or live in Prague but to lead his native city. His membership in ANO, or perhaps a pragmatic sense of political survival, led him to curtail support of immigrants. I did not broach these subjects.

Kateřina had told me that Meeting Brno covered the hotel and meals for only the direct descendants of the owners of the houses and their children. She assumed other family members had paid their own way and was astonished to learn from me that the lodging and meals for everyone had been covered. She responded that the city must have stepped in. Hollan confirmed it, saying that once the city had decided the reunion would take place, half a million crowns [c. $35–36,000] more or less didn't make a big difference. Mayor Vokřál expressed his great satisfaction with the reunion and his delight that so many people attended. Instead of being put out by the numbers, it was quite the reverse. I think the sentiment was genuine.

Mayor Vokřál said: "This was Brno. It had Jews and Germans – and we lost both, first the Jews and then the Germans. Then under communists many more people left as well, especially from the intelligentsia." In celebrating the house and the reunion, city officials wanted to bring back a missing part of the city, at least symbolically. People needed to be made aware how much the present city owes to the enterprise of those who were gone. Concerning the house, he said: "Professor Hammer [Ivo] keeps us moving." On the one hand the city wants more visitors, but on the other, more visitors make it more difficult to keep the house in shape. In any case, the house brings in money. Later Hollan told me they shared a long-term plan for establishing the villa as an independent organization with an executive board that would include representation from the family. But given complex bureaucratic structures, it would be difficult to establish.

Mayor Vokřál said he hoped to develop relations with other families, from other minorities. He affirmed that our family was part of the city and that we were always welcome, as is our input concerning the house. "For us, you are our family." We shook hands, and he presented me with a lovely painting of Brno. The publicist then took me aside for a short interview and posted online photographs and a story about my project and visit with the mayor.[16]

Absence, Presence, and Property

How citizens viewed our visit was most evident at the 2017 town hall, which some 300 to 400 people attended out of a population of around 300,000. The crowd was diverse and included many young people. Why had they come? Petr Kalousek from Meeting Brno said people were curious and cared about their history. Roman said they wanted the experience of seeing family members in person. Kateřina said it was touching for Brno citizens to encounter us, to see we are present and not just dead history. Our story is Brno's story. They wanted to see the living descendants of the people who made the great buildings. And they wanted to learn what we think about Brno now. She received many satisfied responses after the town meeting, although some people had expected a deeper discussion.

Why is the family relevant, I asked? The fame of the building helps, she replied. People built the industry and the architecture, and elevated Brno from a simple provincial city. She went on, very movingly: "And then suddenly the house became an empty building. So much was lost. It can't be fixed by money, only by gesture. To put life back in the walls is to put life back in the city."

Anna Šabatová, the highly distinguished ombudsman of the Czech Republic, first heard of the villa only at the Czech/Slovak divorce. From the 1960s through the 1980s, she said, there was no recognition of the quality and value of the place. Šabatová offered additional reasons for the popularity of the town hall. First, while we might not like it, people were intrigued by *The Glass Room*, and it provides a kind of access to the villa. Second, the larger question of the past, especially the German past, has been opened more and more. Even though the family are Jewish, we are linked to this reconciliation process. Finally, there is increased awareness of the industrial legacy of the interwar period, visible more in Brno than in Prague.

I asked Šabatová if she was pleased with the family's response. "It's not a matter of your response," she replied. "What is important was the event, the gesture, and especially the act of the city to repair the villa." For Šabatová, the event is a small piece on a much broader canvas. She was intrigued by Grete's human rights work and linked the family story to the contemporary issue of immigration. She called herself "a part of the community who is ashamed of the way the government treats refugees." Šabatová told us about an initiative in which her father, a prominent intellectual and dissident, had been involved, the Bernard Bolzano Foundation. Bolzano (1781–1848) was a priest, mathematician, and noted pacifist who stood against ethnic or linguistic nationalism, advocating civic participation in the place one lived regardless of particularist identity. This idea was submerged by the subsequent growth of German and Czech ethnonationalisms. Her father thought the only way forward was to foster a culture of dialogue, and he helped create a forum that brought together intellectuals, politicians, and activists. The Bolzano Foundation facilitated conversation between Czechs and Germans in the 1990s and, from 2005, on the future of the European Union, always drawing on Bolzano's idea that instead of dividing people, ethnic and other particular identities could enrich everyone.

When David looked at a photo of the townhall, he identified another notable dissident in the audience, the distinguished writer and politician Milan Uhde. Uhde granted us a long interview in which it became clear that for him it was the Jewish aspect of the story that most resonated. He recounted the tragic history of his parents' struggles against anti-semitism from both Germans and Czechs, and how, despite his own success, he too has had to face anti-semitism, even after 1989. He would have asked the (rhetorical) question why we didn't get the property back in 1945 but didn't want to spoil the atmosphere of the town hall. Uhde said that many Czechs didn't want to know about the brutalities perpetrated by other Czechs. He was nine years old in 1945, and he remembers. The Czechs say they have never committed violence, that they are "decent people," while people like him are depicted as "flagellants."

Uhde was curious how my relatives dealt with their fate, different from his. As he put it, I didn't have the ghosts of his family. Maybe other ghosts, but not those ones.

On my side, there was embarrassment that despite our losses, we were better off for having lived outside Czechoslovakia since 1938. This insight was reinforced by the conversations we were privileged to have with Šabatová and Uhde, each of whom has struggled for a better society and suffered for it, and they now saw a country in which, at the national level, their ideals were betrayed.

In some respects, "the Jews" are simply the figure of what Roman and Radovan precisely call absence. Jews either fled or were killed;

what remained is their material property – houses, buildings, objects. Our reappearance creates ambiguity. Whose property was it, and whose property has it become? David put it rather cynically, remarking that at some level most Czechs want to ensure they don't have to return property to the original owners. They want us to visit and legitimate their occupation and administration of the buildings. They don't want us to stay, except in some passing fantasies that we might invest in industry and create large numbers of jobs.

Yet property is not exclusively material. In an anthropological lexicon, it is also symbolic. With respect to symbolic property we do benefit – in reputation and cachet, in our ability to continue to coalesce as a family – from the hospitality the city offers us. The mayor and Mojmír called us the moral owners. But as Mojmír also observed, the reality is different. Affectively it is ours; effectively it is theirs.[17]

Four Films

The house and family have been subject to much representation on film. German director Dieter Reifarth drew on Fritz Tugendhat's gorgeous photographs to create the documentary *Haus Tugendhat*, described in previous chapters. It is a film the family approves, even though it shows some disagreement among us. Family members have suggested the film be shown to visitors of the villa; there is space in the basement where it could run. The film would serve to enliven the house and to present the house over time rather than as a static or "authentic" object. To date, the curators have been opposed, likely because the film is not wholly laudatory of Czech efforts at conservation.

The city called upon Roman and Radovan to film the reunion. They produced a short, excellent film for the city, previewing excerpts with relevant family members to ensure their permission. The city sent us each copies, and it was shown at the 2018 Meeting Brno festival and the Czech Centre in Vienna. Keeping their promise to anxious family members, Roman and Radovan refused to hand over the full footage to the city and are continuing their longer project.

I gingerly asked Mayor Zoubek about the family's reaction to the film *The Löw-Beer Villas and the Story of the Found Suitcase* that he had produced. Zoubek gave a straightforward reply. He had been surprised and hoped he managed to explain its purpose, namely, to show local citizens who the Löw-Beers were and "what they did for us." It was made, in effect, for themselves, to show their children something about the beautiful houses in the park and the people who had inhabited them. The film may have been produced by amateurs, Zoubek admitted, but they wanted to revisit the past and to acknowledge that Svitávka wouldn't be what it is today without the family. Three of them wrote the script together and filmed with a budget of 80,000 crowns (c. CAN$4,500). They enjoyed making it and held the premiere on a big screen in the park in July 2014, exactly four years before we spoke; Fritz's son John attended from New York.

The film's narrative hinges on the discovery of a suitcase in the attic. I learned, to my surprise, that such a suitcase exists. It arrived in 1939, addressed to a former servant in the villa who had been close to the family before they left. No one knew who sent it. As Alfred was the last to leave, they assumed it was his. Of its contents, only two shirts remained. This additional piece of the mystery of Alfred's death explains why the film hinges on Alfred rather than Fritz or Rudolf. Yet the family protested that the reasons for Alfred's flight and death were not made explicit; a family tragedy is turned into light entertainment. Zoubek takes the family's response seriously and wants to change the ending but doesn't have the money for it. As someone from Brno said in the filmmakers' defence, at least they mentioned the family; no one had done so for the previous forty years.

Dani and Ivo were not among those offended by the film, and they pointed to an astute remark by my cousin Jonas that the film was not really about our family but about themselves. I asked Mr. Zoubek which role he had played. He squirmed and, smiling coyly, admitted that "maybe" he was Rudolf. His evident pride reinforces my view that one way to understand the film is as a carnivalesque reversal of hierarchy, a salutary inversion in which the former workers perform as the former bosses.[18]

I began this book with a response to *The Glass Room*. Local responses to the Czech edition were variable. One person dismissed it as ahistorical trash. Uhde called it a bad novel, parasitical and calculated. He described it as "written with a cold pen," meaning that it exploited the story of the family without empathy. But Szaló observed that the novel showed a part of Jewish heritage in Brno and offered one of the first ways to speak about the Holocaust there. He pointed out that on his first visit to the villa in the 1990s, he was not informed of any Jewish connection; the villa was discussed only in relation to functionalist architecture. The book, he said, had a generative public impact with respect to the Holocaust, especially because it portrays events in a way that is neither pathetic nor tragic. The family are treated as "just people," and the depiction of the sexual affairs renders them more human. Szaló referred to György Lukács argument that what makes a good historical novel is not factual documentation but its ability to evoke something true of the age. The point here is that what family members take for granted, or what Jews elsewhere take as public discourse about the Holocaust, operated in Brno as a kind of dissonant rhetoric, providing an opening to the subject that shifts people's frame of understanding.[19] Šabatová attributed the current popularity of the villa directly to the book and confessed that she too was influenced by it, even though she knew it was fiction. She was uncomfortable about her reaction because she knew some members of the family were offended by the book.

Despite Dani's petition to Mayor Vokřál to stop it, a film of *The Glass Room* was made in the Tugendhat House only a few weeks before my visit. It was done under the watchful eye of Iveta and her staff, who worked hard to protect the house and furniture, albeit the actresses wore stiletto heels and smoked, practices otherwise forbidden to visitors. Iveta said that Mawer himself felt somewhat betrayed because the director changed the story. Roman and Radovan's request to film the filming was denied.

The proposal to make the film passed city council with little debate as it was considered good publicity for the city. Only Hollan voted against. Vokřál admitted the decision was difficult as he knew Dani was opposed. But not only did he come out in favour, he gave the producers a million Czech crowns in support. This funding was part of a larger strategy to attract the international film industry to Brno.[20] Although it was a Czech production with a Czech director, the actors came from across Europe, and the film was shot in English. The book had already brought tourists and publicity, and Vokřál hoped that if the film proved of high quality, it would further heighten Brno's reputation as a city of culture. As others said, it would also serve as part of his legacy. He told me he would regret his decision if the film turned out badly, which it did.[21]

Mayor Vokřál wanted to offend the family as little as possible. He spoke to the director about the family's concerns and hoped he would further change identities. But this intervention did not address my aunts' concerns. Dani sees the story and film as a betrayal of her parents' memory. "You couldn't do more to hurt them," she said. One can reply that the book and film are pure fiction and have nothing to do with the actual inhabitants. But that is not how the public sees it. Iveta reported that visitors to the villa often correct the guides when their account does not accord with the book. Even as sophisticated a reader as Šabatová confessed that her impressions of the house and family were mediated through the novel, though she knows better. Mojmír, who was caught between the mayor and Dani, said the problem is that the story both is and isn't about the family; the genre is too mixed. The film would create even more interest in the house but, at the same time, further confuse fact and fiction.

Kateřina said it was very surprising to her and the Meeting Brno team that the mayor supported the filming. "It wasn't fair – just after we've said we want good relations with the Jewish families." The double messaging and quick about face are disconcerting. This situation may be why the local Jewish community is reluctant to participate in the broader cultural affairs of the city and why Dani is reluctant to place family memorabilia in the museums. There is also the knowledge that beyond the admirable group of activists and idealists, one finds not only amoral forces of capital but deep xenophobia and illiberal politics. The ways in which these forces and ideas reinforce each other are all too evident in some of the Czech Republic's neighbours.

※

On my last evening I attended a jazz concert held on the terrace below the Tugendhat House. Sitting on the broad steps under an open sky and listening to music from the 1920s and 1930s, I was taken back both to the period when my mother ran through the garden and to the wonderful family party held there the previous year. Two phrases from the conversation we had just held with Milan Uhde stayed with me. He said at one point: "Your family lost the most beautiful house in Europe." He also said: "Don't leave us. Don't return, but don't leave either."

Chapter Seventeen

Looking Back: Conundrums of Identity and Representation

During the reunion it seemed as though we were somehow two families, the one gathered on the lawns and herded into the buses and the imagined family of the pre-war period, affluent, invested in the world, making and doing and thinking important things. And before that family, a much more shadowy third one, living in a ghetto, tied to practices long since abandoned. Who knows now how comfortable or how confined they felt, spatially, socially, or with respect to religion and ideas? In sum, a kind of layering, a palimpsest of families.

Is our family the "same" family today that it was in 1848, 1900, 1939, or 1945? What has enabled a sense of continuous identity across time or encouraged mutual identification among living members? Is this book a confirmation or – like so much historical or ethnographic writing – an obituary?

My gaze has been turned to the past, oriented towards generations before mine. I have not noted the existence of many younger members. Perhaps they will barely see themselves as part of the family described here, will not comprehend this family as a whole, will not see *their* family as *this* whole. It is in the nature of families to forget antecedents, for branches to break off and begin anew, much as the children of Max and Pauline broke off from their parents' respective siblings, much as Eveline's descendants separated from those of her brothers, and as the brothers' descendants gradually separated from each other. That is as it must be.

Families are not essentially existing things in the world. I have argued that family – any family – is constituted through its representations of itself. Such representations happen in what is said and done (and what is kept silent and not done); at events of social reproduction like baptisms or circumcisions, birthdays, weddings, and funerals; in the ways people name each other and are named (as in the posted death notices I showed); in the course of everyday life, in the ways people care and are cared for, share, bequeath and inherit property, build and inhabit homes, manage domestic lives, visit, write letters, assist each other with migration, visas, and remittances, and, in my mother's family, respond to calls from lawyers, from the City of Brno, and even, as it were, from the Tugendhat House itself.[1]

The family persists as well through its representation by others and its responses to those representations. Indeed, the family (any family) could be called both a subject and an object of representation, constituted in the first instance through the acts and images that put it under description as a family and that commit new members to it. This family has been observed, as it were, through the windows of the glass house. But the family is not the house. Like the proverbial river, and unlike a house, one cannot step into the same family twice. It is neither as circumscribed nor as stable (though the Tugendhat House has not been stable either). Powerful forces have shaped and reshaped this family's representations of itself and by others. But if representations are historically constituted, they also perdure; they have lingering effects, and they overlap, like waves on a beach. The patriarchy, sibling marriages, financial consolidation, and patterns of residence and consumption that characterized the family up to the Second World War continued to cast their shadow long after. The house Grete commissioned disappeared from view for many decades, only to return to render us subjects of representation in new, periodically intense, and sometimes misleading ways. This book too brings the past into the present for a time, composing and recomposing the family in the process.

Representation has carried weight in the life of this family for reasons that have to do with the cultural, political, and economic circumstances at which successive generations lived. Before the First World War these included shared ownership of an expanding firm, rapid emergence into the upper bourgeoisie, and consolidated marriages and residence. Between the wars, there were expanded horizons and new achievements of individual members. Internal relations remained intense, and the family was seen, and saw itself, as a world unto itself and as somehow special. During and after the Second World War, the family was fractured and reconstituted in a diasporic spread that thinned some ties but intensified others, especially around the nodal figures who returned to Europe and came to signify a common identity and past. For some, the dispersal was undoubtedly liberating, freeing the younger adults from the demands of the firm and the larger family. Eventually, there emerged the aura of the highly valued cultural artefact that is the Tugendhat House, and the family gained salience for citizens of Brno in thinking about the past and future of their society.

Our Jewish Question

One way we have been represented in Brno, for good and for ill, is as Jews. However, that is not the primary way most of us identify ourselves, and even if we did, we are hardly *representative* Jews; once richer, more privileged, and simply luckier than those who were unable to emigrate, who were murdered by Nazis, harassed and imprisoned by the communist regime, or wary enough to keep a low profile in the Czech Republic today.

In this family, I think identification *as* a family has been more salient than being Jewish, or indeed than any religious, ethnic, or national identity. It could be said that *family* took their place as our most singificant collective imaginary. A specifically Jewish identity has been or becomes salient only for individuals who choose it or insofar as we are collectively attacked for it, as we were in print when we reclaimed the Lehmbruck statue.

Today we are dispersed across Austria, Canada, England, Germany, Switzerland, the United States, and, if I include the broader family who showed up for the reunion, Australia, Brazil, and

France as well. There was not a single family member from Israel. But national identification has not been central for most of us. In inter and post-war Czechoslovakia family members were faced with an impossible situation: a demand that they become Czech in the face of an imposed definition as German. We learned to be sceptical of national identifications. I am a Canadian but consider myself an accidental one. My parents happened to end up and meet in Montreal. My mother tongue is English largely because they preferred the lesser amount of religion taught in the anglophone Protestant schools to the greater amount taught in francophone Catholic schools in Quebec in the 1950s. Each a native speaker of German, my parents spoke to each other and to us in English. Hanna was equally fluent in French and Spanish. We were evidently not Québécois, but neither were we fully part of the anglophone community of our suburb who took for granted Protestant Christianity and a good deal else that did not pertain to us. My father's world was one of intellectuals, largely mathematicians and logicians, a truly international and transnational community. My mother came to engage with increasing intensity in public life in Quebec, but when I was young her primary identification was with her family, an identification reinforced for me through our trips to Europe.

My parents did not tell us we were Jewish, though they never hid or denied it either. We followed none of the Jewish holidays and never set foot inside either a synagogue or a church. My father came from a family with a stronger Jewish identity than my mother's. He maintained a muted interest in Israel, where he had cousins, but he was not Zionist and became increasingly critical of Israeli policy. Moreover, he was an outspoken atheist and anti-ritualist. My mother described herself as agnostic. She maintained her family tradition of a Christmas tree. Holidays were marked most strongly for us by the eagerly awaited arrival and consumption of foil-wrapped chocolate tree ornaments and Easter eggs sent by Grete from Switzerland. Hanna rolled marzipan rings that we dipped in chocolate and added to the tree. We had no connection to the large, observant, and partly Yiddish-speaking Jewish community in Montreal.

And yet each member of the larger family, at every generation, has had to take a position with respect to "being Jewish." We have each acknowledged it and simultaneously acknowledged our distance from it, refusing to be overdetermined by it. Hence, I prefer to speak of being ~~Jewish~~ rather than of being Jewish.[2] I do not mean this disrespectfully.

There is a good deal of moralization about this position from outsiders. But we are not false Jews or self-hating Jews, as those who essentialize or politicize identity might have it. Our distinctiveness is neither accidental nor willful but has a legitimate history. The generation who moved out of the Moravian ghettos into Austro-Hungarian society experienced a sense of freedom. They began to relinquish the practices and commitments that had defined the world of the ghetto and to take on features of the wider world. They tried to disentangle being Jewish in a religious or observant sense from being Jewish in a genealogical sense, but it was unclear what, beyond religious observance, Zionism, or suffering anti-semitism could substantiate a Jewish identity. Specifically Jewish practices became less relevant as the family rose in the class hierarchy and as they embraced the exciting currents of rationalism, modernism, and universalism. In any case, they refused to let the Jewish component of their social identity be an encompassing one and, like many Jewish intellectuals from central Europe, remained highly sceptical of any form of nationalism.[3]

Were we fallen from the world of the shtetl, risen from it, or did we simply slip out sideways? There is no fascination for orthodox life, no passion for reciting the Torah (though my father loved it as a secular reader) or for celebrating the annual round of Jewish holidays, and no direct memory of doing so. Judaism emerges only in brief, unexpected moments, like Paul's deathbed blessing. Once God and ritual were forsaken, what then could it mean to "be" Jewish? For most of us it had little meaning except as a kind of historical legacy, and insofar as being of Jewish descent made one vulnerable to prejudice and enjoined identification with its victims. To be Jewish was to accede to the label and labelling practices of those who denigrated it, but also to exhibit solidarity with other Jews, as when Grete worked on behalf of refugees in Brno or

Helene with psychiatric patients in Geneva. Mutzi never showed any sign of being Jewish, but she left money to several Jewish charities in her will.

Even though objective Jewish practices like speaking Yiddish, observing dietary rules, or attending synagogue were abandoned, the family did not simply assimilate to Austrian or German society. Unlike other wealthy Jewish families such as the Wittgensteins and Gutmanns, the Löw-Beers did not convert. Culturally, my great-grandparents through Grete were Viennese, but to meet Catholic Austrians is immediately to note a difference. (We bake a much more delicious *Sachertorte* than what is served in the Hotel Sacher.) My grandparents' generation were more likely to participate in German cultural life than in Austrian, but they never became German (as did the Weiss family, however). In my parents' generation, passionate about German philosophy, Ernst moved to Germany and became part of that tradition, but he spent years feeling an outsider and eventually came to regret how much of a German he had let himself become. He attempted to counter that with identification as South American, and he drew explicitly on his Jewish identity to support Palestinian causes. All the post-war European returnees retained a kind of cosmopolitanism that differentiated them from ordinary Germans, Austrians, or Swiss, albeit anxious to participate in national, political, and civic life. My cousin Lukas Hammer is currently a member of the Austrian Parliament for the Green Party. One thing that links us with other Jews is the affectation that being Jewish affords a critical angle towards the mainstream.

Each generation responded to their Jewish question as the times enabled or demanded. Until Moses Löw-Beer left the ghetto, family members were unproblematically Jewish, though Boskovice was full of intense internal debate over practice and piety. The last member of the family people recalled being a practising Jew was Pauline, the mother of my great-grandfather, but the extent of her practice was relative to the perspective of her non-observant grandchildren. Her grandson Paul had his bar mitzvah in her synagogue at the factory; her great-granddaughter Margaret recalled being taken to see the room: the ceiling was painted blue, with silver stars.

Pauline's sons had bar mitzvahs, but their wives came from a family that was already less identified with Judaism. As Paul recollected, "my mother was non-religious. Her family were completely assimilated. It was different with my father; he went once a year to temple [on Yom Kippur] but otherwise he hardly cared about religion. He did not mind that my mother was an active assimilant. According to the registration form we were all 'Mosaic.' We would not have been baptized, as one had reservations; baptismal water has never touched me or anyone else in the immediate family [but see below]. My father had some knowledge of religion, because his mother [Pauline], although not pious, came from a very old Jewish family that led her family tree back to the famous Rabbi Löw [of Prague], though this was never proven. She was a very educated woman, but we had little contact with her."

Here is Paul's cousin Fritz on the social context. "When I encountered the social anti-semitism existing in Canada and the USA, I was horrified and convinced that this kind of segregation had not existed in pre-Hitler Europe. But one day I suddenly asked myself whether this was really true, and I checked the people who had made up the social group around Alfred and Marianne in Brno. Although a non-Jew ... might be invited once in a while, the 'regulars' were all Jews. This finally opened my eyes to the fact that social segregation had in fact been as bad as it was over here ... In reality, the Jews were not accepted by anyone. The industrial workers hated them as being rich, the peasants regarded them with suspicion if only because they were different, the bourgeois and professional people saw in them unwelcome competitors who were only too often more successful than they themselves, and only the aristocracy regarded them with toleration – as long as they kept their place in the divine order of things."

Fritz speculates on his great-grandfather's experience. "I cannot imagine what the situation may have been in the first years after emancipation when the Jews were allowed to leave the ghettos for the first time after centuries of strict segregation. I suppose that they must have been very humble, very careful and probably hypocritical vis-à-vis every Gentile. It probably required a certain courage for Moses L-B to go and settle in a village like Svitávka among the peasants who were certainly different and whom he must have regarded as potential enemies. The ghetto had not really ended; there was still very little mixing of Gentiles and Jews even in 1938. The L-Bs in Svitávka lived entirely apart from the people around them. Moses must have been fully aware of the general anti-semitism, but sixty years later the situation was likely rather different partly because probably at least 80 per cent of Brno industry and finance were in Jewish hands so that the anti-semitism, though scarcely diminished, must have appeared less threatening, less important than before. I know that Alfred and Marianne realized the existence of anti-semitism but I think they did not like to talk about it."

The First World War was a turning point. One effect of the breakup of the Habsburg Empire was the creation of national borders. Assimilated Jews could no longer enjoy a kind of anonymous citizenship, a non-national identity in an empire characterized by cultural and linguistic pluralism. The new states were ideologically based on national homogeneity; Jews had to choose a national affiliation and, even then, were likely marked as foreign. Historian William McCagg suggests that Jews who had identified as Habsburg faced an identity crisis and painful choices; in Galicia, Poles and Ukrainians each suspected Jews of being allied with their rivals for national claims, and in Moravia, it meant deciding whether to switch from speaking German to Czech.

In McCagg's view, to engage in a secular way of life was to cast aside one's "national" identity as a Jew. This identity could be regained through Zionism, which became an attractive option for many in the former empire, though less so in Czechoslovakia because of relatively good relations. Czechoslovakia's first president, Thomas Masaryk, was a lawyer who had defended Jews from blood libel, and the new country was better governed, more democratic, and more stable than either Austria or Hungary. Many Jews cast their lot with Czechoslovakia, as evidenced in the domestic architecture that Grete and her cousins Fritz and Ernst commissioned. The antipathy that grew through the 1930s took them by surprise.

Those in my grandparents' generation had little Jewish identity. Ernst Löw-Beer had a bar mitzvah, said his daughter, only for the presents and was an atheist. Paul and Helene never fasted on Yom Kippur. Fritz recalled: "Walking to school in Brno, workers' boys often shouted 'Zide' after me and once I was attacked by them (nothing much happened though) but that sort of thing did not impress me particularly. I had no great consciousness of being 'a Jew' and did not realize that civilized and educated Gentiles really saw any difference between Jews and themselves. In short, I was living in a non-existing world, protected by my isolation in Svitávka and by the Löw-Beer name."

The members of this generation did not bring up their children with a religious or Jewish identity. Grete put up a Christmas tree, and Hanna's best friend was a blonde Christian girl. Hanna's first cousin Margaret said no one in her immediate family attended synagogue in Czechoslovakia. She thought her great-grandparents might have, and her grandparents on high holidays, but she also recalled them serving ham. Margaret is unusual among family members in that she married a man of orthodox Jewish background and some years later, as she put it, "returned to the faith of my ancestors."

Margaret reflected, I think correctly, that her parents' position was less about rejecting Jewish identity than about being modern. That generation threw themselves into art, science, and politics. Most of their friends were Jewish, but "being Jewish" had little to do with it.

After the war, in North America, Hans Löw-Beer raised his children as Unitarians. Max in Vancouver joined the Anglican Church. Ernst Löw-Beer married a non-Jew who raised their children Protestant. Their daughters became respectively Jewish and Catholic to suit their husbands. Ernst's son Peter became a Unitarian. Helene's daughter Joan said her parents didn't tell her she was Jewish. Later her father Kusi, himself of Japanese background, advised her: "The Jews are always going to suffer prejudice. You don't look Jewish and your name isn't Jewish, so just pass." But Joan said that she does identify as Jewish, though she celebrates Christmas. Her sister Eva added: "I attended Jewish Sunday school briefly because I wanted to see what it was like … I was later baptized and confirmed an Episcopalian – this religious phase lasted about a year.

Ironically, my Christian godparents had a daughter who converted to Judaism and is currently married to a cantor. My father was Buddhist and practised in his own way ... My Jewish identity is mostly limited to the family history." Family identity trumps Jewish identity.

Of my mother's siblings, Ernst requested and received a bar mitzvah and spent his life actively thinking through what it meant to be religious but never fully taking it on. Hanna's younger sisters went through periods in early adolescence when they identified as Jews, joined Jewish youth groups, and considered Zionism, to the great consternation of the older generation. As an adult, Dani told me that her identity is not Jewish because she rejects the whole concept of identity. She says there are many parts to her; she recognizes the Jewish heritage or background as significant, but as only one piece of who she is. She had no problem marrying a German. Like Ernst, Ruth, and my father, she became increasingly opposed to Israeli policy with respect to the Palestinians. In a phrase that may sound paradoxical but resonates strongly with me, Dani said she knew she was Jewish when she realized she couldn't visit Israel; she would take it all too personally and too hard. Being Jewish comes to include legitimately criticizing Israeli policy and standing in affective yet also ironic relationship to the identity.

Marriages with non-Jews increased at each generation. There were none in my great-grandparents' generation. Two of the eight double cousins in my grandparents' generation had non-Jewish partners, and so too did two of Fritz Tugendhat's siblings. In my mother's generation, of nine cousins descended from Alfred and Marianne, only three had Jewish partners (plus one partly Jewish). None of my mother's four siblings on her father's side married Jews. In my generation, of twenty descendants of Alfred and Marianne, only two have Jewish partners. One European relative explicitly does not want her children to be identifiable as Jews. She thinks anti-semitism is passed from one generation to the next and said that "something very threatening is on the rise."

Things can also go the other way. Ellen Pollak, great-granddaughter of Alfred's sister Eveline, grew up in New York, out of contact with us but quite similar with respect to being Jewish. As she wrote me, "the Pollak's were also very assimilated and not particularly religious, although it seems that as factory owners [before the war], they were influential members of the Jewish community in Bielsko-Biala and affiliated in some way with the ornate and imposing synagogue just down the street from the family home (now ... a pile of rubble). Roger and I had little to no Jewish education and no formal bar/bat mitzvahs and went to Seders only at other people's houses. We had a Xmas tree in our home every year." Yet Ellen married a man who was "sent for 3 years to a religious school in Israel as a teenager, so he speaks gorgeous Hebrew and does quite a bit of the Torah reading for the rather eclectic Reconstructionist synagogue where our daughters were bat mitzvahed [in the United States]. He managed to convey his great love for the language and traditions to our children and, in the process, I garnered a bit of education too ... I wouldn't say I'm religious, but I do identify strongly as Jewish."

What renewal of Jewish identity there is in the family comes through marriage, which is evident when marrying practising Jews, as Margaret or Ellen did, but sometimes even when marrying non-Jews. Rachel, the daughter of my mother's brother Robin Weiss and his wife (also named Margaret), a practising Roman Catholic from Kerala, said the children and grandchildren of Hans Weiss considered themselves Jewish only insofar as Hitler called them so. She thinks she might not feel Jewish at all if it weren't for the Holocaust; it links up with her experience of racism in the United Kingdom against South Asians. Only recently has the category "mixed race" become available for her to think about herself. Otherwise, the Weiss family never considered these things; they were rationalists. Nevertheless, her South Asian mother was appreciative of the Jewish side. Once when we were in London, Margaret produced a Passover meal for all of us non-practitioners.

The person for whom the family's Jewish identity held the most positive significance was possibly Irene Kalkofen, the nanny for Grete's children in Brno. As a German non-Jew, she made a positive attachment to a Jewish family, a decisive act that placed her in exile and then into work with Jewish survivors in England.

Wealth and Class

From the time of Max through the Second World War, the salient forms of identification were class and family, and these reinforced each other. In a description that is astonishingly accurate for my family, European historian Leonore Davidoff speaks of "kinship-rich class societies" and argues that class formation was based not only on the confrontations between workers and capitalists, but also on the fact that "kinship endogamy formed the nucleus of class endogamy."[4] For Christians and Jews alike, she argues, a sense of belonging derived more from kinship than faith.[5]

Sylvia Yanagisako makes a similar point when she proposes a "theory of capitalist motivation in which sentiments operate as forces of production that incite particular kinds of capitalist action ... [T]he productive capacities of the bourgeoisie are, like those of the workers, produced and reproduced through cultural processes in which kinship and gender are crucial."[6]

In her account of the "long family," one that included many siblings, born across a lengthy period, Davidoff writes: "Groups of siblings, cousins, and friends contributed to people's feelings of inclusion, sense of security, and assumptions about social place. From infancy boys and girls within such families had learned to deal with a variety of temperaments and relationships. They took part in creating and living with elements of authority, power, favouritism, bullying, rivalry, and competitiveness. They were also given opportunities to develop a capacity for concern, empathy, and insight. As childhood turned into youth, the sense of place within the sibling and kin group carried over into a perception of inviolable personal and social distinctiveness ... On no small measure such formative experiences in early life forged the consciousness of position and class-belonging that was a defining feature of nineteenth- and early twentieth-century political as well as social and personal life."[7]

Davidoff's perceptive depiction applies directly to the Löw-Beers, and the consciousness it describes continued through my grandparents' lives and on to some of my mother's cousins. They could either accept capitalism and their class position or try to find a compromise with it. Thereafter, there have been significant shifts in both class and class consciousness as lived experience.

After the war, family assets were distributed in stock portfolios rather than concentrated in means of production. As such, wealth was relatively concealed. Family members invested independently of one another; because of differences in spending and in skill and luck in investment, as well as the professions people took up, disparities in wealth shifted. There were times when the vagaries of investments determined different fortunes between siblings or cousins.

As a child it appeared to me that having money was connected to a sense of confidence and superiority. Some (not all) wealthier relatives appeared to look down on my immediate family, whether because we had much less (my father starting from nothing after the war) or because we lived unselfconsciously in a style and comportment that revealed class difference or worse, class indifference. We inhabited a small bungalow and ate hot dogs at least once a week to manage the household budget. Hanna kept aside what money she had for our university education. She said simply that *we* were not money minded. She also averred that being happy was far more important than being rich.

Questions of money remain largely unspoken within the family. In her anthropological study of family-owned textile firms in northern Italy, Sylvia Yanagisako observes that "betrayal and estrangement are as much a regular part of the organizational dynamics of … family capitalism as are trust and kinship solidarity."[8] With the obvious exception of Paul's son, betrayal and estrangement are too strong to describe our family's experience. However, feelings of financial injustice and envy have appeared. Grete's brother Max resented the division of money in his generation. I resented that his widow convinced Mutzi not to pass on her diamond ring to my mother. Some people suspect that the houses Grete was able to build indicate that she received more than her share. Since finances were hardly transparent, and the principles of distribution unclear, there is no way to resolve these issues. Ultimately, they are overridden by feelings of common identification with "family."

There is a common saying that one generation makes money and the next spends it. This scenario is sometimes called the Buddenbrooks effect, after Thomas Mann's fictional four-generational portrait of a north German family, but it is a story heard in Italy and in China and no doubt elsewhere.[9] Younger generations have less urgency and are possibly less ambitious or less industrious. Phrased positively, intellectual and artistic pursuits are ones that the children or grandchildren of successful businesspeople can access and afford. I don't know how such pursuits would have unfolded had historical events been otherwise, but already in Brno there was some resistance to expected roles, and one young man, Fritz Löw-Beer, successfully opted out of business. Several women of his generation, like Lene, Anni, Helene, and Ala, pursued higher education and careers.

High achievement was expected of everyone, but there were tensions between succeeding through business or via intellectual or artistic activity and connoisseurship. More than a simple division of interests, in this setting of sharp convictions, the choices were moralized. Some family members were interested in and very good at business but felt looked down upon by those with intellectual or artistic leanings. Those who engaged in intellectual activity or art were sometimes resented and envied, sometimes depreciated by those in business. The intellectuals placed art or philosophy above money, but they needed money to collect art or live in the world of ideas. As Hans Löw-Beer said to me, "it was all based on business, and yet business was looked down upon." Feeling unacknowledged as a serious intellectual, and perhaps even as a son, Paul's younger son Peter made the point by absconding with the family fortune.

There was also a distinction between living relatively luxuriously, or at least comfortably, and living relatively ascetically, and in either case, sometimes ostentatiously so. Was wealth something to be disdained, ashamed of, enjoyed, or flaunted? The same great aunt who appropriated the diamond ring flew from Vancouver to celebrate the post-war opening of the Vienna opera house. Others scorned such pretensions.

Sometimes these predilections followed from parent to offspring, and sometimes they were reversed. Rudolf and Elise were very wealthy yet personally modest, though they slid with ease into life in the best Swiss hotels. Their children also lived modestly, Helene extremely so, while some of their grandchildren reacted against that lifestyle. Alfred rode horses; one of his grandsons played polo, while another gave away most of his money. Benno loved cars; his sons spent wildly on their automobiles and other luxuries. Two of his grandsons turned to lives of public service, albeit one still drives a low-slung sports car.

All these matters are complex and deeply personal. Paul was simultaneously the owner and manager of factories and the "red sheep" of the family, as his daughter put it. The tension between an appreciation for making money and a disdain for it, and between luxury and moderation, was evident in Grete's life. Depending on one's perspective, the respective values remained in contradiction or were successfully resolved. With an austerity about their persons and a seriousness in their approach to life, Grete and Fritz built houses that were showy precisely in their absence of show, adhering to Mies's adage that less is more but never compromising on quality.

Money aside, we were all subject to the high expectations that family members placed on one another and that as members of the family, many of us came to place on ourselves. One relative told me she determined not to pressure her children to succeed academically – until they told her they knew full well that she was trying to suppress her desire to do so. We worry that our achievements are insufficient. The bright side of this pressure is when we are able to serve as exemplars. The Tugendhat House is exemplary, and Grete herself has been an exemplar, even if in ways that we could not always follow.

Anthropologist Veena Das has remarked: "It is not as if a representation can coincide with what is represented."[10] But then, how do we acknowledge the relation between representation, representer, and represented? What is the relationship between this book and its subject? Between this family and its self-representations? Or between my representation of this family – extensive, demanding, privileged with wealth, intelligence, and a high opinion of itself – and *any* family, or perhaps the European bourgeois family, the capitalist family, the diasporic family? In what ways can representation avoid stereotype, especially when lives are used in projects of national and historical imagination, as in Brno? To be available to an audience, Das observes, some sort of typification is necessary, meeting certain expectations of narrative and description.[11]

Only great works of art manage to transcend this typification; that is how they are great. The Tugendhat House is a great work of art, neither representing nor representative, simply itself. But it has not escaped the indignities of being represented. Nor have its inhabitants.

Throughout the manuscript there have been silences. Some of them reproduce the silences encountered in life. One of my cousins said that her father never spoke to her about the past or about the family. She wrote me that "the impact of the diaspora and the family reticence to share has been a feeling of struggling to find a context." That is what I contribute to rediscovering here.

Sometimes silence should be respected. As the anthropologist Vincent Crapanzano put it, "we should respect in the Other the same mystery we expect others to respect in ourselves."[12]

The biggest lesson I have learned in the course of writing is how difficult, indeed impossible, it is to do justice to the life and character of another person. Some of my relatives I see only from a distance, and they come to stand unfairly for a general point I want to make, never fully for or as themselves. Others I have had the privilege to view from closer up, but the closer I look, the greater the injustice seems, not only in violating their privacy but also in the inaccuracy – painting a picture so much less rich, complex, and vibrant than the actual human beings they were and that as a chronicler I owe them. It is hard to disagree with painter Mark Rothko's observation that "silence is so accurate."

I feel greatest inadequacy when it comes to Grete, who is, after all, the central figure in this narrative. As I wrapped up a set of revisions to the manuscript, I dreamt, for the first and only time, of Grete. She singled me out to walk alone with her, the only way, she had said, to truly get to know someone. I began by asking her about her time in Berlin. But she kept getting distracted, enthused, or annoyed by this or that, so the conversation could not proceed. We stopped for lunch at a country inn, and she patted the place next to her for me to sit. But her back was to the chimney, and she was now too hot, now too cold, and she stood up to speak to the manager about it. The feeling of the dream was that she was ready to talk, better disposed towards me than I have unfairly portrayed her, and that she approved my project. She invited me to the table. But it was too late. There were so many questions I wanted to ask, so much to fill in, but her need for perfection got in the way, and it didn't happen.

Acknowledgments

A version of chapter 1 was first presented in 2014 at a workshop on representation organized by Bianca Dahl at the Centre for Ethnography, University of Toronto Scarborough. That essay transformed definitively into a book project during a fellowship at the Wissenschaftskolleg zu Berlin in 2016–17, thanks to a mischievous suggestion from Rogers Brubaker, the examples set by Carey Harrison and Frédéric Brenner, the enthusiastic encouragement of Cheryl Misak and David Dyzenhaus, and the support of Luca Giuliani, Daniel Schönpflug, and Sonja Grund. Special thanks to Sonja Asal who facilitated access to the Deutsches Literaturarchiv in Marbach, accompanied me there, and kindly translated many of the letters in the archives. My thanks to Arnulf Heidegger and to Ernst Tugendhat for their permission to examine the Heidegger and Tugendhat correspondence housed there.

In Berlin I also received particularly valuable insights from Avishai Margalit and Stefan Gosepath, as well as generous responses from Michal Bodemann, James Conant, Lorraine Daston, Gertrud Grünkorn, Fritz Kramer, Matthias Kroß, Thomas Meyer, and Stephan Schlak, among others. In Aarhus and elsewhere I have benefitted from wonderful conversations with Thomas Wentzer.

In Brno I am indebted to Iveta Černá, Matěj Hollan, Mojmír Jeřábek, Petr Kalousek, Monika Koppová, Radovan Kramář, Jaroslav Ostrčilík, Jakub Pernes, Anna Šabatová, Bohumír Smutný, Csaba Szaló, Kateřina Tučková, Milan Uhde, Petr Vokřál, Roman Zmrzlý, and in Svitávka, to Mayor Jaroslav Zoubek. I cannot thank them enough for their forthright engagement with the project, and I admire their contributions to civic life.

My time in Brno was facilitated enormously by the participation of David Henig, with whom it was an honour to work. David has been an exceptionally generous colleague and wonderful sounding board then and since.

I have also been able to draw on the excellent Czech websites and documentation concerning the houses and family. Readers wishing more detail or more images than I can provide here should check out the Villa Tugendhat website (https://www.tugendhat .eu/en/) as well as the many excellent publications produced in Brno, such as the recent *Exploring the History of the Textile Industrialists in Brno*, published by the Muzeum Brněska in 2017.

In Toronto Christoph Emmrich very kindly translated much of the Heidegger-Tugendhat correspondence, and Sandra Bamford, Joshua Barker, Ritu Birla, Katie Kilroy-Marac, Srilata Raman, Jack Sidnell, and Donna Young each offered perceptive suggestions. I also thank Rogers Brubaker, Gillian Feeley-Harnik, Rena Lederman, Carola Lentz, Isidore Lobnibe, Birgit Meyer, and Dietrich Neumann for helpful conversations. Howard Norman, Alisse Waterston, and an anonymous reviewer gave feedback on an unwieldy first draft, and David Henig on a later one. My editor, Jodi Lewchuk, has offered impeccable judgment and steadfast support throughout; Janice Evans, Carolyn Zapf, and the rest of the University of Toronto Press team have been outstanding to work with as well. Larry Lambek kindly proofed the manuscript.

Research and writing were conducted while I was beneficiary of a Canada Research Chair from the Social Sciences and Humanities Research Council of Canada.

Of my family I can say only that they have proved themselves even more admirable than I describe in the body of the work. Of those who have since died, I am indebted to Robert Fuhrmann, Jonas Guggenheim, Margaret Libbert, Hans (John) and Edith Low-Beer, Paul and Ala Löw-Beer, Patricia Gercik, Irene Kalkofen, Iain Smith, Kathy Tugendhat, Minnie Tugendhat, and Peter Weiss.

Enormous thanks to Eva Colacicco, Michael Fuhrmann, Lukas Hammer, David Löw-Beer, Jane Low-Beer, John (Johnny)

Low-Beer, Martin Löw-Beer, Joan Lowber Berkowitz, Peter Lowber, Joan Musitano, Leif Parsons, Ellen Pollak, Anna Sagemuller, Kitty Schmidt, Andy, Eduardo, and Marcia Tugendhat, Martin Tugendhat, and Margaret, Rachel, and Robin Weiss. Susan Low-Beer (Parsons) has been particularly encouraging over many years, and Roger Pollak has been very generous in sharing his photo archive.

I have been discussing the family with Ruth Guggenheim-Tugendhat and Zwi Guggenheim for as long as I can remember, and I thank them for much insight and hospitality over the years. Ernst Tugendhat has been extremely kind and generous in putting up with this intrusion into his affairs; he offered advice on this project as early as 1988. Dani Hammer-Tugendhat and Ivo Hammer have responded with characteristic energy and enthusiasm to all my questions and requests for photographs. They are the true curators of the family's legacy, and readers should also turn to their writing on the Tugendhat House, which they have done so much to conserve and protect.

This book is about my mother's family, but I am equally a member of my father's family and of my wife's, not to say of my own. I am grateful to all of them. My late father Jim Lambek, my brothers Larry and Bernie Lambek, and sister-in-law Linda Sproul have each provided encouragement and feedback. Nadia Lambek, Simon Lambek, Carey DeMichelis, and Geraldo Gonzalez have looked on with bemusement at my obsession but have also offered much good advice and support. Jackie Solway's role has been invaluable. She has sustained me all the way through, providing insight and scepticism in good measure and keeping me from many errors of judgment. Needless to say, all failings are my own.

My greatest debt must be to my late mother, Hanna, through whom I became a part of this family, which she loved and which she exemplified for me. She died much too early. This book is both in her memory and for all her grandchildren and great-grandchildren.

Timeline

1746	**Salomon is born (d. 1832)**
1788	Jews had to select surnames
1793	**Moses is born (d. 1851)**
c. 1820	Aron-Jakob firm founded
c. 1825	Moses starts wool washing in Svitávka
1829	**Max is born (d. 1887)**
1838	**Pauline is born (d. 1919)**
c. 1839/41	Moses L-B cloth manufacturing firm founded
1848	residence rules officially rescinded
1851	Max takes over the firm
1856	**Anna is born (d. 1939)**
1859	**Eveline is born (d. 1925)**
1862	Max founds factory in Brno
1864	**Cilla is born (d. 1942)**

1865	**Rudolf is born (d. 1953)**
1872	**Alfred is born (d. 1939)**
1874	**Benno (d. 1916) and Elise (d 1957) are born**
1876	Max establishes factory in Sagan
1882	**Marianne is born (d. 1975)**
1887	Rudolf takes over the firm
1888	**Max Hože is born (d. 1942)**
1895	**Fritz T. is born (d. 1958)**
1898	**Lene W. is born (d. 1951)**
1900	**Hans W. is born (d. 1980)**
1901	marriage of Alfred and Marianne
1902	completion of Grosse Villa
	Max L-B is born (d. 1954)
1903	marriage of Benno and Hansi
	Grete is born (d. 1970)
1905	marriage of Rudolf and Elise
1906	Kleine Villa built
	Fritz L-B is born (d. 1976)
1908	**Helene is born (d. 1980)**
1909	**Irene K. is born (d. 2004)**
1910	**Paul L-B is born (d. 2003)**
1911	**Hans L-B is born (d. 1993)**
1922	marriage of Grete and Hans Weiss
1924	**Hanna is born (d. 1991)**
1928	Grete meets Mies, divorces Hans, marries Fritz Tugendhat
1929	construction of Villa Tugendhat begins
1930	family moves into the villa (December)
	Ernst T. is born
1933	**Herbi is born (d. 1980)**

1935	Ernst L-B's house constructed in Brno
1936	Grete and Fritz spend four weeks in Palestine
1938	12 March: Germans march into Austria
	13 March: Hanna leaves with Hans for England
	May: Grete leaves for St. Gallen, Switzerland
1939	15 March: Germans occupy Brno
	17 March: Hitler parades in Brno
1941	January: Grete, Fritz, and family depart for Caracas, Venezuela
1950	June: Grete, Fritz, and family return to St. Gallen
1957	Helene and Kusi move from New York to Switzerland
1967	Grete revisits the Tugendhat Villa
1969	Grete conditionally offers the Tugendhat Villa to the City of Brno
2001	Tugendhat House becomes a UNESCO World Heritage site
2012	renovation of Tugendhat Villa completed
2017	Brno hosts the family for a reunion

Notes

Preface

1 "The past is a foreign country: they do things differently there." L.P. Hartley, *The Go-Between* (Hamish Hamilton, 1953), 1. See also historian David Lowenthal, *The Past Is a Foreign Country* (Cambridge University Press, 1985).

1. People Who Live in Glass Houses

1 Simon Mawer, *The Glass Room* (Little, Brown, 2009), front matter, unpaginated.
2 Daniela Hammer-Tugendhat and Wolf Tegethoff, eds., *Ludwig Mies van der Rohe: The Tugendhat House* (Springer, 2000). I will cite from the new expanded edition: Daniela Hammer-Tugendhat, Ivo Hammer, and Wolf Tegethoff, eds., *Tugendhat House: Ludwig Mies van der Rohe* (Birkhäuser-De Gruyter, 2020). Hereafter HTT.
3 *Last Week Tonight with John Oliver*, season 1, episode 20, "Civil Forfeiture" (HBO), 6 October 2014, https://www.youtube.com/watch?v= 3kEpZWGgJks. Lévi-Strauss saw houses in these societies as "moral persons." Claude Lévi-Strauss, "The Social Organization of Kwakiutl," in *The Way of the Masks* (University of Washington Press, 1982), 163–87. See also Janet Carsten and Stephen Hugh-Jones, eds., *About the House: Lévi-Strauss and Beyond* (Cambridge University Press, 1995); Janet Carsten, "House-Lives as Ethnography/Biography," *Social Anthropology* 26, no. 1 (2018): 103–16.
4 However, consider the country houses of British nobility.
5 Letter to Frantisek Kalivoda, 11 November 1968, as cited by Wolf Tegethoff in HTT, 138–9n62.

6 See Ivo Hammer, "Surface Is Interface," in HTT, 140–61, for full discussion of the struggle over conservation. For another thorough discussion of the house, including what the editors call its rehabilitation, see Iveta Černá and Dagmar Černoušková, eds., *Mies in Brno: The Tugendhat House* (Muzeum Města Brna, 2013). On the excellent Villa Tugendhat website developed by the museum (https://www.tugendhat.eu/en/), one can learn a great deal about the house and even take a virtual tour (https://www.tugendhat.eu/en/photogallery/virtual-tour.html).

7 Martin Gayford, "Living the Highly Expensive Life," *The Spectator*, 4 August 2018, https://www.spectator.co.uk/article/living-the-highly-expensive-life.

8 Sarah Crown, "Interview with Simon Mawer," *The Guardian*, 3 October 2009, http://www.theguardian.com/culture/2009/oct/03/simon-mawer-life-in-books.

9 The film of *The Glass Room* goes even further, described as "a love story between two women." Will Tizard, "'The Glass Room's' Historic Czech Building Provided Context, Atmosphere," *Variety*, 18 October 2018, https://variety.com/2018/artisans/production/czech-movie-the-glass-room-1202982141/. It was subsequently retitled *The Affair*.

10 Crown, "Interview."

11 Dieter Reifarth, dir., *Haus Tugendhat*, Pandora Film, 2013.

12 Ingeborg Messerschmidt speaks with no regret or acknowledgment of what else was going on.

13 Unfortunately, they both died before they could begin the project.

14 Clifford Geertz, "Blurred Genres: The Refiguration of Social Thought," in *Local Knowledge: Further Essays in Interpretive Anthropology* (Basic Books, 1983), 19–35.

15 Bianca Dahl, "There Are No Heroes Here: Introductory Remarks to the Conference on The Ethnographic Pact," Centre for Ethnography, University of Toronto Scarborough, 7 November 2014; Philippe Lejeune, *Signes de vie: Le pacte autobiographique 2* (Seuil, 2005).

16 Here and throughout the book I use "Czech" to refer to citizens of Czechoslovakia, irrespective of whether they identified as Czech or Slovak. Brno was inhabited largely by speakers of Czech and is now located in the Czech Republic.

17 Amalia Herrmann, email 4 May 2012.

18 Walter Benjamin, "Eduard Fuchs: Collector and Historian," *New German Critique* 5 (1975): 27–58, original 1937. Fuchs was friendly with Rosa Luxemburg.

19 He had designed Fuchs's house for its original owner, Hugo Perls. Fuchs may have introduced Grete to the architect.

20 HTT, 21. However, subsequent occupants have complained about heating costs.

21 The designer was Lilly Reich, partner to Mies and equally fastidious.

22 HTT, 5.

23 HTT, 20.

24 HTT, 21.

25 Daniela Hammer-Tugendhat, "Family-Life in the Tugendhat-House," Lecture 2019 in Chicago, Washington, New York, and Los Angeles (Invitation of the Mies van der Rohe Society and Dr. David Hensler).

26 HTT, 36–7. I use the translation from the earlier edition.

27 HTT, 47.

28 Stanley Cavell, *A Pitch of Philosophy* (Harvard University Press, 1994); Robert K. Merton, *A Life of Learning: Charles Homer Haskins Lecture*, ACLS Occasional Paper 25 (American Council of Learned Societies, 1994).

29 HTT, 44. Both my mother and my daughter have also worked closely on human rights issues.

30 Paul Henry Dukes, *An Epic of the Gestapo* (Cassell, 1940). Dukes was later known for introducing yoga to the United Kingdom.

31 HTT, 55.

32 HTT, 70.

33 HTT, 71. Meanwhile in the United States, Philip Johnson, in the catalogue of MOMA's Modern Architecture: International Exhibition that opened 10 February 1932, waxed on about the "magnificent" Tugendhat House that was "epoch-making as the most luxurious house in the modern style." Cited by Dietrich Neumann, "Can One Live in the Villa Tugendhat?" *Wolkenkuckucksheim – Internationale Zeitschrift zur Theorie der Architektur* 17, no. 32 (2012): 87–99, quotation on 97. The house appeared on the cover of the MOMA catalogue. Fritz and Grete were among the sponsors of the exhibition (Neumann, 97). Presumably they did not know of Johnson's Nazi connections. Martin Filler, "The Godfather: Mark Lamster's 'The Man in the Glass House: Philip Johnson, Architect of the Modern Century,'" *New York Review of Books*, 18 April 2019, https://www.nybooks.com/articles/2019/04/18/philip-johnson-godfather/.

34 The bedrooms were closed.

35 The replies were published in *Die Form: Zeitschrift für gestaltende Arbeit* 11, 15 January 1931, 437–8. They are reprinted in English in HTT, 76–7. As Neumann notes, "neither of them responded to the accusations of squandering enormous amounts of money on luxury at a time when many workers in their factories had just been laid off" (Neumann, "Can One Live in the Villa Tugendhat?" 93). However, the house was begun before the Wall Street crash of autumn 1929, and it is unclear whether their factories were downsized.

36 HTT, 76, 77.

37 HTT, 77.

38 HTT, 83. "Architekt und Bauherr" in *Was gibt Ihnen/Co Poskytuie Architekt?* (Architekten-Interessengemeinschaft, 1934), 10–11.

39 HTT, 72. See also Rostislav Švácha, "The Tugendhat House's Space," in Černá and Černoušková, *Mies in Brno*, 74–97.

40 HTT, 72–3. See Martin Heidegger, "The Origin of the Work of Art," in *Martin Heidegger: The Basic Writings*, ed. David Farrell Krell (HarperCollins, 2008; original 1950), 143–212; Mies inaugural speech to the Armour Institute of Technology in 1938, as reprinted in Fritz Neumeyer, *The Artless Word* (MIT Press, 1991; original, Berlin, 1986).

41 Fiona MacCarthy, "The Glass Room Restored," *The Guardian*, 2 November 2012, https://www.theguardian.com/books/2012/nov/02/glass-room-villa-tugendhat-restored.

42 Hans Sluga, *Wittgenstein* (Wiley-Blackwell, 2011), 6. The Wittgenstein house was influenced by the architect Adolf Loos, who adhered much more stringently to a purely functionalist approach than did Mies.

43 "Im Dastehen des Tempels geschieht die Wahrheit. Dies meint nicht, hier werde etwas richtig dargestellt und wiedergegeben, sondern das Seiende im Ganzen wird in die Unverborgenheit gebracht und in ihr gehalten." Martin Heidegger, *Der Ursprung des Kunstswerks* (Stuttgart, 1992), 54, as cited and translated by Hammer-Tugendhat, HTT, 72. This text was written a few years after the house, which would not have been to Heidegger's taste, was built.

44 HTT, 73.

45 MacCarthy, "Glass Room."

46 Ivo Hammer, HTT, 170. See also his extensive documentation of the struggles over conservation.

2. Writing the Family

1 Historian of the European family, Lenore Davidoff, calls the distinction between the nuclear and extended family "highly problematic." Lenore Davidoff, *Thicker than Water: Siblings and Their Relations, 1780–1920* (Oxford University Press, 2013), 21.

2 Michael Lambek, "Pinching the Crocodile's Tongue: Affinity and the Anxieties of Influence in Fieldwork," *Anthropology and Humanism* 22, no. 1 (1997): 31–53.

3 I am less troubled by my proximity to the subject matter than historians might be. As Rena Lederman writes, "canonical proximity to our sources … appears self-evidently edifying to many anthropologists. But intimacy as a scholarly knowledge practice appears intellectually sloppy

and ethically suspect from the perspective of mainstream sociology, social psychology, and other social and behavioral sciences, all of which have invested enormous creative energy in devising ways of bracketing the relational character of research work." Rena Lederman, "Deception and Objectivity in the Social and Behavioral Sciences," paper presented to the workshop on Fakery, Insincerity, and the Anthropology of Humbuggery, Capri, September 2017.

4 By auto-ethnography I mean an account in which the anthropologist's eye is turned on their own cultural conditions of being, bringing to light the tacit assumptions on which their way of life is based as it might be viewed by an anthropologist from afar.

5 Janet Malcolm, *The Impossible Profession* (Knopf, 1977) and *Iphigenia in Forest Hills* (Yale University Press, 2011); W.G. Sebald, *The Emigrants* (The Harvill Press, 1996); Jamaica Kincaid, *A Small Place* (Farrar, Strauss, and Giroux, 1988) and *My Brother* (Farrar, Strauss, and Giroux, 1997); John Berger, *A Fortunate Man* (Allen Lane, The Penguin Press, 1967) and *Pig Earth* (Pantheon, 1979); Caroline Steedman, *Landscape for a Good Woman* (Rutgers University Press, 1987); Edmund de Waal, *The Hare with Amber Eyes: A Hidden Inheritance* (Chatto & Windus, 2010); Philippe Sands, *East West Street: On the Origins of "Genocide" and "Crimes Against Humanity"* (Knopf, 2016). For family accounts by anthropologists, see Steven Robins, *Letters of Stone: From Nazi Germany to South Africa* (Penguin, 2016); Alisse Waterston, *My Father's Wars: Migration, Memory and the Violence of a Century* (Routledge, 2014); Clara Han, *Seeing Like a Child: Inheriting the Korean War* (Fordham University Press, 2020); Carola Lentz and Isidore Lobnibe, *Imagining Futures: Memory and Belonging in an African Family* (Indiana University Press, in press). See also Alisse Waterston and Barbara Rylko-Bauer, "Out of the Shadows of History and Memory: Personal Family Narratives in Ethnographies of Rediscovery," *American Ethnologist* 33, no. 3 (2006): 397–412, https://doi.org/10.1525/AE.2006.33.3.397; Alisse Waterston, "Intimate Ethnography and the Anthropological Imagination: Dialectical Aspects of the Personal and Political in *My Father's Wars*," *American Ethnologist* 46, no. 1 (2019): 7–19. See also Janet Carsten, Sophie Day, and Charles Stafford, eds., *Reason and Passion: The Parallel Worlds of Ethnography and Biography*, special issue of *Social Anthropology* 26, no. 1 (2018); Daniel Bertaux and Paul Thompson, *Between Generations: Family Models, Myths and Memories* (Transaction Publishers, 1993); Deborah Reed-Danahay, ed., *Auto/ethnography: Rewriting the Self and the Social* (Berg, 1997).

6 Ludwig Wittgenstein, *Philosophical Investigations*, 3rd ed., trans. G.E.M. Anscombe (Blackwell, 2001 [1953]).

7 Lederman compares the ethical challenges for anthropologists of writing about people we have come to know well with those faced by writers of fiction whose characters are drawn from people they know. Rena Lederman, "Comparative 'Research': A Modest Proposal Concerning the Object of Ethics of Regulation," *PoLAR: Political and Legal Anthropology Review* 30, no. 2 (2007): 305–27.

8 For a different but compelling approach to the child's perspective, see Han, *Seeing Like a Child*.

9 For "diffuse solidarity," see David Schneider, *American Kinship: A Cultural Account* (University of Chicago Press, 1980); for "mutuality of being," see Marshall Sahlins, *What Kinship Is – and Is Not* (University of Chicago Press, 2013). For recognition of ambivalence by anthropologists, see Meyer Fortes, *Kinship and the Social Order* (Routledge, 2004 [1969]); and Michael Peletz, "Ambivalence in Kinship since the Forties," in *Relative Values*, eds. Sarah Franklin and Susan McKinnon (Duke University Press, 2001), 555–602. Recent overviews of anthropological positions on kinship are found in Janet Carsten, *After Kinship* (Cambridge University Press, 2003); Susan McKinnon and Fenella Cannell, eds., *Vital Relations: Modernity and the Persistent Life of Kinship* (SAR Press, 2013); and Sandra Bamford, ed., *The Cambridge Handbook of Kinship* (Cambridge University Press, 2019). On kinship and memory, see, inter alia, Janet Carsten, ed., *Ghosts of Memory: Essays on Remembrance and Relatedness* (Blackwell, 2007); Joëlle Bahloul, *The Architecture of Memory: A Jewish-Muslim Household in Colonial Algeria, 1937–62* (Cambridge University Press, 1996).

10 Rogers Brubaker, *Trans: Gender and Race in an Age of Unsettled Identities* (Princeton University Press, 2016), 143.

11 See Davidoff, *Thicker than Water*.

12 The distinction between what he called corporate kin groups and the axis of amity was made explicit by Fortes, *Kinship and the Social Order*.

13 My mother had four paternal half-siblings: Ernest, Marian, Peter, and Robin Weiss.

14 Marilyn Strathern, *The Gender of the Gift: Problems with Women and Problems with Society in Melanesia* (University of California Press, 1988).

15 Pierre Bourdieu, *Distinction: A Social Critique of the Judgement of Taste* (Harvard University Press, 1987).

16 Isaac Löw-Beer (1811–98), son of Jacob. Isaac and Leah had only one child, who died young. Leah is mentioned in Ernest Jones's biography of Freud.

17 My father disapproved of psychoanalysis, but his sister and her husband co-authored books with Anna Freud. See Joseph Goldstein, Albert Solnit,

Sonja Goldstein, and Anna Freud, *The Best Interests of the Child* (The Free Press, 1996).

18 Georgia Hunter, *We Were the Lucky Ones* (Viking, 2017).

19 Daniel Low-Beer, *The Arks: The Löw-Beer Story behind Schindler's List and Villa Tugendhat* (Books & Pipes, 2020).

20 Bernie Lambek, *Uncivil Liberties: A Novel* (Rootstock Publishing, 2018).

3. Before Löw-Beers

1 Herman Freudenberger, *The Industrialization of a Central European City: Brno and the Fine Woollen Industry in the 18th Century* (Edington Wiltshire, Pasold Research Fund Ltd., 1977), 25.

2 "Virtual Jewish World: Moravia, Czech Republic," *Jewish Virtual Library*, https://www.jewishvirtuallibrary.org/Moravia. The source of material on this website is listed as Meir Lamed/Yeshayahu Jelinek, *Encyclopaedia Judaica*, 2nd ed. (The Gale Group, © 2008).

3 Neighbouring Silesia has had a more complicated history. The Prussians took most of it from Austria in 1742; part went to Poland after the First World War, and part remained German until the end of the Second World War, when most of the rest was incorporated into Poland. However, a small portion, known as Czech Silesia, was never conquered by the Prussians, remained closely connected to Moravia, and today is located within the Czech Republic.

4 "Virtual Jewish World: Moravia, Czech Republic." See also "Jewish Families from Brno (Brünn), Moravia, Czech Republic," *Geni*, https://www.geni.com/projects/Jewish-Families-from-Brno-Br%25C3%25BCnn-Moravia-Czech-Republic/13167.

5 Michael L. Miller, "Boskovice," *YIVO Encyclopedia of Jews in Eastern Europe*, 2010, https://yivoencyclopedia.org/article.aspx/Boskovice.

6 William McCagg, *A History of Habsburg Jews, 1670–1918* (Indiana University Press, 1989), 14.

7 McCagg, *History of Habsburg Jews*, 15.

8 McCagg, 19–20.

9 Freudenberger, *Industrialization*, 29.

10 "Virtual Jewish World: Moravia, Czech Republic."

11 Freudenberger, *Industrialization*, 71.

12 Michael Miller, *Rabbis and Revolution: The Jews of Moravia in the Age of Emancipation* (Stanford University Press, 2010), 333.

13 McCagg, *History of Habsburg Jews*, 29.

14 McCagg, 86.

15 McCagg, 96.

16 McCagg, 147.

17 McCagg, 176–7. The first students bearing family names listed at the Deutschen Staats-Ober-Gymnasiums in Brno are Nathan Löw-Beer and Emil Tugendhat. *Geschichte des Deutschen Staats-Ober-Gymnasiums in Brünn* (Druck von R.M. Rohrer, 1878).

18 McCagg, *History of Habsburg Jews*, 122.

19 McCagg, 145–6.

20 McCagg, 156.

21 McCagg, 200.

22 Freudenberger, *Industrialization*, 186.

23 Freudenberger, 13.

24 Freudenberger, 1, 110.

25 Freudenberger, 151, 172.

26 Freudenberger, 181.

27 Freudenberger, 3.

28 McCagg, *History of Habsburg Jews*, 77.

29 McCagg, 72.

30 Miller, "Boskovice"; see also Město Boskovice, "Boskovice," https://web .archive.org/web/20060206212934/http://www.concentus-moraviae .cz/en/Mesta/Boskovice.htm.

31 Boskovice: Festival for the Jewish Quarter, https://www.boskovice-festival .cz/cs. I have not been able to recover the original Brno tourist website from which I took the quotations.

32 See "Hermann Ungar," Twisted Spoon Press, https://www.twisted spoon.com/ungar.html. By contrast, municipal autonomy was subsequently revoked in Prague and in Galicia. See "Virtual Jewish World: Moravia, Czech Republic."

33 Miller, "Boskovice." A descendant of the count made the news in 2011 when he won a settlement for false imprisonment in the United Kingdom for bribery in respect to an arms deal. He is described in *The Telegraph* as a multi-millionaire Austrian count, with a castle in Perthshire and a house in Sloane Square, who complained he wasn't given decent underwear during his six days of imprisonment. See Tom Whitehead, "Austrian Count Who Complained over Prison Underpants Wins Damages, Says Lawyer," *The Telegraph*, 27 May 2011, http://www.telegraph.co.uk /news/uknews/law-and-order/8542570/Austrian-count-who -complained-over-prison-underpants-wins-damages-says-lawyer.html.

34 Miller, "Boskovice."

35 Miller.

36 Miller, "Boskovice" and more generally, *Rabbis and Revolution*.

37 Adler is remembered today as the teacher of Moses Sofer, who followed him briefly to Boskovice and later founded the very active and strongly anti-reform yeshiva of Pressburg (Bratislava), where many of the Hungarian rabbinate were subsequently trained.

38 Boskovice was also the birthplace of Hirsch Bär Fassel (1802–83), who became an influential rabbi and philosopher, contributor to Austrian Jewish newspapers, and author of many books. Fassel's moderate reformism brought him into conflict with the chief rabbis of Moravia at the time. He promoted German-language sermons, synagogue choirs, indoor weddings, and a modernized circumcision ritual. Michael L. Miller, "Fassel, Hirsch Bär," *YIVO Encyclopedia of Jews in Eastern Europe*, 2010, https://www.yivoencyclopedia.org/article.aspx/Fassel_Hirsch_Bar.

39 Aleš Gottvald and Mikhail Shifman, *Georg Placzek: A Nuclear Physicist's Odyssey* (World Scientific Publishing, 2018).

40 See Vladimír Velešík, "The Beginnings of Enterprise of the Löw-Beer Family Members," in *Löw-Beer's Villas and the History of an Entrepreneurial Family*, eds. Dagmar Černoušková, Petra Svobodová, Vladimír Velešík ml., and Vladimír Velešík (MAS Boskovicko Plus and MAS Svitava, 2014), 7–12; Jaroslav Bránský, *Zidé v Boskovicich* [The Jews of Boskovice] (Klub Pratel Boskovic, Nakladatelstvi Albert, 1999).

41 "Loew Geneology and Loew Family History Information," *Geni*, 2022, https://www.geni.com/surnames/loew.

42 Like many illustrious rabbis, he was also called by an honorific title and was known to his followers as MaHaRaL, the Hebrew acronym for Moreinu HaRav Löw, "Our teacher, Rabbi Löw." Such titles were marks of singular distinction and did not pass on.

43 Alden Orech, "Modern Jewish History: The Golem," *Jewish Virtual Library*, http://www.jewishvirtuallibrary.org/the-golem. The article draws from *The New Standard Jewish Encyclopedia*, *Encyclopedia Judaica*, and *The New Jewish Encyclopedia*. I learned this story originally from Roy Rappaport.

44 His name indicates that he was a Levite, although also bearing the name Löw. The website (www.geni.com/surnames/loew) offers an alternative etymology for the name Löw. It suggests that in some cases Löw might not refer to Judah but be the German rendering of the Hebrew *Levi*, which came to serve as the root of many other last names, from Levy through Levine, Lewin, and even Lewis, but also transformed to Loewi, Löwy, and perhaps sometimes to Löw. The original Levi was a brother of Judah, among the twelve sons of Jacob and founders of the twelve tribes of Israel. In the Torah, the descendants of Levi were assigned priestly service in the temple, while those of Judah were rulers. However, as

their descendants thoroughly intermingled, for a given individual either source for the name Löw could be appropriate.

45 Gotthard Deutsch and S. Mannheimer, "Löw, Samuel (called also Samuel Kollin, or Kelin)," *Jewish Encyclopedia*, https://jewishencyclopedia.com /articles/10137-low-samuel.

46 Gotthard Deutsch, A. Freimann, and Richard Gottheil, "Boskowitz," *Jewish Encyclopedia*, 1906, https://www.jewishencyclopedia.com /articles/3589-boskowitz.

47 Bedřich Nosek, "Kolin, Shemu'el ben Natan ha-Levi," *YIVO Encyclopedia of Jews in Eastern Europe*, 2010, http://www.yivoencyclopedia.org/article .aspx/Kolin_Shemuel_ben_Natan_ha-Levi.

48 Samuel's son Wolf was indeed a significant rabbi, but he became a Boskowitz, not a Löw-Beer.

49 "Rabbi ha-levi Kolin soll der Vater von Salomon Löbl (1746–1832) gewesen sein, der sich dann Löw Beer nannte und Wollhändler war. Dieser wiederum war der Vater von Moses Löw Beer (1793–1851)." Traudl Schmidt, *Das Schicksal hat mich verschont … Versuch einer politischen Biographie. Die Lebens- und Familiengeschichte von Paul Löw-Beer (1910– 2003)* [Fate Spared Me … An Attempt at a Political Biography. The Life and Family History of Paul Löw-Beer] (master's thesis, Fakultät für Sozialwissenschaften der Universität Wien, 2005), 7. My translation.

50 One remaining problem is that 1746 is also the birthdate given for Samuel's son Wolf, who did become a rabbi. However, it is possible that one or the other were born in 1740. Other possibilities are that Salomon was the son of one of Samuel's brothers, that he was an illegitimate son of Samuel's, with a different mother from Wolf, or that he was Samuel's son-in-law.

51 Nela Ledvinová, *Židovská podnikatelská rodina Löw-Beer od konce 18. století do první poloviny 20. Století* [The Löw-Beer Jewish Business Family from the End of the 18th Century to the First Half of the 20th Century] (Masarykova univerzita, Pedagogická fakulta, Katedra historie, 2018). I draw on Google for my translation.

4. Founding the Firm

1 Leopold eventually moved to Vienna and became a banker. Nela Ledvinová, *Židovská podnikatelská rodina Löw-Beer od konce 18. století do první poloviny 20. Století* [The Löw-Beer Jewish Business Family from the End of the 18th Century to the First Half of the 20th Century] (Masarykova univerzita, Pedagogická fakulta, Katedra historie, 2018), citing Jaroslav Bránský, *Zidé v Boskovicich* [The Jews of Boskovice] (Klub Pratel Boskovic, Nakladatelstvi Albert, 1999), 212.

2 Salomon's remaining son, Abraham, moved to Topolčany in Slovakia.

3 I draw extensively on chapter seven of Traudl Schmidt's master's thesis, *Das Schicksal hat mich verschont ... Versuch einer politischen Biographie, Die Lebens- und Familiengeschichte von Paul Löw-Beer (1910–2003)* [Fate Spared Me ... An Attempt at a Political Biography. The Life and Family History of Paul Löw-Beer] (master's thesis, Fakultät für Sozialwissenschaften der Universität Wien, 2005). Schmidt draws also on oral translations provided to her of sections from Bránský, *Židé v boskovicích*, which I have not consulted directly. Hans Löw-Beer told his daughter Susan that Moses created the first woollen mill in Austro-Hungary in 1836.

4 See the comprehensive chapters by Vladimír Velešik in *Löw-Beer's Villas and the History of an Entrepreneurial Family*, eds. Dagmar Černoušková, Petra Svobodová, Vladimír Velešík ml., and Vladimír Velešík (MAS Boskovicko Plus and MAS Svitava, 2014). The Czech edition is Dagmar Černoušková, Petra Svobodová, Vladimír Velešík, eds., *Löw-Beerovy vily a historie jedné podnikatelské rodiny*, 2014.

5 Another son of Jakob Aron, named Max, had some eleven children. A granddaughter of one of them, Ricky, is married to fashion magnate Ralph Lauren.

6 Daniel Low-Beer, *The Arks: The Löw-Beer Story behind Schindler's List and Villa Tugendhat* (Books & Pipes, 2020).

7 Černoušková et al., *Löw-Beer's Villas*, 17.

8 Černoušková et al., 16n31.

9 Petra Svobodová, Petr Svoboda, et al., *Exploring the History of the Textile Industrialists in Brno* (Muzeum Brnenska, 2017), 18–19. The authors list ten siblings, including Joseph, Max, Salomon, two other brothers, and five sisters.

10 This anecdote is an example of the common phenomenon of remembering "famous" relatives, though in this case it is only me doing so.

11 George Sauer, *Handbook of European Commerce: What to Buy and Where to Buy It* (Sampson Low, Marston, Searle, and Rivington, 1876; reprinted Bibliobazaar, 2008), 293, 295. The Brünn section appears to have been prepared by Gustavus Schoeller, consular agent of the United States.

12 Černoušková et al., *Löw-Beer's Villas*, 17–19.

5. The Patriarch and His Siblings

1 This approach is akin to my strategy in *Island in the Stream: An Ethnographic History of Mayotte* (University of Toronto Press, 2018). That book contains a discussion of the nature of historical horizons and experience in a flow of overlapping age cohorts.

2 Traudl Schmidt, *Das Schicksal hat mich verschont ... Versuch einer politischen Biographie. Die Lebens- und Familiengeschichte von Paul Löw-Beer (1910–2003)* [Fate Spared Me ... An Attempt at a Political Biography. The Life and Family History of Paul Löw-Beer] (master's thesis, Fakultät für Sozialwissenschaften der Universität Wien, 2005).

3 Herman Freudenberger, *The Industrialization of a Central European City: Brno and the Fine Woollen Industry in the 18th Century* (Edington Wiltshire, Pasold Research Fund Ltd., 1977), 188.

4 Dagmar Černoušková, Petra Svobodová, Vladimír Velešík ml., and Vladimír Velešík, eds., *Löw-Beer's Villas and the History of an Entrepreneurial Family* (MAS Boskovicko Plus and MAS Svitava, 2014), 20.

5 From Schmidt, *Das Schicksal hat mich verschont*, 39. All translations are my own.

6 A *Kommanditgesellschaft* is a limited partnership business entity used in German, Austrian, and some other European legal systems. Whereas in other kinds of partnerships all partners are fully liable for the partnership's debts, "in a limited partnership there are general partners (*Komplementär*) with unlimited liability and limited partners (*Kommanditisten*) whose liability is restricted to their fixed contributions to the partnership. Although a partnership itself is not a legal entity, it may acquire rights and incur liabilities, acquire title to real estate and sue or be sued." "*Kommanditgesellschaft*," Wikipedia.org, https://en.wikipedia.org /wiki/*Kommanditgesellschaft*.

7 According to Bohumír Smutný, the factory was founded in 1877, Cornelius Hože joined in 1907, and Pavel Kohn and Max Hože in 1927. It became a limited partnership with Rudolf, Alfred, Max, Fritz, Ernst, Paul, and Hans Löw-Beer, all members of the Moses L.-B. firm, from 1933. Bohumír Smutný, *Brnenstí podnikaltelé a jejich podniky 1764–1948* [Brno's Entrepreneurs and Their Partners] (*Statutární mesto Brno, Archiv mesta Brna*, 2012), 72.

8 "The Commissioners," *Villa Tugendhat*, https://www.tugendhat.eu /en/o-dome/stavebnici/.

9 Černoušková et al., *Löw-Beer's Villas*, 29.

10 This routine was presumably during the period after the death of the third brother, Benno, who had been in charge at Svitávka, and before Alfred's son Max came of age to run it.

11 His daughter Helene told Eva that he visited Vienna only every third weekend.

12 Černoušková et al., *Löw-Beer's Villas*, 26–7. Nela Ledvinová gives many more detailed criteria for receiving financial assistance. Ledvinová

describes working conditions as follows, drawing from the archive of the Löw-Beer Villa Association, but unfortunately without dates: "Young workers and women did not work night shifts; only at the age of 18 could young people work overnight. The working hours of the employees were fixed. From Monday to Thursday, they worked from seven in the morning to six in the evening, but on Friday work started at half past six in the morning and ended at six in the evening.

"On Saturday, they worked from six in the morning until half past four in the afternoon. Work breaks took place at noon from twelve to one o'clock. The staff also had a quarter-hour breakfast break. The night shift lasted twelve hours. On Easter Saturday and December 24, work ended at 12 noon. The sign for the beginning and end of work was announced by a steam whistle. On New Year's Eve, Easter Monday, the Ascension Day, Whit Monday … and Christmas, workers were free. Workers received their wages every week on Saturday at half past four, when the working week ended. They received the payment in cash." The Rules of Procedure said that "supervisors 'have the right to rebuke and impose fines on workers who made a mistake. Swearing is prohibited.' The Rules of Procedure also set out general rules of conduct for company employees. 'Workers are to come to the factory in a sober state and to behave in it morally, decently and in such a way that they do not disturb other workers doing their jobs. It is strictly forbidden to take brandy to the workplace. In factory rooms so designated by the employer, smoking is forbidden. In others, workers are only allowed to smoke with pipes, but they must stop smoking one hour before the end of work.'" Nela Ledvinová, *Židovská podnikatelská rodina Löw-Beer od konce 18. století do první poloviny 20. Století* [The Löw-Beer Jewish Business Family from the End of the 18th Century to the First Half of the 20th Century] (Masarykova univerzita, Pedagogická fakulta, Katedra historie, 2018), 27. I draw on Google translation.

13 Karl Kraus, "Brünn," *Die Fackel* 6 (Ende Mai 1899): 5–12. My translation.

14 Ledinová, citing the Archive of the Svitávka Township Office, Memorial Book of the Svitávka Township, 30–1. My translation.

15 Schmidt, *Das Schicksal hat mich verschont*, 37–8, citing Jaroslav Bránský, *Zidé v Boskovicich* [The Jews of Boskovice] (Klub Pratel Boskovic, Nakladatelstvi Albert, 1999), 121; and Černoušková et al., *Löw-Beer's Villas*, 22–3.

16 However, for Fritz, "Rudolf was quite blind to the Nazi danger and refused to do anything which would have saved some of our Central European assets. In 1937–38 he tried to found and build a small woollen

factory in Switzerland, but the existing Swiss firms did not want new competition and the Swiss authorities refused our application. It was probably just as well because the whole Western textile industry has not done very well through the years."

17 Paul said that Sagan was owned 50/50 by the L-B and Weiss families.

18 They were also related to the influential Bernays family, from which Leah married Izak Löw-Beer and her niece Martha married Sigmund Freud.

19 I take the latter from a remark by Paul quoted in Traudl Schmidt's master's thesis, *Das Schicksal hat mich verschont*, 58. The text reads as though it were Prague, but it must refer to Brno. On the Villa Tugendhat website, Alfred is listed as a manufacturer and founding member of the *Spolek Dum utechy v Brne*.

20 His name is borne by one of nineteen 15-tonne 13T buses that were baptized on 22 December 2016 with the names of prominent Brno personalities.

21 Ellen Pollak, email, 26 April 2016.

22 Max Pollak is described as "an affluent journalist and philosophical pedagogue." See "Who Was Benjamin's Wife?" *Benjaminology*, 2 February 2012, http://benjaminology.blogspot.com/2012/02/who-was -benjamins-wife.html.

23 Ellen Pollak, emails, 24 April 2016 and 6 November 2020. Jan Sedlák and Libor Teplý, *Vila Tugendhat: prostor ducha a umění* [*The Tugendhat House: A Space for Art and Spirit*] (Fotep, 2014). Ellen and her brother Roger, like many other family members, are highly educated. Roger is a retired research scientist and Ellen emeritus professor of English. Ellen's daughters are respectively a medical doctor and an art historian. Ellen's uncles were a travel agent and a taxi driver.

24 "Dora Sophia Kellner," *Wikipedia*, https://de.wikipedia.org/wiki/Dora _Sophie_Kellner, citing Eva Weissweiler, *Das Echo deiner Frage. Dora und Walter Benjamin. Biographie einer Beziehung* (Hoffmann und Campe, 2020). Dora and Walter's marriage did not last long.

25 I don't know how Haiti was connected to Max Pollak's stay there.

6. The Wiedmann Sisters

1 It was a small social world. Ahron's mother had been born a Tugendhat.

2 See Sylvia Yanagisako, *Producing Culture and Capital: Family Firms in Italy* (Princeton University Press, 2002). It is notable that in this excellent anthropological study, the subjects are all textile manufacturers.

3 The Wittgensteins had converted to Christianity.

4 A Google search immediately brought forward anti-semitic conspiracy theories about them.

5 On the elaborate Porges family website (http://www.porges.net /HomeGeneral.html), it says of Dr. Robert Carl Porges that "he received his M.D. in 1886 and became a close friend of the Queen mother of Emperor Franz Joseph. He converted to Catholicism." Hans Porges "received his medical doctorate at the University of Vienna in 1922," married the artist Suzanne Oberländer, and emigrated to New York in 1938.

6 Also in New York were Percy and Paul, sons of a cousin of Heinrich Wiedmann. Percy was considered a disreputable character who tried to embroil family members in dubious schemes.

7. The Double Cousins, before the War

1 Single cousins – the children of the other sisters of these wives and husbands – were mentioned in the previous chapter. There were four on the Löw-Beer side and two on the Wiedmann side.

2 Letter from Fritz to Joan, 21 July 1974.

3 Dagmar Černoušková and Iveta Černá, "The Large Löw-Beer Villa and the Small Löw-Beer Villa in Svitávka," in *Famous Villas of the South Moravian Region*, ed. Jan Sedlák (Foibos 2007), 32–8. See also Dagmar Černoušková, Petra Svobodová, Vladimír Velešík ml., and Vladimír Velešík, eds., *Löw-Beer's Villas and the History of an Entrepreneurial Family* (MAS Boskovicko Plus and MAS Svitava, 2014).

4 There were shorter holidays elsewhere. In 1912 Marianne and Hansi took their children for several weeks to a beach resort on the Baltic. With nannies and trunks, Marianne described it as an enormous expedition.

5 At an earlier period, Berta and Heinrich stayed with Marianne in the Kleine Villa, where Marianne organized bridge and other card games for her father every morning.

6 Fritz also recalled performing "Haydn's *Kindersymphonie* on one of Marianne's birthdays … I blew a water-filled pipe as the nightingale." "Ernst Latzko was for years *Musikdirektor* in Weimar … [and] some sort of cousin of the Wiedmann sisters."

7 Marianne made her own money post-war through wise investment in IBM.

8 Lotte Schenke-Danzinger, Hildegarde Hetzer, and Helene Löw-Beer, *Pflegemutter und Pflegekind* [Foster Mother and Foster Children] (Hirzel, 1930); Helene Löw-Beer and Milan Morgenstern, *Heilpädagogische Praxis,*

Methoden und Material (Sensen Verlag, 1936); translated as *Practical Training for the Severely Handicapped Child*. According to Joan, Helene wrote the text and was unhappy with the translation; her contribution, ahead of its time (but in line with Anni Weiss), was on the importance of developing relationships with mentally disabled children.

9 Email from Eva Colacicco, 1 December 2019.

10 He may also have been sent for experience to the factory in Sagan.

11 Interview with Margaret Libbert, conducted by Arlene Gladstone, Jewish Museum and Archives of British Columbia, 17 May 2001. See also Margaret Libbert (nee Low-Beer): UBC Legacy Project interview, https://open.library.ubc.ca/collections/ubcavfrc/items/1.0368668.

12 On another occasion Hans told me that he and Paul chose their respective studies on their own accord.

13 He may have spent time at a factory in New Jersey to improve his knowledge of chemical engineering.

14 Fritz Low-Beer, *Chinese Lacquer of the Early 15th Century* (Museum of Far Eastern Antiquities, Bulletin 22, 1950). See also Patricia Frick, "Fritz Low-Beer (1906–76): A Collector and Connoisseur of the First Generation," *Orientations: The Magazine for Collectors and Connoisseurs of Asian Art* 37, no. 8 (2006); Dagmar Černoušková and Iveta Černá, "Not Seeing the Trees Because of the Forest: The Other World of the Collector Fritz Löw-Beer," in *ORBIS ARTIUM. On the Anniversary of Lubomír Slavíček*, eds. Jiří Kroupa, Michaela Šeferisová Loudová, and Lubomír Konečný (Masarykova univerzita, 2009), 755–65. See also the beautiful photographs of his apartment in the Grosse Villa in Černoušková et al., *Löw-Beer's Villas*.

15 Černoušková and Svobodová describe the house as follows: "With its living space layout and refined details," it recalls the Villa Tugendhat. "The house with built-in furniture, cherry wood panelled walls, elegant lighting by the Lobmeyr company, and with atypical iron fittings for windows and doors, modern air-conditioning, and exclusive roof terrace belongs among the most remarkable villas in Brno." Černoušková et al., *Löw-Beer's Villas*, 52.

8. Departures and After

1 Their escape was facilitated by Tess Simpson, a Quaker born of Lithuanian Jews, in Leeds who assisted refugees.

2 Astonishingly, they appear to have made at least one post-war trip to North America. Susan Low-Beer remembers meeting them as a child in a hotel in Quebec City.

3 These views were confirmed by Irene Kalkofen, who remarked of the pre-war period that "Max was neurotic, perhaps because he had such a beautiful and intelligent sister. There were always big problems with him; he lacked confidence." This comment was the kind of "common knowledge" that circulated within the family.

4 "Svitávka," written for Marianne's eightieth birthday, 2 September 1962.

5 Susan and Jane are close to me in age but a generation older. Jane and I were good friends in childhood. In adulthood, they and their respective families have been my neighbours in Toronto. Both sisters are talented artists. Fred was plagued by mental illness and died young.

6 I explore our "Jewish question" in the final chapter.

7 In 1940 Hans spent time at Bethlehem Steel but returned to Montreal, where he and Edith married at city hall in fall 1942.

8 On their departure from Svitávka, see Johnny's account as reported in Daniel Low-Beer, *The Arks: The Löw-Beer Story behind Schindler's List and Villa Tugendhat* (Books & Pipes, 2020). On the *Athenia*, see "SS *Athenia* (1922), *Wikipedia*, https://en.wikipedia.org/wiki/SS_Athenia_(1922). Mimi spoke of the experience in the film *Outbreak 1939*, directed by Martina Hall, which was made for television and broadcast in 2009.

9 Monika Kopplin and Margarete Prüch, eds., *Im Zeichen des Drachens: von der Schönheit chinesischer Lacke. Hommage an Fritz Löw-Beer* [*In the Sign of the Dragon: On the Beauty of Chinese Varnishes. Homage to Fritz Löw-Beer*] (Linden-Museum Stuttgart, 2006).

10 A *Doboschtorte* is a labour-intensive twelve-layer cake with buttercream filling and a glazed top. It was traditional for birthdays in the family.

11 All the letters here are in possession of Susan Low-Beer.

12 Wolff was the Swiss husband of Grete's friend Käte Victorius and a lawyer.

13 Marianne did reach England, and from there she was able to get a visa to rejoin Grete in Switzerland.

14 Vladímir Velešík ml. (jr.) places the reburial on 19 May 1950. See Vladímir Velešík ml., "The Period of 1938–1945," in *Löw-Beer's Villas and the History of an Entrepreneurial Family*, eds. Dagmar Černoušková, Petra Svobodová, Vladimír Velešík ml., and Vladimír Velešík (MAS Boskovicko Plus and MAS Svitava, 2014), 84.

9. The Patriarch's Son

1 Traudl Schmidt, *Das Schicksal hat mich verschont … Versuch einer politischen Biographie. Die Lebens- und Familiengeschichte von Paul Löw-Beer*

(1910–2003) [Fate Spared Me … An Attempt at a Political Biography. The Life and Family History of Paul Löw-Beer] (master's thesis, Fakultät für Sozialwissenschaften der Universität Wien, May 2005). Translations from Schmidt are my own; I quote liberally but do not cite page numbers.

2 Email from David Löw-Beer, 23 January 2022.

3 Schmidt describes the visit. The factories were shabby but still running. "The Löw-Beers were the object of curious observation by many workers. The manager and the mayor officially welcomed us and made friendly speeches. Paul was led through the director's office where an image of the Löw-Beers hung, as if nothing had happened. As word spread rapidly in town that the Löw-Beers were there, many older people came by to greet Paul, often with emotion. We were able to walk freely through the house, where the original furniture was still standing. The daughter of the housekeeper of Paul's parents was there. A large spread was laid out at a nearby restaurant. It was a real party in a very cordial atmosphere." On a second, unannounced visit in 2002, the factory had bankruptcy signs, and Schmidt described the Grosse Villa as big and gloomy.

4 Paul Broda, *Scientist Spies: A Memoir of My Three Parents and the Atom Bomb* (Matador, 2011).

5 Paul has much more of interest to say on the heady mix of politics, class, and art in Schmidt's thesis.

6 Schmidt points out that "the arrest of Löw-Beer had been arranged by the 'leader' of the German student body, Kühn-Steinhausen." Source: Humboldt University Archive. Quoted in Prof. dr. Rüdiger vom Bruch, Classmates of 1933: The expulsion of students from the University of Berlin, documentation of the exhibition in the foyer of the Humboldt University of Berlin from 21 May to 21 June 2002.

7 From a letter from the American Embassy to MI5 in March 1955, quoted in Broda, *Scientist Spies*, 258.

8 The same passage is translated in Broda, 41. Paul Broda adds that "it was Hilde who energetically mobilised Paul's father and also Berti's uncle Ferdy Marek, the Austrian minister in Prague, to effect their release by a combination of financial and diplomatic influence" (41).

9 Broda, 45, 60.

10 Reference: KV 2/2186 [dated 1945–46]. It continues: Note: Serial 207b: LOEW-BEER's relationship with Edith TUDOR-HART and others. Serial 208d: summary of LOEW-BEER's case and photograph. Serial 212a: LOEW-BEER responsible for liaison between Czech, German and Austrian Communist parties. Serial 218b: LOEW-BEER's various

notable Communist friends and associates 1945 Jan 01 – 1946 Dec 31 (The National Archives Kew, Public Records, former reference PF 48969 Vol 6, opening date 03 February 2006).
I have not examined these documents. Edith Tudor-Hart was part of the network of spies and also a photographer. She took the photographs of Rudolf and Elise (Figures 9 and 16). In his review of Paul Broda's book, Eric Hobsbawm suggests that Edith recruited Berti Broda. Eric Hobsbawm, "Everybody Behaved Perfectly," *London Review of Books* 33, no. 16 (25 August 2011), 17–18.

11 Broda, *Scientist Spies*; John Earl Haynes, Harvey Klehr, and Alexander Vassiliev, *Spies, the Rise and Fall of the KGB in America* (Yale University Press, 2009).

12 In 1979 Melinda Maclean returned to the United States.

13 So Kitty learned as an adult from Anna Mahler, the daughter of Alma and Gustav Mahler, who had been a friend of Paul and Ala's and fellow member of the Austrian Centre in London during the war.

14 Broda, *Scientist Spies*, 67.

15 Berti's brother, Christian, served twice as Austrian minister of justice, implementing gay marriage and other progressive policies.

16 Broda, *Scientist Spies*, 298

17 See Broda, 253, 276, 283–4.

18 David Löw-Beer, 24 January 2022.

10. Grete and Her Family, in Former Times

1 The Art-Nouveau villa was built in 1903–04 for Jewish textile industrialist Moriz Fuhrmann. The property included a vineyard that led up the hillside. Alfred purchased it for 290,000 crowns and renovated it into a single-family dwelling. He did further renovations in the 1930s, designed by Viennese architect Rudolf Baumfeld. See "The Löw-Beer Villa Brno," Muzeum Brěnska, 2020, https://www.vilalowbeer.cz/en/. The house is described in chapters 15 and 16.

2 His uncle died the following year, in 1922.

3 Steve Silberman, *NeuroTribes: The Legacy of Autism and the Future of Neurodiversity* (Penguin, 2015). See also John Elder Robison, "Kanner, Asperger, and Frankl: A Third Man at the Genesis of the Autism Diagnosis," *Autism: The International Journal of Research and Practice* 21, no. 7 (2017): 4.

4 Anni Weiss, "Qualitative Intelligence Testing as a Means of Diagnosis in the Examination of Psychopathic Children," *American Journal of*

Orthopsychiatry 5, no. 2 (1935): 154–79. Lina Zeldovich writes: "By closely observing … children, Frankl and Weiss also described autistic traits in a way we would recognize today. And they did so at least a decade before Kanner and Asperger did." She adds that Asperger likely trained under Frankl. Lina Zeldovich, "How History Forgot the Woman Who Defined Autism," *Spectrum*, 7 November 2018, https://www.spectrumnews.org /features/deep-dive/history-forgot-woman-defined-autism/. The woman in the title is not Anni Weiss but Grunya Sukhareva, who characterized the condition earlier in Russia.

5 See the mention of Anni Weiss-Frankl as a "notable Columbian," https:// blogs.cul.columbia.edu/rbml/2018/10/01/new-resource-notable -columbians/.

6 Information from an email exchange between historian of physics Dean Rickles and Robin Weiss (15 July 2012 and 9 August 2012).

7 Rudi Weiss (1901–68), the middle brother, I have described in earlier chapters.

8 Interview with Irene Kalkofen, 1989.

9 See also Daniela Hammer-Tugendhat, "Fritz Tugendhat as a Photographer," in HTT, 56–67, with many images throughout the book.

10 Hermann was no doubt related to Georg Tugendhat, whose grandfather also came from Bielitz and who moved to the United Kingdom from Vienna and became wealthy. His sons and now a grandson have been prominent in law and Conservative politics. Somewhere along the line they converted to Christianity.

11 Benjamin and Samuel Löw were brothers. Samuel Löw was father of Pauline, who gave birth to Alfred, Grete's father. Benjamin Löw was father of Marie Löw, who gave birth to Emil, Fritz's father. See Kinship Diagram 4.

12 This revelation appeared only in his Australian granddaughter's communication to Marcia Tugendhat; if correct, it may help explain Fritz's personality.

13 See Bohumír Smutný, *Brněnští podnikatelé a jejich podniky: 1764–1948. Encyklopedie podnikatelů a jejich rodin* [*Brno Entrepreneurs and Their Enterprises: 1764–1948. Encyclopedia of Entrepreneurs and Their Families*] (Statutární město Brno, 2012).

14 Grete Tugendhat, "On the Construction of the Tugendhat House," lecture delivered in Brno, 17 January 1969, reprinted in full in HTT, 18–23.

15 Wolf Tegethoff, "The Tugendhat 'Villa': A Modern Residence in Turbulent Times," in HTT, 90–139. The quotes are from pages 95 and 94, respectively.

16 Dani, personal communication, 1988.

17 It was just after the opening of the Barcelona Pavilion in May.

18 Dietrich Neumann, "Can One Live in the Villa Tugendhat?" *Wolkenkuckucksheim – Internationale Zeitschrift zur Theorie der Architektur* 17, no. 32 (2012): 87–99, quotation on 88.

19 Neumann, "Can One Live in the Villa Tugendhat?" 89.

20 As original as the house is, Neumann documents influences from, and parallels with, other houses built at the time. Neumann, 88.

21 Daniela Hammer-Tugendhat, "Family-Life in the Tugendhat-House," Lecture 2019 in Chicago, Washington, New York, and Los Angeles. (Invitation of the Mies van der Rohe Society and Dr. David Hensler).

22 See additional points in the text of Grete's lecture in HTT, 18–23.

23 Irene recalled another proposed visit by Mies when the family thought they should hide the piano lest its presence offend him (HTT, 87).

24 Conversation 1988 and HTT, 29. Neumann in "Can One Live in the Villa Tugendhat?" suggests that the Barcelona plans were delayed and completed at the last moment because Mies was working on the Tugendhat House; conversely, he argues that many of the weaker details of the Tugendhat House were handled by employees once Mies was actually constructing the Barcelona Pavilion. Neumann, in fact, is a critic of the house, arguing that the living areas should have been on the upper story, enabling garden access for the children from bedrooms on a lower floor. The back of the main floor against the slope is too dark and of necessity windowless, and "the entire arrangement on the upper floor seems strangely cumbersome" and would have "trapped parents and children in their bedrooms if they wanted to avoid meeting visitors in the entrance lobby" (94). He adds: "It is the great irony of the Tugendhat Villa, that, while it became one of Mies' most widely known and influential buildings thanks to the dissemination of its striking photographs, at the same time it was his least successful response to the requirements of a functioning home" (96).

25 HTT, 77, as originally published in *Die Form*, November 1931.

26 HTT, 76.

27 Julia Eckert, personal communication, 2017.

28 Elfriede Heidegger determined the plans for the house the Heideggers built in Freiburg in 1928. "The house was a mixture of bourgeois town house and Black Forest homestead. Inside it had wood panelling; outside it was shingled. Martin's room was the biggest one." Gertrud Heidegger, *Martin Heidegger: Letters to His Wife* (Polity Press, 2008), 118.

29 Neumann in "Can One Live in the Villa Tugendhat?" wonders "how difficult it might have been for the wealthy young couple to forgo many

interior design conventions of their peers," displaying family portraits or "exotic travel souvenirs" (94), but in fact Grete and Fritz shared Mies's abhorrence of sentimentality and wouldn't have cared what others thought.

30 As cited in HTT, 169n39.

31 The only evidence that the baby was female comes from Irene.

32 Rudi was Hanna's paternal uncle; Charlotte and Rudi were a couple but not married.

33 Interview with Irene; Neumann, "Can One Live in the Villa Tugendhat?" 87.

34 I suspect he purchased the Daumier through Eduard Fuchs, who was a specialist on Daumier and helped rediscover him (Tegethoff in HTT, 98). The painting is today at the Musée d'Orsay in Paris.

35 "Irene Kalkofen Remembers," in HTT, 87.

36 Some observations in this chapter are taken from HTT, 88.

37 HTT, 87.

38 However, visiting playmates were not allowed in the main room. Hanna said her parents always call it the Saal and never the Wohnzimmer (letter to Dieter Roger).

39 Letter to architect Prof. Dieter Roger, 25 November 1985.

40 The cook had a single room and the maids a double room, adjacent to the kitchen. When Dani visited Brno with her mother in 1969, a former servant came up and cried, saying those had been the best years of her life.

11. Grete and Her Family, the War Years

1 Miriam Lewin, "Kurt Lewin: His Psychology and a Daughter's Recollections," in Portraits of Pioneers in Psychology, vol. 3, eds. Gregory Kimble and Michael Wertheimer (Psychology Press, 1998), 112.

2 Irene thought Hanna had been brought to England once before the war, fetched by Hans for a beach holiday near Bristol. My mother never mentioned this event.

3 Hammer puts his departure a month earlier. HTT, 142n5.

4 Letter translated by Margaret Libbert, in possession of Susan Low-Beer.

5 In another version, he had a secret he wanted to show her; in his closet was a complete Nazi uniform. The anti-semitism has to be placed against the fact that Rolf's mother, Hedwig von Rosen, was half-Jewish. Irene never mentioned that Rolf's son became the well-known conductor John Eliot Gardiner or that Rolf's sister, Margaret Gardiner, was a left-wing

political activist, writer, and mother of historian Martin Bernal. She also wrote a remarkable memoir of the anthropologist Bernard Deacon, *Footprints on Malekula* (Free Association Books, 1987).

6 Letter from Ludwig Glaeser to Hanna Lambek, 12 June 1979. Phyllis Lambert also attended the interview.

7 Hanna to Irene, 7 September 1945.

8 In summers 1946 and 1947 she returned to work in Caracas.

9 Eric Löw-Beer, *Mainly Memories*, unpublished and undated, 168 pages; courtesy of Michael Fuhrmann.

12. Grete and Her Family, after the War

1 The will was written in 1969 and revised in 1971.

2 Dagmar Černoušková and Iveta Černá, "Wartime and Post-War Fate of the House and Its Owners," in *Mies in Brno: The Tugendhat House*, eds. Iveta Černá and Dagmar Černoušková (Muzeum Města Brna, 2013), 136. The authors reprint Fritz's full initial letter and add that in 1948 a certificate of Czechoslovak citizenship was granted Fritz and Grete and their four joint children. According to HTT, 144, Grete filed for restitution in September 1949. In April 1950 the government cancelled the application. Max, Fritz, and Ernst Löw-Beer each also filed for restitution; despite showing they had supported the Czech side during the war, they too were turned down.

3 A lengthy homage in Spanish is to be found in *El Anclita*, of the C.A. de Corretaje Segurosca.

4 We took the Cunard *Ivernia* from Montreal to Liverpool, 20–31 July and returned 2–12 September.

5 See photos in HTT, 54.

6 This financial information is what Ernst told me in 2015.

7 HTT, 147n19

8 HTT, 138–9n62.

9 HTT, 156n49.

10 Cited in HTT, 72n5.

11 Daniela Hammer-Tugendhat, "Family-Life in the Tugendhat-House." Lecture delivered to the Mies van der Rohe Society, Chicago, 29 May 2019.

12 See HTT; see also Černá and Černoušková, *Mies in Brno*; Iveta Černa and Ivo Hammer, eds., *Materiality* (Muzeum města Brna, 2008) for extensive discussion of the political and technical aspects of renovation, conservation, and reconstruction, beginning in 1981.

13 Kathy repeated these remarks word for word to Dani in June 2019, a few weeks before her death.

14 Iris Murdoch, "A Recollection of Ludwig Wittgenstein," in *Portraits of Wittgenstein*, eds. F.A. Flowers and Ian Ground (Bloomsbury 2016), 749.

15 Eva Colacicco, email to me. Gretl is an informal diminutive of Grete, itself a diminutive of Margarete.

16 One might counterpoise the ethical compulsion to truth with philosopher J.L. Austin's remarks that pretence can conceal knowledge that could hurt another. J.L. Austin, "Pretending," in *Philosophical Papers*, eds. J.O. Urmson and G.J. Warnock (Oxford University Press, 1979), 253–71. Compare Veena Das, *Textures of the Ordinary* (Fordham University Press, 2020), 109–10.

17 Ernst Tugendhat, "Whom to Thank? German Philosopher Ernst Tugendhat on Religion as a Need and the Difficulty of Satisfying It," *Sign and Sight*, 27 December 2006, http://www.signandsight.com/features/1107.html. The article originally appeared in German in the *Neue Zürcher Zeitung* on 9 December 2006. Speaking of the "unrelieved sobriety of Heidegger's work," Peter Gordon notes that "throughout all of his seminars, Heidegger – almost – never makes a joke." Peter Gordon, "Fidelity as Heresy: Levinas, Heidegger, and the Crisis of the Transcendental Ego," in *Heidegger's Jewish Followers*, ed. Samuel Fleischacker (Duquesne University Press, 2008), 191.

18 My thanks to Dani for the point.

19 Eva Colacicco, email 2018.

20 Laurent was devoted to Hanna, albeit for reasons of discretion he virtually omitted her from his autobiography, *Un Matématicien aux prises avec le siècle* (Éditions Odile Jacob, 1997); English edition, *A Mathematician Grappling with His Century* (Springer, 2001).

13. The Philosophers: Helene Weiss, Käte Victorius, Ernst Tugendhat, Martin Heidegger

1 On Heidegger's attraction and the power of his early ideas for Jewish students, see Samuel Fleischacker, ed., *Heidegger's Jewish Followers* (Duquesne University Press, 2008). Fleischacker notes that most of Heidegger's well-known students from the 1920s were Jews. He selected essays on Hannah Arendt, Leo Strauss, Hans Jonas, and Emmanuel Levinas, in part because, as he explains, they were all "strongly committed to their Jewish heritage" (26). The relevant members of my family had little affinity with Jewish thought.

2 More than one philosopher, German and American, have told me that Ernst was Germany's greatest living philosopher. But, as a distinguished American philosopher added, German philosophy was not so great after the war compared to its heritage.

3 Arnulf is the official family trustee; his father Hermann (1920–) is not actually Heidegger's biological son.

4 I am indebted to Amalia Herrmann for sharing the CV. Lene also took courses in history, classical philology, theology (from Bultmann), art history, and archaeology.

5 In his memoirs Gadamer mentions students gathering in Marburg in 1924, among them Lene and Käte, and Hannah Arendt in a green dress. Hans-Georg Gadamer, *Philosophical Apprenticeships*, trans. Robert R. Sullivan (MIT Press, 1985).

6 Heidegger had prepared written notes for some lectures but not for others. According to Thomas Meyer (personal communication), after the war Heidegger asked Ernst for a copy of Lene's notes, which Ernst provided.

7 The Stanford archives contain Lene's transcripts from 1920 to 1935. The collection is described as "notes taken by Helene Weiss and her associates during a series of courses taken from Heidegger; it forms a complete and clearly presented corpus of Heidegger's teaching and philosophy in one of the most important periods of his career." There are some 3,000 pages of handwritten notes, not including those she copied from Loewald and Mörchen, as well as several hundred pages of typed notes from 1928 on. For example, Lene transcribed Heidegger's lectures given in the winter of 1930–31 at Freiburg that became *Hegel's Phenomenology of Spirit*. These transcriptions were one of the sources for the book and almost identical to MH's own text and the transcription of Curd Ochwadt. See Ingtraud Görland, "Editor's Epilogue," in Martin Heidegger, *Hegel's Phenomenology of Spirit* (Indiana University Press, 1988 [1980]), 150–3. In a conversation in 2017 Ernst insisted that he sold the notes to Stanford, but I suspect they were a donation.

8 Another time he said he did know her but didn't elaborate.

9 See Peter Gordon, *Continental Divide: Heidegger, Cassirer, Davos* (Harvard University Press, 2010).

10 The thesis was titled *Der Zufall in der Philosophie des Aristoteles*; it was published in 1942 as a book, *Kausalität und Zufall in der Philosophie des Aristoteles* [*Causality and Coincidence in the Philosophy of Aristotle*]. On the recommendation letter and the acknowledgments, Thomas Meyer, personal communication. Lene appears to have been Heidegger's

last Jewish student before the war, although in 1933 there was also an American, Marjorie Glickstein, who subsequently had a distinguished career as Marjorie Grene.

11 Amalia Herrmann, email 4 May 2012. In 1948 Lene published an article in English on "Aristotle's Teleology and Uexküll's Theory of Living Nature" in the *Classical Quarterly* 42, nos. 1–2 (1948): 44–58. Other publications include "Democritus' Theory of Cognition," *Classical Quarterly* 32 (1938): 47–56; "The Greek Conceptions of Time and Being in the Light of Heidegger's Philosophy," *Philosophy and Phenomenological Research* 2 (1941): 173–87; and "An Interpretative Note on a Passage in Plotinus on Eternity and Time," *Classical Philology* 36 (1941): 230–9.

12 Nun wünsche ich Ihnen von Herzen, daß die Nähe der Liebsten u. die Umgebung des Landes Ihnen Genesung und Ruhe bringt und vor allem die innere Freimütigkeit zu dem, was uns täglich abverlangt wird. Jeder hat seine Last an Scheitern zu tragen.

Wir wissen nie, ob solche Wege nicht schließlich zu wesentlichen Erfahrungen führen, an denen wir sonst vorbeigingen.

13 DLA Marbach, A: Heidegger, 92.73.5/2. The letter is in difficult handwriting. I am indebted to Sonja Asal for transcribing and initially translating this and other letters.

Heute sprach ich nach der ersten Übungsstunde meines Privatissimums, das ich in kleine Kreise versuche, Ernst Tugendhat u. fragte zuerst nach Ihnen. Ich bin froh für Sie, daß in diesen schweren Wochen und Tagen Menschen um Sie sind und Sorgen u. Helfen.

Sie dürfen dessen gewiss sein, daß ich in den vergangenen Wochen oft an Sie dachte. Jetzt, wo etwas mehr Luft ist nach angestrengter Arbeit, möchte ich Ihnen diesen ganz besonderen Gruß senden u. Ihnen von Herzen die rechte [unlesbar] Ruhe und Geduld wünschen; denn was ist die Geduld anderes als das Sichsammeln ins reinere Dulden, das uns immer bei allem Schweren ein Geschenk bringt, nämlich die Erfahrung, daß der Schmerz das große Tor zum Sein bleibt.

Und wenn Sie es auch kennen, möchte ich Ihnen doch eigens das Wort Hölderlins aus dem Schluß des Hyperions aufschreiben: "… daß, wie Nachtigallgesang im Dunkeln, göttlich erst, in tiefem Leid das Lebenslied uns tönt."

Da seit Kurzem der Grenzübertritt und Aufenthalt erleichtert ist, möchte ich in den nächsten Wochen doch versuchen, nach Basel zu kommen u. Sie zu begrüßen. Aber Sie müssen selber ganz von sich aus darüber entscheiden. Vielleicht bitten Sie Käte Victorius, mir kurz mitzuteilen, ob und wann und wie ein Besuch möglich ist.

Mit herzlichen Grüßen u. Wünschen für Sie auch im Namen meiner
Frau
Ihr Martin Heidegger.
Grüßen Sie auch Käte V. von uns.

14 Sonja Asal, personal communication.
15 There is no dedication included in the English version, published in David
Farrell Krell, ed., *Martin Heidegger: Basic Writings* (Harper Collins, 1993).
16 Frau Helene Weiss war eine meiner ausgezeichnetsten Schülerinnen, die
über zehn Jahre bei mir gearbeitet hat. Im Sommer 1934 habe ich ihre
Dissertation bei der philosophischen Fakultät der Universität Freiburg
vorgelegt. Diese hielt es für angebracht aus formalen Gründen – nach
einem ministeriellen Erlass des damaligen Badischen Kultusministeriums
waren jüdische Studenten nur in einer bestimmten beschränkten Anzahl
zur Promotion zugelassen – der Verfasserin eine ausserdeutsche Universität
zur Promotion zu empfehlen. Ich hebe daraufhin Frau Helene Weiss zur
Universität Basel geratem. Die Arbeit wurde in Erweiterter Form "Kausalität
und Zufall in der Philosophie des Aristoteles" 1942 in Basel gedruckt.
17 For the former view, see Miriam Lewin's letter to the *New York Times*
(11 February 1990). She writes: "My aunt Helene Weiss was one of
Heidegger's students whose whole life was affected by his anti-Jewish
prejudice. Heidegger accepted her as his doctoral student, but when she
completed her Ph.D. dissertation under him, he refused it and forced her
to leave the university without any degree. He shamelessly admitted that
only her Jewish birth caused him to reject her thesis.

She managed to escape from Germany before Hitler took power and to
enter England. There she discovered that without credentials she could not
be employed in her field. She was forced to make her living selling pots
and pans door-to-door, and she died in England at a rather young age."

Much of this letter is wrong. Lene did have a degree. Lene no doubt
had a difficult time, but both she and her brother Paul Weiss were
supported by the Council for At-Risk Academics (CARA) as well as by
Hans Weiss (Miriam's uncle) during their studies at Cambridge (Robin
Weiss, email 10 December 2016). CARA was established by William
Beveridge in 1933. Peter Weiss said Lene saved money and also received
some reparations. Moreover, Lene died in Switzerland, not England.

Heidegger's motives remain unclear. The other two philosophy
professors at Freiburg at the time appear to have been overt Nazis.
Presumably Heidegger lacked the courage to defend Lene and perhaps
didn't want his name attached to a Jewish supervision. In any case, the
positive consequence was that she was able to leave Germany.

The quotation from Heidegger comes from "'Only a God Can Save Us': *Der Spiegel*'s Interview with Martin Heidegger"; originally published 31 May 1976; English translation in Richard Wolin, ed., *The Heidegger Controversy: A Critical Reader* (Columbia University Press, 1991), 97–8. There is an error in the text when he says he "visited Dr. Weiss several times in Brussels before her death"; it was actually in Basel.

18 Robin Weiss recalls his father saying so (email 10 December 2016).

19 See K. Victorius, "Der 'Moses des Michelangelo' von Sigmund Freud," in *Entfaltung der Psychoanalyse*, ed. A. Mitscherlich (Klett, 1956), 1–10.

20 Someone suggested to me that Hannah Arendt might have removed those from KV to MH and perhaps some of his to her, but I have no evidence for this surmise.

21 Ernst Tugendhat, letter to Irene Kalkhofen, 22 June 1941, age eleven.

22 He read a draft of this chapter, and Dani reported (1 October 2019): "As I expected, he was not enthusiastic, but on the other side not really negative. I asked whether he wishes to change anything, he said no. Then I asked him whether he permits you to publish it. He said, he does not have to allow you anything; of course you can publish it. He is not sure whether anybody would be interested."

23 While one relative found this memory a terrible story of crushing a boy's spirit, another remarked that at thirteen Ernst should have known better and that Fritz was quite right.

24 Dani, who was a child at the time, does not believe seders could have taken place.

25 This institution later evolved into the school directed by Kathy.

26 Ernst Tugendhat, "The Time for Philosophising Is Over," interview by Ulrike Herrmann, *Sign and Sight*, 20 August 2007, translated by Claudia Kotte from *Die Tageszeitung*, 28 July 2007, http://www.signandsight.com/features/1487.html.

27 "Für mich war die Konfrontation mit "Sein und Zeit" schon sehr früh, als ich 15 Jahre alt war, prägend. Das hat mich überhaupt zur Philosophie gebracht." Michael Hesse, "Philosoph Ernst Tugendhat wird 85: „Es wird zu viel geschwafelt," *Berliner Zeitung*, 6 March 2015.

28 These were standardized packages containing tins of meat and other foods. Ernst simply ordered and paid for them. He would have just turned seventeen at the time of the first package.

29 An exclamation point was normal punctuation for salutation in a letter.

30 Christoph Emmrich, who has kindly translated the letters between Heidegger and Ernst, makes the comparison here to Hegel's *lebendiger Geist*.

31 It may be that Hannah Arendt and Herbert Marcuse were also sending CARE packages (Thomas Mayer, personal communication).

32 Lene was not Ernst's aunt in the literal sense. She was the sister of Grete's first husband and not of Ernst's father. I assume, however, that Ernst also used the kin term.

33 All quotes in this paragraph are from the Herrmann interview in *Sign and Sight* with minor adjustments in the translation by me.

34 Herrmann interview.

35 The sentence is taken from a summary of a five-page letter, as prepared by the Marbach archivists and placed in the file.

36 As summarized in the archives.

37 The invitation came from Frithjof Bergmann, whom Ernst had met in Germany but who taught at Michigan. Several years later, and knowing nothing about their connection, I audited Bergmann's graduate seminar on Freud.

38 Als ich jetzt diese Vorlesung von 1925 las, fand ich mich wieder in die alte Werkstatt zurückversetzt, aus der ich mich verstehe.

39 Dass Sie an meiner Entwicklung weiter Anteil nehmen, bedeutet mir sehr viel, und dass Sie auch meine abweichenden Überlegungen und Intentionen so positive aufnehmen, hat für mich etwas ganz Unverhofftes. Ich weiss nicht, ob ich die Kraft habe, etwas Vernünftiges zustandezubringen und denke immer wieder daran, von der Philosophie ganz abzuspringen.

40 Das hängt mit der Frage zusammen, deren Klärung mir sehr wichtig wäre: wieweit die "ontischen" Gegebenheiten, von denen wir in der "Ontologie" auszugehen haben, als "Seiendes" zu verstehen sind oder als "Sätze" (Sinneinheiten); wie man hier ansetzt, das wirkt sich dann auch das Weltproblem aus: ob man die Welt primär als das Offene der Anwesenheit von Seiendem versteht oder als das Offene des Verstehens von Sinn, bzw. wie beides zusammenhängt. Gerade auch darüber würde ich mir von einem Gespräch manche Klärung erhoffen.

41 Ernst told me that Gadamer was a very nice man, although he once also questioned my interest in Gadamer's philosophy, calling the work very conservative.

42 "Heideggers Idee von Wahrheit," in *Heidegger*, ed. Otto Pöggeler (Berlin, 1969); republished in English in *Critical Heidegger*, ed. and trans. Christopher Macann (Routledge, 1996), 227–40. The quotation is from 238–9. Thomas Meyer (personal communication) pointed out that Heidegger himself famously said that after reading Ernst's essay he changed his own views.

43 Herrmann interview in *Sign and Sight*.

14. Tugendhat, after Heidegger

1 Laureano Ralón and Mario Teorodo Ramírez, "Interview with Günter Figal," *Figure/Ground*, 18 August 2015, http://figureground.org/fg /interview-with-gunter-figal/.

2 Ernst Tugendhat, "The Time for Philosophising Is Over," interview by Ulrike Herrmann, *Sign and Sight*, 20 August 2007, translated by Claudia Kotte from *Die Tageszeitung*, 28 July 2007, http://www.signandsight .com/features/1487.html.

3 Herrmann interview in *Sign and Sight*.

4 The German edition is *Vorlesungen zur Einführung in die sprachanalytische Philosophie* (Suhrkamp, 1975). Habermas's remarks are found in "Eine philosophische Existenz: Autonomie und Gerechtigkeit – zum 90. Geburtstag von Ernst Tugendhat," *Die Zeit*, 5 March 2020.

5 Among the people who responded, in more or less depth, were Erdmute Alber, Sonja Asal, Michal Bodemann, James Conant, Lorraine Daston, Julia Eckert, Georg Elwart (at an earlier time), Luca Giuliani, Stefan Gosepath, Gertrud Grünkorn, Fritz Kramer, Matthias Kroß, Avishai Margalit, Thomas Meyer, Stephan Schlak, and Thomas Wentzer (in Aarhus).

6 These and subsequent observations come as well from a further conversation with Avishai at which Jackie, my wife, was also a participant.

7 Ernst turned later to G.H. Mead on this subject. Margalit made some amusing remarks about Buber and Scholem. Both men were connoisseurs of chocolate. Scholem was sent chocolate by his admirers and kept it in a cupboard. You knew where you stood with him according to the quality he offered you. Buber would surreptitiously sneak a piece into his mouth and didn't offer to share. I can identify with both.

8 German philosophy does have a different concept of "anthropology," but Ernst didn't stop to think that mine might be equally legitimate.

9 Until then, they got along very well, but their respective students formed distinct parties: one was either MT's student or ET's. According to a former student of Theunissen, ET had easier relations with his students; MT was friendly but somewhat disengaged.

10 Herrmann interview in *Sign and Sight*.

11 As recounted in Michael Hesse, "Philosoph Ernst Tugendhat wird 85: „Es wird zu viel geschwafelt," *Berliner Zeitung*, 6 March 2015.

12 Herrmann interview in *Sign and Sight*. However, before he left for Chile he did make accusations of anti-semitism.

13 Herrmann interview. In fact, as he had never lived there, he did not literally "come back" to Germany.

14 In retrospect, his daughter Marcia suggests, it is possible that Herbi too suffered from a bipolar condition.

15 Ernst brought Martin, age twelve, on what Martin remembered as a fantastic trip to Chile. At thirteen, his mother took Martin to live in Tenerife, where Ernst visited twice a year. Martin then wanted to live with Ernst, but Ernst refused. Martin felt too that once he decided not to pursue an academic career, interest in him waned. In 1983 Ernst was still sufficiently under Heidegger's spell to name his son Martin.

16 Presumably a family heirloom.

17 In the Herrmann interview in *Sign and Sight*. The letter from Peru was typed on full length sheets.

18 Michael Hesse, "Philosoph Ernst Tugendhat wird 85: „Es wird zu viel geschwafelt," *Berliner Zeitung*, 6 March 2015.

19 Ernst Tugendhat, Celso López, and Ana María Vicuña, *Manuel y Camila se preguntan: ¿Cómo deberíamos vivir? Reflexiones sobre la Moral* (Planeta, 1998).

20 In the Herrmann interview in *Sign and Sight*. Ernst had another manic crisis in Vienna, around 1996.

21 Hans-Martin Gauger as cited in Christian Geyer, "Ernst Tugendhat wird 90: Was meint "ich"?" *Frankfurter Allgemeine*, 8 March 2020.

22 Ernst Tugendhat, *Egozentrizität und Mystik. Eine anthropologische Studie* (C.H. Beck, 2003). English translation: Ernst Tugendhat, *Egocentricity and Mysticism: An Anthropological Study*, trans. Alexei Procyshyn and Mario Wenning (Columbia University Press, 2016).

23 Herrmann interview in *Sign and Sight*.

24 Hesse in the *Berliner Zeitung* makes the former point; the latter is in the interview with Herrmann.

25 Ernst Tugendhat, *Anthropologie statt Metaphysik* [Anthropology Instead of Metaphysics] (C.H. Beck, 2007).

26 Delivered 5 December 2005; published in *Le Monde diplomatique*, German edition, 13 January 2006.

27 It is the Talitha Kumi Evangelical Lutheran School (Arabic: قومي طاليثا also known as *Evgl. Luth.-Sekundar-Schule*), a German international school in Beit Jala, West Bank, Palestinian territories. The name "Talitha Kumi" is from Aramaic "Little girl, get up!" spoken by Jesus as he resurrected the daughter of Jairus (Mark 5:38). The donation was to subsidize more places for Muslim students.

28 Interview with Herrmann in *Sign and Sight*.
29 Interview with Herrmann.

15. The Reunion

1 The program is appended at the end of this chapter.
2 The convert's brother was grandfather to Ricky Loew-Beer Lauren, who was presumably far enough removed not to have heard about the event.
3 In contrast to the large number of Löw-Beers, very few Stiassnys turned up.
4 This view is evident in the lengthy memoir by Eric Low-Beer, a first cousin of Daniel's father. Eric's lifestyle also illustrates the considerable capital his branch extracted and later further retrieved.
5 See Marcel Mauss, *Essai sur le Don* (1925); *The Gift*, trans. Jane Guyer (Hau Books, 2016). Thanks to David Henig for the reminder.
6 See "Hilary Mantel: Why I Became a Historical Novelist," *The Guardian*, 3 June 2017, https://www.theguardian.com/books/2017/jun/03/hilary-mantel-why-i-became-a-historical-novelist.
7 The Jewish population of Brno was 11,102 in September 1941. "The mass deportation of Jews from Brno and its surrounding commenced on Nov. 26, 1941, when 1,000 Jews were sent to the Minsk ghetto. Another 2,000 were sent to Theresienstadt on Dec. 2 and 5, and 7,000 more were deported between Jan. 28 and May 27, 1942, most perishing in Auschwitz ... The survivors who returned to Brno after the Holocaust numbered 1,033 in 1948." "Jewish Families from Brno (Brünn), Moravia, Czech Republic," *Geni*, https://www.geni.com/projects/Jewish-Families-from-Brno-Br%25C3%25BCnn-Moravia-Czech-Republic/13167.
  Jews deported from Boskovice included ten with the last name Weiss, four Löw-Beer, and four Hanak. Benjamin and Vladka Meed Registry of Jewish Holocaust Survivors, c. 1994.
8 An amusing recollection of the windows comes from Valerie Furhmann (as passed on to me by her grandson Michael Fuhrmann in an email 28 May 2005: "It needed an engineer to cope with all the push-button windows – which the children pressed when they should not have done. It could be opened like being on the deck of a ship ... Tugendhat had a photographic studio in the basement and took the best photo I ever had of me."
9 One can see what Grete and Fritz were rejecting in the photo "Interior of a typical middle-class German home, late nineteenth century," reproduced in Walter Benjamin's *Berlin Childhood around 1900* (Belknap, 2006), 87, from Hans-Adolf Jacobsen and Hans Dollinger, eds., *Hundert Jahr Deutschland 1870–1970: Bilder, Texte, Dokumente* (Verlag Karl Desch, 1969).

10 Written in Czech, the Brno Architectural Manual website (https://www
.bam.brno.cz/) gives good architectural history and maps of all the
interwar modernist buildings in Brno.

11 Neumann says Brno had at the time "probably the highest number of
modern buildings anywhere in Europe." Dietrich Neumann, "Can One
Live in the Villa Tugendhat?" *Wolkenkuckucksheim – Internationale Zeitschrift
zur Theorie der Architektur* 17, no. 32 (2012): 87–99, quotation on 90.

12 The forum was filmed. See "Meeting Brno," https://www.youtube.com
/watch?v=dYmBj1W7uS4.

13 See "Brno's Villa Tugendhat Reopens after Two Year Renovation," Radio
Prague International, 1 March 2012, http://www.radio.cz/en/section
/curraffrs/brnos-villa-tugendhat-reopens-after-two-year-renovation.

14 *The Löw-Beer Villas and the Story of the Found Suitcase*, produced by
Petr Břetislav, ARTV Film Studio, 2017, https://www.youtube.com
/watch?v=n5i33sCpgYk.

15 Some days after the reunion, we received an email from the curators at
the Löw-Beer Villa that showed a curator also dressed as Alfred. This
costumed "actor" seemed much more incongruous.

16 A less well-off relative stayed in modest lodgings and joined them during
the day.

17 Karl Marx, *The Karl Marx Library*, vol. 1, ed. Saul K. Padover (McGraw
Hill, 1972), 245–6.

18 Carey added the salient point that this idea is exactly why Brno feels the
need to "meet" its past. On ideas of the future characteristic of the past,
that is, on a history of concepts of the future, see Reinhart Koselleck,
Futures Past (Columbia University Press, 2004).

19 Anthropologist Danny Miller has observed that where kinship was once
a given, in contrast to friendship, which was voluntary, it is now the
case that we can select from among our kin and maintain relationships
with those with whom we are friends. Daniel Miller, "The Ideology of
Friendship in the Era of Facebook," *Hau: Journal of Ethnographic Theory* 7,
no. 1 (2017): 377–95.

16. Reconciliations in Brno

1 He was released only when the authorities became afraid he might die
in prison. Damaged mentally and physically, he spent his remaining five
years of life in a care home.

2 Daniel has since made a strong start. See "Saving Schindler's Ark,"
https://arksfoundation.net/.

3 Compare Rita Astuti, *People of the Sea: Identity and Descent Among the Vezo of Madagascar* (Cambridge, 1995).
4 In the 1920s you had to be baptized to teach at the University of Brno. Theodore K. Rabb, "Rabinowicz, Oskar K," *YIVO Encyclopedia of Jews in Eastern Europe*, 2010, http://www.yivoencyclopedia.org/article.aspx /Rabinowicz_Oskar_K.
5 A great book on this subject, from another part of the world, is Richard Handler, *Nationalism and the Politics of Culture in Quebec* (University of Wisconsin Press, 1988).
6 "The national composition with its majority German bourgeoisie can be seen in the list of city representatives: Mayors – democratically elected since 1851 – were almost all Germans until the inception of the First Republic." See "A Speech by the Mayor of the City of Brno Richard Svoboda on the Evening Session on 'The Tradition of German-Jewish and Czech Culture in Brno,'" in *The Tradition of German-Jewish and Czech Culture in Brno* (Brno Centre for European Studies, 2005), 5–6, http:// dumbell.physics.muni.cz/placzek/papers/city_hall.pdf. German may also have been seen as "higher"; Petr Spielmann writes: "German … was used by many Brno Jews. But not only by them: even President Masaryk wrote letters to his mother in German." See "Some Remarks to the Tradition of Relations between the German, Jewish, and Czech Cultures in George Placzek's Hometown Brno," in *The Tradition of German-Jewish and Czech Culture in Brno*, 27–36, quotation on 28.
7 This description is taken from the article by Strakoš Martin on German House, translated by Jan Purkert, https://www.theatre-architecture.eu /en/db/?theatreId=432.
8 The Jews had long been caught in the tension between Czech speakers and "Germans." Historian Michael Miller observes that in the late nineteenth century, Moravian Jews were deplored by Czech nationalists for their attachment to schooling in German and for their power in determining closely contested elections. He concludes: "In theory, emancipation had transformed Moravia's Jews into Jewish-Moravians, but ironically, this occurred just as the regional and *supra*national Moravian identity began to give way to mutually exclusive Czech and German national identities." Michael Miller, *Rabbis and Revolution: The Jews of Moravia in the Age of Emancipation* (Stanford University Press, 2010), 343.
9 Kateřina Tučková, *Vyhnání Gerty Schnirch* [*The Expulsion of Gerta Schnirch*] (Host, 2009), https://www.katerina-tuckova.cz/en/the-expulsion -of-gerta-schnirch-en-2/. Kateřina has written several more novels on historical and feminist themes.

10 For comparable contemporary issues of commemoration in Sudetenland, see Barbara Spalová, "Remembering the German Past in the Czech Lands," *History and Anthropology* 28, no. 1 (2017): 84–109.

11 I learned this detail also in a letter to me from Robert Fuhrmann, 9 March 1994. Hans Fuhrmann was murdered in Auschwitz. For the genealogical connections, see Kinship Diagram 3.

12 "Speech by the Mayor of the City of Brno Richard Svoboda."

13 See David Altshuler, "Tunneling towards Capitalism in the Czech Republic," *Ethnography* 2, no. 1 (2001): 115–38.

14 Zoubek appeared not to know about the earlier strikes described in chapter five.

15 This kind of claim through suffering is not specifically Czech; it is all too familiar elsewhere.

16 Both Mattej Hollan and Petr Vokřál failed to be re-elected in fall 2018.

17 For accounts of property in post-socialism, see Katherine Verdery, "Fuzzy Property: Rights, Power, and Identity in Transylvania's Decollectivization," in *Uncertain Transition: Ethnographies of Change in the Postsocialist World*, eds. Michael Burawoy and Katherine Verdery (Rowman & Littlefield, 1999), 53–82; and Katherine Verdery, *The Vanishing Hectare: Property and Value in Postsocialist Transylvania* (Cornell University Press, 2003).

18 See Peter Stallybrass and Allon White, *The Politics and Poetics of Transgression* (Cornell University Press, 1986).

19 On dissonant rhetoric, see Simon Lambek, "Nietzsche's Rhetoric: Dissonance and Reception," *Epoché: A Journal for the History of Philosophy* 25, no. 1 (Fall 2020): 57–80.

20 Scenes in *Hannibal Rising* were filmed in the house in 2007.

21 Retitled *The Affair*, the film received poor reviews and was called "architecture porn" on RogerEbert.com. See Odie Henderson, "Reviews: The Affair," rogerebert.com, 5 March 2021, https://www.rogerebert .com/reviews/the-affair-movie-review-2021.

17. Looking Back: Conundrums of Identity and Representation

1 For a more analytic account of the constitution of kinship, see Michael Lambek, "Kinship, Modernity, and the Immodern," in *Vital Relations: Modernity and the Persistent Life of Kinship*, eds. Susan McKinnon and Fenella Cannell (School of Advanced Research Press, 2013), 241–60.

2 Following Heidegger and Derrida, I write this "under erasure" (*sous rature*), signifying that the word is inevitable yet inadequate, its

meaning undecidable and constituted through difference rather than substantively.

3 In the late nineteenth century many Jews supported Habsburg liberals and cosmopolitans against nationalists. See, in what is otherwise a deeply flawed book, Ernest Gellner, *Language and Solitude: Wittgenstein, Malinowski, and the Habsburg Dilemma* (Cambridge University Press, 1998). On nationalism and the ethnic movement in a regional context, see Rogers Brubaker, "Aftermaths of Empire and the Unmixing of Peoples: Historical and Comparative Perspectives," *Ethnic and Racial Studies* 18, no. 2 (1995): 189–218. Brubaker gives a good account of the Germans in Czechoslovakia. See also Rogers Brubaker, *Nationalism Reframed: Nationhood and the National Question in the New Europe* (Cambridge University Press, 1996).

4 Lenore Davidoff, *Thicker than Water: Siblings and Their Relations, 1780–1920* (Oxford University Press, 2013), first quote, 28, and second, citing Jon Mathieu, 27.

5 Davidoff, *Thicker than Water*, 77.

6 Sylvia Yanagisako, *Producing Culture and Capital: Family Firms in Italy* (Princeton University Press, 2002), 32.

7 Davidoff, *Thicker than Water*, 131–2.

8 Yanagisako, *Producing Culture and Capital*, 114.

9 Thanks to Stefan Gosepath for the *Buddenbrooks* reference. The Italian case is evident in Yanagisako, *Producing Culture and Capital*. The Chinese case has been subject to research by Charles Stafford (personal communication).

10 Veena Das, "The Grains of Experience," *Somatosphere*, 10 February 2018, http://somatosphere.net/forumpost/the-grains-of-experience/.

11 Das, "The Grains of Experience."

12 Vincent Crapanzano, *Tuhami: Portrait of a Moroccan* (University of Chicago Press, 1980), 152.

Index

conservation. *See* restoration

cosmopolitanism, 50, 290, 311, 323–4, 332, 337, 354, 410n3

Crapanzano, Vincent, 364

Czech and German ethnolinguistic divisions, 46, 85, 88, 135, 198, 298, 319–22, 336, 343, 376n16, 408n8. *See also* German language; nationalists

Czechoslovakia: historical composition, 46; interwar industry, 82–4, 135–7; interwar relations, 352, 356; post-war, 322, 343; Soviet invasion, 171

Czech/Slovak partition, 6, 288, 342, 376n16

Dani. *See* Hammer-Tugendhat, Daniela

Das, Veena, 363–4

Daumier painting, 189, 396n34

Davidoff, Leonore, 360, 378n1

Davos, 103, 141, 213, 241

DeMichelis, Carey, 305–6, 310, 407n18

dining table, 13–14, 222, 293

divorce: Hans and Grete, 38, 189; scandalous, 116

double cousins: Löw-Beer, 11, 37, 79, 99, 119, 123, 131–2, 136, 158, 177, 215; Weiss, 180

dowry, 37, 82, 97, 108, 129

Dukes, Sir Paul, 15–16, 156, 203, 377n30

Dussauze, Lotte Weiss, 181

Dvorzak, Gretl, 195–6

ebony. *See* Macassar panels

entrepreneurs, 51, 63, 72, 87–8, 112, 214, 335–7

escape, from Vienna: Fritz's, 146; Helene's, 401n17; Marianne's, 152–5; Paul's, 139

espionage, 166, 171

ethics, 29, 232–3, 326, 398n16; Ernst, 260, 266, 267; Grete, 226, 229, 232; of representation, 20, 29, 379n3, 380n7

ethnography, 22, 26, 29

ethnonationalism, 343. *See also* Czech and German ethnolinguistic divisions; German language; nationalists

exposure, 29–30, 187

factories: in Canada, 142, 145; cellulose, 82, 164, 167; cement, 82, 83, 97, 135–7, 184, 298, 386n7; conditions in, 87–9, 337, 386–7n12; as domicile, 80, 108, 119, 177, 297, 298; history of, 48, 51–2; L-B textile, 38, 65–8, 71, 72, 75–6, 81–3, 89–90, 136, 182–3; post-Communist, 302–4, 335; post-war, 140, 158, 160, 164, 167, 168, 173, 219, 223; running of, 84–8, 113, 121, 134, 146, 178; screws, 82, 99–100; success of, 285; sugar, 75, 81–2, 89, 137, 139; in Venezuela, 204, 208, 210, 221. *See also* Svitávka

family: bilateral, 78; conceptualization and representation, 22–30, 40–1, 285, 287–8, 293, 306, 309, 333, 349–51; corporate, 36; enclosed, 119, 123, 131, 215; Grete's 33–4; and kinship, 32–3; knowledge in, 31, 97; as primary identification, 132, 149, 307, 351, 358;